DATE DUE

INTERNATIONALIZATION: FIRM STRATEGIES AND MANAGEMENT

THE ACADEMY OF INTERNATIONAL BUSINESS

Published in association with the UK Chapter of the Academy of International Business

Titles already published in the series:

International Business and Europe in Transition (Volume 1)
Edited by Fred Burton, Mo Yamin and Stephen Young

Internationalisation Strategies (Volume 2)
Edited by George Chryssochoidis, Carla Millar and Jeremy Clegg

The Strategy and Organization of International Business (Volume 3)
Edited by Peter Buckley, Fred Burton and Hafiz Mirza

Internationalization: Process, Context and Markets (Volume 4)
Edited by Graham Hooley, Ray Loveridge and David Wilson

International Business Organization (Volume 5)
Edited by Fred Burton, Malcolm Chapman and Adam Cross

International Business: Emerging Issues and Emerging Markets (Volume 6)
Edited by Carla C.J.M. Millar, Robert M. Grant and Chong Ju Choi

International Business: European Dimensions (Volume 7)
Edited by Michael D. Hughes and James H. Taggart

Multinationals in a New Era: International Strategy and Management (Volume 8)
Edited by James H. Taggart, Maureen Berry and Michael McDermott

International Business (Volume 9)
Edited by Frank McDonald, Heinz Tüselmann and Colin Wheeler

Internationalization

Firm Strategies and Management

Edited by

Colin Wheeler

Frank McDonald

and

Irene Greaves

First published 2003 by
PALGRAVE MACMILLAN
Houndmills, Basingstoke, Hampshire RG21 6XS and
175 Fifth Avenue, New York, N. Y. 10010
Companies and representatives throughout the world

PALGRAVE MACMILLAN is the global academic imprint of the Palgrave Macmillan division of St. Martin's Press, LLC and of Palgrave Macmillan Ltd. Macmillan® is a registered trademark in the United States, United Kingdom and other countries. Palgrave is a registered trademark in the European Union and other countries.

ISBN 1–4039–0671–8

This book is printed on paper suitable for recycling and made from fully managed and sustained forest sources.

A catalogue record for this book is available from the British Library.

Library of Congress Cataloging-in-Publication Data
Internationalization:firm strategies and management/editors, Colin Wheeler, Frank McDonald and Irene Greaves.
    p.   cm.—(Academy of International Business series)
Papers from the 29th Annual Conference of the UK Chapter of the Academy of International Business held at the University of Central Lancashire.
Includes bibliographical references and index.
ISBN 1–4039–0671–8
    1. International business enterprises—Management—Congresses.   I. Wheeler, Colin, 1949–   II. McDonald, Frank, 1951–   III. Greaves, Irene.   IV. Academy of International Business. UK Chapter. Conference (29th : 2002 : University of Central Lancashire)   V. Academy of International Business (Series) (Palgrave (Firm))
HD62.4 .I578 2003
658'.049—dc21

                                                                2002035517

10   9   8   7   6   5   4   3   2   1
12   11   10   09   08   07   06   05   04   03

Printed and bound in Great Britain by
Antony Rowe Ltd, Chippenham and Eastbourne

S0693085
122203

Contents

List of Tables

List of Figures

Foreword

This book will be on display (and on sale) at the 30th Annual Conference of the UK Chapter of the Academy of International Business. Established in 1973 by Michael Z. Brooke, the founding chairman, AIB UK has come a long way during the intervening period. It is among the most active chapters in the AIB's worldwide organization.

International business, and with it the academic discipline dedicated to its study, has grown spectacularly in the last 30 years. From an early emphasis on economic theory and econometric methods, research now incorporates scientifically rigorous qualitative research methods drawing on numerous contributory disciplines. A broad community of international business scholars has developed, and the initial spotlight has enlarged to encompass a whole host of special topic areas and issues related to the processes in international business. International business research has matured from a preoccupation with explaining why international business exists to making a contribution to its effectiveness. New frontiers exist, notably in scientific research on processes and new forms in international business. Thus in this collection we have papers covering performance, location, market structure, and also issues of strategy, employee relations, the process of internationalization, de-internationalization, small and high-technology firms, and e-commerce. This is not, of course, exhaustive of the proliferation of areas of scholarly enquiry within international business, but it is a powerful demonstration of the academic health of international business research and of AIB UK.

The breadth and depth of scientific enquiry in international business within the UK – perhaps unique amongst regional chapters in publishing annually an edited conference volume with a leading academic publisher – is a fitting tribute to the organization founded by Michael Brooke. His commitment to issues of the effective management of international business is strongly echoed in this volume. This is honoured at the 30th anniversary annual conference with a special panel session to celebrate Michael's contribution to the subject of international business, and to our academic and professional community in the UK and worldwide.

JEREMY CLEGG
Chair Academy of International Business
United Kingdom Chapter

Acknowledgements

Many thanks to the Department of International Business and Accounting and Lancashire Business School, University of Central Lancashire, for holding the 29th Annual Conference of the Academy of International Business. Thanks, also, to the staff of the Business Services Unit, in particular Liz Kelly and Emma Woodward, for coordinating operations and compiling the proceedings and at the University of Strathclyde, to Pavlos Dimitratos for his advice on the preparation of the manuscript and to Ruth Kerr and Aisla Cullen for their help with word-processing and proof-reading.

The editors acknowledge and thank Taylor & Francis Ltd (*http://www.tandf.co.uk/journals*) for permission to publish a version of the article 'The Relative Economic Performance of Foreign Subsidiaries in UK Manufacturing', by Chengqi Wang, Pamela Siler and Xiaming Liu, *Applied Economics* (2002).

Notes on the Contributors

Zuhair Al-Obaidi is Professor of International Business at the Helsinki School of Economics. His business experience includes 13 years of work and consultation for Middle Eastern and Finnish firms, governments, and international organizations. His current teaching and research interests include technology transfer, the globalization of high-tech SMEs, IT applications to internationalization, and business in developing countries.

Jim Bell is Professor of International Business Entrepreneurship at the University of Ulster, Magee College, Northern Ireland. His research interests are in the area of small-firm internationalization and public policy in support of internationalization.

Luis Bernardino is Assistant Professor of International Marketing and Marketing Management at ISCTE-Management School of Lisbon, Lisbon, Portugal. He is currently studying for a PhD with the Department of Business and Management at the University of Glasgow. His research interests include the internationalization of SMEs, international entrepreneurship and international business strategy.

Arrti H. Billimoria has an MA in international business analysis from University College Northampton. Her research interests are global and international economics, particularly foreign direct investment.

Sue Bridgewater is a Lecturer in Marketing and Strategy at Warwick Business School, Warwick University. Her research interests lie in the areas of internationalization, networks, e-business and brand strategies.

Chris Carr is Professor in Corporate Strategy, University of Edinburgh. His main research interest is strategic approaches to globalization. He has published two books in the field and articles in several academic journals including the *Strategic Management Journal.*

Helen Chen-Mansolas is a PhD student at Warwick Business School. Her research interests are in the area of e-business and internationalization.

Mark Cook is Principal Lecturer in Economics at University College Northampton. His teaching and research interests are focused on international business, the economics of Europe and small and medium-sized enterprises (SMEs). He has written a number of texts including *International Business*

Economics, Managerial Economics and *Supply-side Economics*. His work has been published in a number of journals, including the *International Small Business Journal*, the *Journal of European Business Education* and the *International Small Business Journal*.

Adam R. Cross is Senior Lecturer in International Business in the Centre for International Business at the University of Leeds (CIBUL), UK, and Deputy Director of the Centre for Chinese Business and Development. He teaches international business at undergraduate level and on MBA programmes in the UK, Singapore, France and Poland. His research interests include licensing and franchising as foreign market servicing strategies, and foreign direct investment in Europe and China. He has co-edited a volume and published in *Management International Review* and *International Business Review*.

Claudio De Mattos is Research Fellow at the Jean Monnet European Centre of Excellence at the Leeds Business School, The University of Leeds, and Assistant Professor at Candido Mendes Business School, Rio de Janeiro, Brazil. His current research focuses on international alliances in high-technology sectors, with an emphasis on SMEs and emerging economies. His work has been published in a number of journals including the *European Management Journal* and the *Thunderbird International Business Review*.

Pavlos Dimitratos is Research Fellow at the Strathclyde International Business Unit, University of Strathclyde. His research interests are international management and strategy, international entrepreneurship and internationalization of smaller firms.

Grahame Fallon is Senior Lecturer in International Business at University College Northampton and Co-Director of the Centre for Research into East European Management. His teaching and research interests are foreign direct investment at the national and regional level in Eastern and Western Europe and in the former Soviet Union, together with international political economy, and the political and economic transition problems of former communist countries. He has also carried out research into the international strategies and operations of small and medium-sized enterprises (SMEs) and into ethnic business. His work has been published in a number of journals, including the *Journal of Small Business and Enterprise Development*, the *European Business Review, Qualitative Research* and the *Journal of Further and Higher Education*.

Jedrzej George Frynas is Lecturer at the Birmingham Business School at the University of Birmingham. His research interest is the activities of multinational enterprises in developing countries. He is the author of *Oil in Nigeria: Conflict and Litigation Between Oil Companies and Village Communities* (Münster/Hamburg: LIT, 2000) and has published articles in politics, law and development journals such as *Third World Quarterly, African Affairs, Review of African Political*

Economy and *Social and Legal Studies*, amongst others. He has also published in mainstream business journals including *Thunderbird International Business Review* and *Management Decision*.

Mika Gabrielsson is Professor of International Business at the Helsinki School of Economics, Finland. His teaching covers areas such as export, international and global marketing, and his research interests include international sales channel strategies and rapid globalization. Before joining the academic world he held several senior positions in high-tech marketing and purchasing, including acting as a product line manager for Fujitsu ICL.

Peter Gabrielsson is Research Fellow at the Centre for International Business Research, Helsinki School of Economics, Finland. He has held several senior management positions in the ICT industry and is currently on study leave from Nokia Mobile Phones, where he holds a position as Senior Product Marketing Manager. His research interests focus on globalization processes and strategies. More recently, he has conducted research on the so-called globalizing internationals and their product strategies.

Irene Greaves is Senior Lecturer in International Business in the Department of International Business, University of Central Lancashire. Her research interests include international business strategy, cross-cultural management and innovation and business continuity management in smaller firms.

Arne Heise is Professor of Economics at the University of Hamburg. His research interests are macroeconomics and employment in Germany. He has worked as a research fellow at the Hans Bockler Foundation and has held the post of Professor in the Universities of Cologne and Vienna. His work has been published in journals such as *WSI Mitteilungen, Wirtschaft und Gesellschaft* and *Journal of Industrial Relations*.

Kevin I.N. Ibeh is Lecturer in the Department of Marketing, University of Strathclyde, Glasgow. His current research interests are export and international entrepreneurship behaviour among small firms, including developing country and agribusiness firms.

Marian V. Jones is Senior Lecturer in the Department of Business and Management, University of Glasgow. Her research interests are internationalization of small high-technology firms, export information and international entrepreneurship.

John Knight is Director of the International Business Programme and Lecturer in Marketing, at the University of Otago School of Business, Dunedin, New Zealand. His research focuses on government export promotion.

Xiaming Liu is Senior Lecturer in the Strategic Management Group at Aston Business School, Birmingham.

Sharon Loane is doctoral candidate at the University of Ulster. Her research interest is the rapid internationalization of Internet-enabled start-ups and she is undertaking a cross-national study in four countries. She has extensive work experience with both large international manufacturing firms and small international service providers.

Frank McDonald is Principal Lecturer and Head of the International Business Unit at Manchester Metropolitan University Business School. His research is focused on the process of internationalization, especially with regard to the impact of institutional factors on FDI inflows. He has published several books in the area of International Business and has published in journals such as *Wirtschaft und Gesellschaft, Journal of Small Business Management* and *Personnel Review*.

Rod McNaughton is the Eyton Chair in Entrepreneurship at the University of Waterloo, Ontario, Canada. His research interests are in the area of SME internationalization and financing international expansion.

Kamel Mellahi lectures at Loughborough University Business School, Loughborough University. His research interests are the management of crisis, failure and decline, de-internationalization and international first-mover advantage/disadvantage. He has recently written a book entitled *The Ethical Business: Challenges and Controversies* (London: Palgrave, 2002) and has published articles in a number of journals including the *British Journal of Management, Thunderbird International Business Review, Total Quality Management*, and *International Review of Retail, Distribution and Customer Research*.

Shan Pan has a PhD from Warwick Business School and is a Lecturer at the National University of Singapore. His research interests are e-commerce, m-commerce, and knowledge management.

Dennis Sakalauskas is Associate/Consultant with Putnam Associates, Inc., Boston, Massachusetts. He has over seven years of experience in management and strategy consulting in Canada, the UK and the USA. He holds a Bachelor of Commerce degree of Mount Allison University in New Brunswick, Canada, and a Master of Science in international marketing of the University of Strathclyde in Glasgow, Scotland, UK.

Pamela Siler is Divisional Leader in Economics in the School of Social and Health Sciences at the University of Abertay, Dundee.

Roger Strange is Senior Lecturer in Economics, and formerly Head of the Management Centre, at King's College London. He has published widely on Europe–Asia economic relations. His most recent books are *Japanese Manufacturing Investment in Europe: Its Impact on the UK Economy* (Routledge, 1993), *Trade and Investment in China* (Routledge, 1998, edited with Jim Slater and Limin Wang), *The European Union and ASEAN: Trade and Investment Issues* (Macmillan, 2000, edited with Jim Slater and Corrado Molteni), and *Small-scale Enterprises in Developing and Transitional Economies* (Palgrave, 2002, edited with Homi Katrak).

Romeo V. Turcan is a PhD student in the Marketing Department at the University of Strathclyde. His research interests are entrepreneurial growth and development, and international competitiveness and the de-internationalization process of small high-technology firms.

Heinz-Josef Tüselmann is Reader in the International Business Unit at Manchester Metropolitan University Business School. His research interests are employee relations in multinational corporations and the location decisions of German multinational corporations. His work has been published in journals such as the *Journal of World Business, Journal of Industrial Relations* and *Transnational Corporations*. He has been involved in work with the German Ministry of Economics on the development of rules for foreign investments and is also an adviser to a Bundstag committee investigating employee relations systems in Germany.

Chengqi Wang is Research Fellow at the Centre for Chinese Business and Development, University of Leeds.

Colin Wheeler is Senior Lecturer in the International Business Unit, University of Strathclyde. His research interests include export marketing strategy and performance, and international marketing strategies in the food and drink industry.

Pakfei Yeung has an MSc in international management from King's College London. She was awarded a distinction for the dissertation and the 'Best Project Prize'. Since graduating, she has worked for Johnson & Johnson.

List of Abbreviations

CLM	conditional logit model
CRN	concentration ration for 'n' firms
DOE	domestically owned firm
D, R&D	design, research and development
EMU	economic and monetary union
EPO	export promotion organization
ER	employee relations
EU	European Union
EUR	other European countries
FDI	foreign direct investment
FOS	foreign-owned subsidiary
GATS	General Agreement on Trade in Services
GATT	General Agreement on Trade and Tariffs
GDP	gross domestic product
HI	Herfindahl index
HRM	human resources management
HTSF	high-technology small firm
IB	international business
ICT	information and communication technology
IDV	International Distillers and Vintners
IJV	international joint ventures
ILO	International Labour Office
IOV	industrial organization-based view
IR	industrial relations
ISP	internet service provider
IT	information technology
JV	joint venture
LEM	large emerging market
MAA	mergers, acquisitions and alliances
MNC	multinational company
MRP	material requirement planning
NAFTA	North American Free Trade Area
NBV	network-based view
NIDL	new international division of labour
OECD	Organization for Economic Cooperation and Development
PGA	Professional Golfers Association
PM	product mandate
PSF	professional service firm
RDAs	regional development agencies

R&D	research and development
RPM	regional product mandate
RBV	resource-based view
RS	rationalized subsidiary
SEAFIC	New Zealand Seafood Council
SG	strategic group
SIC	Standard Industrial Classification
SME	small and medium-sized enterprise
SMOPEC	small open economies
SSTP	strategic stable time period
TCA	transaction-cost approach
TRIPS	Trade Related Intellectual Property Rights
UDG	United Distillers Guinness
UNCTC	United Nations Centre for Transnational Corporations
WERS98	Workplace Employee Relations Survey 1998
WPM	world product mandate
WTO	World Trade Organization

1 Introduction: Internationalization, Firm Strategies and Management

Colin Wheeler, Frank McDonald and Irene Greaves

This volume of the Academy of International Business (AIB) series is organized broadly around the theme of internationalization and is based on a selection of the best papers presented at the 29th Academy of International Business UK Chapter Conference. The book is divided into four parts or sub-themes. Part One focuses on subsidiary location and performance and begins with the study that won the Best Paper Award at the conference. Part Two deals with internationalization and firm strategy and Part Three examines practices and policies associated with the internationalization of small and medium-sized enterprises. The contributions in Part Four focus on the role of the Internet and e-commerce in international business and internationalization.

PART ONE: SUBSIDIARY LOCATION AND PERFORMANCE

In Chapter 2, Chengqi Wang, Pamela Siler and Xiaming Liu compare the economic performance of UK and foreign-owned firms in UK manufacturing industry. Using a panel dataset covering 14 233 firms for the period 1992–96 they examine the influences of firm, industry and country-specific advantages on productivity. They find that the relative performance of foreign subsidiaries is jointly determined by both home and host-country conditions, consistent with the 'double diamond model', and that labour productivity is higher in foreign subsidiaries than in UK-owned firms. Foreign subsidiaries as a whole also employ higher levels of human capital and enjoy greater economies of scale than UK-owned firms.

While there are no significant differences in the productivity gap between foreign subsidiaries of different nationalities, the results show that the reasons for foreign superiority do vary across nationalities, indicating that the ownership advantage of foreign subsidiaries may take different forms. A further source of productivity advantage for US subsidiaries is their higher level of intangible assets, and for European and Japanese subsidiaries their higher level of capital intensity.

In Chapter 3, Pakfei Yeung and Roger Strange focus on the factors that affect the choice of location of Japanese-affiliated manufacturing firms, one of the most dynamic sources of new FDI within the United States in the last decade. They argue that, since 1973, FDI has had a significant impact on State economies in the

United States, yet very few rigorous statistical analyses have been undertaken of the geographical dispersion of this investment. They use conditional logit analysis to model the location choices of Japanese firms between nine 'divisions' of the United States. The effects of the introduction of the North American Free Trade Agreement (NAFTA) are also investigated by contrasting the location determinants of those affiliates established prior to 1994 with those established after January of that year. They conclude that the educational standard of the workforce, the size of the local divisional market, and the state of the transportation infrastructure all have highly significant positive effects upon location choice, whilst both taxation and average labour costs have significant negative effects. The importance of labour costs appears to diminish markedly after the introduction of NAFTA, and this may perhaps reflect the relocation of labour-intensive Japanese manufacturing investment away from the United States to Mexico. Although they caution that such a conclusion is speculative and merits further study.

In Chapter 4, Grahame Fallon, Mark Cook and Arrti Billimoria explore a range of factors which influence the regional location of inbound foreign direct investment (FDI) in the West Midlands and Scotland. They examine official inward investment agency publications in order to identify those factors which public policy-makers believe attract FDI to each region. The influences on multinational corporation (MNC) decision-makers' FDI location decisions are also explored by means of multiple regression analysis. Elasticity analysis is then used to explore the sensitivity of FDI inflows with regard to a range of regional policy instruments. The results show that MNCs are attracted to the West Midlands and Scotland by different factors, and suggest that official inward investment agency thinking does not give sufficient attention to the key factors which have determined MNCs' direct investment location decisions. The authors conclude that central government, inward investment agencies and regional development agencies may need to adapt their thinking, their policies and their literature in order to address the main issues which influence the regional distribution of FDI in the UK context. In particular, central government should be flexible in its approach to inward investment policy, allowing regional development agencies the autonomy to operate distinctive direct investment strategies, related more strongly than at present to those differing factors which in reality appear to be attracting FDI to their regions.

Heinz-Josef Tüselmann, Frank McDonald and Arne Heise examine in Chapter 5 whether nationality of ownership still matters in the shaping of employee relations in German subsidiaries in the UK, or whether instead they adopt an Anglo-Saxon model of employee relations. The study is based on a representative survey of German subsidiaries in the UK, their parent companies and a comparative analysis based on the Workplace Employee Relations Survey (WERS98). In contrast with previous studies, this research reveals a pronounced country-of-origin effect in employee relations approaches and style. Furthermore, there are indications that employee relations in German subsidiaries increasingly reflect the emerging new German employee relations approach; that is, a flexible collective approach with a human resources management dimension, rather than an individualistic Anglo-Saxon approach.

PART TWO: INTERNATIONALIZATION AND FIRM STRATEGY

In Chapter 6, Chris Carr assesses the issue of global concentration, arguing that it is a central issue for any competitive strategy. He refutes recent claims of global fragmentation in sectors such as oil production, oil refining, automobiles and aluminium. Herfindahl index–based evidence is countered by more recent data. Broader, complementary measures, particularly the concentration ratio of the four largest firms in an industry likewise confirm patterns of global concentration, as does commercial and historical data. Similar concentration patterns are found in other sectors, though the extent varies with their economic characteristics. Chris Carr concludes by suggesting that internationally-orientated strategies, rather than global strategies, are still important since outright market domination or even niche strategies demand resources beyond the reach of many companies.

In Chapter 7, Peter and Mika Gabrielsson discuss how information and communication technology (ICT) companies originating from small open economies such as Finland, have faced a considerable challenge when moving from international to global product and marketing strategies. Both their environment and their resources and capabilities (strategic levers) have triggered a change in their corporate-level strategies, which has also had an effect on the degree of standardization of their business-level product strategies and marketing. They describe the ICT companies' development from the 'international market penetration' stage towards the 'global alignment' stage, and the drivers are examined. They review the standardization debate, concluding that both content and processes should be standardized to achieve increased global competitiveness. The authors describe and illustrate this phenomenon in the ICT equipment-manufacturing field and draw conclusions regarding the change from international to global product, channel and branding strategies.

In Chapter 8, Claudio de Mattos and Adam Cross consider the contribution of firm-specific factors to the viability of strategic alliances between firms from developed countries and those of large emerging markets/countries. They isolate and evaluate firm-specific factors associated with biotechnology firms from the UK and Germany in the context of possible alliance formation with similar firms from Brazil, and compare firms identified as 'most compatible' and 'least compatible'. Their findings show that firm-specific characteristics have an impact upon the compatibility of respective firms as they contemplate a strategic alliance. In particular, firms that have a strong expansionist strategy are found to be more compatible with large emerging market (LEM) firms than those who do not. The degree of specialization, size and human resources allocated to production are found to have a similar effect.

In Chapter 9, Pavlos Dimitratos, using data from an in-depth investigation of Greek firms that operate abroad, analyses the features associated with the effective management of internationalization ventures, utilizing two theoretical frameworks from organization theory, namely agency and stewardship theories. Four closely interrelated characteristics, which are associated with the application of the two theories, are examined as relevant success features: (a) consensus on objectives and strategy between the focal company and its partners abroad; (b) a 'situational' decision-making approach based on which partner has the best knowledge of a specific issue; (c) provision of appropriate incentives to partners; and (d) suitable performance measurement to ensure that partners are rewarded appropriately. Both the agency and the stewardship theories illuminate different aspects of these features. The author suggests that international partners should combine aspects of both the 'agent' and the 'steward' roles to secure better performance in the international marketplace.

Using a case study of how Marks and Spencer's withdrew from France during a period of crisis, Kamel Mellahi in Chapter 10 examines the process of de-internationalization and the interaction between the organization and its wider operating environment. The company initially had a standardized approach to de-internationalization across Europe, but in France the company was eventually forced to respond to local legislation and practice and change its initial approach to withdrawal.

In Chapter 11, Sharon Loane, Jim Bell, Mika Gabrielsson and Zuhair Al-Obaidi replicate a Finnish study of multiple export channels conducted by Gabrielsson and Al-Obaidi. Using case studies they explore the international channel strategies of small and medium-sized design companies in Northern Ireland. The authors describe the emergence of multiple channel structures and examine this process using four theoretical approaches: the internationalization process; sales channel economic structures; long-term channel relationships and the product life-cycle. The study highlights the impact of environmental changes and the advances in communications technology, such as the Internet, on channel structures.

PART THREE: THE INTERNATIONALIZATION OF THE SMALL FIRM

In Chapter 12, Luis Bernardino and Marian Jones explore the impact of high-technology small firms' internal resources/capabilities on international performance taking into consideration that this relationship is mediated by the type of foreign market entry mode utilized by the firm. Following the resource-based approach, they suggest that it is the idiosyncratic, often intangible resources that form the basis of firm capabilities, and consequently underpin other, more tangible sources of competitive advantage. In that context the study considers that the firm's organizational, technological, financial and human resources can be major sources of competitive advantage. They also suggest that firms may augment their resource base through access to external resources held by partners, through utilization of cooperative modes of foreign market entry. The implications are that the international performance of small high-technology firms will be greater where cooperative modes of foreign market entry are utilized. Propositions for future empirical work are put forward.

In Chapter 13, Romeo Turcan explores the nature of the de-internationalization process in small high-technology firms and develops a conceptual framework of the de-internationalization process in small firms. Three constructs form the basis of the proposed conceptual framework, namely: commitment, change and time. He suggests that in order to develop a better theoretical understanding of small firm de-internationalization there is a need for a paradigm shift from positivism to realism.

In Chapter 14, John Knight, Jim Bell and Rod McNaughton argue that official sources of export information are generally held in low regard by firms and that experiential knowledge gained by exporters themselves through visiting and working in foreign markets cannot be effectively substituted for by consultants – either governmental or commercial. Nevertheless, government organizations in many countries, including New Zealand, continue to focus their efforts on provision of export information. The authors examine perceptions held by New Zealand seafood exporters of the usefulness of government export assistance services, particularly information services, provided to them on a semi-commercial basis.

The New Zealand case is of particular interest because of a growing trend towards charging for services among other national export promotion organizations. The firms in this study report widespread dissatisfaction with the cost-effectiveness of these services. Firms advocate a return to a 'helping hand' approach, and express a willingness to pay for commercial results.

PART FOUR: THE INTERNET AND E-COMMERCE

In Chapter 15, Helen Chen, Sue Bridgewater and Shan Pan suggest that the open and connected nature of the Internet suggests parallels with business-to-business networks. The challenges of building positions in the latter are used as a framework to identify issues for building positions in international Internet networks. They analyse three small Hong Kong-based firms that have used the Internet to expand into international markets. The actors, activities and resources framework suggests that these firms operate in rapidly changing networks with uncertainty as to which will be successful positions. As a consequence, resource commitment tends to be incremental. They conclude that to operate effectively in the international e-marketspace, firms need to create more stable, trusting relationships.

In Chapter 16, Dennis Sakalauskas and Kevin Ibeh investigate the use of the Internet for realty – that is property-buying – purposes, and the effect of usage on buyer–realtor (estate agent) relationships in Canada and the UK. The findings suggest an appreciably higher level of Internet usage among the surveyed property buyers and a positive link between online realty experience and buyer–realtor relationship strength. Opportunities (or prospects) for e-commerce were, however, found to be minimal. The authors argue that realtors need to deploy Internet-enabled capabilities in ways that complement and support their existing (or traditional) channels.

In Chapter 17, the last Chapter, George Frynas analyses some of the most important political and legal challenges faced by internationally operating internet firms today. In addition to dealing with an important but rarely discussed issue, George Frynas attempts to provide a fresh perspective on this topic by utilizing the concept of political risk. Using evidence from exemplary court cases on topics such as consumption tax and intellectual property rights, the discussion demonstrates that internet firms face serious political and legal uncertainties, which differ considerably between different markets. In terms of methodology, the paper portrays how legal materials can be used to understand the impact of legal and political processes on international firms. It is suggested that future business research could make greater use of factual evidence from litigation as an alternative methodology in the study of the business environment.

Finally, we would like to say that preparing this book for publication on the 30th Anniversary of UK AIB, has made us very aware of the contribution that Michael Brooke has made to the UK Chapter of the Academy of International Business. His foresight in founding AIB UK 30 years ago, has provided a vibrant and flourishing forum for the development and support of research in international business in the UK.

Part One

Subsidiary Location and Performance

2 The Relative Economic Performance of Foreign Subsidiaries in UK Manufacturing*

Chengqi Wang, Pamela Siler and Xiaming Liu

INTRODUCTION

There is now considerable evidence to show that domestically-owned firms (DOEs) have lower levels of labour productivity than foreign-owned subsidiaries (FOSs) in UK manufacturing industry. In explaining these productivity differences, most studies refer to the firm-specific advantages which multinationals possess, allowing them to succeed in foreign environments. In fact, as Barrell and Pain (1997) point out, if foreign-owned assets are no more productive than those that are locally-owned, the rational for FDI, particularly among developed countries, disappears. Superior foreign-owned assets are also important from a policy viewpoint in that there is a perception that host countries can benefit from the potential for spillover effects to domestic firms. Given the importance of firm-specific advantages to FDI theory, it is surprising that there has been little attempt to directly measure these assets in studies of relative productivity performance.

According to Davies and Lyons (1991), foreign-owned enterprises held a 48.6 per cent productivity advantage over domestically-owned enterprises in the late 1980s. The authors point out, however, that the superior performance of FOSs may simply reflect the fact that they are clustered in industries with above average productivity. This is what is often labelled the 'structural' effect. Applying a two-tier decomposition analysis, Davies and Lyons (1991) find that if the two types of firms had identical employment distributions across industries, the productivity gap would fall to 23.5 per cent. The gap remaining is attributed to 'ownership' effects defined by the authors above as 'pure efficiency' and technology differentials. Davies and Lyons (1991) recognize that the observed productivity gap might equally be due to differences in other firm-level variables such as labour skills, capital inputs or monopoly power.

* The editors acknowledge and thank Taylor & Francis Ltd (*http://www.tandf.co.uk/journals*) for permission to publish a version of the article 'The Relative Economic Performance of Foreign Subsidiaries in UK Manufacturing', by Chengqi Wang, Pamela Siler and Xiaming Liu, *Applied Economics* (2002).

A number of studies have considered the home base of the multinational corporations when investigating sources of productivity advantages. Griffith (1999), after controlling for industry differences, finds 1992 value-added per worker to be: 39 per cent higher in French-owned establishments; 32 per cent higher in German-owned establishments; and 41 per cent higher in US-owned establishments. Value-added per worker in Japanese-owned establishments is not significantly different from those that are UK-owned in the Griffith paper. Oulton (1998), using a large cross-section of 1995 firm-level data, found that after controlling for industrial composition, US ownership raised labour productivity by 26 per cent in UK manufacturing industries and 34 per cent in non-manufacturing industries. Firms under other (non-US) ownership had advantages of 14 per cent and 31 per cent respectively in manufacturing and non-manufacturing. Oulton (1998) notes that ownership may have a direct effect on productivity if foreign firms have access to superior assets, including those that are knowledge-based. He finds, however, the indirect effects of foreign ownership to be more important in explaining the superior performance of foreign firms. These are the effects associated with a higher level of capital intensity and a labour force that is more skilled.

UK domestically-owned firms are not the only ones to lag behind their foreign-owned counterparts. Globerman *et al.* (1994) find that, after correcting for sectoral differences, foreign-owned firms operating in Canada have significantly higher productivity than Canadian-owned establishments. The authors use factor proportion and scale differences to explain the superior performance of FOSs from the USA, the EC and Japan. While proxies for capital intensity, labour force participation and firm size are used, the difference in technology levels is not included as an explanatory variable. This exclusion seems inconsistent with the conventional FOS ownership advantage assumption. In addition, although two labour input-related explanatory variables are used to measure the active workforce and the share of male employees, the potential role of human capital is not considered.

In contrast to other studies, Kim and Lyn (1990) suggest that foreign-owned multinational enterprises do not necessarily enjoy 'monopolistic advantages' over their domestic competitors. They find foreign firms operating in the USA to be less profitable than randomly selected US firms, and that they spend more on R&D and less on advertising. The findings, according to the authors, imply that foreign firms are attracted to the USA because of its brighter economic prospects and by the possibility of gaining access to US technology. When Kim and Lyn (1990) subdivide the foreign-based multinationals into those from Canada, Japan and Western Europe, their findings indicate that motivations for investing in the USA may differ by country of origin.

This study represents an attempt to overcome some of the shortcomings of previous research by examining a panel data-set, which consists of 14 233 firms operating in 14 broad UK industries for the period 1992–96. We first investigate whether there is a significant labour productivity gap between FOSs and UK DOEs, and then quantify factors likely to be important in explaining the gap. Unlike previous work, this study attempts to directly measure the role of firm-specific assets in explaining productivity differences by making use of an intangible assets variable.

The issue of a FOS's nationality is also of particular relevance to this study. The knowledge of whether and how the home country of a FOS affects the benefits from FDI may help a host country to target subsidiaries of certain home countries more effectively. As in Globerman *et al.* (1994), we control for ownership effects by identifying foreign-owned establishments in terms of the owner's home country. Subsidiaries from other European (EUR) countries, Japan, and the USA are compared with UK indigenous firms. In addition, we control for the influences of industry distribution by using dummy variables corresponding to 14 SIC sub-manufacturing industries.

The rest of the chapter is organized as follows. The next section outlines the major theoretical considerations and the third section describes the sample. The fourth section sets out the empirical models, while the empirical results are presented next, followed by the conclusions.

THEORETICAL CONSIDERATIONS

Firm-specific ownership advantages have played a dominant role in the theory of FDI. Hymer (1976) argues that the MNC is a creature of market imperfections, which lead a firm to possess monopolistic advantages. Because of this, it is possible for the firm to overcome economic and/or cultural/social distance and to earn a higher rate of return than local competitors in the host country. Dunning's eclectic paradigm (1981, 1988a, 1988b) combines ownership (firm-specific), internalization and location (country-specific) advantages to explain the existence and growth of MNCs' competitors. He suggests that all three conditions should be present for firms to have a strong motive to undertake FDI.

As emphasized by Markuson (1995), with respect to firm-specific assets, those that are 'knowledge-based' have played a key role in explanations of FDI. He notes that multinational enterprises can be identified with a high ratio of intangible assets to market value. Process and product innovations, along with intangible assets such as marketing skills and reputation, act as joint inputs across a geographical range of plants, leading to firm-level scale economies. The importance of these types of assets also leads to internalization strategies to minimize transactions costs (see Rugman, 1980, or Casson, 1987). Imperfections in markets for human capital, knowledge, marketing and managerial expertise mean that these intermediate outputs can be best exploited by overseas production rather than by licensing. One objective of the current study is to explore the relationship between firm-specific assets, particularly those that are knowledge-based, and the productivity advantages of FOSs.

The performance of FOSs is affected not only by firm-specific assets, but also by country-of-origin characteristics. As expressed in his work on the competitive advantages of nations, Porter's (1990) 'single diamond' view alleges that the strong global competitiveness generated by the core competences of an MNC, results from the characteristics of the MNC's home base. According to Porter, multinational status is a reflection of a company's ability to exploit strengths gained in one nation in order to establish a position in other nations.

The technological profile of a creative subsidiary will reflect the distinctive specialized technological capacities of its home country.

Davies and Lyons (1991) acknowledge that in this 'world best-practice view', FOSs represent the best-practice technology available in their country of origin (for example German machine tools). If this is the case, the productivity of FOSs should mirror that of their home firms whether they are multinational or produce strictly for national markets. An implication of this perspective is that an MNC's advantage when producing in a host country is positively correlated with the international productivity differential between its home and host country.

Challenging Porter, Rugman and Verbeke (1993) use a 'double diamond' approach in contrast to the single diamond framework. They argue that, while multinational subsidiaries benefit from global learning and global scope economies, they are becoming increasingly independent from individual countries. Multinational firms engaged in international competition need to take into account demand conditions, production factors and the forces driving industry competition in both the home and host country.

Given the contrasting views noted above, another objective of the current study is to investigate whether the relative performance of FOSs depends on their countries of origin, assuming all other factors such as market conditions remain constant. Of particular interest is whether the results from our empirical investigation are consistent with a 'single diamond' or 'double diamond' approach.

THE SAMPLE

Data and Sample

This study uses a panel data-set which contains 14 233 firms across 14 industries for the period 1992–96. The empirical data used in this study are taken from FAME (Financial Analysis Made Easy), the financial database available on CD-ROM containing major public and private companies from the Jordan Watch and the Jordan Survey database. Industry effects are captured by classifying firms to 14 sub-manufacturing industries – the broadest classification of the SIC.

Firms are categorized by ownership, with FOSs defined as those firms with at least 50 per cent of their share capital in foreign ownership. In our data-set, the 'foreign firms' include those subsidiaries from other European countries (EUR), the USA and Japan. The number of firms in the sample accounts for approximately 26 per cent of the total number of manufacturing firms in the FAME database. Our sample contains 4267 FOSs and 9966 DOEs, which represent about 30 per cent of the total number of foreign firms and about 23 per cent of the total number of UK-owned firms in the database respectively. Thus the sample is fairly representative of UK manufacturing industry. Table 2.1 shows the distribution of sample firms by industry and ownership. A data Appendix at the end of the chapter provides a more through description of the data and sources used.

Table 2.1   Distribution of sample firms by industry and nationality

Industry: SIC name		Number of firms					
		UK	EUR	USA	Japan	Foreign	Total*
DA	Food, beverage, and tobacco	805	206	66	8	280	1085
DB	Textile products	610	50	48	12	110	720
DC	Leather products	93	8	7	0	15	108
DD	Wood products	206	33	4	0	37	243
DE	Pulp, paper, publishing	1605	344	130	8	482	2087
DF	Coke, petroleum and nuclear	41	26	20	0	46	87
DG	Chemical products	736	297	216	29	542	1287
DH	Rubber and plastic products	503	121	54	6	181	684
DI	Other non-metallic mineral products	293	72	34	2	108	401
DJ	Basic metals	1821	378	265	17	660	2481
DK	Machinery and equipment	710	252	179	22	453	1163
DL	Electrical and optical products	1292	325	390	93	808	2100
DM	Transport equipment	343	92	51	5	148	491
DN	Other	908	220	151	26	397	1305
Total		9966	2424	1615	228	4267	14233

* Total of UK, EUR, USA and Japan.

Summary Statistics

Table 2.2 shows the average labour (LP), capital (CP) and total factor (TFP) productivity advantage that FOSs have over UK indigenous firms by industry and by nationality of the subsidiary. Clearly there is a great deal of diversity across industries, but nevertheless a number of patterns emerge. First, foreign subsidiaries, whatever their nationality, benefit from higher average labour productivity (LP) in almost every industry. Both US and European (EUR)-owned firms are more efficient than UK-owned firms, but there is no obvious difference between US and EUR firms. Japanese-owned firms outperform UK firms, but they have lower labour productivity than their European and US counterparts. Second, with respect to total factor productivity (TFP), the average gap is generally smaller, except in the case of Japanese-owned firms. In fact, EUR-owned firms have a lower level of TFP than UK-owned firms. This is partly because capital productivity (CP) is higher in UK-owned firms in ten industries of our sample

Since most previous studies in the area have focused on labour productivity, for purposes of comparison we do the same. In the next section, empirical models are developed to examine the relationship between the firm's level of labour productivity and its nationality, controlling for industrial structural effects. We then empirically investigate the factors that are likely to be important in explaining the generally inferior labour productivity in UK domestically-owned firms.

Table 2.2   Comparative levels of productivity (UK level = 1)

Industry	LP			TFP			CP		
	EUR	USA	Japan	EUR	USA	Japan	EUR	USA	Japan
Food, beverage	0.93	1.74	1.49	0.73	1.07	0.91	0.75	1.07	0.65
Textile products	1.26	1.27	1.15	0.74	1.07	0.78	0.56	0.95	0.61
Leather products	2.58	1.11		1.23	0.61		0.96	0.46	
Wood products	1.21	1.06		0.78	1.43		0.66	1.80	
Pulp, paper, publishing	1.28	1.05	0.92	1.27	0.98	1.34	1.30	0.96	1.87
Coke, petroleum, nuclear	1.75	2.16		1.44	1.04		1.61	0.84	
Chemical	1.02	1.09	1.04	1.04	1.13	1.90	1.07	1.22	3.36
Rubber, plastic	1.17	1.12	2.91	0.98	0.95	0.79	0.96	0.94	0.74
Other non-metallic mineral	1.03	1.15	1.89	0.82	1.30	4.78	0.77	1.49	13.69
Basic metals	1.01	1.08	0.82	0.80	1.05	0.65	0.70	1.08	0.55
Machinery, equipment	1.16	1.15	1.46	1.17	1.17	1.37	1.39	1.25	1.23
Electrical	1.13	1.32	1.38	1.00	1.19	1.22	0.89	1.20	1.33
Transport equipment	0.92	0.88	1.33	0.81	3.33	0.45	0.75	1.43	0.21
Other	1.20	1.27	1.08	1.06	1.09	1.06	0.43	1.06	0.63
Manufacturing averages*	1.25	1.25	1.11	0.92	1.17	1.29	0.91	1.13	1.78
Standard error	0.33	0.33	0.12	0.33	0.70	1.26	0.33	0.32	3.55

* Figures include 14 industries for the EUR and the USA and 11 industries for Japan.
The EUR and US figures are almost unchanged if leather, wood products and coke, petroleum and nuclear industries are excluded.

EMPIRICAL MODELS

As noted above, the labour productivity of a firm depends to some extent on the characteristics of the industry it competes in and its nationality. Following Globerman *et al.* (1994) we adopt a model using both industry and nationality dummy variables. For the industry dummy, 'food products, beverages, and tobacco' is taken as the base industry. UK ownership is used as the constant when considering nationality. Since we use a panel data-set, our first empirical model is as follows:

$$LP_{ij} = \alpha + \sum_{k=1}^{13} \gamma_{kij} I_{kij} + \sum_{h=1}^{3} \delta_{kij} N_{hij} + \varepsilon_{ij} \tag{2.1}$$

where LP_{ij} is the labour productivity of firm i at time j. It is measured by value-added per worker. The intercept term, α, includes the average effect of a UK establishment in the food product, beverages and tobacco industry. The dummy variable I_{kij} is equal to one if firm i is in industry k, and zero otherwise. Likewise, dummy variable N_{hij} is equal to one if firm i is of nationality h, and zero otherwise. In our sample, $i = 1, 2, \ldots, i(= 14\ 233)$ firms in $k = 1, \ldots, 14$ industries, and $j = 1, 2, \ldots, J(= 5)$ covering the years 1992–96.

In our second empirical model, we test for the influence of a number of other factors on labour productivity in addition to the nationality variables. With reference to more sophisticated versions of the production function, labour productivity depends on the following variables: physical capital intensity (*CI*); intangible assets per worker (*INT*); human capital (*HC*); and firm size (*SIZE*):

$$LP_{ij} = \alpha + \beta_1 CI_{ij} + \beta_2 INT_{ij} + \beta_3 HC_{ij} + \beta_4 SIZE_{ij} + \sum_{k=1}^{13} \gamma_{kij} I_{kij}$$

$$+ \sum_{h=1}^{3} \delta_{kij} N_{hij} + \varepsilon_{ij} \qquad (2.2)$$

Assuming that some of the home-country differences in productivity can be attributed to these differences in firm-specific factor intensities, then we would expect the influence and significance of the nationality variables to decline.

A variable of particular interest and one which is unique to this study is intangible assets per worker (*INT*). This is a proxy for the firm-specific knowledge-based assets that have been so important in explaining the theory of FDI. Recent work by Liu *et al.* (2000) at the UK industry level shows a positive and significant relationship between labour productivity and intangible assets. We would expect the same positive relationship in this firm-level study. In fact an interesting question concerns the significance of the ownership variables in equation (2.2) above, when this variable is added, given the importance placed on ownership advantages as embodied in intangible assets in the theoretical literature. With respect to knowledge-based assets, our empirical measure of the intangible assets variable includes the value of patent rights and capitalized development costs. It also includes the value of other intangible assets such as trademarks and brand names, which also give the firm 'monopolistic advantages', increasing value-added per employee.

Another variable of interest is human capital (*HC*). A higher value of human capital may be seen as evidence of higher learning efforts, or a larger effective labour force. Theoretical models of economic growth such as Lucas (1988) emphasize that the engine of growth is the unlimited accumulation of human capital. A standard proxy for labour quality or human capital is average wages, assuming factors are paid according to their marginal products. However, since wages may be simultaneously determined with output (value-added), regressing a value-added-based measure of productivity on average wages may raise simultaneity problems. To avoid this problem, we follow Hausman (1978) and Rault (1995) and use the residuals from the regression of the log (average wages) on *CI, INT, SIZE* as the proxy for human capital. This proxy reflects the average wages (therefore labour quality or human capital) that are not explained by all the other explanatory variables.

A positive relationship is also expected between the dependent variable and physical capital intensity (*CI*), measured by the value of physical capital stock per employee. The average firm size (*SIZE*) variable, measured by sales and representing economies of scale is usually assumed to be positively related to labour productivity.

As noted earlier, ownership factors may indirectly affect the performance of foreign subsidiaries because FOSs are associated with higher levels of factor intensities. We establish the links between the individual determinants of labour productivity and nationality by estimating the following equations, again controlling for industry effects:

$$CI_{ij} = \alpha + \sum_{k=1}^{14} \gamma_{kij} I_{kij} + \sum_{h=1}^{3} \delta_{kij} N_{hij} + \varepsilon_{ij} \tag{2.3}$$

$$INT_{ij} = \alpha + \sum_{k=1}^{14} \gamma_{kij} I_{kij} + \sum_{h=1}^{3} \delta_{kij} N_{hij} + \varepsilon_{ij} \tag{2.4}$$

$$HC_{ij} = \alpha + \sum_{k=1}^{14} \gamma_{kij} I_{kij} + \sum_{h=1}^{3} \delta_{kij} N_{hij} + \varepsilon_{ij} \tag{2.5}$$

$$SIZE_{ij} = \alpha + \sum_{k=1}^{14} \gamma_{kij} I_{kij} + \sum_{h=1}^{3} \delta_{kij} N_{hij} + \varepsilon_{ij} \tag{2.6}$$

In all equations the variables are in logarithmic form except for the ownership dummies. The equations are estimated through pooled ordinary least squares (POLS).

EMPIRICAL RESULTS

Equation (2.1) in Table 2.3 shows labour productivity to be higher in foreign subsidiaries than in UK-owned firms, holding industry influences constant. This finding is consistent with other studies. Somewhat more surprising are the relatively small differences in productivity advantage amongst multinationals of different nationalities. If we convert coefficients in equation (2.1) to percentages $[\exp(\beta)- 1]$, then Japanese-owned firms lead with a 31 per cent productivity advantage over UK-owned firms, followed by US-owned firms with a 25 per cent advantage and European-owned firms with a 23 per cent advantage. While our findings for US-owned firms mirror those of Oulton (1998), they contrast with Griffith's (1999) finding of no productivity advantages for Japanese-owned firms.

Equation (2.1) = in Table 2.3 highlights the fact that productivity differences among FOSs of different home countries, controlling for industry effects, are not statistically significant. As a crude test of Porter's single diamond approach we can compare the differences between DOEs and FOSs of different nationalities with international productivity differences in manufacturing. Crafts and O'Mahony (1999) report labour productivity advantages over the UK in manufacturing in 1996 to be: 71 per cent in the USA; 47 per cent in Japan; and 26 per cent in France and Germany. The authors noted above use output per hour worked in manufacturing as their labour productivity measure. Using a different measure, Barrell and Pain

Table 2.3   Regression results

Equation	Results	
(2.1)	$LP_{ij} = 0.21\ EUR_{ij} + 0.22US_{ij} + 0.27Japan$ (4.51***) (4.67***) (5.25***)	$\bar{R}^2 = 0.47$
(2.1)	$LP_{ij} = -0.01EUR + 0.08\ Japan$ (−0.20) (1.54)	$\bar{R}^2 = 0.47$
(2.2)	$LP_{ij} = 0.10CI_{ij} + 0.03INT_{ij} + 0.52HC_{ij} + 0.04SIZE_{ij}$ $+ 0.10EUR + 0.13US + 0.21Japan$ (4.78***) (4.35***) (8.32***) (1.53) (2.49***) (3.13***) (4.48***)	$\bar{R}^2 = 0.66$
(2.3)	$CI_{ij} = 0.45EUR + 0.08US + 0.50Japan$ (3.42***) (0.64) (3.48***)	$\bar{R}^2 = 0.30$
(2.4)	$INT_{ij} = 0.01EUR + 0.02US - 0.01JAPAN$ (1.29) (2.15)** (− 0.91)	$\bar{R}^2 = 0.44$
(2.5)	$HC_{ij} = 0.12EUR + 0.17US + 0.20Japan$ (2.51***) (3.64***) (3.98***)	$\bar{R}^2 = 0.26$
(2.6)	$SIZE_{ij} = 0.19EUR + 0.40US + 0.45Japan$ (1.84**) (3.77***) (3.87***)	$\bar{R}^2 = 0.49$

Note: (a) equation (2.1) = reports the results of comparison among FOSs of different nationalities by substituting the USA for the UK as the base country; (b) *, **, and *** denote significance at 10 per cent, 5 per cent and 1 per cent levels respectively; (c) figures in parentheses are the *t* statistic; (d) to facilitate clarity, industry dummy variable coefficients are not reported.

(1997) report gross product per employee in the UK to be 12 per cent lower than the European average across all sectors, and 28 per cent lower in manufacturing in 1996.

The limited evidence reported above shows the productivity gaps between DOEs and FOSs from the USA and Japan to be modest and not directly proportional to the gap between the UK and the corresponding home countries in manufacturing. In fact the productivity advantages among all FOSs are close to the European average. This may indicate that the original productivity advantages of some foreign firms may be negatively affected by European market conditions. Another explanation might be that European integration and geographical adjacency help FOSs from the EU to offset some of their disadvantages relative to FOSs from the USA and Japan. All of this suggests that the relative performance of foreign subsidiaries is jointly determined and is likely to be influenced by both their home-country bases and host-country market conditions. These findings, which should be interpreted with caution, seem to coincide with the spirit of the 'double diamond' framework (Rugman and Verbeke, 1993).

As expected, equation (2.2) of Table 2.3 shows that capital intensity, intangible assets per worker, human capital, and large firm size contribute positively to value-added per employee. All these explanatory variables except the size variable are statistically significant at the 0.01 level. In contrast to the studies of Globerman *et al.* (1994) and Oulton (1998), the nationality variables are still statistically significant when these explanatory variables are added to equation (2.1). Again, converting nationality coefficients to percentages [exp (β) − 1], gives FOSs from Japan a 23 per cent productivity advantage over UK DOEs, followed by US-owned firms with a 13 per cent advantage and EU-owned firms with an 11 per cent advantage. This suggests that, when one holds some obvious conditioning factors constant, UK-owned firms are still less efficient than foreign subsidiaries. It is also apparent that not all of the advantages of foreign ownership are reflected in the intangible assets variable. In fact the relatively high coefficient remaining for Japanese nationality may reflect the advantages associated with superior managerial practices.

We follow Globerman *et al.* (1994) and estimate equations (2.3)–(2.6) to examine the extent to which the differences in relative productivity performance can be attributed to the differences in factor intensities across nationalities. Equation (2.3) shows that there is no significant difference in capital intensity between UK and US-owned firms. While this is a bit surprising, it is consistent with the finding of Kim and Lyn (1989) that foreign subsidiaries in the USA are more capital-intensive than their indigenous counterparts. In contrast, European and Japanese-owned firms are significantly more capital-intensive than UK indigenous firms.

Equation (2.4) shows that US subsidiaries enjoy higher levels of intangible assets per employee. This is consistent with recent work by the Department of Trade and Industry (DTI, 1999) which shows UK firms to trail US firms in terms of their spending on R&D per worker and their patenting per head of population. However, FOSs from Europe and Japan do not demonstrate significant differences from UK DOEs in their stock of intangible assets. This is inconsistent with the DTI report noted above which shows UK firms to lag behind both Japanese and European firms generally with respect to their innovative activities. These inconsistencies may be partially explained by our measure of intangible assets, which includes trademarks and brands in addition to knowledge related assets. Also, FOSs may be able to obtain access to more advanced technologies through parent firms in their home countries. If this is the case, then FOSs may still enjoy higher labour productivity even though there is no significant difference in the stock of intangible assets at the subsidiary level.

Turning to human capital in equation (2.5), the result shows that the lower level of human capital in DOEs may be one important reason for their inferior performance. This result is consistent with other evidence. Crafts and O'Mahony (1999) conclude that there are a 'number of mechanisms' linking human capital accumulation and productivity, not all of which can be quantified. Nevertheless, they find that Britain has a serious shortfall in human capital relative to both the USA and Germany. Our result is also consistent with those studies which highlight the higher levels of technical and scientific skills in the workforce of FOSs (Carr, 1992; Mason *et al.*, 1994). Equation (2.6) shows that the relatively smaller scale of operations in DOEs may also contribute to the observed productivity gap through the relationship with ownership.

CONCLUSIONS

We have compared the performance of foreign and UK-owned firms operating in UK manufacturing industry. Holding industry influences constant, FOSs outperformed DOEs in terms of their labour productivity. This finding is consistent with the conventional ownership advantage assumption from FDI theory and also with other empirical findings. However, in contrast to other studies, our regression analysis shows that there are no significant differences between the productivity advantages of FOSs of different nationalities. This is despite the fact that there are significant international differences in labour productivity in manufacturing between the USA, Japan and Europe. While foreign firms may bring best practices from their countries of origin, this study indicates that the relative performance of foreign subsidiaries is jointly determined by both home and host country conditions. This is consistent with the 'double diamond model'.

Another finding of interest relates to the role of factor intensities in explaining the labour productivity advantages of FOSs. Physical capital intensity, human capital and the value of intangible assets per worker are all positively and significantly related to the firm's labour productivity. However, even with the addition of these explanatory variables to the regression analysis, the nationality dummies remain positive and significant. In contrast to other studies, this suggests that ownership advantages are not 'explained away' by factor proportion differences. In particular they are not explained away by the addition of our intangible assets variable, which is of particular interest to this study. These findings suggest that further research is needed to capture empirically the firm-specific advantages of FOSs. The relatively high coefficient for the Japanese nationality dummy indicates that there may be a role for managerial practices in studies of this type.

While there are no significant differences in the productivity gap between FOSs of different nationalities, the results show that the reasons for foreign superiority do vary across nationalities. We argue that the ownership advantage of FOSs may take different forms, depending on the relative characteristics of both host and home country and heterogeneous motivations underlying FDI in the UK. Not all FOSs of different home countries enjoy technical advantages over DOEs in terms of the level of intangible assets. While the superior performance of US subsidiaries is associated with higher levels of technology and other firm competence variables, European and Japanese affiliates do not demonstrate significant technical advantages over UK-owned firms in terms of intangible assets. The labour productivity advantages of European and Japanese-owned firms are due to higher capital intensity, a more skilled staff and the larger size of operations.

The fact that multinationals of different origins have distinct sources of productivity advantage has policy implications for targeting the promotion of FDI into the UK. If FOSs with high levels of firm-specific intangible assets is desired, then a goal might be the attraction of more FOSs from the US. On the other hand it appears that European and Japanese-owned firms bring productivity advantages associated with higher capital intensity. These results, however, need to be viewed with caution, as more empirical work is needed in this area. More certainty can be associated with the importance of human capital as a source of labour productivity. Our results show that human capital is generally associated with higher levels of productivity and that foreign firms of all nationalities have higher levels of this variable than UK-owned firms. Here the policy implication is clear and consistent with other work.

Appendix

The following variables are used in the study:

LP is labour productivity, which is measured as the ratio of value-added to the number of employees.

TFP is total factor productivity, which is measured as value-added per composite unit of labour and capital: $TFP = \dfrac{V}{C^{\beta} L^{(1-\beta)}}$, where *V* is value-added, *C* is the stock of capital, and *L* is employment. The coefficient β is the average share of capital income from 1992–96.

CP is capital productivity, which is measured as the ratio of value-added to the physical capital stock.

CI is capital intensity, which is measured as the ratio of physical capital stock to employment.

INT is intangible assets intensity, which is measured as the net book value of intangible assets to employment. Intangible assets may include unwritten off goodwill and issue expenses as well as patents, trademarks and the value of publication rights and brands where capitalized as well as development costs where capitalized.

HC is human capital. A standard proxy for labour quality or human capital is average wages. However, as Globerman *et al.* (1994) and Rault (1995) point out, regressing a value-added-based measure of productivity on average wages raises potential simultaneity problems, since wages may be simultaneously determined with the output (value-added). To avoid this problem, we follow Hausman (1978) and Rault (1995) and use the residuals from the regression of the log (average wages) on *CI*, *INT*, and *SIZE* as the proxy for human capital. This proxy reflects the average wages (therefore labour quality or human capital) that are not explained by all the other explanatory variables.

SIZE is the average size of the firm over the period 1992–96, and is measured in terms of total sales.

Note

1. This study uses a panel data-set which contains 14 233 firms across 14 industries for the period 1992–96. The empirical data for this study are from the FAME database. The original source is the accounts firms must legally supply to Companies House. The sample of manufacturing firms was drawn with the requirement that each firm report sufficient data in all five years of the study. Each firm was assigned to one of 14 SIC sub-manufacturing categories based on its primary product.

   The data are broken down by ownership. FOSs are defined as those where at least 50 per cent of share capital is in foreign ownership. The 14 233 firms account for approximately 26 per cent of the total number of manufacturing firms in the database. There are 4267 FOSs and 9966 DOEs, which represent about 30 per cent of the total number of foreign firms and about 23 per cent of the total number of UK-owned firms in the database respectively. Thus the sample is fairly representative of UK manufacturing industry.

REFERENCES

Barrell, R. and Pain, N. (1997) 'The Growth of FDI in Europe', *National Institute Economic Review*, 160, 63–75.

Carr, C. (1992) 'Productivity and Skills in Vehicle Component Manufacturers in Britain, Germany, the USA and Japan', *National Institute Economic Review*, 139, 79–87.

Casson, M. (1987) *The Firm and the Market: Studies in Multinational Enterprise and the Scope of the Firm* (Oxford: Blackwell).

Crafts, N. and O'Mahony, M. (1999) 'Britain's Productivity Performance Separating the Contributions of Different Factors is Difficult', *New Economy*, 3–16.

Davies, S.W. and Lyons, B.R. (1991) 'Characterising Relative Performance: The Productivity Advantage of Foreign Owned Firms in the UK', *Oxford Economic Papers*, 43, 584–95.

Department of Trade and Industry (1999) *UK Competitiveness Indicators 1999* (London: HMSO).

Dunning, J.H. (1981) *International Production and Multinational Enterprise* (London: Allen & Unwin).

Dunning, J.H. (1988a) 'The Eclectic Paradigm of International Production: A Restatement and Some Possible Extensions', *Journal of International Business Studies*, 19, 1–32.

Dunning, J.H. (1988b) *Explaining International Production* (London: Unwin Hyman).

Globerman, S., Ries, C.J. and Vertinsky, I. (1994) 'The Relative Performance of Foreign Affiliates in Canada', *Canadian Journal of Economics*, 27, 143–55.

Griffith, R. (1999) 'Using the ARD Establishment Level Data to Look at Foreign Ownership and Productivity in the United Kingdom', *Economic Journal*, 109, 416–42.

Hausman, J.A. (1978) 'Specification Tests in Econometrics', *Econometrica*, 46, 1251–71.

Hymer, S.H. (1976) *The International Operations of National Firms, A Study of Direct Foreign Investment* (Cambridge, MA: MIT Press).

Kim. W.S. and Lyn. E.O. (1990) 'FDI Theories and the Performance of Foreign Multinationals Operating in the US', *Journal of International Business Studies*, 21, 41–54.

Liu, X., Siler, P., Wang, C and Wei, Y. (2000) 'Productivity Spillovers from Foreign Direct Investment: Evidence from UK Industry Level Panel Data', *Journal of International Business Studies*, 31(3), 407–25.

Lucas, R.E.J. (1988) 'The Mechanics of Economic Development', *Journal of Monetary Economics*, 22, 3–42.

Markuson, J.R. (1995) 'The Boundaries of Multinational Enterprises and the Theory of International Trade', *Journal of Economic Perspectives*, 9, 169–89.

Mason, G., van Ark, B. and Wagner, K. (1994) 'Innovation and the Skill Mix: Chemicals and Engineering in Britain and Germany', *National Institute Economic Review*, 148, 61–72.

Oulton, N. (1998) 'Labour Productivity and Foreign Ownership in the UK', National Institute for Social and Economic Research, Discussion Paper 143.

Porter, M.E. (1990) *The Competitive Advantage of Nations* (New York: Free Press Macmillan).

Rault, L.K. (1995) 'R&D Spillovers and Productivity Growth: Evidence from Indian Private Firms', *Journal of Development Economics*, 48, 1–23.

Rugman, A.M. (1980) 'Internationalisation as a General Theory of Foreign Direct Investment: A Reappraisal of the Literature', *Weltwirtschaftliches Archiv*, 116(2), 365–79.

Rugman, A.M. and Verbeke, A. (1993) 'Foreign Subsidiaries and Multinational Strategic Management: An Extension and Correction of Porter's Single Diamond Framework', *Management International Review*, 2, 71–84.

3 The Location of Japanese Direct Investment in the United States

Pakfei Yeung and Roger Strange

INTRODUCTION

Most scholarly work on Japanese FDI in the United States has focused on its industrial organization, management–labour relations, and entry-mode aspects, or on US policy towards inward investment; however the spatial distribution of this investment has received less attention. There are now Japanese affiliates in all US states with the exception of North Dakota, but the geographical dispersion is not uniform. This study investigates the location choices of 1297 Japanese manufacturing affiliates established between 1990 and 1997 with a view to identifying the main locational determinants, and assesses the impact of the North American Free Trade Agreement (NAFTA). The NAFTA was established on 1 January 1994, with the aim of eliminating nearly all tariffs on trade between the United States and Canada by 1998, and between the United States and Mexico by 2008. In addition many non-tariff barriers were to be removed.

This topic is of interest for several reasons. First, Japanese FDI in the United States rose substantially during the 1980s, growing faster than inward investment from other countries (Yamamura, 1989). Second, an understanding of the spatial behaviour of Japanese-affiliated firms will provide further insights about what distinguishes Japanese firms from US firms. Third, this study contributes to recent advances in empirical location analysis by considering the effects of regional integration (that is, NAFTA) on foreign direct investment.

The structure of the chapter is as follows. The next section provides a litera-ture review. The following section outlines the rationale for the inclusion of each of the explanatory variables, and specifies their expected effects upon the choice of location. The fourth section presents a brief overview of the conditional logit model (CLM), which has been used to analyse the location choices, and identifies the sources of the data on the Japanese affiliates. The penultimate section contains the empirical results from the regression ana-lyses, together with a discussion of the most important findings. The final section offers a summary with a consideration of the policy implications. The practical limitations of the project and various suggestions for future research are also discussed.

LITERATURE REVIEW

As inward investment in the United States has surged since the late 1970s, and several researchers have investigated its locational determinants (Little, 1978, 1983 and 1986; McConnell, 1980; Luger and Shetty, 1985; O'hUallachain, 1985; Moore *et al.*, 1987; Glickman and Woodward, 1988; Bagchi-Sen, 1989; Swamidass, 1990; Coughlin *et al.*, 1991; Woodward, 1992). These studies vary both in their methods of analysis and in the disaggregation of the data. In some cases (e.g. Luger and Shetty, 1985), the sample sizes are very small making the results potentially unreliable.

Notwithstanding these limitations, the analyses have identified certain regional characteristics responsible for sub-national geographical patterns. Mandell and Killian (1974, cited by Ondrich and Wasylenko, 1993) found that foreign investors ranked locational factors in the following order: nearness to markets, availability of labour, transportation facilities, and government aid. A more comprehensive survey of foreign manufacturers pointed to similar locational factors (Arpan and Ricks, 1986). The major influence on the decision to locate in a state was market proximity, followed in importance by transportation facilities, labour factors, and taxes. In a still larger sample of foreign manufacturing firms, respondents rated 32 different plant location factors (Tong, 1979). The five most important factors found in this study were the availability of transportation services, labour attitudes, ample space for future expansion, nearness to markets within the United States, and the availability of suitable plant sites. In a later study, Swamidass (1990) found that market size was strongly associated with the locational decisions of foreign manufacturers, and remarked that foreign manufacturers tended to become more like their domestic counterparts.

One of the earliest statistical studies on the spatial patterns of FDI within the United States was carried out by Little (1978), later updated in Little (1983, 1986). Using aggregate data, various state characteristics were regressed against state shares of inward foreign investment relative to shares of domestic manufacturing for 1975 and 1976. She concluded that foreign and US investors did not focus their investments in the same areas, or even within the same industries, because they appeared to assign different significance to various locational characteristics. In particular, foreign investors were seen to give relatively high weight to state wage differentials and to the availability of port facilities, whilst US investors were comparatively more concerned about regional differences in fuel and power costs.

McConnell (1980) used stepwise regression to test a large number of locational factors against state shares of foreign investment using data for 1976. The significant explanatory variables included regional labour conditions, industrial agglomeration and market demand. The dependent variable was the number, rather than the value, of foreign investments. McConnell noted that FDI in the United States had shifted away from the previous investment concentrations in the industrial heartlands of New England, the Mid-Atlantic, and the Great Lakes states to the Sunbelt and Pacific states. This conclusion was also confirmed in O'hUallachain's (1985) study, in which he investigated the lag dispersion hypothesis, and concluded that FDI in the southeast, southwest, and far west had actually led to domestic shifts in manufacturing investment. More recently, Glickman and Woodward (1988) found that the spatial distribution of FDI increasingly resembled that of domestic firms as a result of simultaneous convergence processes. This finding was confirmed by Chang (1989) for Japanese direct manufacturing investment in the United States. He found that the distribution of Japanese plants correlated well with US manufacturing, and that the Japanese presence in US manufacturing was most prominent in consumer electronics, steel, automobiles and high-technology industries.

The influences of state corporate income tax rate, and of the form of the income tax base structure, on FDI in manufacturing were investigated in a study by Moore *et al.* (1987). Their empirical results suggested that tax structures that used the unitary method of accounting had a substantial impact on the amounts of FDI, whereas business income tax appeared to have little impact.

Various studies have addressed the issue of domestic branch location (Carlton, 1983; Bartik, 1985, 1989; Schmenner *et al.*, 1987; McConnell and Schwab, 1990). Bartik (1985) used a conditional logit model (CLM) and found that differences in unionization across states had a major impact on industrial location within the United States. Furthermore, his results also indicated that state taxes modestly affected business location, contradicting the conventional wisdom. Schmenner (1982) also used a CLM and found that the plant-location decision could be usefully modeled as a staged process, and that geographically defined differences were not sufficient by themselves to explain why some states did better than others in attracting new plants. He concluded that when plant-specific characteristics were used in addition to the state-based factors, the explanatory power of the model improved substantially.

There have been only a few attempts to apply CLMs to the analysis of foreign-owned branch locations. For example, Coughlin *et al.* (1991) developed a CLM of the factors affecting the locational choices of foreign direct investors in the US manufacturing sector between 1981 and 1983. They found that the number of potential sites was a key determinant, but that the *dartboard theory* of industrial location did not apply generally. However, Bartik (1985, p. 18) estimated that the land area elasticity of domestic branch plants was approximately unity, and stated that the 'dartboard theory works almost perfectly. A 10 per cent increase in State land area causes almost exactly a 10 per cent increase in the number of new plants.' Coughlin *et al.* (1991) also found that land area had a positive influence, but estimated that the elasticity was considerably less than unity. This study also found that states with higher per capita income and higher densities of manufacturing activity attracted relatively more FDI but that higher wages and higher taxes deterred FDI. Higher unemployment rates and unionization rates, more extensive transportation infrastructures, and larger promotional expenditures were associated with increased FDI.

Woodward (1992) examined the location of Japanese manufacturing firms using US data on 540 plants established between 1980 and 1989. He performed two levels of analysis: state choice and the selection of the county within the state. For the state analysis, he found that higher per capita income in the region, a state economic development office located in Japan, the state's land area, and the state's location close to the Pacific region attracted Japanese manufacturing plants. Higher levels of unionization of the labour force, and unitary taxation, were shown to deter Japanese manufacturing investment. For the county-level analysis, Woodward included all counties that had a Japanese manufacturing plant and a random sample of nine counties in each state that did not have a Japanese manufacturing plant. He first examined all the counties in a pooled analysis, and then separated them into two groups: those counties within the auto-alley in the states between Michigan and Tennessee, and those not. Counties with manufacturing agglomeration economies, an interstate highway connection, and with larger land areas were shown to attract more plants in each of the analyses. Furthermore, higher population density attracted more plants in the pooled and non-auto-alley county analyses, whereas higher rates of poverty and unemployment deterred Japanese manufacturing plant locations. Property taxes were, however, shown not to have a significant influence on plant location.

In addition, Woodward concluded that a higher percentage of African-Americans in the population deterred the location of Japanese manufacturing plants in the auto-alley counties. Cole and Deskins (1988) argued that Japanese locational patterns reveal a distinct racial bias, and remark that it is not uncommon for Japanese investors to take into account minority population ratios when making a locational decision. They conclude that Japanese investors, particularly automotive transplants, can effectively inhibit the employment of the African-American population, and thus exclude them by locating in so-called low minority ratio rural areas. Cole and Deskins (1988) also claim that states offering subsidies to foreign investors who locate in certain rural counties may, in effect, have been subsidizing discrimination against African-Americans and other minority populations. Japanese firms publicly deny that their location decisions within the United States are racially determined, and cite only fundamental economic variables as relevant factors.

The two most recent CLM studies are those by Head *et al.* (1995) on the effects of agglomeration benefits on the location choice of Japanese firms in the United States, and by Ford and Strange (1999) on Japanese manufacturing firms within the European Union. Head *et al.* (1995) examined the location choices of 751 Japanese manufacturing plants built in the United States since 1980, and found that a diverse set of Japanese investors preferred to site their plants in areas where they found concentrations of previous Japanese investments in the same industry and, in some cases, previous investments made by keiretsu affiliates. In addition, Head *et al.* (1995) confirmed the hypothesis that state borders did not define the relevant economic boundaries for agglomeration effects.

Ford and Strange (1999) investigated the factors that Japanese firms took into account when deciding upon the location of their affiliates within the European Union. Using a data-set comprising 520 manufacturing affiliates established between 1980 and 1995, and located in the seven most popular host EU countries, they concluded that agglomeration economies, local industry output, educational attainment, English language ability, and especially national GDP per capita had significantly positive effects on location choice. They also found that local industry productivity, wage levels and unionization had significantly negative effects.

In summary, there have been several studies that have addressed the question of what determines the location of foreign affiliates within the United States. The present study focuses on the choices of Japanese firms, and aims to extend the extant literature by investigating the effects of NAFTA on the location choice.

EXPLANATORY VARIABLES AND HYPOTHESES

In this section, the rationale behind the inclusion of each of the independent variables in the model is explained. A common perception about Japanese investors is that they tend to prefer rural sites (Mair *et al.*, 1988). Supported mainly by manufacturing studies, it is often remarked that Japanese investors mistrust urban workers due to their undesirable work habits. However, there are numerous economic reasons for an urban orientation when deciding location choice. Urban areas provide affiliates with more utilities, travel, communication links and various other resources. Urban areas also provide a larger collection of readily available professional services, such as accountants and lawyers that Japanese firms may need, and a more diverse range of cultural amenities. Population density (POP) was included in the model as a proxy for urban areas, and is expected to have a positive influence upon location choice.

It is well-known that Japanese firms look very carefully at the characteristics of the local workforce, and tend to screen a large number of candidates during recruitment. Among the more important factors that the Japanese look for are positive attitudes towards work, company loyalty, and commitment to continual improvement. Given the emphasis that Japanese investors place on mental as well as manual skills, a well-educated population might be hypothesized to influence location choice. Educational attainment (EDU) is here measured by the percentage of the population over 25 years of age with a bachelor's degree or more. This variable is expected to have a positive effect upon location choice.

Economic theory suggests, *ceteris paribus*, that Japanese firms would prefer to locate their affiliates in wealthier markets. Haitani and Marquis (1990) further conclude through survey research that market opportunities rank above all other variables on the investment decision, and subsequently hypothesize that regional markets are a primary influence on affiliate location. Two variables were used to measure local market demand: state per capita income and gross state product.

State per capita income (INC) is a measure of average consumer income in the state and is expected to have a positive influence on FDI location. Woodward and Rolfe (1993) suggest that per capita income figures also reflect the general quality of infrastructure. The size of the local market is captured by gross state product (GSP), and this is also expected to have a positive effect upon location choice.

One would expect taxes to have a negative effect on location decisions, yet the empirical evidence is not conclusive. Newman (1983) and Bartik (1985, 1989) reported that high corporate tax rates inhibited employment growth and location choice. Luger and Shetty (1985) found that higher tax rates were related negatively to FDI in one industry, but also found a positive relationship in another industry, and no relationship in a third industry. Newman and Sullivan (1988) concluded that taxes had an insignificant effect on location selection.

There are numerous conceptual problems in attempting to assess the impact of taxation on business location decisions including identifying the incidence of tax, the possibility that taxes finance the provision of goods and services valued by the business, and the use of tax incentives. In addition, there are special tax issues associated with FDI such as the introduction of unitary taxation by a number of states (Glickman and Woodward, 1987; Coughlin *et al.*, 1990). The former study found that unitary taxation reduced FDI in 1981, while the latter study found that it reduced the employment growth of foreign-owned firms (Tannenwald, 1984). Although anecdotal information suggests that Japanese investors do not rate taxes as a high priority in their location search, the variable (*TAX*) was nonetheless considered to be worth investigation in this study and was expected to have a negative effect upon location choice.

Labour market conditions such as wage rates and the availability of labour are often cited as important considerations for potential investors. Many studies (for example Bartik, 1985) have found that higher wages have a negative influence, and Little (1978) concluded that state wage differentials were relatively more important for foreign investors than for domestic investors, though Glickman and Woodward (1987) came to the opposite conclusion. We include average wage rates (*WAGE*) as an explanatory variable, and expect it to have a negative effect upon location choice.

It is also hypothesized that higher unemployment rates (*UNEM*) will be related negatively to FDI. Woodward (1992, pp. 699–700) suggested that 'Japanese firms are not concerned about tight labor markets, but rather seek to avoid high unemployment areas . . . [that] are viewed as offering less-competitive industrial conditions and a lower quality of life.' One complicating factor relates to the effects of unemployment insurance. Ehrenberg and Oaxaca (1976) concluded that higher benefits encouraged the unemployed to seek higher-paying employment, and thus increased the average duration of unemployment. If this were so, the empirical association between unemployment rates and FDI would be ambiguous.

The geographical size of a division (*LAND*) may affect the number of potential sites available to investors (Bartik, 1985; Coughlin *et al.*, 1991), and it is expected that this variable will have a positive influence on the probability of

Table 3.1   Locational determinants of Japanese-affiliated firms in the USA

Variable	Definition	Expected effect	Source
POP	Population density (number of persons per acre)	Positive	US Bureau of the Census; CPH-2, P25-1106, & CB96-10 (1989–96)
EDU	Educational attainment (% of population over 25 years of age with a bachelor's degree)	Positive	US Bureau of the Census, P-20 (1989–96)
INC	Average income per capita ($)	Positive	US Department of Commerce Website; Bureau of Economic Analysis (1989–96)
GSP	Gross state product ($ million)	Positive	US Department of Commerce Website; Bureau of Economic Analysis (1989–96)
TAX	Taxation per capita ($ million)	Negative	US Bureau of the Census; GF (1989–96)
UNEM	State unemployment rate (% of population)	Negative	US Department of Commerce Website; US Bureau of the Census (1989–96)
HWAY	Highway mileage (urban & rural)	Positive	US Federal Highway Administration; Highway Statistics (1989–96)
LAND	Land area excluding federal land (thousand acres)	Positive	US General Services Administration; Inventory Report (1989–96)
WAGE	Average wage rate ($ per job)	Negative	US Department of Commerce Website; Bureau of Economic Analysis (1989–96)

location. Other researchers have criticized the use of this variable as a proxy for the number of potential sites, on the grounds that a larger division does not necessarily have more 'suitable' sites. However, this argument overlooks the inclusion of other variables (for example, population density, unemployment rate) that relate to the quality of sites.

Another variable included here, as in a number of other studies (McConnell, 1980; Moriarity, 1983; Bartik, 1985; Woodward, 1992), is the existence of a highly developed transportation network. The existence of transportation linkages is a proxy for the accessibility to regional and national markets. The existence of a highly developed transportation infrastructure depends on public funding, and thus may have repercussions on public taxes. The indirect effect through taxation could in turn affect business location decisions, but will not be considered. We focus here on greater highway mileage (*HWAY*), adjusted for state size, which is expected to be related positively to FDI. Other variables measuring railway mileage and/or public airport facilties might also be included.

The definitions of all the explanatory variables, and their expected impact upon location choice, are given in Table 3.1. It is assumed that prospective Japanese investors make location choices based on the values of these variables in the year before the establishment of the affiliate – for example the location of an affiliate established in 1994 is chosen on the basis of the relative attractiveness of the alternative locations in 1993.

DATA AND METHODOLOGY

Due to the size and diversity of the United States, location selection requires an extensive search. This is especially true for Japanese investors who have less initial knowledge than most domestic firms, and there is considerable evidence that they engage in thorough and systematic fact gathering before they make their final location choice.

It is assumed that Japanese firms rationally evaluate all relevant characteristics from a set of alternative locations to seek divisional locations with the highest expected profits. Following earlier studies (Bartik, 1985; Coughlin *et al.*, 1991; Woodward, 1992; Head *et al.*, 1995; Ford and Strange, 1999), the CLM pioneered by McFadden (1974) is adopted to estimate the location probabilities. The location decision of the Japanese-affiliated firms is modelled as a conditional logit problem, where the dependent variable is the *division* chosen by each investor: New England, Middle Atlantic, East North Central, West North Central, South Atlantic, East South Central, West South Central, Mountain, and Pacific. The divisions are as defined by the US Census Bureau, viz: New England (Connecticut, Maine, Massachusetts, New Hampshire, Rhode Island, Vermont), Middle Atlantic (New Jersey, New York, Pennsylvania), East North Central (Illinois, Indiana, Michigan, Ohio, Wisconsin), West North Central (Iowa, Kansas, Minnesota, Missouri, Nebraska, North Dakota, South Dakota), South Atlantic (Delaware, Florida, Georgia, Maryland, North Carolina, South Carolina, Virginia, West Virginia), East South Central (Alabama, Kentucky, Mississippi, Tennessee), West South Central (Arkansas, Louisiana, Oklahoma, Texas), Mountain (Arizona, Colorado, Idaho, Montana, Nevada, New Mexico, Utah, Wyoming), Pacific (Alaska, California, Hawaii, Oregon, Washington). For data management reasons, the choice was restricted to these nine divisions, rather than considering the choice between 50 states.

Toyo Keizai (2000) provides data on all the Japanese-affiliated firms established within the United States since 1886. The relevant information was computer-coded according to state, then division, for each of the 1297 affiliates established within the United States between January 1990 and December 1997. Each affiliate forms a separate observation comprised of *J* alternatives, with

1 assigned to the chosen location and 0 otherwise. The data set used in this paper is summarized in Table 3.2.

It is assumed that each Japanese investor chooses to locate in the division that will yield the highest profit. Let i represent the Japanese affiliate faced with the choice of J possible locations. Formally, the jth division is chosen by the ith firm if and only if:

$$\pi_{ij} = max\{\pi_{ik}; k = 1, \ldots, 9\}$$

where π_{ij} denotes the profit earned by the ith firm given that it locates in the jth division. Following McFadden (1974), the profits earned in the jth division are a function of a vector of observed characteristics X_j of the division, and of a random disturbance term ϵ_{ij}. The disturbance term reflects measurement and/or specification errors, and is assumed to be independent log-Weibull distributed. Carlton (1983) argued that the random disturbance term might also be considered as a firm-location specific effect, differing across divisions for any one firm and across firms for any one division, thus capturing the unique advantages of the location for each affiliate. The vector β is unknown parameters to be estimated. In formal terms:

$$\pi_{ij} = \beta X_j + \varepsilon_{ij}$$

McFadden further shows that the probability of locating an affiliate i in location j is given by:

$$P_j = \exp\{X_j\beta\} / \sum_{k=1}^{9} \exp\{X_k\beta\}$$

Table 3.2   Number and percentage of Japanese-affiliated firms in the USA

Division	1886–2000		1990–97		1990–93		1994–97	
New England	97	2.7%	39	3.0%	25	3.7%	14	2.2%
Middle Atlantic	805	22.1%	249	19.2%	151	22.5%	98	15.6%
East North Central	642	17.6%	197	15.2%	92	13.7%	105	16.8%
West North Central	55	1.5%	21	1.6%	13	1.9%	8	1.3%
South Atlantic	383	10.5%	150	11.6%	73	10.9%	77	12.3%
East South Central	152	4.2%	57	4.4%	22	3.3%	35	5.6%
West South Central	155	4.3%	77	5.9%	36	5.4%	41	6.5%
Mountain	72	2.0%	34	2.6%	14	2.1%	20	3.2%
Pacific	1279	35.1%	473	36.5%	244	36.4%	229	36.5%
USA	3640	100%	1297	100%	670	100%	627	100%

Source: Toyo Keizai (2000).

where P_j denotes the probability of locating in division j, which depends on the attributes of that division relative to the attributes of the other nine divisions in the discrete choice set. In simpler terms, if each firm i is located in order to maximize profit, then P_j is the probability that a particular division j is chosen. Estimates of β may be obtained by maximum likelihood estimates (Greene, 1997).

The test statistic λ provides a measure of the overall significance of the estimated equations (Greene, 1997):

$$\lambda = 2\,[L(\text{max}) - L(0)\,]$$

The statistic λ follows a chi-square distribution, with degrees of freedom equal to the number of restrictions determined by the null hypothesis. $L(\text{max})$ is the maximum log-likelihood of the selected model, and $L(0)$ is the log-likelihood of the constrained model:

$$L(0) = -n \cdot \ln J$$

where n is the number of observations. In the constrained model, the slope coefficients are set equal to zero, and the selection probability of each division is equal to $1/J$ (Berry and Lindgren, 1996; Greene, 1997; Ford and Strange, 1999).

EMPIRICAL RESULTS

The empirical results of the conditional logit estimation are presented in Table 3.3. The coefficient estimates and the *t*-statistics (in brackets) for the explanatory variables are shown for three different regression equations:

- Equation 3.1 is estimated for the full sample of 1297 affiliates established between 1990 and 1997.
- Equation 3.2 is estimated for the 670 affiliates established between 1990 and 1993 – that is, before the introduction of the NAFTA.
- Equation 3.3 is estimated for the 627 affiliates established between 1994 and 1997 – that is, after the introduction of the NAFTA.

All three regression equations are highly significant ($p < 0.01$) according to the chi-square test. Furthermore, the coefficient estimates for all the explanatory variables in all three regressions have the expected signs, though not all are statistically significant.

As regards equation 3.1, a number of variables are statistically significant: educational attainment (*EDU*), gross State product (*GSP*), and highway mileage (*HWAY*); all have highly significant positive effects upon location choice, whilst both per capita taxation (*TAX*) and average wage costs (*WAGE*) have significant negative effects.

Table 3.3   Coefficient estimates of the conditional logit model

Variable	Equation (years)		
	1 (1990–97)	*2 (1990–93)*	*3 (1994–97)*
POP	0.036	0.056	0.096
	(1.104)	(1.096)	(1.559)
EDU	0.170***	0.042	0.245**
	(4.122)	(0.665)	(2.414)
INC	0.144 E-03	0.559 E-03**	0.382 E-04
	(1.126)	(2.430)	(0.132)
GSP	0.198 E-05***	0.160 E-05*	0.352 E-05***
	(4.063)	(1.693)	(4.623)
TAX	−0.216 E-02***	−0.362 E-02***	−0.195 E-02***
	(−4.099)	(−3.473)	(−2.832)
UNEM	−0.876	−0.180	−0.324
	(−1.233)	(−1.426)	(−1.581)
HWAY	0.480 E-03***	0.130 E-03	0.562 E-03*
	(4.889)	(0.943)	(1.761)
LAND	0.695 E-06	0.186 E-05	0.904 E-05**
	(0.321)	(0.503)	(2.153)
WAGE	−0.222 E-03**	−0.468 E-03***	−0.653 E-04
	(−2.326)	(−2.859)	(−0.326)
Number of observations	1297	670	627
Number of alternatives	11673	6030	5643
Restricted log-likelihood	−2849.80	−1472.14	−1377.66
Maximum log-likelihood	−2343.33	−1186.92	−1135.18
Chi-square	1012.92***	570.44***	242.48***

Note: *t*-statistics are in brackets. *** denotes significance at the $p < 0.01$ level, ** at the $p < 0.05$ level, and * at the $p < 0.10$ level.

If the coefficients of equations 3.2 and 3.3 are compared, it appears that the coefficients of market size (*GSP*) and taxation (*TAX*) have been little affected by the introduction of NAFTA. Wage costs were significant in the earlier period, but had a minimal effect upon location choice in the latter period. In contrast, the effects of educational attainment (*EDU*), potential sites (*LAND*) and infrastructure (*HWAY*) became both stronger and significant from 1994 onwards. The interpretation of these results is not clear-cut, but one suggestion that would merit further study is that Japanese FDI within the United States became less labour-intensive after the introduction of NAFTA (with any labour-intensive FDI being diverted to Mexico), with the result that wage costs have become less-important determinants of location within the United States whilst other factors such as educational attainment have become more important.

Finally it is interesting to note that both the population density (*POP*) and unemployment (*UNEM*) variables are statistically insignificant in all three regressions, though their coefficients do have the expected signs. Perhaps these findings gainsay the conclusions of Cole and Deskins (1988) regarding the racial bias of Japanese investors.

CONCLUSIONS

This research is an initial exploration into a topic that is of great relevance to the economic development efforts of US states, counties and divisions. The study has focused on the location selection of Japanese affiliates, one of the most dynamic sources of new FDI during the past decade. We have not considered why there has been FDI growth in the United States, nor tried to assess the benefits (and/or costs) for the host economies and thus the wisdom of welcoming inward FDI. The empirical results broadly confirm the importance of many of the variables that were hypothesized to be important factors in the location decisions. One important conclusion is that differences in taxation across locations have a major negative impact on affiliate location. Labour costs too have a significantly negative effect, whereas educational attainment, market size and a developed transportation network have significantly positive effects.

The policy implications of these empirical results are as follows. First, the results contradict the common view that state and local taxes exert no influence on business location patterns. These more general measures of the overall levels of taxation were shown to have a strongly significant negative affect on affiliate location. Second, higher wage rates appeared to act as deterrence to FDI at least before the formation of NAFTA. However, this is not to argue for lower wages, but it does have implications for the type of FDI that a high-wage economy might seek to attract within a free-trade area. Third, the results confirm that Japanese firms are much more likely to select locations characterized by concentrations of well-educated workers, therefore suggesting an active role for education policy. Fourth, the results also indicate that Japanese investors prefer locations with stronger markets suggesting an active role for industrial policy. Fifth, the *dartboard theory* of industrial location does not seem to be supported.

The study is not without its limitations. Future research might consider additional explanatory variables (for example agglomeration effects, unionization, minority population densities, energy prices, state promotion expenditure, productivity) in the model, and include data on affiliates established before 1990 and after 1997. In particular, agglomeration effects may well have become more important with regard to FDI in the United States after the formation of NAFTA, when the more labour-intensive FDI is being drawn towards Mexico. The location choice could also be modeled as a sequential process: first division, then state, then county, and the entry mode could be considered. It is possible that the factors affecting the location choices of greenfield ventures will differ from those pertinent to mergers and acquisitions. Friedman *et al.*, (1996) found that certain locational characteristics were relatively more important for certain entry modes, particularly greenfield ventures, than others. Finally, given the likely effects of the formation of NAFTA, it would be instructive to include explicitly both Mexico and Canada as alternative investment locations within North America.

REFERENCES

Arpan, J.S. and Ricks, D.A. (1986) 'Foreign Direct Investment in the U.S., 1974–1984,' *Journal of International Business Studies*, 17, 149–53.

Bagchi-Sen, S. (1989) 'Foreign Direct Investment in U.S. Metropolitan Areas, 1979–83', *Urban Geography*, March/April, 121–37.

Bartik, T.J. (1985) 'Business Location Decisions in the United States: Estimates of the Effects of Unionization, Taxes, and Other Characteristics of States', *Journal of Business and Economic Statistics*, 3 (1), 14–22.

Bartik, T.J. (1989) 'Small Business Start-Ups in the United States: Estimates of the Effects of Characteristics of States', *Southern Economic Journal*, April, 1004–18.

Berry, D.A. and Lindgren, B.W. (1996) *Statistics: Theory and Methods* (2nd edn) (London: Duxbury Press).

Carlton, D.W. (1983) 'The Location and Employment Choices of New Firms: An Econometric Model with Discrete and Continuous Endogenous Variables', *The Review of Economics and Statistics*, 65 (3), 440–9.

Chang, K. (1989) 'Japan's Direct Manufacturing Investment in the United States', *The Professional Geographer*, August, 41 (3), 314–28.

Cole, R.E. and Deskins, D.R. Jr (1988) 'Racial Factors in Site Location and Employment Patterns of Japanese Auto Firms in America', *California Management Review*, Fall, 9–22.

Coughlin, C.C., Terza, J.V., and Arromdee, V. (1990) 'State Government Effects on the Location of Foreign Direct Investment', *Regional Science Perspectives*, 20, 194–207.

Coughlin, C.C., Terza, J.V., and Arromdee, V. (1991) 'State Characteristics and the Location of Foreign Direct Investment within the United States', *The Review of Economics and Statistics*, 73 (4), 675–83.

Ehrenberg, R.G. and Oaxaca, R.L. (1976) 'Unemployment Insurance, Duration of Unemployment, and Subsequent Wage Gain', *American Economic Review*, 66 (5), 754–66.

Ford, S. and Strange, R. (1999) 'Where do Japanese Manufacturing Firms Invest within Europe, and Why?', *Transnational Corporations*, 8 (1), 117–42.

Friedman, J., Gerlowski, D.A., and Silberman, J. (1992) 'What Attracts Foreign Multinational Corporations? Evidence from Branch Plant Location in the United States', *Journal of Regional Science*, 32 (4), 403–18.

Friedman, J., Fung, H., Gerlowski, D.A., and Silberman, J. (1996) 'State Characteristics and the Location of Foreign Direct Investment within the United States', *The Review of Economics and Statistics*, 78 (2), 367–8.

Glickman, N.J. and Woodward, D.P. (1987) *Regional Patterns of Manufacturing Foreign Direct Investment in the United States*, Special Report for U.S. Department of Commerce, Economic Development Administration (www.bea.doc.gov).

Glickman, N.J. and Woodward, D.P. (1988) 'The Location of Foreign Direct Investment in the United States: Patterns and Determinants', *International Regional Science Review*, 11 (2), 137–54.

Greene, W.H. (1997) *Econometric Analysis* (3rd edn) (New Jersey: Prentice Hall).

Haitani, K. and Marquis, C.T. (1990) 'Japanese Investment in the Southeast United States: Factors, Obstacles, and Opportunities', *Economic Development Review*, Summer, 44–8.

Head, K., Ries, J., and Swenson, D. (1995) 'Agglomeration Benefits and Location Choice: Evidence from Japanese Manufacturing Investments in the United States', *Journal of International Economics*, 38 (3/4), 223–47.

Japan External Trade Organization (2000) *Japanese Manufacturing Plants in U.S.: Annual Survey*. (London: JETRO).

Little, J.S. (1978) 'Location Decisions of Foreign Investors in the United States', *New England Economic Review*, July/August, 43–63.

Little, J.S. (1983) 'Foreign Investors' Locational Choices: An Update', *New England Economic Review*, January/February, 28–31.

Little, J.S. (1986) 'The Effects of Foreign Direct Investment on U.S. Employment during Recession and Structural Change', *New England Economic Review*, November/December, 40–8.

Luger, M.I. and Shetty, S. (1985) 'Determinants of Foreign Plant Start-Ups in the United States: Lessons for Policy-makers in the Southeast', *Vanderbilt Journal of Transnational Law*, 18 (2), 223–45.

Mair, A., Florida, R., and Kenney, M. (1988) 'The New Geography of Automotive Production: Japanese Transplants in North America', *Economic Geography*, October, 352–73.

Mandell, S.L. and Killian, C.D. (1974) *An Analysis of Foreign Investment in Selected Areas of the United States: A Research Project on behalf of the New England Regional Commission* (Boston: The International Center of New England).

McConnell, J.E. (1980) 'Foreign Direct Investment in the United States', *Annals of the Association of American Geographers*, June, 70 (2), 259–70.

McConnell, V.D. and Schwab, R.M. (1990) 'The Impact of Environmental Regulation on Industry Location Decisions: The Motor Vehicle Industry', *Land Economics*, February, 67–81.

McFadden, D. (1974) 'Conditional Logit Analysis of Qualitative Choice Behavior', in P. Zarembka (ed.) *Frontiers in Econometrics*, 105–42 (New York: Academic Press).

Moore, M.L., Steece, B.M., and Swenson, C.W. (1987) 'An Analysis of the Impact of State Income Tax Rates and Bases on Foreign Investment', *The Accounting Review*, October, 62 (4), 671–85.

Moriarity, B.M. (1983) 'Hierarchies of Cities and the Spatial Filtering of Industrial Development', *Papers of the Regional Science Association*, 53, 59–82.

Newman, R.J. (1983) 'Industry Migration and Growth in the South', *The Review of Economics and Statistics*, February, 76–86.

Newman, R.J. and Sullivan, D.H. (1988) 'Econometric Analysis of Business Tax Impacts on Industrial Location: What Do We Know, and How Do We Know It?', *Journal of Urban Economics*, March, 215–34.

O'hUallachain, B. (1985) 'Spatial Patterns of Foreign Direct Investment in the United States', *Professional Geographer*, May, 37 (2), 154–62.

Ondrich, J. and Wasylenko, M. (1993) *Foreign Direct Investment in the United States* (Michigan: W.E. Upjohn Institute for Employment Research).

Schmenner, R. (1982) *Making Business Location Decisions* (Englewood Cliffs, NJ: Prentice Hall).

Schmenner, R.W., Huber, J.C., and Cook, R.L. (1987) 'Geographic Differences and the Location of New Manufacturing Facilities', *Journal of Urban Economics*, January, 21, 83–104.

Swamidass, P.M. (1990) 'A Comparison of the Plant Location Strategies of Foreign and Domestic Manufacturers in the U.S.', *Journal of International Business Studies*, second quarter, 21, 301–17.

Tannenwald, R. (1984) 'The Pros and Cons of Worldwide Unitary Taxation', *New England Economic Review*, July/August, 17–28.

Tong, H.M. (1979) *Plant Location Decisions of Foreign Manufacturing Investors* (Ann Arbor: University of Michigan International Press).

Toyo Keizai (2000) *Kaigai Shinshutsu Kigyo Soran (Japanese Overseas Investment)* (Tokyo: Tot Keizai Shinposha).

Woodward, D.P. (1992) 'Locational Determinants of Japanese Manufacturing Start-Ups in the United States', *Southern Economic Journal*, 58 (3), 690–708.

Woodward, D.P. and Rolfe, R.J. (1993) 'The Location of Export-Oriented Foreign Direct Investment in the Caribbean Basin', *Journal of International Business Studies*, 24 (1), 121–44.

Yamamura, K. (1989) *Japanese Investment in the United States: Should We Be Concerned?* (Seattle: Society for Japanese Studies).

4 The Regional Distribution of Inbound FDI in the United Kingdom: Evidence from the West Midlands and Scotland

Grahame Fallon, Mark Cook and Arrti H. Billimoria

INTRODUCTION

A growing number of studies have been published that focus on the determinants of inbound foreign direct investment (FDI) at the national level, but relatively few studies investigate the forces affecting the distribution of FDI between UK regions. This chapter seeks to rectify this omission, by identifying a set of factors that may be expected to influence the regional distribution of FDI based on an analysis and synthesis of existing theoretical and empirical literature.

LITERATURE REVIEW

Theoretical developments in the study of FDI at firm level began in 1960, with a pioneering study by Hymer in his PhD thesis, the main thrust of which was published in 1976 (Hymer, 1976). Numerous writers have subsequently contributed to the understanding of FDI, focusing both on MNCs (from the transactions cost, network and resource-based perspectives) and on their impact on the economic development of host countries.

Buckley and Casson (1976) made an important contribution to the development of *transaction cost theory*, following which Dunning (1977 and 1988) put forward an 'eclectic paradigm' derived from the theory of the firm, organizational theory and location theory that integrated market- and cost-orientated explanations of FDI. The paradigm still provides a valuable framework for examining theories of MNC activity and FDI (Dunning, 2001).

For FDI to occur, Dunning argues that MNCs must possess *ownership-specific advantages* not possessed by competing firms. These advantages could include assets such as technology (Hymer, 1976), a strong brand image (Caves, 1971) and production experience and know-how (Giddy and Young, 1982). MNCs can, secondly, be best placed to exploit their particular ownership-specific assets by *internalizing market transactions* or bypassing the market. FDI can allow MNCs to reduce the degree of uncertainty otherwise associated with the availability, price or quality or of the prices obtained for its products (Dicken, 1992); to maintain control over their own technologies and knowledge (Buckley and Casson, 1976); and to exercise tight control over internal costs and prices (Lall, 1973). FDI can enable MNCs to make use of *location-specific factors* in order to exploit their assets more fully (Dunning, 1988). Host-country characteristics, such as the size and level of economic development, the presence of an established and varied industrial base, government policies and cluster and local supplier development can help to draw in FDI (Crone, 2001; Tavares and Young, 2002). These factors can also help to generate ownership-specific advantages for locally-based subsidiaries that can subsequently be internalized by the MNC (Hedlund, 1984; Rugman and Verbeke, 1992).

Much recent research into FDI has focused on a *network perspective* (Birkinshaw and Hood, 1997; Gupta and Govindarajan, 2000), according to which MNC subsidiaries are seen as playing an increasingly active role in creating and maintaining ownership advantages. Rather than being essentially dependent on decisions taken and resources controlled by corporate head-quarters, subsidiaries are seen as developing into a 'node in a network', possessing direct links with 'internal and external actors' and hence 'greater degrees of freedom' than before (Tavares and Young, 2002, p. 691). Interaction with outside parties and the building of market relationships can also help promote competence and technology development for appropriately located subsidiaries, creating potential internalized benefits for the MNC as a whole (Grant, 1996; Anderson *et al.*, 2001).

Connections are also being made based on the resource-based view of the firm-specific resources and competencies that can create competitive advantage (Barney, 1991), provided that they are valuable, rare and difficult to imitate (Birkinshaw *et al.*, 1998). Studies linking resources-based advantages to FDI have focused on a range of resources owned by MNCs, in the manufacturing, marketing, organizational, human resources and technology fields (Rugman, 1981; Cantwell, 1989, 2001; Dunning, 1993). Some such resources are location-bound (Rugman and Verbeke, 1992), in that they can only add value in a particular country or region of operation. Others are capable of being leveraged by MNCs to deliver ownership advantages in a range of different locations (Birkinshaw *et al.*, 1998). The importance of natural resources and unskilled labour to FDI location is, however, thought to be diminishing at present, whereas that of networking opportunities with local firms is steadily increasing (Dunning, 1994, 1995).

Development economists and economic geographers have added to the literature on FDI by focusing on the beneficial impact on host-country economic development through interfirm linkages with local suppliers (Crone, 2001; Gorg and Ruane, 2001). The development of clusters has received attention (Enright 1995, 1996, 1998), especially with the ability of host regions to act as 'sticky places in slippery space' (Markusen, 1996). Participation in internationally competitive clusters by FDI can enable MNCs to take advantage of proximity benefits thereby enhancing their competitiveness (Krugman and Venables, 1995; Ivarsson,

1999). Shared access to information and knowledge networks, supplier and distributor chains, markets and marketing intelligence, competencies and resources can play an important part in this process (Enright and Roberts, 2001). Where host regions are technologically advanced, MNCs can also take advantage of locally-available R&D expertise which can generate substantial spillovers for subsidiaries located in technologically advanced regions (Cantwell and Janne, 1999). Government policies supporting cluster development therefore have the potential to exercise an important influence on the location decisions of MNCs (Young and Hood, 1994; Tavares and Young, 2002).

Locational Choice of FDI by MNCs

Stopford and Strange (1991) and Dunning (1993) suggest that four main factors determine the location of FDI by MNCs: the search for markets (following customers, suppliers or competitors abroad, seeking increased familiarity with the local business environment or reducing their costs of supplying a foreign market); the search for resources (physical, labour or technological); the search for efficiency (exploiting different factor endowments, cultures, institutional arrangements, economic systems and policies, market structures and geographical specialization so as to reduce costs and enhance competitiveness); and finally the search for strategic assets (such as local scientific, technological or management expertise, enabling MNCs to sustain and advance their international competitive advantages). National and regional resource endowments; market access and potential; favourable competitive positions; strong consumer demand; and favourable host government policies can also help to attract FDI to specific locations.

The model tested in this chapter focuses on four of the main 'drivers' of FDI location which are markets, resources, efficiency and host-government policies. Strategic asset-seeking FDI is excluded from the study, since it proved incapable of measurement using the published UK data that is available.

Empirical Studies of FDI Location

The potential importance of market-seeking, resources-seeking and efficiency-seeking FDI is reflected in the findings of a range of econometric and survey-based studies (drawing on both UK and US data) based on the determinants of FDI location decisions at the country and regional levels. There is also some empirical support for the view that host-government policies, whether intentionally or not, may influence the levels of inbound FDI entering particular locations.

Market-related factors such as market size and growth, population density, per capita income, retail spending levels and economic growth rates have all been shown to exercise a substantial, positive effect on inbound FDI (McConnell, 1980; Culem, 1988; Bagchi-Sen and Wheeler, 1989; Swamidass, 1990; Haitani and Marquis, 1990; Wheeler and Mody, 1992; Friedman *et al.*, 1992; Woodward,

1992; Billington, 1999; Ford and Strange, 1999). Market-seeking FDI may be attracted to locations with greater proximity to the host country and good market access (Hill and Munday, 1992; Arpan and Ricks, 1995), and where competition from rival firms and imports is relatively low (Milner and Pentecost, 1994). Infrastructure factors, related to the degree of development and quality of transport and communications systems have also been found to exert a positive and significant effect on location decisions (Coughlin *et al.*, 1991; Hill and Munday, 1992; Woodward and Rolfe, 1993; Arpan and Ricks, 1995; Mudambi, 1995).

Resource-related factors in host nations or regions have also been suggested as an important determinant of FDI location (Glickman and Woodward, 1988; Mudambi, 1995; Billington, 1999). Labour-market conditions can be particularly influential (McConnell, 1980; Arpan and Ricks, 1995; Yeung and Strange, 2003), encompassing the supply of local labour, educational attainment levels and the quality of human skills capital, and local workforce characteristics and trade union strength. High unemployment may help to draw in FDI by increasing the availability of labour and the willingness of employees to work harder and to accept lower wages (Glickman and Woodward, 1988; Coughlin *et al.*, 1991; Friedman *et al.*, 1992; Billington, 1999). Any resultant deterioration in living standards, the labour skills base and local competitive conditions may deter FDI (Woodward, 1992; Billington, 1999), but the overall impact of unemployment on FDI is nonetheless assumed to be positive for the purpose of this study. MNCs can be attracted by the presence of a well-educated and trained workforce in particular countries or regions, and by the possession of English language ability (Bachtler and Clement, 1990; Ford and Strange, 1999). The possession of positive workforce attitudes towards employment, company loyalty and continuous improvement may also have a positive effect (Mair *et al.*, 1988). The impact of trade union strength is less predictable, however, since high levels of unionization can both attract foreign investors by raising worker morale and labour productivity (Billington, 1999), and deter them due to their capacity to increase worker militancy and raise average wage levels (Ford and Strange, 1999).

Efficiency-related factors including the cost of labour, the regional industrial mix and agglomeration economies can exercise an important influence on the geographical location of FDI. The decision to locate FDI in a particular country can also be motivated by a so-called 'bandwagon effect', involving a response to or an attempt to preempt location in a particular country by a MNC's major sectoral competitors (Bagchi-Sen, 1995.)

High labour costs and resultant wage differentials may deter FDI (Hill and Munday, 1992; Collis and Noon, 1994; Mudambi, 1995; Billington, 1999) although high levels of labour productivity may offset this effect (Ford and Strange, 1999). Increasing host-country industrialization can act as a stimulus to FDI, as can high geographical concentrations of manufacturing or services activity (Coughlin *et al.*, 1991; Wheeler and Mody, 1992; Billington, 1999). Agglomeration economies, associated with interfirm proximity, networking and interactions in regionally-based sectoral clusters are also an important influence on FDI location (McConnell, 1980; Hill and Munday, 1992; Woodward, 1992; Taylor, 1993; Head *et al.*, 1995, Ford and Strange, 1999; Crone, 2001; Gorg and Ruane, 2001). Regionally concentrated technological strengths and R&D activities can reinforce the agglomeration effect (Scott, 1993; Enright and Roberts, 2001).

However, interregional spillovers can complicate the picture. Head *et al.* (1995) argue, for example, that regional borders do not define the relevant economic boundaries for agglomeration effects.

Host-government policies including regional promotional activities, financial assistance to investors, and variations in taxation and government spending levels may have the effect of increasing the volume and value of inbound FDI entering particular countries or regions and the resultant spillover benefits. Empirical studies suggest that government promotional activity has the ability to raise the levels of inbound FDI committed by MNCs to particular locations (Coughlin *et al.*, 1991; Hill and Munday, 1992; Friedman *et al.*, 1992; Woodward, 1992). Financial assistance to MNCs may also be influential (Mandell and Killian, 1974; Hill and Munday, 1992; Friedman *et al.*, 1992; Billington, 1999) together with government spending on goods and services valued by MNCs such as infrastructure improvements (McConnell, 1980; Yeung and Strange, 2003). The impact of taxation on FDI decisions is uncertain due to the inconclusive nature of existing empirical findings (Luger and Shetty, 1985; Newman and Sullivan, 1988; Yeung and Strange, 2003). Taxation is therefore excluded from the model used in this chapter although a number of authors (including Coughlin *et al.*, 1991 and Arpan and Ricks, 1995) argue that regional taxation structures can have a substantial impact on FDI (which can be deterred by high taxation levels).

The Impact of the Regional Development Agencies

The Regional Development Agencies (RDAs) established in England in 1999, and the agencies responsible for attracting FDI in Scotland and Wales (established in the late 1970s), have a potentially important role to play in the attraction of inbound FDI. The RDAs' responsibilities include marketing their regions to foreign investors, promoting technology transfer and investment (including inbound FDI), building internationally competitive businesses, enhancing workforce skills, and coordinating regional infrastructure development (Foley, 1998; *Economist*, 1999). The RDAs are also responsible for the coordination of sites, finance, training and infrastructure services in support of FDI (Caborn, 1999).

The creation of the RDAs has facilitated the rationalization and coordination of economic development at the regional level, as well as the management of FDI. However, their effectiveness has been restricted by a lack of funding, together with a lack of direct control over important elements of the development process (Foley, 1998) and over policy areas vital to the attraction of inbound FDI (Islam, 2002). RDAs' individual budgets are relatively small, and are insufficient for the achievement of the ambitious goals set for them by central government in the management of inbound FDI and in other areas of activity. The new RDAs are also hampered by their lack of strategic control over their regions' educational and vocational training systems, taxation and infrastructure spending, the levels and availability of regional assistance in their regions and average wage rates, making it more difficult for them to compete effectively for inbound FDI in the global marketplace (Foley, 1998; *Economist*, 1999, Islam, 2002).

Changes in the Attraction of Inbound FDI to UK Regions

An increasing body of evidence (Roberts *et al.*, 1988; Collis *et al.*, 1989; Hill and Munday, 1992; Meyer and Qu, 1995) suggests that changes are now occurring in the regional distribution of inbound FDI in the UK, on which the influence of the new English RDAs has yet to be determined. An initial concentration of FDI in the South-East region of the UK has been broadly maintained, although peripheral regions such as Scotland, Wales and the North of England, and latterly regions such as the West Midlands, have been increasingly favoured by foreign investors. These findings form the basis for the present study, and for the choice of regions.

UK FDI INFLOWS AND STOCK AT NATIONAL AND REGIONAL LEVELS

Table 4.1 shows the net foreign investment by regions in the UK during the period 1996–2000, expressed in percentage terms. Europe had 47.1 per cent of the UK's total FDI stock in 2000 (up from 32.5 per cent in 1996), followed by the USA with 34.4 per cent (down from 41.5 per cent in 1996), Asia with 5.2 per cent (6.0 per cent), Australasia and Oceania with 4.0 (5.72 per cent) and Africa with 0.4 per cent (0.57 per cent).

Table 4.1   UK FDI stock levels by regions of origin (net foreign investment position by value in £ million, percentages)

Region	1996	1997	1998	1999	2000
EU	32.5	29.4	34.1	45.0	47.1
United States	41.5	45.9	46.1	39.2	34.4
Asia	6.0	6.0	5.1	3.0	5.2
Australasia and Oceania	5.72	4.8	3.86	3.0	4.0
Africa	0.57	0.64	0.81	0.4	0.4

Source: ONS (2001) *Foreign Direct Investment.*

Table 4.2 UK FDI stock levels by countries of origin (net foreign investment position by value in £ million, percentages)

Country	1996	1997	1998	1999	2000
Austria	0.2	0.05	0.16	0.11	0.2
Belgium/Luxembourg	0.92	1.2	1.49	1.74	1.3
Denmark	0.63	0.6	0.77	0.83	0.97
Finland	0.25	0.3	0.36	0.39	0.36
France	6.79	9.1	8.0	8.3	16.8
Germany	7.06	6.6	5.7	15.2	8.9
Greece	0	0	0	0.02	0
Irish Republic	0.52	1.2	0.1	1.3	1.2
Italy	0.73	0.53	0.69	0.64	0.8
Netherlands	13.9	7.9	13.9	14.2	14.0
Portugal	0	0	0	0.08	0
Spain	0.06	0.16	0.23	0.43	0.76
Sweden	1.4	1.6	1.43	1.7	1.3

Source: ONS *Foreign Direct Investment* Inquiries (2001).

Amongst the European countries, France was the biggest direct investor in the UK in 2000, with 16.8 per cent of the total net FDI stock (substantially higher than 6.79 per cent in 1996). The Netherlands occupied second place with 14 per cent of FDI (up from 13.9 per cent in 1996), followed by Germany with 8.9 per cent (7.06 per cent) (see Table 4.2).

Table 4.3 shows the sectoral distribution of net FDI stocks held in the UK between 1997 and 2000 in percentage terms. Manufacturing maintained the greatest concentration of FDI throughout the period, followed by financial services, although both suffered a fall in their share of total FDI stocks. Transport and communications, real estate and business services, and retail and wholesale trade and repairs all experienced a rise in their share of FDI stocks over the four-year period, while the share of primary production declined.

Table 4.3 Distribution of UK FDI stocks by sector (£ million, percentages)

	1997	1998	1999	2000
Primary	13.2	12.6	10	9
Manufacturing	41	39.1	35	32
Financial services	28.3	22.2	20	21
Real estate and business services	6.7	8.9	6	9
Transport and Communications	1.3	6.7	17	19
Retail/wholesale trade and repairs	9.5	9.7	12	10

Source: ONS, MA4 *Foreign Direct Investment* (2002).

Table 4.4   Net UK FDI inflows by countries and regions of origin, 1996–2000 (£ million, percentages)

	1996	1997	1998	1999	2000
Europe	44.2	41.4	51.0	72.5	70.1
of which EU	29.8	34.0	48.3	72.9	67.2
The Americas	46.0	52.3	41.8	31.6	21.2
of which USA	43.0	49.5	41.4	29.3	18.3
Asia	2.6	2.0	3.2	−4.0	6.2
of which Japan	1.3	1.4	2.2	−4.9	3.7
Australasia and Oceania	6.4	3.5	2.2	−0.2	2.0
Africa	0.8	0.8	1.8	0.2	0.5
Totals	100.0	100.0	100.0	100.0	100.0

Source: Adapted from ONS, *Foreign Direct Investment* (2001).

Table 4.4 shows net FDI inflows into the UK by regions and selected countries of origin over the period from 1996 to 2000 in percentage terms. Taken overall, the table shows a similar pattern to that of FDI stock holdings. The share of Europe rose steadily over the four years to 1999, although a minor fall was experienced in 2000. The share of the Americas rose initially but declined steadily between 1997 and 2000. Asia and Japan, Australasia and Oceania and Africa had only a relatively small share in FDI inflows over the four-year period.

DETERMINANTS OF FDI IN THE WEST MIDLANDS AND SCOTLAND: THE 'OFFICIAL' VIEW

Data from two UK regions, the West Midlands and Scotland, were gathered to assess the importance of the various factors considered to attract FDI inflows. To set the scene for this investigation the sections below outline the main character-istics of FDI inflows into these regions and official views of the RDAs on the importance of these characteristics.

The West Midlands

The West Midlands has long been established as a major European region for attracting inbound FDI, and in 2000 it ranked amongst the top five locations for FDI in Europe (Advantage West Midlands, 2000). Of the 40 per cent of EU foreign direct investment projects attracted to the UK, the West Midlands has consistently secured 20 per cent in recent years (Government Office for the West Midlands, 2001). Tables 4.5, 4.6, and 4.7 show the volume, geographical origins and sectoral balance of inbound FDI into the West Midlands.

Table 4.5 shows (1994 to 2001) that 584 FDI projects were undertaken in the region, leading to planned investment levels of £9097 million, and to the creation

Table 4.5   FDI inflows into West Midlands, 1994–2001

	1994–95	*1995–96*	*1996–97*	*1997–98*	*1998–99*	*1999–2000*	*2000–2001*	*Totals*
No. of projects	70	76	74	87	82	92	103	584
Size or value of planned investments (£ million)	1 094	848	2 654	936	1 084	275	2 206	9 097
Jobs created or safeguarded	13 445	11 501	19 426	18 267	14 731	17 730	25 093	120 193

Source: Invest UK, Invest in Britain Bureau and Advantage West Midlands (1999–2001).

or safeguarding of 120 193 jobs (Invest in Britain Bureau and Advantage West Midlands, 1999 to 2001). Table 4.6 shows the geographical origin of FDI inflows into the West Midlands between 1994 and 2001, by numbers of new projects. European and North American companies are dominant, but Asia-Pacific investment also make a continuing if numerically less important contribution to FDI throughout the seven-year period (Invest in Britain Bureau 1999 and Advantage West Midlands, 2001).

Manufacturing FDI inflows have remained consistent in terms of new project numbers throughout the period 1994–2000, although there has been an increase in services FDI (Table 4.7). These trends reflect the retreat of manufacturing from an overwhelmingly dominant share of West Midlands FDI inflows in 1994–95 to a lesser share by 2000–01, while the share of services has risen steadily over the same period (Advantage West Midlands, 2000 and 2001).

Much of the FDI entering the West Midlands has traditionally been concentrated in a narrow range of manufacturing sectors in which the region is strong, such as the automotive sector, engineering, rubber and plastics, manufacturing and food and drink. Since the late 1990s, however, the region found growing success in attracting business-services companies and in particular companies in the information technology and software sectors. In 2000, for example, Advantage

Table 4.6   FDI inflows into the West Midlands by source countries, 1994–2001 (number of projects)

	1994–95	*1995–96*	*1996–97*	*1997–98*	*1998–99*	*1999–2000*	*2000–2001*	*Totals*
N America	30	32	36	36	40	50	36	260
Europe	35	31	28	48	33	32	59	266
Asia Pacific	5	13	10	13	9	10	8	68

Source: Invest UK, DTI/FEO Invest in Britain Bureau and Advantage West Midlands, 1999–2001.

Table 4.7   FDI inflows into the West Midlands by sector, 1994–2001 (number of projects)

	1994–95	1995–96	1996–97	1997–98	1998–99	1999–2000	2000–2001	Totals
Primary	0	0	0	0	0	1	0	1
Manufac-								
turing	64	65	57	64	58	69	70	447
Services								
/Other	6	11	17	23	24	22	33	136

Source: Advantage West Midlands, 1999–2001.

West Midlands received 116 enquiries from potential investors in the software industry compared to 97 from engineering companies and 81 connected to the automotive industry (Advantage West Midlands, 2001).

The stock of FDI in the West Midlands contains six of the top-ten global software companies, together with 18 of the top-20 global automotive suppliers, 25 of the top-30 global automotive plastics suppliers and a host of global telecommunications companies (Advantage West Midlands, 2000). The region also has the strongest financial services sector in the UK outside London. In 2000, a total of more than 223 000 people were employed through inbound FDI in the West Midlands within 1925 companies (over a third of which have moved into the region since 1991) from a range of host economies including the USA, Germany, Japan, France, Taiwan, the Netherlands, Switzerland and Sweden. These companies include BMW, Denso, Ford, Fujitsu, Magneti Marelli, NEC, Oracle, Peugeot, GAP and OSI Pharmaceuticals (Advantage West Midlands, 2001).

Official investment agency sources argue that the West Midlands' attractiveness for FDI is largely explained by resources-related factors:

> The region boasts a skilled and dedicated workforce of more than 2.4 million people, who have consistently demonstrated their versatility, flexibility and competitive instinct over many years. They are ready to be flexible in working practices and committed to meeting targets. (Advantage West Midlands, 2000)

The workforce is obviously highly skilled, with the region generating 34 000 new high-quality graduates from its nine universities each year. These institutions, together with the region's 60 higher and further education colleges, provide a sound base of well-educated graduates for companies to draw upon, particularly those in the information technology sector. The West Midlands is also seen as a relatively low-cost area to live in (compared to the south-east) and this further strengthens its appeal as a magnet for FDI.

Official sources also consider market-related factors to be important in attracting inbound FDI to the West Midlands. Much is made of the region's location at the very centre of the UK's transport infrastructure together with the fact that 75 per cent of the UK's population is within a half-day truck drive of the region's centre. 'High quality and highly reliable road, rail and sea connections are all part of the region's well-developed and extensive transport infrastructure, all supported by an advanced telecommunications network' (Advantage West Midlands, 2000).

Efficiency-related factors are also seen as playing an important role in attracting FDI to the West Midlands, particularly in sectors in which the region has traditionally been strong. The region's traditional role as a centre for manufacturing and motor vehicle production contributes to its continuing status as a prime location for inbound FDI in these sectors, linked to the manufacturing and distribution of products destined for the UK and mainland European markets. There has recently been a concerted effort, however, to attract more high-value-added jobs in business services and IT to the region, and to diversify away from more traditional manufacturing activities (Advantage West Midlands, 2000).

Official sources finally point to the work carried out by Advantage West Midlands in marketing the region to potential MNC investors, drawing attention to the volume and value of FDI attracted with investment agency support. Attention is also drawn in official publications to the potential availability of government financial assistance to direct investors in the region (Advantage West Midlands, 2000).

Scotland

Investment agency sources suggest that Scotland, like the West Midlands, has achieved considerable success in attracting inbound FDI. Over 900 foreign-owned companies have bases in Scotland, including Motorola, Compaq, NEC, IBM and Sun Microsystems (Invest UK, 2001). Table 4.8 shows that 625 FDI projects were undertaken in the region between 1994 and 2000, leading to planned investment levels of £9416 million and to the creation or safeguarding of 101 678 jobs (Locate In Scotland, 1995 to 2001). These figures show that the

Table 4.8   FDI inflows into Scotland, 1994–2001

	1994–95	*1995–96*	*1996–97*	*1997–98*	*1998–99*	*1999–2000*	*2000–2001*	*Totals*
No. of projects	97	84	86	87	78	91	102	625
Size or value of planned investments (£ million)	£1 127	£981	£3 122	£1 012	£761	£650	£1 763	9 416
Jobs created or safeguarded	12 329	12 560	14 295	17 947	10 867	19 334	14 346	101 678

Source: Locate in Scotland, *Annual Reviews* (1995 to 2001).

48   *Inbound FDI in the UK*

Table 4.9   FDI inflows into Scotland by source countries, 1994–2001 (number of projects)

	1994–95	1995–96	1996–97	1997–98	1998–99	1999–2000	2000–2001	Totals
N America	41	27	28	36	29	39	52	252
Europe	47	48	48	42	43	46	38	312
Asia Pacific	9	9	10	9	6	6	12	61

Source: Locate in Scotland, *Annual Reviews*, 1995 to 2001.

volume and value of Scotland's FDI inflows were both greater than for the West Midlands during the same period, although the number of jobs created or safeguarded is somewhat lower in the case of Scotland (see Tables 4.5 and 4.8).

Table 4.9 shows that the market for FDI in Scotland is dominated by European and North American donor companies (with many of the former consisting of non-Scottish, UK-based concerns, according to Locate in Scotland, 2001). Smaller inflows of FDI also continue to be attracted from companies based in the Asia-Pacific region (Locate In Scotland, 2001). This broad pattern is consistent with that of the West Midlands (see Tables 4.6 and 4.9).

Table 4.10 indicates the breakdown of FDI inflows into Scotland on a sectoral basis during the period from 1994 to 2001. Manufacturing FDI inflows have fallen from 77 new projects at the beginning of the period to 67 at the end, whilst services inflows have in contrast risen steadily from 18 to 35 new projects. However, inbound FDI in the primary sector appears to be of little significance to Scotland (Locate in Scotland, 1995–2001). These trends broadly reflect those exhibited by West Midlands FDI during the same period.

In the manufacturing sector, Scotland has achieved particular success in attracting inbound FDI to its electronics and services industries. Together, these sectors accounted for 46 per cent of all new foreign direct investment projects in the region between 1994 and 2000, during which time electronics brought in 23 per cent of FDI, and services 25 per cent (Locate in Scotland, 2001). Scotland is

Table 4.10   FDI inflows into Scotland by sector, 1994–2001 (number of projects)

	1994–95	1995–96	1996–97	1997–98	1998–99	1999–2000	2000–2001	Totals
Primary	2	4	2	2	0	0	4	12
Manufac- turing	77	67	61	62	49	56	67	439
Services/ Other	18	13	23	23	29	35	35	176

Source: Locate in Scotland, *Annual Reviews*, 1995 to 2001.

now home to a cluster of over 420 electronics companies (158 owned by overseas firms) which together make up 'Silicon Glen', arguably 'the largest concentration of electronics companies anywhere in Europe' (Invest UK, 2001). Scotland's electronics industry has achieved this position due to a decade of rapid and sustained growth in output and product sales, while the region is now at the forefront of global technology developments in the electronics sector (Locate In Scotland, 2001). The industry also claims to possess strength in diversity, having 'Europe's largest concentration of semiconductor fabricators', together with a number of leading global players in the 'computer, consumer electronics, office products and telecommunications equipment' markets (Locate In Scotland, 2001).

In the years since 1996, Scotland's services industry has replaced electronics as the prime target for inbound FDI in both volume (number of new projects), value (capital investment) and employment (job-creation and safeguarding) terms. Service-sector activities now account for 38 per cent of inbound FDI projects, 19 per cent of investment and 39 per cent of planned jobs (Locate In Scotland, 2000). Services FDI that enters Scotland covers a broad compass, including higher value-added activities such as electronics design and biotechnology research, design and development (R,D&D). The financial services sector has also shown strong interest in investing in the region, as has the dot.com sector (until recently), while Scotland is attracting increasing attention as a location for major call centres (Locate In Scotland, 2000).

Official sources suggest that a range of factors have been important in attracting FDI to Scotland, including market-related factors such as the size of its population (5.1 million) and the quality of its distribution infrastructure. The availability of a high-speed distribution infrastructure is also thought to act as a powerful incentive for the location of FDI in the region.

Resources-related factors, such as its 'highly skilled, flexible workforce'; and efficiency-related factors, including Scotland's status as a 'major centre for high-tech R,D&D' are thought to play an important role in attracting FDI to Scotland (Invest UK, 2001). High-value-added activities in the electronics and R&D sectors are seen as being attracted to Scotland by the sophistication of Scotland's telecommunications network, the high quality of Scotland's human skills capital, and by the agglomeration economies available in 'Silicon Glen'. On the other hand, lower-value-added activities such as financial services and call centres are regarded as being drawn in by resources-related factors alone. Prominent amongst these, in the official view, is the availability of a pool of affordable labour in the region due to its relatively high unemployment and relatively low wage rates (Locate In Scotland, 2001).

Official sources finally draw attention to the role of the inward investment agency in marketing Scotland to potential FDI investors. Reference is also made to the availability of governmental assistance for FDI in the region (Locate in Scotland, 2001).

THE STUDY

The empirical research underlying the second part of this study was designed to answer the following questions:

1 Does the search for markets, resources and efficiency provide a statistically significant explanation for the attraction of Scotland and the West Midlands?
2 Which, if any, of the factors suggested by the literature in the field provide a significant explanation of the decision to locate in one or both of these two regions?
3 To what extent does official RDA thinking on the determinants of FDI reflect the realities of the regional investment location choices being made by MNCs?

The basic functional relationship described in the equation is that flows of FDI (using the proxy of the number of new projects per year) in UK regions are a *positive* function of: government regional assistance (*RPA*); spending on infrastructure (*ROAD*); size of regional population (*POPN*); levels of unemployment (*UN*); the extent of regional industrialisation (*MAN*) reflecting agglomeration economies; and levels of education (*EDU*); and are a *negative* function of average regional wage earnings (*AWC*). The functional relationship was initially estimated using OLS regression analysis.

New FDI projects were used as a proxy for FDI inflows to the regions, following the example of Hill and Munday (1991, 1994). A choice has had to be made between proxies recorded in *Regional Trends*, the annual number of foreign investment project successes (www. statistics.gov.uk/regional trends) or by Invest UK, the annual number of new investment projects (www.dti.gov.uk/ibb/). The latter measure was chosen for this study as it quantifies inbound FDI projects on a current-year basis rather than recording the number of project 'successes' in a particular year, the actual investment for which is likely to have taken place at least one year before.

The analysis of data in the study is based on the estimation of the empirical relationship between inbound FDI and the seven independent variables for the West Midlands and Scotland between 1980 and 1998.

FINDINGS

The estimated coefficients for inbound FDI are shown in Tables 4.11 and 4.12. The estimates suggest that a significant proportion of the variation in the dependent variable can be explained by the independent variables in the case of both UK regions. The model's explanatory power is stronger for the West Midlands, as demonstrated by the goodness of fit statistics (unadjusted coefficient of determination, $R^2 = 0.884$; adjusted coefficient $R^2 = 0.802$) than for Scotland ($R^2 = 0.816$; adjusted $R^2 = 0.687$).

Table 4.11   Multiple regression results – West Midlands

Variable	Coefficient	T ratio
Constant	1754.6	1.998
Government regional assistance (*RPA*)	220.9	2.880*
Spending on infrastructure (*ROAD*)	−4.8	−0.357
Size of regional population (*POPN*)	0.4	−2.136
Level of unemployment (*UN*)	−1.0	−0.488
Extent of regional industrialization (*MAN*)	0.2	0.286
Levels of education (*EDU*)	2.8	2.328*
Average regional earnings (*AWC*)	54.6	0.731
R^2	0.884	
Adjusted $\underline{R}^2$	0.802	

* Statistically significant at the 0.05 level.

Given the small sample sizes the results provide evidence on the relative influence of the seven 'independent' variables on FDI inflows into the West Midlands and Scotland. The *t*-test results suggest that the key influences on FDI vary considerably between these two regions. In the West Midlands, the regional assistance levels (*RPA*) and education (*EDU*) are statistically significant. In Scotland, market size (*POPN*), level of unemployment (*UN*), regional assistance (*RPA*) and average wage costs (*AWC*) are all significant. Taken together, these findings suggest that it may prove difficult to explain the regional distribution of inbound FDI in the UK using a common set of independent variables.

The signs of some of the coefficients also point to the existence of potential difficulties for inbound-FDI policy-makers. It might be expected that rising average wage costs would act as a deterrent to FDI, but the results suggest that this variable has a positive influence on FDI in Scotland. This apparent contradiction may be

Table 4.12   Multiple regression results – Scotland

Variable	Coefficient	T ratio
Constant	−3845.7	−3.974
Government regional assistance (*RPA*)	−18.4	−2.835*
Spending on infrastructure (*ROAD*)	−10.8	−0.587
Size of regional population (*POPN*)	0.7	3.743**
Level of unemployment (*UN*)	9.2	3.665**
Extent of regional industrialisation (*MAN*)	1.7	1.653
Levels of education (*EDU*)	0.2	0.667
Average regional earnings (*AWC*)	75	2.325*
R^2	0.816	
Adjusted $\underline{R}^2$	0.687	

* Statistically significant at the 0.05 level, **Statistically significant at the 0.01 level.

explained by reference to the possibility that labour costs may have an ambiguous effect on FDI. On the one hand, high labour costs might lead to a reduction in resource-seeking FDI, as they raise the total costs of the investing firms. On the other hand, they will help to create higher real incomes and purchasing power at the regional level, so providing a possible stimulus to market-seeking FDI.

The coefficient of *RPA* also has an unexpectedly negative sign in the case of Scotland, suggesting that increasing levels of government regional assistance are associated with lower inflows of FDI into the region. This result may be explained, at least in part, by the heterogeneity of the Scottish economy which cannot be reflected by its treatment as one unified region in published official statistics. RPA may be expected to attract FDI to core areas of the Scottish economy (such as the Central Lowlands), but this effect may be masked by its inability to overcome the inherent disadvantages of peripheral areas (such as The Highlands and Islands) as locations for inbound FDI (due to their remoteness from markets, relatively poor infrastructure and lack of agglomeration economies). These circumstances would appear at first glance to argue strongly for the adoption of a more geographically-focused approach to RPA in the case of Scotland. However, it is possible that the negative relationship suggested here between RPA and FDI is due to data and/or estimation problems, therefore this finding should be treated with caution.

Although both in Scotland and the West Midlands the results suggest that a relationship exists between FDI inflows and a number of 'independent' variables, the direction of causality cannot be inferred from these findings. For example, in the case of Scotland inbound FDI appears to be influenced by RPA. However, it is possible that reverse causality applies and that the findings indicate that changes in the level of FDI lead to changes in the level of RPA made available to direct investors in the region.

The results of the adjusted R^2 tests are supported by the F-test results for both the West Midlands and Scotland (see Table 4.13). The F-test results, used as a measure to test for the significance of the explanatory variable together within an equation, are significant for both the West Midlands and Scotland albeit at different levels (0.01 for the West Midlands; 0.05 for Scotland). These findings offer further support for the view that the model provides a better explanation of inbound FDI in the West Midlands than in Scotland.

Evidence of intercorrelation is provided by the analysis of the findings for both regions. There appears, for example, to be a strong intercorrelation between average gross weekly earnings (*AWC*) and education levels (*EDU*) in both the

Table 4.13 F-test results

Region	F-ratios	Significance of F-values
West Midlands	10.851	0.01
Scotland	6.339	0.05

Table 4.14 Multicollinearity tests

Region	Intercorrelated variables*
Both regions	AWC:EDU
West Midlands only	POPN:AWC; POPN:EDU; ROAD:AWC; ROAD:POPN; ROAD:EDU; MAN:AWC; AWC:RPA
Scotland only	EDU:RPA; EDU:UN; EDU:MAN

* Pearson correlation coefficient = 0.70 or above; 0.05 confidence level.

West Midlands and Scotland. These results cast doubts on the significance and reliability of individual coefficients, and on the ability of some of the independent variables to add much to the overall fit of the model (see Table 4.14).

Stepwise multiple regression analysis was used in order to help overcome problems of multicollinearity. Each variable was introduced separately into the equation and other variables were omitted or excluded if the explanatory power of the equation was not improved. This procedure provided an opportunity to maximize the explanatory power of the model, and to gain further insights into the relative importance of the independent variables at the regional level.

In the case of the West Midlands, the results obtained from the stepwise analysis support the earlier findings from the multiple regression analysis, indicating that RPA and EDU exercise the most important influence in attracting inbound FDI. For Scotland, the *stepwise* analysis contradicts the OLS findings, suggesting that only average wage costs (*AWC*) exert a statistically significant influence over inbound FDI. *POPN, UN* and *RPA* may still have a role to play in FDI decision-making, however, since *AWC* would only appear to explain approximately 40 per cent of the inbound FDI that enters the Scottish region (see Table 4.15).

Using the results from Tables 4.11 and 4.12, it is possible to estimate regional elasticity measures in order to help determine the responsiveness of inbound FDI to changes in the statistically-significant independent variables included in the regional FDI location model. For the West Midlands, Table 4.16 shows the elasticities of FDI with respect to *RPA* and *EDU*, the elasticities calculated are point elasticities ($E = $ dFDI/d explanatory variable $\times$ explanatory variable/FDI) based on 1986/87 data. These results suggest that a marginal increase in education provision would in principle lead to a greater impact on FDI inflows into the region than would a marginal increase in spending on RPA. These findings do not point

Table 4.15 Stepwise regression results

Region	Significant factors affecting the location of inbound FDI, 1990–98
West Midlands	RPA*(+ve), EDU*(+ve)
Scotland	AWC*(+ve)

* Statistically significant at the 0.05 level.

Table 4.16　Elasticities for the West Midlands and Scotland

Region	Elasticity
West Midlands	*RPA* (0.2985), *EDU* (2.57)
Scotland	*POPN* (99.57), *UN* (3.32), *RPA* (−1.17), *AWC* (3.33)

to an obvious response at regional level, however, since the West Midlands RDA has little direct control over education spending. Table 4.16 also provides support for the view that *POPN, UN* and *AWC* all have the potential to attract FDI to Scotland, although none are under RDA control. The remaining variable, *RPA*, is under greater RDA control but the perverse sign (−1.17) indicated by the elasticity estimate suggests that its impact on FDI is complex, making it difficult to propose policy recommendations for Scotland.

POLICY RECOMMENDATIONS

The results provide tentative support for the view that the attraction of FDI inflows into the West Midlands and Scotland is related to the search for markets, resources efficiency, and government policies. Official thinking on the determinants of inbound FDI does not appear, however, fully to reflect the realities of the investment location choices being made by MNCs. Advantage West Midlands, Locate in Scotland, Invest UK and Invest in Britain bureau literature provides a broad indication of the regional determinants of FDI in these two regions. Little light is cast, however, on the relative importance of the factors that influence investment location decisions, or on how these factors differ between the West Midlands and Scotland. Similarly, little indication is provided as to why MNCs in particular sectors may prefer one potential UK investment location to the other. These findings suggest that central government, inward investment agencies and RDAs alike may need to adapt their thinking, their policies and their literature in order to focus more clearly on the key influences on the regional distribution of FDI in the UK context.

The findings presented in this paper may help guide policy-makers' thinking by identifying a set of key (but not common) factors which appear to be influencing FDI location decisions in the West Midlands and Scotland. In the case of the West Midlands, the elasticities suggest that levels of education and government regional assistance are significant positive determinants of FDI from the MNCs' perspective. For Scotland, the results indicate that the size of the regional population, levels of unemployment and average regional wage earnings all have positive impacts on FDI, while government regional assistance affects FDI levels negatively.

Investment agency publications suggest that each region has distinct sectoral strengths: engineering, automotive and software activities in the case of the West Midlands, and electronics and services activities in that of Scotland. Both regions, it is argued, exhibit path dependency in terms of the sectoral composition of their FDI, showing an apparent tendency to draw FDI into sectors that are already significantly represented in their regional economies. However, the findings reported in this paper suggest that the sectoral character of regional industrialization shown by the variable *MAN* is not significant in attracting inbound FDI to either region. One reason for this may be that the use of time-series analysis hides the fact that changes are taking place over time in the structure of both the West Midlands and Scottish economies, leading to gradual changes in the industries into which FDI is being attracted. In the West Midlands, there has been a growing emphasis on FDI in the business services sector, and in particular by IT and software companies. In Scotland, the services sector has come to the fore in recent years as the prime target for inbound FDI. Economies of agglomeration may therefore be of importance in explaining the regional location of inbound FDI, but this effect may be difficult to model econometrically during such a period of sectoral transition, leading to the statistically insignificant findings for *MAN* estimated in the current study.

The findings reported in this chapter point to a major difference of emphasis over the locational determinants of FDI as seen by inward investment agencies in the West Midlands and Scotland and MNCs. There is a clear difference between the factors that appear to be attracting FDI and the sectors of industry which these two UK regions are attracting FDI inflows. This suggests that central government should be flexible in its approach to FDI policy by allowing RDAs the autonomy to operate distinctive FDI strategies related more strongly than at present to those factors that appear to be attracting more FDI to their regions.

CONCLUSION

This chapter has pointed to a number of policy areas over which RDAs have relatively little control, but which it appears can exercise an important influence over FDI location decisions. These include education and vocational training, the average wage rates within their regions, the level and availability of government assistance to industry and the level of spending on transportation and communications infrastructure at the regional level. The findings suggest that if RDAs were given greater strategic control over these areas by central government, supported by appropriately enlarged budgets and an enhanced ability to raise revenue from independent sources, their effectiveness in attracting inbound FDI could be substantially improved.

The study has been limited by problems of data comprehensiveness, consistency and reliability. RDA data sometimes appear in anecdotal form making it difficult to categorize FDI by sector, size and country of origin. FDI can also be both new to the region or an extension of existing investment activity and the allocation of published data between these two categories are not always clear.

The data included in this study do not reflect any spillover effects from FDI to other areas of the regional economy. The study also neglects the possibility that when FDI is established at a regional boundary it will affect two regions but may be allocated only to one. The 12-month time period for data on FDI inflows can also vary between sources.

There is a need for further research into the issues raised by this paper and in particular for in-depth studies into the key influences determining the regional distribution of FDI inflows. Survey-based research may help to overcome at least some of the data problems identified above, while future econometric studies could usefully focus on alternative specifications of both the dependent and the independent variables in order to improve the reliability and value of the findings. The potential impact of RDAs on the volume and value of FDI at the regional level and the likely implications of new government policies increasing their ability to operate distinctive direct investment strategies also needs further exploration. Further research into the spillover effects and country-of-origin questions raised here could provide useful information to scholars and government policy-makers at regional and national levels.

REFERENCES

Advantage West Midlands (2000) *Inward Investment Annual Review* (Birmingham: Advantage West Midlands).

Advantage West Midlands (2001) *Inward Investment Annual Self Monitoring Report, April 2000–March 2001* (Birmingham: Advantage West Midlands).

Anderson, U., Holm, U. and Holmstrom, C. (2001) 'Relationship Configuration and Competence Development in MNC Subsidiaries', in H. Hakansson and J. Johanson (eds) *Business Network Learning* (Oxford: Pergamon), 185–205.

Arpan, J. and Ricks, D.A. (1995) *Directory of Foreign Manufacturers in the United States* (Atlanta: School of Business Administration, Georgia State University).

Bachtler, J. and Clement, K. (1990) 'Inward Investment in the UK and the Single European Market', *Regional Studies*, 24 (2), 173–80.

Bagchi-Sen, S. and Wheeler, J.D. (1989) 'A Spatial and Temporal Model of Foreign Investment in the US', *Economic Geography*, 65 (2), 113–29.

Barney, J.B. (1991) 'Firm Resources and Sustained Competitive Advantage', *Journal of Management*, 17(1), 99–120.

Billington N. (1999) 'The Location of Foreign Direct Investment: An Empirical Analysis', *Applied Economics*, 31 (1), 100–20.

Birkinshaw, J. and Hood, N. (1997) 'An Empirical Study of Development Processes in Foreign-owned Subsidiaries in Canada and Scotland', *Management International Review*, 37 (4), 393–64.

Birkinshaw J., Hood, N. and Jonsson, S. (1998) 'Building Firm-specific Advantages in Multinational Corporations: The Role of Subsidiary Initiative', *Strategic Management Journal*, 19 (3), 221–41.

Blair, A.R., (1987) 'The Relative Distribution of US Direct Investment: The UK/EEC Experience', *European Economic Review*, 31 (5), 1137–44.

Buckley, P.J. and Casson, M. (1976) *The Future of Multinational Enterprise* (London: Macmillan).

Caborn, R. (1999) 'The Role of the New Regional Development Agencies', *Management Services*, 43 (5), 8–9.

Cantwell, J.A. (1989) *Technological Innovation and Multinational Corporations* (Oxford: Basil Blackwell).

Cantwell, J.A. (2001) 'Innovation and Information Technology in MNE', in Rugman A.M. and Brewer T. (eds) *Oxford Handbook of International Business* (Oxford: Oxford University Press), 431–56.

Cantwell, J.A. and Janne, O.E.M. (1999) 'Technological Globalisation and Innovative Centres: The Role of Corporate Technological Leadership and Locational Hierarchy', *Research Policy*, 28, 119–44.

Caves, R.E. (1971), 'International Corporations: The Industrial Economics of Foreign Investment', *Economica*, 51 (1), 1–27.

Collis, C.G. and Noon, D. (1994) 'Foreign Direct Investment in the UK Regions: Recent Trends and Policy Issues', *Regional Studies*, 28 (8), 843–8.

Collis, C.G., Noon, D., Roberts, P. and Gray, K. (1989) *Overseas Investment in the West Midlands Region* (Birmingham: West Midlands Industrial Development Association, Centre for Local Economic Development).

Coughlin, C.C., Terza, J.V. and Arromdee, V. (1991) 'State Characteristics and the Location of Foreign Direct Investment in the United States', *The Review of Economics and Statistics*, 73 (4), 675–83.

Crone, M. (2001) 'Local Learning from Multinational Plants: Knowledge Transfers in the Supply Chain', *Regional Studies*, 35 (6), 535–48.

Culem, C.G. (1988) 'The Locational Determinants of Direct Investments among Industrialised Countries', *European Economic Review*, 32 (4), 885–904.

Dicken, P. (1992) *Global Shift: The Internationalisation of Economic Activity*, 2nd edn, (London: Paul Chapman Publishing).

Dunning, J.H. (1977) 'Trade, Location of Economic Activity and the MNE: A Search for an Eclectic Approach', in Ohlin, B., Hesselborn, P.O. and Wijkman, P.M. (eds), *The International Allocation of Economic Activity* (London: Macmillan, 395–418).

Dunning, J.H. (1988) 'The Eclectic Paradigm of International Production: A Restatement and Some Possible Extensions', *Journal of International Business Studies*, 19 (1), 1–31.

Dunning, J.H. (1993) *Multinational Enterprises and the Global Economy* (Wokingham, UK, and Reading, MA: Addison Wesley).

Dunning, J.H. (1994) 'Re-evaluating the Benefits of Foreign Direct Investment', *Transnational Corporations*, 3 (1), 27–51.

Dunning, J.H. (1995) 'Reappraising the Eclectic Paradigm in the Age of Alliance Capitalism', *Journal of International Business Studies*, 26 (3), 461–93.

Dunning, J.H. (2001) 'The Eclectic (OLI) Paradigm of International Production: Past, Present and Future', *International Journal of the Economics of Business Studies*, 8 (2), 173–90.

The Economist (1999) 'Towards a Federal Britain: An England of Regions', 25 March, www.economist.com

Enright, M.J. (1995) 'Organisation and Coordination in Geographically Concentrated Industries', in Raff D. and Lamoreux N. (eds) *Coordination and Information: Historical Perspectives on the Organisation of Enterprise* (Chicago: Chicago University Press).

Enright, M.J. (1996) 'Regional Clusters and Firm Strategy', in Staber, U., Schaefer, N. and Sharma, B. (eds) *Business Networks – Prospects for Regional Development* (New York: de Gruyter), 190–213.

Enright, M.J. (1998) 'Regional Clusters and Firm Strategy', in Chandler, J., Solvel, A.D. and Hagstrom, P.A. (1998) *The Dynamic Firm: The Role of Technology, Strategy, Organisation and Regions* (Oxford: Oxford University Press).

Enright, M.J. and Roberts, B.H. (2001) 'Regional clustering in Australia', *Australian Journal of Management*, 26, 65–86.

Foley, P. (1998) 'The Impact of the Regional Development Agency and Regional Chamber in the East Midlands', *Regional Studies*, 32 (8), 777–82.

Ford, S. and Strange, R. (1999) 'Where do Japanese Manufacturing Firms Invest within Europe, and Why?', *Transnational Corporations*, 8 (1), 117–42.

Friedman, J., Gerlowski, D. and Silberman, J. (1992) 'What Attracts Foreign Multinational Corporations? Evidence from Branch plant Location in the United States', *Journal of Regional Science*, 32 (4), 403–18.

Giddy, I.H. and Young, S. (1982) 'Conventional Theory and Unconventional Multinationals: Do New Forms of Multinational Enterprise Require New Theories?', in Rugman, A.M. (ed.), *New Theories of the Multinational Enterprise* (London: Croom Helm) ch. 4.

Glickman, N.J. and Woodward, D.P. (1988) 'The Location of Foreign Direct Investment in the United States: Patterns and Determinants', *International Regional Science Review*, 11 (2), 137–54.

Gorg, H. and Ruane, F. (2001) 'Multinational Corporations and Linkages: Panel Data Evidence for the Irish Electronics Sector', *International Journal of the Economics of Business*, 8 (1), 1–18.

Government Office for the West Midlands (2001) 'Invest in Britain' (London: HMSO.)

Grant, R. (1996) 'Prospering in Dynamically Competitive Environments: Organizational Capability as Knowledge Integration', *Organization Science*, 7 (4), 375–87.

Gupta, A.K. and Govindarajan, V. (2000) 'Knowledge Flows within Multinational Corporations', *Strategic Management Journal*, 21 (4), 473–96.

Haitani, K. and Marquis, C.T. (1990) 'Japanese Investment in the Southeast United States: Factors, Obstacles and Opportunities', *Economic Development Review*, Summer, 44–8.

Head, K., Ries, J. and Swenson, D. (1995) 'Agglomeration Benefits and Location Choice: Evidence from Japanese Manufacturing Investments in the United States', *Journal of International Economics*, 38 (3–4), 223–47.

Hedlund, G. (1984) 'Organization In-between: The Evolution of the Mother-Daughter Structure of Managing Foreign Subsidiaries in Swedish MNCs', *Journal of International Business Studies*, 15 (2), 109–23.

Hill, S. and Munday, M. (1991) 'The Determinants of Inward Investment: A Welsh Analysis', *Applied Economics*, 23 (1), 761–9.

Hill, S. and Munday, M. (1992) 'The UK Regional Distribution of Foreign Direct Investment: Analysis and Determinants', *Regional Studies*, 26 (6), 535–68.

Hill, S. and Munday, M. (1994) *The Regional Distribution of Foreign Manufacturing Investment in the UK* (London: Macmillan).

Hymer, S.H. (1976) *The International Operations of National Firms: A Study of Direct Foreign Investment* (Cambridge, MA: MIT Press).

Invest in Britain Bureau (1999) *UK Inward Investment*, http://www.dti.gov.uk/ibb/

Invest UK (2001) *UK Regional Information, Scotland and West Midlands*, http://www.Invest.uk.com/investing/uk_regional

Islam, F. (2002) 'Resisting the Pull of the South', *The Observer*, 12 May, 4.

Ivarsson, I. (1999) 'Competitive Industry Clusters and Inward TNC Investments: The Case of Sweden', *Regional Studies*, 33 (1), 37–49.

Krugman, P.R. and Venables, A.J. (1995) 'Globalisation and the Inequality of Nations', *Quarterly Journal of Economics*, 90 (4), 857–79.

Lall, S. (1973) 'Transfer Pricing by Multinational Manufacturing firms', *Oxford Bulletin of Economics and Statistics*, 35 (3), 173–95.

Locate in Scotland (1995–2001) *Inward Investment Annual Reviews*, http://www.lis.org.uk.

Luger, M.I. and Shetty, S. (1985) 'Determinants of Foreign Plant Start-ups in the United States: Lessons for Policy-makers in the Southeast', *Vanderbilt Journal of Transnational Law*, Spring, 223–45.

Mair, A., Florida, R. and Kenney, M. (1988) 'The New Geography of Automotive Production: Japanese Transplants in North America', *Economic Geography*, 64 (4), 352–73.

Mandell, S.L. and Killian, C.D. (1974) *An Analysis of Foreign Investment in Selected Areas of the United States, A Research paper on Behalf of the New England Regional Commission*, (Boston, MA: The International Center of New England, Inc.).

Markusen, A. (1996) 'Sticky Places in Slippery Space: A Typology of Industrial Districts', *Economic Geography*, 72 (3), 293–313.

McConnell, J.E. (1980) 'Foreign Direct Investment in the US', *Annals of the Institute of American Geography*, 70 (2), 259–70.

Meyer, S. and Qu, T. (1995) 'Place-specific Determinants of FDI: The Geographical Perspective', in Green, M.B. and Norton, R.D. (eds) *The Location of Foreign Direct Investment: Geographic and Business Approaches* (Aldershot: Avebury).

Milner, C. and Pentecost, E. (1994) 'The Determinants of the Composition of the US Foreign Direct Investment in UK Manufacturing', in Balasubramanyam, V.N. and Sapsford, D. (eds), *The Economics of International Investment* (Aldershot: Edward Elgar).

Mudambi, R. (1995) 'The Multinational Investment Location Decision: Some Empirical Evidence', *Managerial and Decision Economics*, 16 (3), 249–27.

Newman, R. and Sullivan, D.H. (1988) 'Econometric Analysis of Business Tax Impacts on Industrial Location: What Do We Know, and How Do We Know It?', *Journal of Urban Economics*, 23 (2), 215–34.

Office for National Statistics (2001) *Foreign Direct Investment*, http:// www.statistics .gov.uk/statbase

Office for National Statistics (2001) *Foreign Direct Investment, MA4*, http:// www.statistics .gov.uk/pdfdir/fdi

Roberts, P., Noon, D. and Irving, P. (1988) *Overseas Investment in the West Midlands Region* (Birmingham: West Midlands Industrial Development Association, Centre for Local Economic Development).

Rugman, A.M. (1981) *Inside the Multinationals: The Economics of Internal Markets* (London: Croom Helm).

Rugman, A.M. and Verbeke, A. (1992) 'A Note on the Transnational Solution and the Transaction Cost Theory of Multinational Strategic Management', *Journal of International Business Studies*, 23 (4), 761–71.

Scott, A.J. (1993) *Technologies: High Technology Industry and Regional development in North America and Western Europe* (London: Pion).

Stopford, J. and Strange, S. (1991) *Rival States, Rival Firms: Competition for World Market Shares* (Cambridge: Cambridge University Press).

Swamidass, P.M. (1990) 'A Comparison of Plant Location Strategies of Foreign and Domestic Manufacturers in the U.S.', *Journal of International Business Studies*, 21 (2), 301–17.

Tavares, A.T. and Young, S. (2002) 'Sourcing Patterns of Multinational Subsidiaries in Europe: Testing the Determinants', *UK Chapter, Academy of International Business*, 29th Annual Conference, University of Central Lancashire, 12–13 April, 689–714.

Taylor, J. (1993) 'An Analysis of the Factors Determining the Geographical Distribution of Japanese Manufacturing Investment in the UK, 1984–91', *Urban Studies*, 30 (1), 209–24.

Wheeler, D. and Mody, A. (1992) 'International Investment Location Decisions: The Case of US Firms', *Journal of International Economics*, 33 (1–2), 57–76.

Woodward, D.P. (1992) 'Locational Determinants of Japanese Manufacturing Start-ups in the United States', *Southern Economic Journal*, 50 (3), 690–708.

Woodward, D.P. and Rolfe, R.J. (1993) 'The Location of Export-oriented Foreign Direct Investment in the Caribbean Basin', *Journal of International Business Studies*, 24 (1), 121–44.

Yeung, P. and Strange, R. (2003) in this volume.

Young, S. and Hood, N. (1994) 'Designing Developmental After-care Programs for Inward Investors in the European Community', *Transnational Corporations*, 3 (2), 45–72.

5 Employee Relations in German Multinationals in an Anglo-Saxon Setting and the New German Model of Labour Relations*

Heinz-Josef Tüselmann, Frank McDonald and Arne Heise

INTRODUCTION

Against the background of increased globalization pressures, the growing internationalization of German multinational companies (MNCs) and the current problems and erosion of the traditional German industrial relations (IR) system, there has been growing interest in the employee relations' (ER) approaches and practices of German MNCs, especially those operating in an Anglo-Saxon setting. A key issue is whether nationality of ownership still matters in ER approaches and practices of German MNCs or whether ER patterns in MNCs are converging towards the Anglo-Saxon approach, irrespective of MNCs' countries of origin. This issue is connected to the wider debate on the fate of national ER models in an era of heightened global competition where MNCs are seen as powerful transmission belts for transnational convergence. The unresolved question is whether national models will retain their national distinctiveness by responding to the pressures of globalization in a path-dependent trajectory of change (Lane, 1995; Whitley and Kristensen, 1996). An alternative view is that these pressures lead to the disappearance of tightly regulated and densely institutionalized models with their emphasis on a collective ER approach, such as the German one, and their convergence to the orthodox Anglo-Saxon deregulated market-led model with its emphasis on an individualistic human resource management (HRM) style (Streeck, 1997). The consensus on the benefits of the traditional German collective ER approach has declined and employers have demanded a more flexible, deregulated and decentralized IR system (Wirtschaftswoche, 1995; Institut der deutschen Wirtschaft, 2000). This literature often refers to British experience, therefore research into ER in

* This chapter is based on a research project funded by the Hans-Böckler Foundation, Düsseldorf, Germany, and has been carried out in cooperation with the Economic and Social Research Institute (Wirtschafts- und Sozialwissenschaftliches Institut), Germany. Infrastructural support was provided by the German–British Chamber of Commerce and Industry in London.

German-owned subsidiaries in the UK provides a fruitful means to investigate whether German MNCs perceive their traditional home-based ER approach as beneficial when operating in an Anglo-Saxon setting; or, alternatively, whether they attempt to drop what they perceive as constraining elements in their home country when operating in host countries that have a permissive IR environment, such as the UK, and adopt the ER approaches of their main international competitors, notably those from the Anglo-Saxon world.

Despite Germany being the world's third largest foreign direct investment (FDI) home country after the USA and the UK (Institut der deutschen Wirtschaft, 2001), research into the ownership effect in German MNCs in the UK and elsewhere is still relatively rare. Investigation of ER approaches in German-owned operations in the UK captures a large proportion of German foreign subsidiaries, thus explaining to a significant extent possible home-country effects in the international operations of German companies. The UK is the fourth most important location for German FDI stock (Deutsche Bundesbank, 2001), and alongside the USA was the most popular destination of German FDI outflows in the 1990s, accounting for one-seventh of all German outward flows in that period (Bundesministerium für Wirtschaft und Technologie, 2000). Furthermore, none of the studies carried out so far has been representative for the total population of German UK-based subsidiaries and none has operated with matched samples of German subsidiaries and British-owned firms. Additionally, the effect of the reform process in Germany on ER in German MNCs' international operations has received little attention. This chapter investigates the ownership effects on the basis of a representative survey of German subsidiaries, their parent companies and a comparative analysis based on the Workplace Employee Relations Survey (WERS98). After the literature review and the discussion of the stereotypical German and British approaches to ER, the chapter compares the ER approaches in German and British-owned establishments on a weighted cross-sectional basis. Thereafter, these findings are examined through a series of comparisons according to industrial activity and size to obtain a fuller picture. This is followed by a detailed intra-German analysis to detect newer developments in ER of the German subsidiaries and variations in the strength of possible country-of-origin effects in line with variables such as control mechanisms, FDI mode and age. The concluding section draws together the main findings and highlights the possible future direction of ER in German MNCs.

THE LITERATURE

Despite the large literature on MNCs and international HRM, relatively little is known about the impact of nationality of ownership. Proponents of the competitive convergence thesis argue that the pressures of globalization have set in motion a convergence process of ER patterns in MNCs towards the individualistic Anglo-Saxon approach, regardless of MNCs' countries of origin (Reich, 1991). This is of particular relevance for MNCs from countries such as Germany where the national business system (including the IR system) is experiencing pressures to change in response to developments in the international economy (Edwards, 1998). Moreover, German MNCs are relative latecomers to the internationalization process, and their home-based ER practices and approaches cannot be easily transferred internationally because of their reliance on a particular national IR institutional system (Streeck, 1997). Therefore, they may seek to adopt the salient characteristics of more mature international companies notable from the Anglo-Saxon world, where ER practices have been developed in a deregulated market-led IR environment.

Another strand of the debate argues that despite global pressures, MNCs are not stateless players but are embedded in their country-of-origin business system which colours behaviour and influences ER approaches in foreign operations (Hu, 1992; Ferner, 1997). Therefore, ER in the international operations of MNCs displays distinctive country-of-origin traits. Other literature emphasizes host-country effects, with subsidiaries blending into the local environment and adopting local approaches (UNCTAD, 1994; Coller and Marginson, 1998). Foreign-owned subsidiaries may also have to comply with host-country rules and regulations where relatively strong institutional and regulatory frameworks may override country-of-origin effects. However, permissive frameworks may allow MNCs to mould ER systems along the lines of home-country practices and arrangements. Alternatively, they may adopt local approaches to mimic their competitors in the host country if this is perceived as beneficial to business success in that country. Furthermore, home-country practices may be unworkable outside the particular IR configuration in which they are embedded.

A significant number of studies have identified an ownership effect showing that MNCs from different home countries behave in a distinctive way in managing ER issues in their international operations (for example Young *et al.*, 1985; Child *et al.*, 1997). Conversely other studies point to the predominance of the host-country effect (Rosenzweig and Noria, 1994; Coller and Marginson, 1998). There is also some evidence that MNCs in industries with high degrees of global exposure are endeavouring to develop ER patterns along the lines of leading global competitors (for example Edwards *et al.*, 2000), which, in turn may lend some support to the convergence thesis. However, the magnitude of either of these effects tends to be contingent on a number of variables, such as FDI mode, age, size, control orientation of the parent company, sector, industrial activity, the specific function of the subsidiary, host-country characteristics and the ER aspect under consideration (for example Traxler, 1996; Edwards *et al.*, 2000).

In contrast to US and Japanese MNCs, German MNCs have been underrepresented in studies of the country-of-origin effect, despite their prominence in the global economy. However, most studies have not found distinctively German patterns in German subsidiaries in the UK or elsewhere, rather they tend to adopt local practices (Beaumont *et al.*, 1990; Innes and Morris, 1995; Guest and Hoque, 1996; Child *et al.*, 2000). A recent study involving in-depth interviews found Germanic traits in several HRM aspects in the UK subsidiaries, but not in relation to collective labour relations (Ferner *et al.*, 2001). This study also suggests a degree of reverse diffusion of certain practices, but this tends to be become transmuted within a managerial repertoire that remains basically German, that is an insertion of a dose of Anglo-Saxon-style HRM into the traditional German ER approach, but in a German manner. However, there is need for further research into the ER of German subsidiaries in the UK. None of the studies carried out so far has been representative of the total population of German UK-based operations and none of these studies has operated with matched samples of German subsidiaries and British firms. Moreover, most studies tend to overlook the possible impact of the recent reforms and developments in Germany on the country-of-origin effect.

THE INDUSTRIAL RELATIONS SETTING AND EMPLOYEE RELATIONS' APPROACHES

Employee Relations in Germany

The traditional collective approach to ER in German companies is deeply rooted in the particular configuration of the German IR system. This is characterized by a high degree of regulation and a dense, encompassing institutional infrastructure that imposes a uniform set of institutional constraints on companies, but at the same time provides incentives for employers to accept institutional constraints (Soskice, 1994; Lane, 1995). The institutional structure is highly integrated with strong linkages, not only within the IR system, but also to the wider German business system. Key elements of the German model, to which the majority of German companies subscribe, are the centrally coordinated sector-based collective bargaining system and employee representation at the domestic level via the works-council system equipped with statutory participation and consultation rights. Indeed, German employers have to negotiate a densely structured institutional framework inside and outside the company level. Since the early 1990s, the effectiveness of the traditional German model has been increasingly contested. The twin pressures arising from heightened international competition and reunification have led to a tendency to erode some of the elements in the German system. Employers' demands for a more flexible, deregulated and decentralized IR system, especially in relation to collective bargaining, seem to have gradually weakened the consensus on the benefits of the traditional collective ER approach (Bispinck, 1995). Throughout the 1990s, a process of incremental reforms to the system has progressively broadened the scope for flexibility and strategic choice in companies (Schulten and Zagelmeyer, 1998; Tüselmann, 2001). However, this has been accommodated within the parameters of the flexible adaptation potential of the current system, taking the form of regulated flexibility and centrally coordinated decentralization, pointing to a path-dependent trajectory of change. Contemporary ER in German companies could be described as a flexible collective approach.

Despite growing interest in an individualistic HRM-style the use of direct employee involvement systems by German companies, thus far, has been modest because of the wide-ranging use of rights of information, consultation and codetermination systems in Germany (Sperling, 1997; Institut der deutschen Wirtschaft, 2000). This has made representative systems based on the use of individual voice mechanisms relatively unimportant in Germany. Therefore, in the international context it may be plausible to infer that German MNCs will have a propensity to support a collective approach to ER in their international operations by recognizing trade unions, engaging in collective bargaining and establishing strong workplace-level employee-representation systems. On the other hand, they may be inclined to put less emphasis on direct employee involvement. However, the reform process in Germany has also widened the scope for introducing direct involvement techniques within a pluralist frame. Indeed, the limited evidence about HRM practices in Germany indicates a gradual uptake of such techniques to complement the traditional emphasis on collective ER (Muller, 1999). Thus, the emerging ER system in Germany may perhaps be summarized as a flexible collective approach with a HRM dimension. In turn, one might expect that German MNCs will increasingly endeavour to blend HRM-style direct employee involvement into collective ER in their foreign subsidiaries.

Employee Relations in the UK

In contrast to Germany, the contemporary British IR system is characterized by a weak regulatory framework with a thin and fragmented institutional infrastructure, which imposes relatively few barriers and constraints on labour-relations practices (Lane, 1995; Soskice, 1994). This fragmentation of the institutional structure is evidently not only in the IR system but also in the wider national business system. Contrary to the German experience, it is less easy to distil the elements of a stereotypical ER approach. Traditionally the cornerstone of labour relations was the pluralist workplace industrial relations system, characterized by the Donovan Report (Royal Commission on Trade Unions and Employers' Associations, 1968), which subsequently collapsed in the 1980s in the wake of the neo-liberal labour market policies under the Thatcher government. These reforms encouraged employers to dispense with collective labour relations and to individualize ER along the lines of US-style HRM (Clark, 1996; Edwards *et al.*, 1998). Indeed, by the end of the 1990s, a collective approach to ER is no longer representative of the economy as a whole, but is increasingly confined to the public sector and a dwindling minority of private-sector companies (Cully *et al.*, 1999; Millward *et al.*, 1999). In the private sector, trade-union recognition collapsed throughout the 1980s and 1990s and with it the incidence of workplace-level trade-union representatives. The use of collective bargaining dramatically declined. By 1998, two-thirds of private-sector employees had their pay fixed by management decision without any union involvement. Non-union channels of interest representation, such as staff representatives or joint consultative committees (JCCs) (the weaker version of the

German works councils), are relatively rare and also in decline. They have not filled the vacuum left by the dramatic decrease in union recognition and workplace-level union representatives. There is a large and growing representation gap in the UK and an absence of any kind of collective voice mechanism in the majority of firms (Millward *et al.*, 1999). In those firms where a collective approach to ER still occurs, it takes place within a changed power balance between employers and collective labour actors and on a decentralized basis.

With the retreat of the collective ER approach there has been much discussion and expectation that HRM-style direct ER may become a major feature of British ER. Although direct employee involvement methods have become increasingly common among UK workplaces, various studies point to a rather *ad hoc* and sporadic adoption of such practices (Sission and Marginson, 1995; Wood and Albanese, 1996). Companies with comprehensive HRM involvement packages are far from the norm, and, furthermore, a large percentage of them tend to be firms with trade-union recognition (WERS98). The combination of the low incidence of a collective approach to ER and the high incidence of comprehensive HRM-style employee involvement schemes found in firms with a collective ER approach indicates that many companies have not developed a coherent alternative approach to collective labour relations other than the unfettered reign of the management prerogative. Here, employees are neither represented by collective voice mechanisms, nor do they enjoy a comprehensive individual voice mechanism. Such workplaces may be described as 'Bleak Houses' (Sission, 1993).

RESEARCH QUESTIONS

In light of the differing findings among the studies relating to ER/HRM in MNCs' international operations, in general, and the shortcomings of studies into ER/HRM of German-owned subsidiaries in the UK (and elsewhere), in particular, it is difficult to arrive at firm expectations. However, on the basis of the salient features and recent developments in the German and British ER models some interesting research questions emerge. The first set of questions relates to the general picture of ER patterns in German subsidiaries compared to those in indigenous host-country firms:

- Do ER practices and approaches in German subsidiaries exhibit a pronounced country-of-origin effect in terms of a greater propensity to operate with collective ER practices and approaches, and a lesser propensity to develop direct employee involvement mechanisms compared to UK owned counterparts?
- Have German-owned establishments developed comprehensive HRM-style direct involvement packages and, if so, has this been done in a unitary fashion or within a pluralist framework, with the latter pointing to a dual ER approach?

- Is there an ownership effect in terms of employees in German subsidiaries enjoying a more comprehensive coverage of voice mechanisms (regardless of whether through collective or individual channels) compared to employees in UK-owned establishments?
- Are there variations in the home-country influence within sub-sets of the sample?

However, the findings to the above questions may conceal a reorientation in the ER patterns in German MNCs' international operations located in an Anglo-Saxon setting. On the one hand, intensified global competition and the accelerated internationalization of German companies since the start of the 1990s has gone hand in hand with the frequently cited dissatisfaction of German employers with the German IR system. On the other hand, the reform process in the German IR system in the 1990s has made the German ER approach more flexible and has also broadened the scope for HRM-style direct involvement within a pluralist frame. Both developments may have a very different effect on the ER of German MNCs' subsidiaries in the UK, which are addressed by the following research questions:

- Do ER patterns in German MNCs in the UK converge towards an individualistic Anglo-Saxon approach with German-owned establishments avoiding/abandoning collective labour relations in favour of either a 'High-Road' HRM approach (that is, a comprehensive and extensive bundle of direct employee involvement mechanisms) or a 'Low-Road' cost-minimizing approach (that is, a Bleak House approach)?
- Do ER patterns in German subsidiaries increasingly reflect the evolving new German approach to ER with German-owned establishments continuing to stress a collective ER approach while at the same time developing HRM-style direct-involvement packages in a complementary rather than in a substitutional manner (that is, a dual-ER approach)?
- In light of the findings to the above questions, what could be the direction of possible spillback effects onto ER in the parent companies German locations and the wider knock-on effects for the German ER model?

In addressing these issues, ER in younger German subsidiaries, greenfield sites, manufacturing plants and establishments with German expatriate managers are of particular interest.

THE STUDY

This cross-sectional study was based on a postal survey, in 1999, of all German subsidiaries in north-west England (based on a list of companies from the German-British Chamber of Industry and Commerce) that employ at least 25 workers

(Tüselmann, McDonald and Heise, 2000). This region of England attracts roughly the same amount of FDI inflows as other regions of the UK and the source countries of FDI in north-west England are similar to the rest of the UK (Invest in Britain Bureau, 1999). Very small subsidiaries were excluded since they are more likely to have informal ER approaches (Millward *et al.*, 1992; Guest and Hoque, 1996). The questionnaire was answered by the managing directors or the human resource managers of the subsidiaries. To ensure comparability to WERS98, this survey was workplace-based (using the WERS definition (see Cully *et al.*, 1999) and the questions asked in the questionnaire were identical to the relevant questions in the Management Questionnaire of WERS98. Forty completed replies were received from a possible response of 105 equalling a 38 per cent response rate. The profile of the survey respondents closely matched that of the total population of German subsidiaries in the UK in terms of size, age, sector and type of activity characteristics (see Table 5.1). The results of the questionnaire are thus broadly representative for ER in German-owned UK subsidiaries. In addition, a short telephone interview was conducted with either the human resource manager or a senior human resource officer of those parent companies whose subsidiaries had returned the questionnaire. A 100 per cent response rate was achieved. To realise this rate, the interview questions were restricted to the incidence of collective labour relations' arrangements in the parent companies.

Table 5.1   Profiles (per cent) of German subsidiaries and British-owned establishments

	German subsidiaries[1]		British-owned establishments[2]	
	Survey respondents	*North-west England*	*UK (weighted data)*	*UK*
Size				
25–99 employees	52	52	53	80
100–499 employees	40	38	37	18
≥ 500 employees	8	10	10	2
Activity				
Manufacturing	41	39	37	21
Sales/distribution	45	47	46	76
Services	13	13	16	
Other	2	3	2	3
Age				
≤ 10 years German-owned	45	42	40	
≥ 11 years German-owned	55	58	60	

Notes: [1] With at least 25 employees; [2] wholly or predominantly British-owned private sector establishments with at least 25 employees.

Sources: Database of the German–British Chamber of Commerce and Industry; Database of the WERS98.

The results from the German subsidiaries were compared to the results contained in the database of WERS98, the largest representative survey on ER in the UK. For the purpose of this study, workplaces with fewer than 25 employees, public-sector enterprises and wholly or predominantly foreign-owned establishments were omitted from the analysis of the WERS98 database. This yielded a total of 659 valid cases. However, the composition of the WERS workplaces differs from that of the survey respondents in terms of size, and industrial activity (see Table 5.1), and studies have shown that ER practices exhibit significant variations according to these characteristics (Rosenzweig and Noria, 1994; Frick and Sadowski, 1995). Thus, for the cross-sectional analysis the results for British establishments were weighted to reflect the composition of the German subsidiaries to ensure that differences in ER between German subsidiaries and British establishments were not merely due to the different composition of the samples. The weighted data is shown in column 3 in Table 5.1. The small sample size of the German study and the large difference between the sample sizes of the German study and WERS98 did not allow for meaningful statistical testing. Thus, the analysis is preliminary and is based on descriptive statistics and comparisons. In the absence of statistical tests for significance, the findings have to be interpreted with a degree of caution. Moreover, the absence of data from the parent companies, other than those on the incidence of collective ER arrangements, implies a further degree of uncertainty in relation to the country-of-origin effect in individualistic ER approaches.

CROSS-SECTIONAL ANALYSIS

Collective Approach to Employee Relations

As expected, nearly all the parent companies of the UK subsidiaries conform to the German model of ER by exhibiting the key German institutional arrangements of prescribing to collective bargaining (thereby implicitly or explicitly recognizing trade unions) and operating works councils (see Table 5.2). However, their UK subsidiaries are less likely to replicate the strong emphasis on collective ER (see Table 5.2). Forty-five per cent recognize trade unions and 40 per cent engage in collective pay bargaining and 38 per cent have trade union representatives at the workplace level. Only 20 per cent of establishments had any kind of formal representative employee participation/consultation systems, such as JCCs, the weaker and voluntary version of German works councils. The low propensity of German subsidiaries to use a collective approach to ER compared to the parent companies can at least in part be explained by the fact that emphasis on collective ER in Germany is largely the result of the particular balance of constraints and incentives generated by the German IR institutional and regulatory system, and that these conditions do not prevail in the UK.

Table 5.2   Incidence of collective employee relations (per cent)

	German subsidiaries[1]	Parent companies	British-owned establishments[2]
Trade union recognition	45	94	35
Collective pay bargaining	40	94	36
Workplace-level trade union representatives	38		27
Non-union employee representatives	18		15
Formal representative employee participation/consultation system (e.g. works council, Joint consultative committee)	20	97	36
Collective voice gap (no collective ER systems)	45	3	60
Comprehensive ER systems (simultaneous use of recognition of trade unions, collective bargaining and either workplace trade union representatives or formal employee representatives)	40	–	20

Notes: [1] With at least 25 employees; [2] weighted responses from WERS 1998 of wholly or predominantly British-owned private sector establishments with at least 25 employees.

A collective ER approach is more widespread among German subsidiaries compared to British-owned firms (see Table 5.2). German subsidiaries seem more inclined to recognize unions and have workplace-level union representatives than British-owned establishments – 45 per cent compared to 35 per cent, and 38 per cent composed to 27 per cent, respectively. In terms of developing formal representative employee participation/consultation systems, German subsidiaries have a lower proportion than British-owned establishments – 20 per cent and 36 per cent respectively. In combination with the rare occurrence of non-union staff representatives (18 per cent German subsidiaries and 15 per cent British-owned establishments), many of which are anyway located in unionized establishments, it seems clear that formal representative systems cannot generally be viewed as alternatives to union recognition and workplace-level union representatives. The collective voice gap (that is the absence of any collective channel of interest representation) is smaller among German subsidiaries (45 per cent) compared to British-owned establishments (60 per cent). This highlights that employees in German-owned workplaces are better represented by collective channels compared to their counterparts in British-owned workplaces. Moreover, 40 per cent of German subsidiaries compared to 20 per cent of British-owned establishments have a comprehensive-style collective ER approach – simultaneously recognizing unions, engaging in collective bargaining and having either workplace-level union representatives or formal representative employee involvement systems (see Table 5.2). There seems to be indeed a recognizable Germanic trait in ER among German subsidiaries.

Individualistic Approach to Employee Relations

The wide-ranging participation, consultation and information rights in the German representative system may explain why employers in Germany tend to make less use of the whole range of direct employee involvement schemes when compared to Anglo-Saxon companies, notwithstanding the gradual uptake of certain HRM practices in Germany. Thus, one would also expect an ownership effect in terms of a lesser emphasis on individualistic HRM-style direct employee involvement compared to British-owned firms. Indeed, on average, German subsidiaries tend to make less use of such practices (see Table 5.3). Although 34 per cent of German as well as British-owned workplaces operate some kind of consultation scheme, German subsidiaries make less use of direct

Table 5.3 Direct employee involvement practices (per cent)

	German subsidiaries[1]	British-owned establishments[2]
Participation		
Partly autonomous		
Teamworking	40	42
Problem Solving Groups	30	38
Average	*35*	*40*
Consultation		
Attitude Surveys	23	42
Suggestion Schemes	35	26
Regular Meetings with the		
Workforce	43	33
Average	*34*	*34*
Information-sharing		
Team Briefing	60	86
Regular Newsletters	58	56
Systematic use of the Management		
Chain	60	64
Average	*59*	*69*
Use of comprehensive direct involvement systems (use at least half of the practices lists above)	50	–
Proportion that recognize trade unions	60	–

Notes: [1] With at least 25 employees; [2] weighted responses from WERS (1998) of wholly or predominantly British-owned private-sector establishments with at least 25 employees.

participation mechanisms (the strongest form of direct involvement), 35 per cent compared to 40 per cent, and information-sharing (the weakest form of direct involvement), 59 per cent compared to 69 per cent. This may point to the existence of an ownership effect. In the absence of comparable data from the parent companies, such a conclusion remains somewhat speculative.

The dissemination of individual practices does not necessarily indicate that German subsidiaries are developing effective individual voice systems that could be considered to be comprehensive HRM direct-involvement packages. To identify the importance of direct involvement systems, subsidiaries that use at least half of the practices listed in Table 5.3 were deemed to have effective direct involvement packages. Using this definition, nearly half of German subsidiaries have developed comprehensive HRM involvement packages (see Table 5.3). However, they tend to be a feature of unionized establishments (60 per cent). This finding is in line with similar results discovered in British firms (Cully *et al.*, 1999). Thus, trade-union presence seems to be compatible with a high commitment to direct employee involvement. It seems that developing an individualistic HRM-style ER is not an alternative; rather, these two approaches seem to be complementary.

The high incidence of such HRM involvement packages in subsidiaries that operate with some form of collective ER implies that a significant minority of subsidiaries have no comprehensive ER approach, with neither collective nor effective individual voice mechanisms (that is, at least half of the practices listed in Table 5.3). The total voice gap amounts to 20 per cent in terms of subsidiaries but to only 5 per cent in terms of employee coverage. In comparison, around one-third of British-owned workplaces have no comprehensive ER approach. The overwhelming majority of employees in German subsidiaries (95 per cent) enjoy some form of voice mechanism. The greater emphasis on a cooperative ER style (regardless of whether through collective or direct channels) among German subsidiaries seems to point to a subtle ownership effect in terms of echoing the nationally embedded culture of cooperation between labour and management in Germany.

VARIABILITY OF COUNTRY-OF-ORIGIN INFLUENCES

The broadly representative nature of both the German subsidiaries and the British owned workplaces and the weighting of the results of the latter to reflect the broad composition of the German subsidiaries allows for a relatively high degree of generalization of the above cross-sectional analysis. However, to obtain a fuller picture, it is also of interest to investigate the variability of the ownership effect detected according to industrial activity and size of the workforce (see Table 5.1 for the composition of the relevant WERS98 workplaces and German subsidiaries). Indeed, surveys in Germany and the UK point to considerable differences in labour relations practices and arrangements according to these variables (see for example Cully *et al.*, 1999).

Employee Relations in German Multinationals

Table 5.4   Employee relations patterns (per cent)[1]

	Activity				Size[2]					
	Manufacturing		services		Small		Medium		Large	
	G	GB	G	GB	G	GB	G	GB	G	GB
Collective arrangements										
Trade union recognition	74	32	22	22	29	20	60	47	72	67
Collective bargaining	65	38	22	24	24	27	60	47	51	58
Workplace level union representatives	70	26	13	14	19	11	53	40	72	67
Non-union employee representatives	23	17	13	9	5	9	33	21	25	17
Works council, joint consultative committee, etc.	18	26	22	27	5	20	40	48	25	58
Collective voice gap										
(no collective ER systems)	23	54	65	71	62	73	30	41	10	20
Direct involvement practices[3]										
Participation	38	33	33	36	31	34	40	42	38	50
Consultation	43	22	26	35	32	30	33	30	42	47
Information sharing	55	46	62	64	38	39	48	52	56	67

Notes: [1] Establishments with at least 25 employees; figures for British-owned establishments: responses from WERS98 of wholly or predominantly British-owned private-sector establishments; [2] small establishments: 25 to 99 employees, medium-sized establishments: 100 to 499 employees, large establishments: 500 and more employees; [3] average of the respective practices listed in Table 5.3.

The incidence of collective and individualistic ER practices seems to be positively correlated to size for both the German subsidiaries and British-owned establishments (see Table 5.4). For example, small firms (both German subsidiaries and British-owned establishments) have low trade-union recognition (29 per cent and 20 per cent respectively), and large firms have a high proportion that recognizes trade unions (72 per cent and 67 per cent respectively). For both, the collective voice gap narrows and the incidence of individual voice mechanisms increases the larger the size of the establishment. Thus, for small firms 62 per cent of German subsidiaries and 73 per cent of British-owned establishments had no collective voice practices, falling to 10 per cent and 20 per cent respectively for large firms.

Across all size categories, a collective ER approach is more pronounced in German subsidiaries when compared with British establishments. Whatever size category, the collective gap is some 10 percentage points smaller among German subsidiaries compared to their British-owned counterparts (see Table 5.4). Therefore, the ownership effect in terms of a greater emphasis on collective ER compared to British establishments applies to all size categories, and seems to remain stable regardless of the category under consideration. In contrast, direct employee involvement practices are more prevalent among British establishments in all size categories. For example, small German-owned firms have 31 per cent direct participation systems compared to 34 per cent of British firms – 38 per cent and 50 per cent respectively for large firms (see Table 5.4). Here, the percentage point differential between British and German-owned workplaces increases in line with the size of the workforce. Notwithstanding the latter point, the home-country effect in terms of a lower inclination to operate direct involvement practices when compared to British-owned workplaces is pertinent across all size categories.

There are considerable variations in the country-of-origin effect when comparing German-owned manufacturing plants and German service-sector operations to their British-owned counterparts. As expected, collective labour relations are more evident in manufacturing plants compared to service-sector operations in both German and British-owned sites. The proportion of German subsidiaries with no collective voice systems for manufacturing is 23 per cent compared to 65 per cent for services – 54 per cent and 71 per cent respectively for British-owned firms (see Table 5.4). However, direct employee involvement practices are more common in German manufacturing plants than in the service-sector establishments, whereas the reverse applies to the British sample. For example, 43 per cent of German manufacturing subsidiaries have direct consultation systems, whereas only 26 per cent of service firms have these systems – 22 per cent and 35 per cent respectively for British firms. In commerce and service-sector establishments, the home-country effect may be judged as rather weak. Compared to British-owned sites in this category, a collective ER approach is only somewhat more widespread, and the use of individual voice mechanisms is moderately lower among German subsidiaries. The differential in both the collective-voice gap and the average incidence of direct-involvement practices amounts to just 6 percentage points (see Table 5.4). NB The figure for the direct involvement practices relates to the average of all practices. German service-sector subsidiaries seem more likely to adopt the approaches of their counterparts in the host country, rather than drawing on the German approach.

In contrast to the above, a strong country-of-origin effect can be detected in German manufacturing plants (see Table 5.4). They are far more likely to operate a collective approach when compared with the British-owned plants. The collective voice-gap differential amounts to 31 percentage points. Seventy-four per cent of German plants recognize trade unions and 65 per cent engage in collective bargaining, compared to 32 and 38 per cent respectively of British plants. Interestingly, German-owned manufacturing plants have also made more progress in developing direct involvement practices compared to British-owned ones. Management in German manufacturing plants seems more likely to take on board individualistic HRM-style involvement practices connected with the Anglo-Saxon approach compared to their British counterparts. For example, 43 per cent of German subsidiaries have direct consultation systems compared to 22 per cent of British firms. At the same time they are also more inclined to operate with a collective ER approach than British plants. Only 23 per cent of German subsidiaries have no collective voice systems compared to 54 per cent of British firms. In many German-owned plants, both collective and individualistic ER practices seem to coexist happily. Rather than replacing collective ER, direct employee involvement practices seem to have added a new dimension to the collective approach. Labour relations in German manufacturing plants in the UK may reflect the evolving new German model of ER, that is a flexible collective approach with a HRM dimension. However, the substantiation of such a prediction requires a more detailed intra-German analysis of the ER approaches of subsidiaries.

INTRA-GERMAN ANALYSIS

Closer inspection of the ER approaches in the German subsidiaries seems to support such a proposition, as well as revealing some interesting findings with regard to the convergence thesis. ER in German subsidiaries exhibit pronounced variations according to size, activity, entry mode and age (see Table 5.5). Greenfield sites, larger establishments, manufacturing plants and younger subsidiaries have a far greater propensity to operate with a collective approach and to develop comprehensive HRM direct involvement packages compared to brownfield sites, smaller establishments, commerce and service-sector outlets and older subsidiaries. Not only are the former types of subsidiaries more inclined to afford their employees collective and effective individual voice mechanisms, as evidenced by the rare occurrence of a 'Bleak House' approach (33 per cent of brownfield sites and 15 per cent of greenfield sites) among those workplaces; they have also made most progress in combining both collective ER practices and direct HRM involvement (30 per cent of brownfield sites and 45 per cent of greenfield sites).

The findings with regard to greenfield sites and younger subsidiaries are particularly informative. Greenfield sites are often considered as especially suitable for an analysis of the country-of-origin effect (see for example Guest and Hoque, 1996). In contrast to brownfield sites, where there may have been a long-established ER pattern prior to the acquisition, greenfield subsidiaries provide the parent company with a clean sheet. The greater emphasis on a collective ER approach in German greenfield sites compared to brownfield subsidiaries indicates that German MNCs tend to draw actively on the home-country model in the design of ER when setting up subsidiaries in an Anglo-Saxon context, rather than using such subsidiaries as a test bed for ER without trade unions, collective bargaining and collective interest representation (see Table 5.5). On the other hand, comprehensive direct involvement packages are more common in greenfield operations compared to brownfield sites (51 per cent and 45 per cent respectively). However, this does not imply a strategy of avoiding collective ER, since German greenfield sites are also more likely to combine collective and individualistic ER compared to brownfield sites. This finding seems to add further evidence to the previously outlined impression of a strong ownership effect in terms of the evolving German approach to labour relations.

This is also confirmed when taking into account the age of the subsidiaries. Thus, only 9 per cent of German subsidiaries that are less than 10 years old have a Bleak House approach, whereas 51 per cent have both collective and direct employee involvement systems (see Table 5.5). Interestingly, the country-of-origin effect seems to have strengthened over time; however, in the absence of longitudinal data such interpretation is somewhat speculative. Since the start of the 1990s, there has been an accelerated internationalization of German companies. In combination with the frequently-cited dissatisfaction of German employers with the IR system since the late 1980s, one might have expected that German subsidiaries in a permissive

Table 5.5 Employee relations approaches in German subsidiaries (per cent)[1]

	Collective approach[2]	Comprehensive direct employee involvement[3]	Collective approach and comprehensive direct employee involvement[4]	Bleak House approach[5]
All subsidiaries	55	55	30	20
Control[6]				
Presence of expatriate managers	70	55	50	11
No expatriate managers	41	41	23	40
Entry mode:				
greenfield sites	67	51	45	15
brownfield sites	45	45	30	33
Age				
≤ 10 years owned	63	63	51	9
≥ 11 years owned	50	39	26	44
Type of activity				
Manufacturing Plants, sales, distribution,	77	65	59	12
Services outlets	46	39	13	35
Size				
≤ 99 employees	38	38	14	38
≥ 100 employees	80	63	53	10

Notes: [1] Subsidiaries with at least 25 employees; [2] with at least one collective arrangement; [3] with at least half of the practices listed in Table 5.3; [4] with at least one collective arrangement and with at least half of the practices listed in Table 5.3; [5] without any collective arrangement and with less than half of the practices listed in Table 5.3;

[6] expatriate presence (%):

greenfield sites:	70	brownfield sites:	38
≤ 10 years owned:	50	≥ 11 years owned:	36
Manufacturing plants:	65	Sales, distribution, services:	30
≥ 100 employees:	67	≤ 99 employees:	24

setting would have endeavoured to avoid/abandon a collective approach to ER in their UK operations and to seek an Anglo-Saxon-style individualistic HRM approach. This would also be in line with the predictions of the convergence thesis. However, the findings in Table 5.5 point to the opposite, with younger subsidiaries being more likely to operate a collective approach than mature ones (63 per cent and 50 per cent respectively). It would appear that German MNCs have responded to the increased international competition of the 1990s by drawing on their home country collective approach in those subsidiaries located in an Anglo-Saxon setting.

At the same time, younger subsidiaries show a far greater propensity than older subsidiaries to develop comprehensive HRM direct-involvement packages (63 per cent and 39 per cent respectively), and to combine these with collective ER systems (51 per cent and 26 per cent respectively). Since younger subsidiaries may be more likely to be a source of ER innovations, emerging ER approaches in German subsidiaries tend to become more multifaceted and more encompassing with the simultaneous strengthening of both the collective and the HRM dimension in a complementary fashion.

Moreover, the strength of the ownership effect seems to be closely associated with the degree of parental control. In line with similar results of other studies (Harzing, 1999; Ferner *et al.*, 2001), the overwhelming majority of parent companies refrain from direct intervention in ER issues. Eighty-five per cent of subsidiaries reported a high degree of autonomy on such issues. Those subsidiaries where parent companies exert indirect control via expatriates are far more likely to operate with a collective ER approach (70 per cent) than subsidiaries where such a control mechanism is absent (41 per cent). Thus, where German companies exert a degree of parental control, they seem to perceive it as beneficial to compete in the UK context by drawing on the German model of ER. These subsidiaries have also made more progress in the development of comprehensive direct involvement packages (55 per cent and 41 per cent respectively) and exhibit a greater propensity to combine collective and individualistic ER systems (50 per cent and 23 per cent respectively). Furthermore, parental control, subsidiary characteristics and an ER approach are interlinked. As discussed before, a collective approach, comprehensive direct-involvement packages and the simultaneous occurrence of these two approaches are more widespread in greenfield sites, larger subsidiaries, manufacturing plants and younger affiliates compared to brownfield sites, smaller subsidiaries, commerce and service-sector outlets and mature subsidiaries. At the same time, in these subsidiaries expatriate presence is also more prevalent (see Table 5.5). Indeed, younger larger-sized manufacturing plants with expatriate managers constitute 13 per cent of all survey respondents, but account for 25 per cent of subsidiaries with collective approaches, 20 per cent of subsidiaries with comprehensive HRM direct involvement and 35 per cent of subsidiaries which operate with both approaches simultaneously. Not only are these the typical German subsidiaries with strong Germanic traits in ER, they may also be viewed as prototypes for emerging ER approaches in German MNCs.

CONCLUSIONS

Contrary to the general tenor of previous studies, this study points to country-of-origin effects in ER of German MNCs' international operations in an Anglo-Saxon setting. A pronounced ownership effect was revealed in relation to the general ER approach and the ER style. Furthermore, there are indications that ER approaches increasingly reflect the emerging new German ER approach, rather than an adoption of an individualistic Anglo-Saxon model. The weighted cross-sectional comparison showed that a collective approach to ER is more widespread among German subsidiaries than British-owned workplaces, and vice versa with regard to individualistic approaches. The nationally embedded culture of cooperation between labour and capital in Germany is reflected by a greater emphasis on a cooperative ER style among German subsidiaries compared to British-owned establishments.

Despite the lower incidence of direct employee involvement practices in German owned establishments, a substantial proportion of German subsidiaries have developed comprehensive HRM-style direct-involvement packages. However, this is generally not connected with the Anglo-Saxon practice of avoiding/replacing collective arrangements. The overwhelming majority of such subsidiaries tend to operate simultaneously with both HRM-style involvement and collective approaches in the UK in a complementary rather than substitutional fashion. This may reflect the developments in the German ER model, where the reform process has not only increased the scope for a more flexible collective ER approach but has also widened the space for the introduction of a pluralist version of HRM to complement collective labour relations.

The findings from the cross-sectional comparison were confirmed across all size categories. However, considerable variations occurred in the comparison of German manufacturing plants and German service-sector operations compared to British counterparts. German service-sector firms seem more likely to adopt the approaches of their British-owned counterparts, whereas German-owned manufacturing plants exhibit a strong country-of-origin effect with regard to collective ER. At the same time, they were more likely to take on board HRM-style involvement practices compared to British-owned plants. With the German manufacturing sector being the core constituent of the German model, the greater occurrence of both collective and direct-involvement practices in their foreign production sites may perhaps be indicative of the evolving new German approach to labour relations. Indeed, the more detailed intra-German analysis showed that the nationality-of-ownership effect and the reflection of the evolving new German approach is particularly pronounced among greenfield sites, larger establishments, younger subsidiaries and manufacturing plants, and is positively associated with parent-company control mechanisms. Furthermore, there are indications that these effects have strengthened over time, signalling that ER in German subsidiaries are becoming more complex and multifaceted with the increasing emphasis on both collective and HRM-style ER. It is possible that the subsidiaries of German MNCs in the UK can act as a focal point of learning and reference for their parent companies for a more comprehensive and complementary infusion of HRM elements into their collective labour-relations approach in German locations. Such reinforcement of the HRM dimension in the flexible collective approach in Germany should not be viewed as an encroachment of the German model, but rather as an enrichment.

However, there is need for further research. A fuller picture about labour relations in German multinationals and the issues raised in this chapter requires a larger survey, the inclusion of longitudinal data and matched responses from parent companies, as well as qualitative research in the form of in-depth interviews with matched pairs of parent companies and subsidiaries to further explore the complexities, linkages and processes involved. Furthermore, similar studies need to be carried out involving other main German FDI host countries to obtain a more comprehensive picture.

REFERENCES

Beaumont, P., Cressey, P. and Jakobsen, P. (1990) 'Key Industrial Relations: West German Subsidiaries in Britain', *Employee Relations*, 12 (6), 3–7.
Bispinck, R. (1995), (ed.) *Tarifpolitik der Zukunft – Was wird aus dem Flächentarifvertrag?* (Hamburg: VSA Verlag).
Bundesministerium für Wirtschaft und Technologie (2000) *Wirtschaft in Zahlen* (Berlin).
Child, J., Faulkner, D. and Pitkethly, R. (1997) 'Foreign Direct Investment in the UK 1985–1994: The Impact on Domestic Management Practices', *Research Papers in Management Studies* (Cambridge: Judge Institute, University of Cambridge).
Child, J., Faulkner, D. and Pitkethly, R. (2000) 'Foreign Direct Investment in the UK: 1985–1994: The Impact on Domestic Management Practice', *Journal of Management Studies*, 37 (1), 141–66.
Clark, T. (1996) *European Human Resource Management* (Oxford: Blackwell).
Coller, X. and Marginson, P. (1998) 'Transnational Management Influence over Changing Employment Practices: A Case Study from the Food Industry', *Industrial Relations Journal*, 22 (1), 4–19.
Cully, M., Woodland, S. Reilly, A. and Dix, G. (1999), (eds) *Britain at Work – As Depicted by the 1998 Workplace Employee Relations Survey* (London: Routledge).
Deutsche Bundesbank (2001) *Kapitalverpflechtung mit dem Ausland*, 10 (Frankfurt).
Edwards, P., Hall, M., Hyman, R., Marginson, P. Sission, K., Waddington, J. and Winchester, P. (1998) 'Great Britain: From Partial Collectivism to Neo-Liberalism to Where?', in Ferner, A. and Hyman, R. (eds) *Changing Industrial Relations in Europe* (London: Blackwell).
Edwards, T. (1998) 'Multinationals and the Process of Reverse Diffusion'. *International Journal of Human Resource Management*, 9 (4), 696–709.
Edwards, T., Rees, C. and Coller, X. (2000) 'Structure, Politics and Diffusion of Employment Practices in Multinationals', *European Journal of Industrial Relations*, 5 (3), 286–306.
Ferner, A. (1997) 'Country of Origin Effects and HRM in Multinational Companies', *Human Resource Management Journal*, 7 (1), 19–37.
Ferner, A., Quintanilla, J. and Varul, M. (2001) 'Country-of-Origin Effects, Host Country Effects and the Management of HR in Multinationals: German Companies in Britain and Spain', *Journal of World Business*, 36 (2), 107–27.

Frick, B. and Sadowski, D. (1995) 'Works Councils, Unions and Firm Performance', in Buttler, F., Franz, W., Schettkat, R. and Soskice, D. (eds) *Institutional Frameworks and Labour Market Performance* (London: Routledge).

Guest, D. and Hoque, K. (1996) 'National Ownership and HR Practices in UK Greenfield Sites', *Human Resource Management Journal*, 6 (4), 50–74.

Harzing, A.W. (1999) *Managing the Multinationals: an international study of control mechanisms* (Cheltenham: Edward Elgar).

Hu, Y. (1992) 'Global or Stateless Corporations: National Firms with International Operations', *California Management Review*, Winter, 107–26.

Innes, E. and Morris, J. (1995) 'Multinational Corporations and Employee Relations: Continuity and Change in a Mature Industrial Region', *Employee Relations*, 17 (6), 25–42.

Institut der deutschen Wirtschaft (2000) *Informationsdienst*, 19, 4–5.

Institut der deutschen Wirtschaft (2001) *Informationsdienst*, 22, 3–4.

Invest in Britain Bureau (1999) *Annual Report* (London: DTI).

Lane, C. (1995) *Industry and Society in Europe. Stability and Change in Britain, Germany and France* (Cheltenham: Edward Elgar).

Millward, N., Steven, M., Smart, M. and Hawes, G. (1992) *Workplace Industrial Relations in Transition* (Dartmouth: Aldershot).

Millward, N., Forth, J. and Byron, A. (1999) 'Changes in Employment Relations, 1980–1998', in Cully, M., Woodland, S., Reilly, A. and Dix, G. (eds) *Britain at Work – As Depicted by the 1998 Workplace Employee Relations Survey* (London: Routledge).

Muller, M. (1999) 'Enthusiastic Embrace or Critical Reception? The German HRM Debate', *Journal of Management Studies*, 36 (4), 465–82.

Reich, R. (1991), *The Work of Nations: Preparing ourselves for the 21st century* (New York: Alfred Knopf).

Rosenzweig, P. and Noria, N. (1994) 'Influences on Human Resource Management Practices in Multinational Corporations', *Journal of International Business Studies*, 25 (2), 229–51.

Royal Commission on Trade Unions and Employers' Associations Report (Donovan) (1968) Cmnd. 362 (London: HMSO).

Schulten, T. and Zagelmeyer, H. (1998) on-line: *http://www.eironline.de*

Sisson, K. (1993) 'In Search of HRM', *British Journal of Industrial Relations*, 31 (2), 210–32.

Sisson, K. and Marginson, P. (1995) 'Management: Systems, Structures and Strategies', in Edwards, P., (ed.) *Industrial Relations* (Oxford: Blackwell).

Soskice, D. (1994) 'Labour Markets in the EC in the 1990s, in European Commission, *Social Europe–Supplement I* (Brussels).

Sperling, H. (1997) *Restrukturierung von Unternehmens – und Arbeitsorganisation – eine Zwischenbilanz. Trend Report Partizipation und Organisation II* (Marburg: Schüren).

Streeck, W. (1997) 'German Capitalism: Does it Exist? Can it Survive', *New Political Economy*, 2 (2), 237–57.

The Economist (1999) 'The Sick Man of the Euro', 5–11 June.

Traxler, F. (1996) 'Collective Bargaining and Industrial Change: A Case of Disorganisation? A Comparative Analysis of Eighteen OECD Countries', *European Sociological Review*, 12 (3), 271–87.

Tüselmann, H. (2001) 'The New German Model of Employee Relations: Flexible Collectivism or Anglo-Saxonisation?, *International Journal of Manpower*.

Tüselmann, H., McDonald, F. and Heise, A. (2000) *The Impact of German Direct Foreign Investment in the United Kingdom on Employment and Employee Relations: The Case of North-West England* (Düsseldorf: Hans Böckler Foundation).

Tüselmann, H. and Heise A. (2000) 'The German Model of Industrial Relations at the Crossroads: Past, Present and Future', *Industrial Relations Journal*, 31 (3), 162–76.

UNCTAD (1994) *World Investment Report 1994: Transnational Corporations, Employment and the Workplace* (Geneva: United Nations).

WERS 1998, *Workplace Employee Relations Survey*, Data File: MQ98 SAV (Essex: Data Archive of the University of Essex, 1999).

Whitley, R. and Kristensen, P. (eds) (1996) *The Changing European Firm: Limits to Convergence* (London: Routledge).

Wirtschaftswoche (1995) 19 October, 27–30.

Wood, S. and Albanese, M. (1996) 'Can We Speak of High Commitment Management at the Shop Floor?', *Journal of Management Studies*, 32 (4), 215–47.

Young, S., Hood, N. and Hamill, J. (1985) 'Decision-making in Foreign-owned Multinational Subsidiaries in the United Kingdom', ILO working paper 35 (Geneva: ILO).

Part Two

Internationalization and Firm Strategy

6 From Global Concentration to Competitive Strategy

Chris Carr

INTRODUCTION

Many writers argue for, imply or sometimes merely assume, a process of almost relentless global concentration driven by scale economies and 'shrinking' geography (Marx, 1919; Hout *et al.*, 1982; Ohmae, 1985, 1990, 2001; Bryan *et al.*, 1999). It is popular (if technically dubious, Kay, 2001a) to cite the statistic that of the world's 100 largest 'economies', 51 are now corporations and only 49 nation states (Hertz, 2001). However, the issue has long been highly controversial and has become intertwined with the complex debate surrounding globalization (Hirst and Thompson, 1996; Held and McGrew, 2000).

Counter-arguments remind us that size alone is insufficient for competitive advantage. Despite $2.4 trillion of mergers in 1998, compared with only $0.57 trillion in 1994, the share of American output attributable to large companies remained at 33 per cent between 1970 and 1990; while well-known firms like USX declined, new competitors and entrepreneurs emerged (Micklethwaite and Wooldridge, 2000, p. 101).

There are a number of other reasons why the process of globalization is not as prevalent as might be supposed. Around 70 per cent of mergers have proved unsuccessful, with integration problems being exacerbated by cross-national cultural insensitivity. For example, Walmart has lost up to $300 million a year 'after misjudging both corporate culture and the market [in Germany]' (*Financial Times*, 2000, p. 25), and some global product launches such as Ford's original world car have failed, and it is still the case that truly integrated multinational corporations (MNCs) remain relatively rare (Hollingsworth and Boyer, 1997). Also, in 1992/3 two-thirds of UK and US MNCs' manufacturing sales derived from their home countries – or three-quarters in the case of German and Japanese MNCs – and these figures having changed little from 1987 (Hirst and Thompson, 1996, p. 96). Truly global brands such as Coke, McDonalds, Mercedes, BMW and Sony are likewise still relatively rare: just seven have more than $3 billion sales, or 12 if we draw the line at $2 billion (*Financial Times*, 2001, p. 30).

So regional and national differences remain acute, creating niches for more local players (Coriale, 1997; Hirst and Zeitlin, 1997; Hollingsworth and Boyer, 1997), and European markets remain relatively heterogeneous and distinct from the USA and Japan. Geographically-based clusters sustain highly competitive smaller players particularly in ceramics, knitwear, footwear and fashion in Italy (Porter, 1998a,b). Many other clusters also sustain a mix of smaller as well as larger companies, notably in carpets in Kidderminster in Britain and in Dalton in the USA (Mair, 2000), toys (in South California) and furniture (in South Carolina). Porter (1990, 1998a,b) also cites vehicle components (particularly Germany's Mittelstand companies) and computers/electronics/software (in Silicon Valley and Silicon Glen). Some argue that innovation within the New Economy has left big, traditional players looking like dinosaurs, or that flexible manufacturing systems and IT likewise advantage nimbler companies better able to exploit subtle and fast-growing segmentation opportunities.

Most academics accept that the balance of forces favouring global rather than national strategies varies from one sector to another (Porter, 1980; Yip, 1989, 1992; Bartlett and Ghoshal, 1991), and recent arguments about overall trends have become extreme. On one hand, Bryan *et al.* (1999) project a radical extension of the 'globalized' sector of business over the next few years, and have correspondingly developed three highly aggressive global options in stark contrast to a fourth 'geographical incumbent' category, not dissimilar to nationally orientated niche positioning.

On the other hand, global sceptics challenge purported patterns of international concentration upon which many international strategies are predicated. Between 1988 and 1998, the top-five high-tech companies' shares of worldwide markets declined by 15–30 per cent in each of three sectors – computer hardware, computer software and long-distance telephony (Ghemawat and Ghadir, 2000, p. 68). Their more detailed analysis of oil, car and aluminium industries argued that (Herfindahl-type) concentration indices have actually fallen in sectors more usually associated with globalization. GM, the global leader in cars, has actually lost share. 'Empirical research indicates that global – or globalising – industries have actually been marked by steady decreases in concentration in the post-World War II period' (Ghemawat and Ghadir, 2000, p. 66). Freed of such biases, executives are urged that 'there are better, more profitable strategies for dealing with globalization than relentless expansions'.

Kay (2000, 2001b) makes the same point, and cites the car industry. Between 1969 and 1996 he argues that shares of the top-three players fell from 51 per cent to 36 per cent, the top nine from 84 per cent to 66 per cent, and there was a slight increase in the number of firms commanding less than 1 per cent market shares. Kay is equally sceptical about megamergers, such as BP Amoco. His more general evidence spans the century, questions the performance of large companies, and again challenges uncritical faith in economies of scale or scope. Variants upon these arguments suggest more positive New Economy, knowledge-based strategies (Nonaka and Takeuchi, 1995, Hamel, 2000, p. 309) or strategic alliances, but the main policy recommendations (just as from Baden and Stopford, 1991) would seem to entail international retrenchment or retreating to niche positions (Ghemawat and Ghadir, 2000).

But which of these two contentious positions is the more correct and how might this vary by type of sector? If well-founded, the latter arguments provide the rationale for a reversion to a more negative international orientation, all the more seductive given an outlook of pessimism particularly in the wake of September 11. This chapter questions these arguments. Is it really so clear that global concentration is not taking place in these specific sectors identified by Ghemawat and Ghadir, and what about other sectors? Arguably the starting point of any robust competitive strategy is indeed a clear understanding of global concentration. The aim of this chapter is, therefore, to re-examine the arguments about global concentration trends.

GLOBAL CONCENTRATION TRENDS

Between 1910 and 1970, the share of the largest 100 firms in manufacturing net output in the USA and particularly in the UK had increased remarkably. In the UK much of this concentration occurred between 1919 and 1930, when the overall CR100 (the share of the largest 100 firms) increased from 56 per cent to 77 per cent, but CR10 measures (the share of the largest 10 firms) continued to increase between 1957 and 1969 for sectors such as food (62 per cent to 80 per cent), drink (41 per cent to 87 per cent), chemicals (81 per cent to 86 per cent) and metals (59 per cent to 74 per cent) (Hannah and Kay, 1977). Mergers and acquisitions account for the vast proportion (especially in the UK) of such increases in concentration, in spite of long-running arguments as to their poor performance (Porter, 1987). Hannah (1976) traces such trends in the UK back to 1880, and industrial economists have since updated our knowledge of such concentration trends in many sectors in both Europe and the USA (Davies and Lyons, 1996; Waldman and Jensen, 1998).

Just as Hannah and Kay (1977) found that between 1953 and 1978 the share of the largest firms in net UK manufacturing output rose from 26 per cent to 41 per cent, Hayward (1995, p. 309) found a similar trend in Europe as a whole. 'The sales of the 50 largest European firms as a percentage of industrial output increased from 15 per cent in 1965 to 25 per cent in 1976'. Moreover, in 1990 'the largest firms in Europe are of a comparable size with those in the US and both are typically larger than those of Japan' (Hayward, 1995, pp. 308–9). Jacobson and Andreosso-O'Callaghan (1996, p. 89) likewise found rising CR100 ratios across Europe between 1962 and 1990 (though with some fall-off after a peak in 1982). However, within Europe at the sector level it is less clear whether or not concentration levels have been increasing or decreasing in recent years. CR4 (the share of the largest 4 firms) concentration levels for Europe declined during the 1970s and 1980s in four sectors (food, drink and tobacco; electrical engineering, office machinery and data-processing; wood furniture and paper; textiles, clothing, leather and footwear), but rose or remained stable in chemicals; and in mechanical and instrument engineering, metals, motor vehicles and other transport (Jacobson and Andreosso-O'Callaghan, p. 90).

Ghemawat and Ghadir's (2000) evidence of global fragmentation would thus seem to fly in the face of historical trends established at national and indeed continental levels, but as the debate moves to the issue of global concentration the choice of concentration measure also merits attention. Their chosen Herfindahl index (HI) represents the sum of the squares of market shares of all players, expressed as a decimal figure between 0 and 1. This is potentially more comprehensive and systematic than CRN measures, though by limiting their HI measures to the top-10 players they risk undermining this more conventional virtue. The measure is problematic in terms of data collected internationally, and interpretation, particularly if used in the absence of other indicators such as CRN measures or simply the trend in terms of number of major participants. There is little historical HI data (particularly internationally) against which to assess trends, and less empirical work clearly establishing linkages with profitability or performance. Such numbers are invariably small and critical numbers are hard to judge. Even small numbers and small changes can represent considerable concentration effects when judged internationally. Thus, whilst the authors suggest a supposedly extreme benchmark of 0.1 of a sector so fragmented that the top-10 companies have equal market shares, this could equally be interpreted as a quite exceptionally concentrated industry in global terms. A final measure sometimes used by companies and consultants such as BCG is relative market share, focusing on the multiple of the leading company's share as compared with that of subsequent players in the sector. This is supposed to give a better indication of market power and likely relative commercial performance (Buzzell and Gale, 1987), but is also useful where often there is only reliable data on the top few companies, particularly internationally.

Deep, longitudinal studies (with international access to more reliable company data) of global concentration and corporate behaviour are still scarce. One such deep study (Schwittay, 1999) comes down clearly in favour of the CR4 measure for reasons already cited, and indeed defines 'globalization' as the point at which this global CR4 measure approaches 40 per cent for any particular sector. The study examined the worldwide spirits industry historically, internationally and throughout this process of 'globalization', as global moves and counter moves became increasingly evident. It is also clear from such studies that global concentration measures need to be interpreted in the light of the number of major worldwide players, and changes taking place such as merger and acquisition trends. Other major studies of global competition do not always provide HI or even CR4 measures, but the perspectives that they do provide rarely suggest global fragmentation over any longer-term time period. In automobiles and in automobile parts, players from countries such as Germany and Japan took time to reestablish themselves after the Second World War, but since then they point to steady reductions in the number of major worldwide players (Altshuler *et al.*, 1984; Womack *et al.*, 1990; Carr, 1993).

GLOBAL CONCENTRATION TRENDS IN ALUMINIUM, AUTOMOBILES AND OIL

Ghemawat and Ghadir (2000) apply their global Herfindahl indices in three seemingly global sectors (oil, automobiles and aluminium extraction) to counter traditional views of global concentration. These HIs are based on just the top-10 companies and on volume (rather than values), both slightly understating conventional figures with some unelaborated amendments in connection with joint ventures. Table 6.1 summarizes their evidence on falling HIs, but then provides more recent data (likewise based on volumes and using just 10 companies), and also CR4 and relative market share measures. Some discrepancy can arise as a result of unelaborated amendments, but the calculations seem straightforward.

Updated Herfindahl index trends provide far less convincing evidence for any thesis of global fragmentation. With relatively high transport/storage costs, aluminium would seem to be less globally concentrated than other sectors, but here Ghemawat and Ghadir's data only goes back to 1975. My calculated HI for 2000 is on a par with their 1975 figure, and my calculated 2001 figure is slightly higher as a result of Alcoa's acquisition of Reynolds Metals and Corland Technologies in 2000 and Alcan's merger with Alusuisse in 2001. The big mergers and acquisitions in this sector took place before 1975 and recent acquisitions are smaller, but even in the last year the global CR4 index has increased from 31 per cent to 36 per cent. This scarcely adds up to a picture of a fragmenting industry; on the contrary it is just approaching Schwittay's (1999) definition of 'globalization' and the point at which international oligopolistic behaviour is likely to increase.

In automobiles, Ghemawat and Ghadir's thesis receives some support from Kay (2000, 2001b) who argues that CR4 and CR8 indices have been falling. He notes quite correctly some decline in market shares for both General Motors the world number 1, and Ford the world number two. However, 1950 figures risk distortion since German and Japanese production was almost bound to recover after the Second World War and markets did not fully open up internationally for quite some years. The global HI for 1997 was broadly on par with 1975 at 0.08, with the figure for 2000 up to 0.13, again scarcely a picture of global fragmentation. On a global basis, HI indices this high are associated with extremely high levels of concentration. The global CR4 index calculated increased from 50 per cent to 53 per cent between 1997 and 2000. With over half of world markets taken by just four players it is inconceivable to argue this sector has not been subject to global concentration: it comfortably passes Schwittay's test.

Even more compelling is evidence for the reduction in the number of significant major players worldwide and the number of global megamergers. IMD's (1999, p. 15) trend graph shows that the number of major automobile manufacturers has fallen from 42 in 1961 to 17 in 1998. Several companies, including Jaguar, Volvo and Saab, have fallen to Ford and GM in recent years. Even since 1998 we have seen DaimlerChrysler (then the largest merger by value of

Table 6.1 Global concentration in oil, automobiles and aluminium

Industry	Year	Herfindahl index	Share of top 4 (CR4)	Sales of no.1 co./no.4	Sales no.1 co./no.10	Other evidence on concentration
Oil production	1950	0.190				Concentration in terms of the 'Seven Sisters' has been long acknowledged, cross-border mergers such as Royal Dutch Shell dating back to the turn of the century. Recent mega-mergers include BP Amoco, Exxon Mobil and, post-Ghemawat and Ghadir (2000), ChevronTexaco and Conoco/Phillips. *Sources: Financial Times*, 9 October 2001, 27 and 20 November 2001, p. 32
	1975	0.045				
	1997	0.035				
New data	2001	0.105	67%	1.5	10.8	
Oil refining	1950	0.105				
	1975	0.010				
	1997	0.015				
New data	2001	0.120	60%	1.4		
Automobile	1950	0.180				IMD (1999, p. 15) trends show steady fall in number of major manufacturers from 42 in 1961 to 17 in 1998. Consolidations since include DaimlerChrysler/Mitsubishi, Renault/Nissan, Ford/LandRover, VW/Rolls-Royce Motors, GM/Daewoo, though some fall short of full equity control. *Source:* Global Market Info Database, INSEAD (2001)
	1975	0.080				
	1997	0.070				
New data	1997	0.080	50%	2.0	4.6	
	2000	0.130	53%	1.8	5.5	
Aluminium	1950	–				Most concentration occurred prior to 1975, though for some reason no data is provided for 1950. During 2000 and 2001, Alcoa acquired Reynolds and Alcan combined with Alusuisse. *Source: Financial Times*, 31 October 2001 Aluminium Supplement II/AME Mineral Economics
	1975	0.041				
	1997	0.027				
New data	2000	0.041	31%	4.0	6.7	
	2001	0.045	36%	3.7	6.9	

all time), in turn extending to virtual acquisition of Mitsubishi Motors. Renault's 30 per cent equity stake in Nissan likewise represents virtually a merger in terms of corporate control. Ford has taken over Land Rover, and VW has acquired Rolls-Royce Motors. GM's acquisition talks with Daewoo appear virtually finalized, and they are also said to be in serious talks with Fiat. Rover is the only major player to have decoupled, but scarcely signifies fragmentation. Again, any predictive value in this thesis appears highly questionable.

The positions in oil production and in refining seem similar. Again, 1950 HI figures seem unusually high. Trends in any single measure over a limited period of time need to be seen against a backdrop of global concentration taking place over more than a century in all three sectors, many of the large mergers resulting in global concentration having taken place well before 1950. My 2001 global HI in oil production is considerably higher than either 1997 or 1975. In oil refining the recent figure is higher still in relation to 1997 or 1975 and higher than 1950. Some discrepancy may arise here, but again the clear trend since 1997 has been global concentration.

Recent mergers/acquisitions include megamergers such as BP Amoco and Exxon Mobil, and in just the last two months Chevron/Texaco and Conoco/Phillips. In respect to Conoco/Phillips, the *Financial Times* (2001, p. 1) reported this:

> $35 billion merger of equals would be the biggest corporate deal this year and extend the trend of consolidation in the oil and gas industry. The deepening consolidation of the industry is being driven by depleting natural gas reserves in the US and a recognition that one must have a certain size to obtain new resources.

According to the article, as the global majors have increasingly used their scale to extend their own reach, Conoco was unique in stressing nimbleness as opposed to scale. Yet even Conoco, it was argued, led the new wave of US acquisitions in Canada, and 'the Phillips merger will now make it the third largest integrated group in the US, the 6th largest energy company and 5th largest global refinery'.

Not only is any predictive value of any thesis of global fragmentation dubious in the extreme, but also with global CR4s substantially over 50 per cent, the oil production and refinery sectors can hardly be described as other than globally concentrated.

From a business economics or commercial perspective, most interesting of all are shares of profits. Are these increasingly appropriated by a small number of players worldwide, or not? Comprehensive profit figures including those for smaller players are harder to find and to analyse, but Table 6.2 analyses all Fortune Global 500 companies for each of these three sectors. In 2000, the top-4 oil companies accounted for just over half of profits from the 29 oil companies making it into the Fortune 500 rankings. This compares with 38 per cent for the top 4 in 1990, though based on 54 listed. In vehicles and vehicle parts the top 4 in

Table 6.2   Global 500 shares of top-4 companies by sector; sales and profits

Sector	Sector rank by revenue in 2000	Year	No.of companies	Sales of no.1/last company X	Top-4 percent of all sales	Top-4 percent of all profits
Oil refining	2	2000	29	19	48	53
		1990	54	40	35	38
Vehicles and parts	3	2000	27	18	50	60
		1990	40	47	43	25
Metals	22	2000	11	2.4	48	20
		1990	41	23	33	28

Source: *Fortune*, 23 July 2001 and 29 July 1991.

2000 took 60 per cent of all profits of 27 companies listed, compared with 25 per cent based on 40 companies listed in 1990. The metals sector here is drawn somewhat more widely than just aluminium, but remains a relatively small sector in terms of turnover contribution. The top 4 accounted for 20 per cent of profits of just 11 participants in 2000, compared with 28 per cent based on 41 companies in 1990. This sector shows less concentration in terms of profit impact, and this indeed has decreased proportionately. Overall, the degree of global concentration in terms of the share of world profits has now become extremely high in oil and automobile sectors, but this would still be less true in the case of metals extraction.

GLOBAL CONCENTRATION TRENDS IN OTHER SECTORS

Ghemawat and Ghadir (2000) cite a database of all sectors, implying perhaps that falling HIs cited may be a more widespread phenomenon, but they present no evidence from these other sectors. Global market-share data is also notoriously difficult to obtain reliably. Certainly some sectors would seem to be highly globally concentrated and there has been much discussion and documentation on shakeouts (for example Day, 1997). By 1998, for example, the top 10 companies commanded 86 per cent of the $262 billion telecoms market, and the top 10 in pesticides held 85 per cent of a $31 billion market (UNDP 2000, p. 343). Table 6.3 therefore presents data collected from a range of sectors where data is relatively accessible. Sectors are arranged broadly in order of globalization as expressed by the global CR4 concentration ratio.

Table 6.3 suggests the global HI index is a fairly insensitive measure. Steel exhibits the lowest figure of 0.008, in line with the lowest global CR4 index of 12 per cent. At the other extreme is aero engines, with global HIs having fallen slightly from 0.308 to 0.291 between 1984 and 2000. With CR4 ratios remaining at 96 per cent, the industry is at the extreme in terms of global concentration,

Table 6.3 Global concentration in other sectors

Industry	Year	Herfindahl index	Share of top 4 (CR4)	Sales of no.1 co./ no.4	Sales of no.1 co./ no.10	Other evidence on concentration
Aero engines	1984	0.308	96%	4.4		Massive global concentration belies fierce competition as major players have changed places.
	2000	0.291	96%	2.5		*Source: Financial Times*, 25 August 2001, p. 12
Mobile phones	2001 Qtr 2	0.153	65%	4.5		*Source: Financial Times*, 21 November 2001.Sup.2/Commerzbank Securities. Handsets
Cruise lines	2001 Qtr 3	0.141	59%	2.8		*Financial Times*, 21 November 2001, p. 25
	2002	0.185	69%			Subject to takeover approval
Spirits	1982	0.054	37%			Schwittay (1999)
	1987		44%			
	1995	0.086	52%			Latest figure is an estimate that could rise in 2002 to just under 65% depending on regulatory intervention affecting outcome of Seagram's acquisition and break-up
	2000		60%			
Tyres	1995	0.099	58%	2.6		*Source: Financial Times*, 14 March 1997, p. 4/EIU

Table 6.3 Continued

Industry	Year	Herfindahl index	Share of top 4 (CR4)	Sales of no.1 co./ no.4	Sales of no.1 co./ no.10	Other evidence on concentration
Brewing	1997	0.078	43%	2.9	4.3	Lynch (2000, p. 347). N.B. Global market estimate based on sales for top 19 and ths understated. True HI and CR4 figures would therefore be higher than these crude estimates
Personal computers	1981	0.025	29%	2.7		*Source:* Successive Harvard case studies
	1991	0.010	12%	3.6		
	2001	0.046	40%	2.0		*Source: Sunday Times*, 9 September 2001. Sec3.9
Pharmaceuticals	1992		15%			*Source:* Wilkinson (2001)/Scripts Reports
	2000					
Anti-depressants	2000	0.107	60%	2.6		Source: Financial Times, 18 September 2001, p. 29 ABN Amro; Thomson Financial Datastream
Steel	1999	0.008	12%	1.2		Johnson and Scholes (2002), p. 597. N.B. global market estimate based on sales for top 12 and thus understated. True HI and CR4 figures would therefore be higher than these crude estimates

regardless of any slight fall in the HI. Yet even steel is now exhibiting major moves towards global concentration in terms of cross-border mergers and acquisitions, which have begun to take place for the first time. Following the Anglo-Dutch merger creating Corus, we are now beginning to see more complex multi-country mergers and the picture is one of rationalization and consolidation, not fragmentation. Of all these sectors, only the personal computer industry appears to have experienced fragmentation – in the period prior to about 1991 after IBM's new standards allowed numerous new entrants. Both HI and CR4 measures dropped for a time as low as steel, but by 2001 the industry is back on track for clear global concentration, the global CR4 hitting 40 per cent. Michael Dell, Dell's chief executive, is openly targeting a 40 per cent global market share, an objective not out of line with the company's performance to date and its highly aggressive marketing campaign. What is clear is that some sectors are much more advanced than others, depending upon economic characteristics, but the overall trend appears decisively towards global concentration.

THE LONG-TERM HISTORICAL PERSPECTIVE

Kay (2000) introduces a further interesting argument against size for the sake of size, by comparing the world's largest companies (in terms of market capitalization) in 1912 with more recent data. One-third of the top 12 in 1912 have, he argues, disappeared. Table 6.4 displays his earlier data, but incorporates even more recent data now available. Table 6.5 shows rankings in terms of long-term capitalization growth and data based on 1917 to 1987, and Table 6.6 shows global rankings for sales and profits for 1990 and 2000.

Table 6.4 Global market capitalization rankings, 1912–2001

Rank	1912 companies	Sector	2001 companies	Sector
1	USX	Steel	General Electric	Conglomerate
2	Exxon	Oil	Microsoft	Software
3	J&J Coates	Textile	Exxon Mobil	Oil
4	Pullman	Rail cars	Pfizer	Drugs
5	Shell	Oil	Citigroup	Banks
6	Anaconda	Copper	Walmart	Retail
7	General Electric	Conglomerate	AOL Time Warner	Entertainment
8	Singer	Sewing m/c.s	Shell	Oil
9	American Brands	Cigarettes	Intel	Micro chips
10	n.a.	Cigarettes	NTTDoCoMo	Telecoms
11			IBM	Computers
12			BP Amoco	Oil

Source: Kay (2000) for 1912, *Financial Times*, 11 May 2001. Top FT 500 Survey for 2001.

Table 6.5   Growth in market capitalization, 1917–87, CAGR per cent p.a.

Rank	Company	Per cent p.a.	Rank	Company	Per cent p.a.
1	General Electric	7.8	8	Procter & Gamble	6.7
2	Eastman Kodak	7.7	9	Amoco	6.5
3	Du Pont	7.2	10	Westinghouse	6.0
4	Sears Roebuck	6.9	11	Chevron	5.9
5	Ford	6.9	12	Mobil	4.8
6	General Motors	6.9	13	Texaco	4.7
7	Exxon	6.9	14	Pacific Gas	4.2

Source: *Forbes*, July 1987.

Certainly simply being big in very old industries, subject to fairly basic technology, proves insufficient for success over the century: USX in steel, Anaconda in copper, J&J Coates in textiles, Pullman in rail cars and Singer in sewing machines have not sustained their formidable size positions from 1912. This is not altogether surprising, but beyond this the thesis that size (and rather the issue should be market share) does not matter is harder to sustain.

Exxon Oil, the world's second largest company in terms of market capitalization in 1912, is still third in 2001, whilst Royal Dutch Shell and BP Amoco likewise remain within the top 12. Focusing on just oil, Exxon, Amoco, Chevron, Mobil and Texaco all feature in the rankings of capital asset growth rates between 1917–87. Exxon ranked third of all global companies in terms of both sales and profits in 1990, and Exxon Mobil ranked first on both counts in 2000. Royal Dutch Shell ranked first on profits and second on sales (again of all global companies) in 1990, though slipping to fourth and sixth respectively in 2000. BP (/Amoco) ranks within the top-8 global companies on both counts for both 1990 and 2000.

Table 6.6   Global sales and profit rankings, 1990 and 2000

Rank	Sales 1990	Sales 2000	Profits 1990	Profits 2000
1	General Motors	Exxon Mobil	Shell	Exxon Mobil
2	Shell	Walmart	IBM	Citigroup
3	Exxon	General Motors	Exxon	General Electric
4	Ford	Ford	General Electric	Shell
5	IBM	DaimlerChrysler	Philip Morris	BP
6	Toyota	Shell	BP	Verizon Comms
7	IRI	BP	PDVSA	Ing Group
8	BP	General Electric	Toyota	Intel
9	Mobil	Matsushita	Du Pont	Microsoft
10	General Electric	Toyota	Chevron	Philips Electric
11	Daimler Benz	Mitsui	Matsushita	Siemens
12	Hitachi	Citigroup	Elf Acquitaine	Philip Morris

Source: *Fortune*, 23 July 2001 and 29 July 1991.

In automobiles, it is true that GM and Ford have slipped a little in terms of recent market share and profit performances. However, they have sustained their first and second positions in the vehicle sector ever since 1920, and both companies ranked within the top 4 of all global companies in terms of sales in both 1990 and 2000. In terms of long term-capital growth between 1917 and 1987, they ranked respectively sixth and fifth. GM was still the world's largest company in terms of sales in 1998 and 1999; Ford was still the world's most profitable company in 1998 (*Fortune*, 1999 and 2000). DaimlerChrysler ranks fifth of all world companies on sales in 2000.

Thus the argument that size doesn't count from a longer-term perspective is quite impossible to sustain in either the oil or automobile sectors. Aluminium as a sector ranks well down and no company figures in terms of these top global rankings, but even looking at the position overall it is extremely difficult to sustain the view that size (and market share would be the more appropriate term here) does not count.

DISCUSSION AND CONCLUSIONS

Ghemawat and Ghadir's refutation of patterns of global concentration in oil, automobiles and aluminium is based on undisclosed market-share data incorporating some undisclosed amendments, so some of the updated Herfindahl indices may not be an entirely comparable basis. In some highlighted instances updated HI indices may therefore be inflated as compared to their data trends and it would be wrong to place too much emphasis on this data alone. However, once (arguably more important) global CR4 concentration ratios are added together with some perspective in respect to company consolidations, this chapter arrives at a diametrically opposite conclusion. Oil production and refining and automobiles display unequivocal global concentration and larger companies are certainly not losing out, either commercially or in terms of their market positions. Some reduction in megamergers and some difficulties in terms of achieving satisfactory results in terms of shareholder value should be expected given the immediate global economic outlook; but the technical arguments countering the thesis of global concentration do not stand up to closer inspection.

Aluminium is substantially behind in these sectors in terms of any process of global concentration and the commercial benefits are less clear-cut, but the indications are that the process is still continuing albeit more slowly. The chapter review of other sectors is necessarily incomprehensive and somewhat unsystematic, because of the difficulty of accessing good information on global market shares. It does span a wide spectrum from some of the most globalized sectors such as aero-engines to some such as steel well down the scale. The overall picture is at least indicative and suggests global concentration, but with sectors again at different levels of advancement. The global CR4 concentration ratio provides arguably the best indication of those that are more advanced and where we might expect to see greater oligopolistic behaviour in terms of competitive interactions (and conceivably further cross-border mergers and acquisitions) worldwide.

In spite of these quite contradictory conclusions, Ghemawat and Ghadir (2000), Kay (2000, 2001b) again highlight (and with new data) one of the most fundamental questions in the history of economics. Given the collapse of Marxism and the triumph of capitalism, it is deeply ironic that Marx's notion of global concentration is indeed becoming more and more evident, whilst Adam Smith's idealization (Skinner, 1970) of large numbers of perfect competitors is becoming less and less realistic. His classic pin industry is today yet one more case study in global concentration. In a sense, moreover, competitive strategy only surfaces as some phenomenon as concentration begins to take effect. Were companies to live in a world characterized by perfect, price-taking commodity markets, there would be little scope for supernormal profits beyond the risk-amended cost of capital.

The question addressed is therefore one which goes to the heart of any competitive strategy as markets become increasingly international. If companies do not know whether their markets are concentrating or fragmenting, then in terms of any coherent competitive strategy they are at sea. At one extreme, should they focus to become globally dominant, at least perhaps in some niche market; or should they retrench internationally, perhaps settling for better profits in safer, closer markets? The conclusions reached here are far closer to those who advocate more aggressive international strategies.

Some indication has been given of how this varies by sector. The Herfindahl index based on global market shares has some virtues as a measure, but this chapter concurs with Schwittay (1999) that using the CR4 concentration measure is both the simplest and clearest in terms of ease of interpretation, and crucially the most predictive of likely future international competitive interaction. As the CR4 based on global market shares begins to approach 40 per cent (and many sectors are well on the way), then the need for a more globally-orientated strategy of some sort becomes increasingly crucial. McKinsey's aggressive picture of a rapid extension of those sectors subject to global competition seems a little extreme given such a downturn in the international environment, particularly in respect to cross-border mergers and acquisitions (Bryan *et al.*, 1999). Avoiding the hype, the findings reported here are somewhat closer to this latter future prognosis than to the opposite more sceptical camp that is in danger of encouraging more defensive, nationally-orientated strategies.

To acknowledge global concentration is not, however, tantamount to advocating aggressive strategies aimed at market domination for all players. Even focusing and niching (Simon, 1996) with the aim of market domination is highly demanding in sectors subject to concentration, and probably well-beyond the resources available to most companies (Carr, 1993). Bryan *et al.* (1999) highlighted three generic options in addition to their more nationally-orientated 'incumbent option' which represent a welcome alternative to the polarized national or global debate, but again they are highly demanding and beyond the resources of many companies. Fortunately, more recent research into 'mixed' industries where the pattern of internationalization is more transitional by Calori *et al.* (2000) suggests a wider range of subtler options. Such options are based on soundly analysed options actually being pursued by executives across Europe, being well-supported in terms of empirical research. Similarly from more defensive international positions, Bartlett and Ghoshal (2000) and Dawar and Frost (1999) both offer nuanced, pertinent international options. A sound appreciation of the stage of global concentration for a given sector is of course a prerequisite in assessing all such options.

Clearly research carried out on concentration trends at national and regional levels now needs to be carried out even more systematically in the global context. The need for more research and indeed for more reliable data is if anything all the more pressing if this chapter is correct in the more bullish picture of global concentration that its presents.

REFERENCES

Altshuler, A., Anderson, M., Jones, D., Roos, D. and Womack, J. (1984) 'The Future of the Automobile', *Report of MIT's International Automobile Programme* (London: George Allen & Unwin).

Baden F.C. and Stopford, J. (1991) 'Globalization Frustrated: The Case of White Goods', *Strategic Management Journal*, 12, 493–507.

Bartlett, C. and Ghoshal, S. (1991) *Managing across Borders: The Transnational Solution* (Boston: Harvard Business School Press).

Bartlett, C. and Ghoshal, S. (2000) 'Going Global: Lessons from Late Movers', *Harvard Business Review*, March, 132–42.

Bryan, L., Fraser, J., Oppenheimer, J. and Rall, W. (1999) *Race for the World* (Boston: Harvard Business School Press).

Buzzell, R.D. and Gale, B. (1987) *The PIMS Principles* (New York: Free Press).

Calori, R., Atamer, T. and Nunes, P. with others (2000) *The Dynamics of International Competition: From Practice to Theory* (London: Sage).

Carr, C. (1993) 'Global, National and Resource-based Strategies: An Examination of Strategic Choice and Performance in the Vehicle Components Industry', *Strategic Management Journal*, 14, 551–68.

Coriale, B. (1997) 'Globalization, Variety, and Mass Production: The Metamorphosis of Mass Production in the New Competitive Age', in Hollingsworth, J.R. and Boyer, R., (eds) *Contemporary Capitalism: The Embeddedness of Institutions* (Cambridge: Cambridge University Press) 240–66.

Davies, S. and Lyons, B. (1996) *Industrial Organization in the European Union: Strategy, Structure and the Competitive Mechanism* (Oxford: Clarendon Press).

Dawar, N. and Frost, A. (1999) 'Competing with Giants: Survival Strategies for Local Companies in Emerging Markets', *Harvard Business Review*, 77 (2), 119–29.

Day, G.S. (1997) 'Strategies for Surviving a Shakeout', *Harvard Business Review*, 75 (2), 92–102.

Financial Times (2000) 12 October.

Financial Times (2001) 1 November.

Fortune (1999) 2 August.

Fortune (2000) 24 July.

Ghemawat, P. and Ghadir, F. (2000) 'The Dubious Logic of Global Megamergers', *Harvard Business Review*, 78 (4), 65–72.

Hamel, G. (2000) *Leading the Revolution* (Boston: Harvard Business School Press).

Hannah, L. (1976) *The Rise of the Corporate Economy* (London: Methuen).

Hannah, L. and Kay, J.A. (1977) *Concentration in Modern Industry: Theory, Measurement and the UK Experience* (London: Macmillan).

Hayward, J. (1995) *Industrial Enterprise and European Integration: From National to International Champion in Western Europe* (Oxford: Oxford University Press).

Held, D. and McGrew, A. (eds) (2000) *The Global Transformation Reader: An Introduction to the Globalization Debate* (Oxford: Polity Press/Blackwell).

Hertz, N. (2001) *The Silent Takeover: Global Capitalism and the Death of Democracy* London: Heinemann.

Hirst, P. and Thompson, G. (1996) *Globalization in Question: The International Economy and the Possibilities of Corporate Governance* (Oxford: Polity Press Blackwell).

Hirst, P. and Zeitlin, J. (1997) 'Flexible Specialization: Theory And Evidence In The Analysis Of Industrial Change', in Hollingsworth, J.R. and Boyer, R. (eds) *Contemporary Capitalism: The Embeddedness of Institutions* (Cambridge: Cambridge University Press) 220–39.

Hollingsworth, J.R. and Boyer, R. (1997) *Contemporary Capitalism: The Embeddedness of Institutions* (Cambridge, UK: Cambridge University Press).

Hout, T., Porter, M. and Rudden, E. (1982) 'How Global Companies Win Out', *Harvard Business Review*, 60 (5), 98–109.

IMD (1999) 'The DaimlerChrysler Merger (A): Gaining Global Competitiveness' Cranfield: European Case Clearing House Case 399–131–1.

INSEAD (2001) 'Renault and Nissan'. Cranfield: European Case Clearing House: 301–050–1.

Jacobson, D. and Andreosso-O'Callaghan, B. (1996) *Industrial Economics and Organization: A European Perspective* (London: McGraw-Hill).

Johnson, G. and Scholes, K. (2002) *Exploring Corporate Strategy: Text and Cases* (Harlow, UK: FT/Prentice Hall, Pearson Education).

Kay, J. (2000) 'Foundations of Corporate Success in the Knowledge Driven Economy', Lecture at University of Edinburgh Management School, Edinburgh, 5 September.

Kay, J. (2001a) 'Choice as Control', *Financial Times*, 21 August, 10.

Kay, J. (2001b) 'The Great Paradox of Globalization: Rich Country Multinationals Benefit from Wider Markets. But They Also Face More Competition', *Financial Times*, 11 November.

Lynch, R. (2000) *Corporate Strategy* (Harlow, UK: FT/Prentice Hall, Pearson Education).

Mair, A. (2000) 'Clustering Processes and Cluster Economics in a Traditional Industry', Paper presented at the British Academy of Management Annual Conference, September, Edinburgh.

Marx, K. (1919) *Capital* (Chicago: Charles H. Kerr).

Micklethwaite, J. and Wooldridge, A. (2000) *A Future Perfect: The Challenge and Hidden Promise from Globalization* (London: Heinemann).

Nonaka, I. and Takeuchi, H. (1995) *The Knowledge-Creating company: How Japanese Companies Create the Dynamics of Innovation* (New York: Oxford University).

Ohmae, K. (1985) *Triad Power: The Coming Shape of Global Competition* (New York: Free Press).

Ohmae, K. (1990) *The Borderless World* (New York: Harper Business).

Ohmae, K. (2001) *The Invisible Continent* (London: Nicholas Brealey).

Porter M. (1980) *Competitive Strategy: Techniques for Analysing Industries and Competitors* (New York: Free Press).

Porter, M. (1987) 'From Competitive Advantage to Corporate Strategy', *Harvard Business Review*, 65 (3), 43–59.

Porter, M. (1990) *The Competitive Advantage of Nations* (London: Macmillan).

Porter, M. (1998a) *On Competition* (Boston: Harvard Business School Press).

Porter, M. (1998b) 'Clusters and the New Economics of Competition', *Harvard Business Review*, 76 (6), 77–90.

Schwittay, B. (1999) 'Globalization and Strategic Groups: The Case of the Spirits Industry', unpublished Ph.D. dissertation, Manchester Business School, Manchester, UK.

Simon, H. (1996) *Hidden Champions: Lessons from the World's Best Unknown Companies* (Boston, MA: Harvard Business School Press).

Skinner, A. (1970) *Adam Smith: The Wealth of Nations. Books I to III* (London: Penguin).

UNDP Report. (2000) 'Globalization with a Human Face', in Held, D. and McGrew, A. (eds) *The Global Transformation Reader: An Introduction to the Globalization Debate* (Oxford: Polity Press. Blackwell) 341–47.

Waldman, D.E. and Jensen, E.J. (1998) *Industrial Organization: Theory and Practice* (Reading, MA: Addison-Wesley).

Wilkinson, D. (2001) *Appraisal of Strategic Options in the Pharmaceutical Industry,* Edinburgh: Edinburgh University Dissertation for the Master of Business Administration Degree.

Womack, J.P and Jones, D.T. and Roos, D. (1990) *The Machine that Changed the World* (New York: Rawson Associates).

Yip, G. (1989) 'Global Strategy in a World of Nations?', *Sloan Management Review*, 31 (1), 29–40.

Yip, G. (1992) *Total Global Strategy* (Englewood Cliffs, NJ: Prentice Hall).

7 Globalizing Internationals: Standardization of Product and Marketing Strategies in the ICT Field

Peter Gabrielsson and Mika Gabrielsson

INTRODUCTION

In the information and communication technology (ICT) industry the pressure to globalize an already international business is great. The industry consists of a range of different companies from manufacturers to service providers, but the focus in this research is on manufacturers of ICT equipment including network infrastructure systems, terminals and personal computers. International companies in particular in these sectors need a well-planned global strategy to be able to leverage their potential fully. The companies have to decide about global market participation, global product and marketing strategies, and the global location of activities as well as global competitive moves. In the ICT field, effective product and marketing strategies are especially important.

The internationalization process has been widely studied (Luostarinen, 1970, 1979 and 1994; Johansson and Vahlne, 1977) with the focus of research mainly on firms in the early phases of internationalization (Melin, 1992), or on multinationals and companies that are already global. However, there is little research on international companies that are becoming global. Globalizing internationals in this study are defined as those companies which were established before 1985, and which had started to internationalize after a period of domestic business, but then started to globalize their operations outside of their domestic continent after 1985 (Luostarinen and Gabrielsson, 2001).

Recent research on the internationalization of firms has concentrated on modes of operation (for example Buckley and Casson, 1998). Much less attention has been paid to either product or marketing strategies, which obviously play a key role when a company is globalized. Product standardization versus adaptation strategies have been studied rather widely with respect to different marketing-mix elements (for example Buzzell, 1968; Keegan, 1969; Levitt, 1983; Jain, 1989). However, research has concentrated on multinationals, often US-based companies, while companies originating from small and open economies (SMOPEC) like Finland have been studied less (Luostarinen, 1979). Furthermore, the change in these strategies when moving from the international to the global stage has not been studied.

The *research problem* can be stated as follows: How can international ICT companies from small and open economies meet the globalization challenge of developing products and marketing them for global markets? The *research questions* that follow from the research problem are as follows: (1) what product strategies are available from the standardization viewpoint and how do these change while international ICT companies globalize? (2) what marketing strategies are available from the standardization viewpoint in general and how do branding and channel strategies in particular change in this process?

The main objective of this chapter is to develop product and marketing strategies for globalizing internationals in the ICT equipment-manufacturing field with a particular focus on possibilities for standardization of products, brands and channels across countries. The first author has developed the conceptual framework and the product dimension, whilst the second author has developed the marketing dimension. The chapter is conceptual in nature but, nevertheless, empirical illustrations are provided throughout the work. Theoretical contributions, managerial implications and suggestions for future research are also set out.

THEORETICAL REVIEW

From International to Global Business Development

We propose that the conversion of an international business to a global business takes place in several stages and that a distinctive strategy is applied in each stage. A pioneer in reviewing the development of different kind of MNCs, Perlmutter (1969) argues that no single criterion of multinationality such as ownership or number of nationals abroad is sufficient to classify MNCs. Quantifiable measures like, for example, investments abroad are useful but not adequate alone. More important is the orientation towards foreigners, ideas and resources in the company at all management levels. These attitudes or orientations may be described as ethnocentric (home-country oriented), polycentric (host-country oriented), geocentric (world-oriented) and regiocentric (region-oriented) (Chakravarthy and Perlmutter, 1985).

Bartlett and Ghoshal (1987) have found that multinational companies face a need for new multidimensional strategic capabilities. Strong geographic management is essential for the development of dispersed responsiveness, but effective management also calls for strong business management with global efficiency and integration. In addition to these capabilities, strong worldwide functional management is needed to build and transfer a company's core competencies. A strategy striving towards simultaneous global efficiency, national responsiveness and worldwide learning may be called a transnational strategy.

Yip (1989) has argued that globalization proceeds in three stages, which are the development of the core strategy, internationalization of the strategy and globalization of the strategy. Also Craig and Douglas (1996) found that global market expansion develops in three phases in addition to the domestic phase, these being: initial market entry, local market expansion and global rationalization. Although global rationalization describes well the phenomena, we prefer to use the term 'global alignment' because there are fewer connotations of a reduction in business activities. Hence we call the main stages, international market entry, international market penetration and global alignment.

The process starts with international market entry (stage 1), in which the company's strategic thrust is to expand geographically to international markets to achieve scale advantages. In the second stage – international market penetration – the company starts to look for new growth potential and expansion in countries where a base has already been established. The idea is to build on existing structures and assets established in each market to achieve scope advantages through spreading administrative overheads (Douglas and Craig, 1989). Product lines and variants may be developed to meet the local market requirements and marketing strategies may be adapted to the local environment.

The development of the international entry and penetration stages has been thoroughly examined by Luostarinen (1970 and 1979) and Johanson and Vahlne (1977), who depict a stepwise process where companies proceed towards higher market involvement. In contrast, Oviatt and McDougall (1994) have argued that some companies may be international from inception, without proceeding through these phases. This phenomenon, often referred to as 'born globals' (for example Luostarinen and Gabrielsson, 2001), is different from the behaviour of the 'globalizing internationals' that have first internationalized their business and only then entered the globalization stage.

The final stage, global alignment (stage 3) is characterized by the adoption of a global orientation in strategy development and implementation. Global expansion becomes a key principle in strategy formulation, and attention focuses on global efficiency without losing local responsiveness. The strategic thrust of the company is to find synergies from operating on a global scale and to take maximum advantage of the multinational nature of its operations. Global alignment includes improving efficiency among its operations across the world and also developing a global strategy that identifies the market segments and customers to be targeted in world markets. Opportunities in identifying segments that are rather regional or global become interesting. A strategic decision relates to the appropriate mix of product businesses worldwide (Douglas and Craig, 1989). At this stage it is also important to note that each country can be seen as a global platform. The focus of the operations in one country is not only on running business in that specific area; and those countries that contribute to the whole company and provide a global competitive advantage are the most successful platforms (Porter, 1986).

The transformation from stage 2 (international market penetration) to stage 3 (global alignment) covers the globalization process of international companies examined in this chapter (see Figure 7.1). (Note! In this research we examine the development from stage 2 to stage 3.)

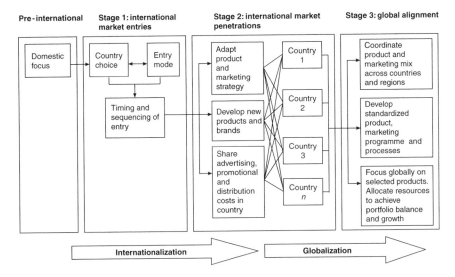

Figure 7.1   Stages in the globalization of ICT companies

Source: Adapted from Douglas and Craig (1989).

The Standardization versus Adaptation Debate

The debate concerning whether to standardize or to adapt the product and marketing mix elements has gone on for a long time and does not seem to be any closer to any conclusive theory or practice. Based on a literature review of articles that appeared from the end of the 1960s to the beginning of 2001 that focus on the standardization of product strategy or marketing mix elements, it is evident that most of the research has focused on the standardization of product strategy, advertising strategy or on the whole marketing mix. This is probably because of the big economic rewards anticipated from the standardization of the product and advertising elements, as well as the difficulties of standardizing the pricing and channel elements. The pricing and channel structures are often country-specific, and therefore companies cannot standardize these across countries. It can also be concluded that most of the studies have been of a purely theoretical nature and empirical evidence is rare except for a few empirical works mainly on MNCs operating in developing countries (see Hill and Still, 1984; Boddewyn *et al.*, 1986; Ozsomer *et al.*, 1991; Chang, 1995) and studies focusing on consumer preferences and segmentation (for example Verhage *et al.*, 1989; Keillor *et al.*, 2001).

The issue of whether standardization is feasible still seems to be unsolved. The most far reaching interpretation has been presented by Levitt (1983), who argued that emerging global markets are providing opportunities to market standardized products across the globe, ignoring regional or national differences. Although increased use of especially product standardization has been supported in the literature (Sorenson and Wiechmann, 1975; Boddewyn *et al.*, 1986; Walters, 1986; Ozsomer *et al.*, 1991; Whitelock and Pimblett, 1997), the empirical evidence is scarce except for a few studies mainly on MNCs. A study of 27 leading US and European multinationals in the consumer packaged-goods industry found that a surprisingly high proportion of the companies, over 60 per cent, reported having a highly standardized marketing programme. Extremely high standardization was found to exist in brands, physical characteristics of products and packaging (Sorenson and Wiechmann, 1975). Also, a series of related surveys of US companies marketing in Europe revealed that product standardization generally increased in 1983 compared to 1973, and standardization of branding had also increased as well.

The proponents of the adapted approach to global marketing claim that as customer and institutional characteristics differ significantly by area, some geographic adjustment is needed to be able to compete successfully (Simmonds, 1985). For instance, market characteristics, industry conditions, product life-cycle stage and the extent of competition vary in each market, as do the marketing institutions available in each country, including distribution channels, advertising media and agencies (Buzzell, 1968). A recent study of consumers in the USA, France and Malaysia also found that only a few product attributes are emphasized across the markets (Keillor *et al.*, 2001).

From the above discussion of the proponents of either full standardization or extreme adaptation, one can conclude that it is more relevant to speak about the degree of standardization on a continuum, for instance from fully standardized products to only loosely agreed product ideas (Quelch and Hoff, 1986). In the ICT industry, one common solution is to standardize the product platform and only make smaller adaptations for different markets, achieving both the benefits of an adapted offering and being able to spread often large outlays for R&D across a large number of countries. The literature indicates that the degree of standardization is expected to differ depending on the nature of the product. First of all, some product types can be standardized more than others. Consumer non-durables have been considered more difficult than consumer durables to standardize because of the influence of culture (Whitelock and Pimblett, 1997). Also, industrial and high-technology products are considered more appropriate than consumer products for standardization (Jain, 1989). Furthermore, in high-technology companies management often lacks both resources and the time to adapt the product to each market. The high-technology market is also very competitive and is characterized by rapid technology shifts, making standardization even more appropriate (Quelch and Hoff, 1986). Secondly, another important aspect is product positioning; it is suggested that standardization is more appropriate when the home market positioning is also meaningful in the target market (Jain, 1989).

An important distinction should be made between standardization of marketing programmes, emphasized by the earlier literature, and standardization of managerial processes put forward by some more recent studies. The focus in process standardization is on the marketing philosophy, principles and technology applied in the planning and preparing of marketing programmes. The conclusion in many of the studies is that it is far easier to standardize the marketing planning process than the content of the programme (Walters, 1986). Sorenson and Wiechmann (1975), for example, conclude that the process of making marketing decisions may be unified; this applies in particular to the system for annual marketing planning. Also, it should be noted that the decision regarding standardization should be made only after carefully considering the advantages and disadvantages and the overall revenues and costs (Buzzell, 1968).

We may summarize the above discussion in that more research is needed on the subject. A better understanding of not only programme standardization but also process-related standardization is important. The world is far more complicated than modelling of the standardization decision in previous research suggests; the standardization alternatives are a spectrum ranging from full standardization to an adaptive approach at different levels of the marketing mix elements. Finally, the question of how the standardization strategy changes when the company moves from international to global has received almost no attention in the literature. This study will attempt to answer these questions.

A THEORETICAL FRAMEWORK EXPLAINING PRODUCT AND MARKETING STRATEGIES

We now examine what factors affect the degree of standardization of global product and marketing strategies when an international ICT company globalizes its activities. This is triggered by a number of drivers which cause the company to change its strategies on different levels, including the corporate, business and functional levels. In Figure 7.2 we present a framework explaining the development of product and marketing strategies (Gabrielsson, 2002).

Environment and Industry-Related Globalization Drivers

Globalization drivers cause the company to reassess its strategy. Homogenization of market need, liberalization of trade and increasing global competition are examples of such drivers. These environment and industry-related globalization drivers are grouped as market, government and competitive factors. Also, the technology life-cycle is expected to be an important factor (Moore, 1998). These factors are expected to influence the company and its strategy at the corporate, business and functional levels. We

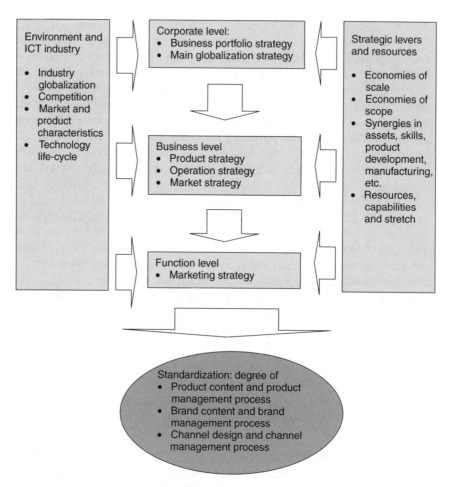

Figure 7.2 The conceptual framework

Source: Adapted from Gabrielsson (2002).

also suggest that the stronger the globalization drivers the higher the standardization degree of both product and marketing strategies (see also Levitt, 1983; Yip, 1992).

In high-technology industries in general and in the ICT companies in particular, it may be assumed that the globalization drivers are relatively strong for the following reasons. First of all, the market need is similar across countries and global or at least regional customers are often present. In, for example, the telecommunication industry, globalization is proceeding rapidly; the needs of the markets are becoming more similar, and, also, segmentation takes place more on the basis of product or customer type than on geographical area

(Alahuhta, 1990). Secondly, trade barriers are relatively low except for restrictions related to technical standards. Also, trade in Europe and in the telecommunication sector in particular is being liberalized and increasing standardization in the telecommunication industry speeds up the globalization process. Thirdly, competition is much more intense in high-technology and ICT fields, so companies utilize all opportunities to achieve competitive advantage through global integration when potential exists. Increasing global competition and increasing speed of the development of new technologies have led to shorter product cycles, higher innovation intensity and increasing importance of economies of scale (Alahuhta, 1990). The cross-subsidization of markets and retaliation to competition are also common tactics in global competition (Hamel and Prahalad, 1985).

Global Strategic Levers and Resources

Strategic levers can be identified as the source for competitive advantage in the global market. Douglas and Craig (1989) introduce the economies of scale, economies of scope and synergies as important levers.

In the international entry stage economies of scale are an important source of competitive advantage. A company often leverages its domestic production base and in this way reduces average unit costs thanks to increasing production volumes. When the company is in the international penetration stage, it expands within the selected geographic markets through adaptive product and marketing strategies as well as by introducing new product lines. The emphasis shifts at this stage to achieving economies of scope by leveraging the established contacts and knowledge of local markets. New products can often be introduced via the same sales channels bringing huge cost benefits.

In the global alignment phase, the company starts to coordinate and rationalize its operations on a global basis to achieve benefits from synergies. Skills or assets that are transferable such as management skills, brand and product knowledge may be leveraged globally (Douglas and Craig, 1989). Global and regional levels of coordination of product and marketing-related requirements become important. These competencies and processes may bring a more sustainable competitive advantage than market-related advantages like economies of scale and/or scope. Recent results, however, indicate that process and competence-related advantages may lose their power if firms use obsolete knowledge in these areas (Christensen, 2001).

Improved coordination and more integrated product and marketing strategies will often lead to economies of scale; centralized product development, production and marketing will eliminate duplication and increase efficiency. In ICT companies, investment in R&D and product development is often high and it is therefore extremely important to spread development costs over the maximum volume of sales from global markets. From this product point of view, this often means reducing the number of product lines and country variants. For example, Motorola announced that they were targeting to reduce their product portfolio in the personal communications sector from 65 products in 2000 to 25 products in 2002; in this way limited resources can be put into developing key products. The importance of global brand dominance has been seen as especially important in fighting global competition. It has also been found that the cost advantages are less durable compared to the brand and distribution advantages (Hamel and Prahalad, 1985).

Resources and capabilities are also expected to impact on global product and marketing strategies (see for example Wernerfelt, 1984). For example, it may be assumed that companies with resources related to global product development skills, an understanding of the use of a modular product platform, mass manufacturing capabilities and global coordination capabilities of different national product requirements will select a highly standardized product strategy when justified by the external environment.

Corporate-Level Strategies

At a corporate level an international ICT company needs to answer the following questions in relation to its globalization strategy. In which businesses does the company want to be and what is the main globalization strategy selected? In a portfolio of different businesses, the corporate management must recognize and cope with strategic variety (Prahalad and Doz, 1987). Corporate strategy is expected to influence business-level product and market strategies, and we develop the following business portfolio strategies for globalizing international companies (Ansoff, 1987):

- Global focus strategy: global geographical expansion in a single or dominant business area with current product technology and market segment.
- *Global-related diversification strategy*: (a) global geographical expansion in a related market segment but with a new product technology; (b) global geographical expansion in a related product technology area but offering this to new market segment(s).
- Global unrelated diversification strategy: global geographical expansion to unrelated market segments and the use of an unrelated product technology.

A recent study investigating 20 large Swedish multinational companies found a strong pattern of product focus in the process of diversifying into a large number of markets (Bengtsson, 2000). This has also been the globalization strategy of, for example, Nokia which has focused on mobile phones and networks and eliminated other product groups from its offering (Häikiö, 2001).

An international company may globalize its businesses utilizing different types of globalization strategies. To start with, a global or multidomestic strategy may be utilized (Hout *et al.*, 1982; Prahalad and Doz, 1987) and then a multifocal

(Prahalad and Doz, 1987)/ transnational strategy is applied (Bartlett and Ghoshal, 1987):

- In a pure global strategy the company is seeking global integration benefits and looking at the whole world as its markets.
- In a multidomestic strategy the company is seeking local responsiveness by adapting its offering and strategies to the local market needs.
- In a multifocal or transnational strategy the company strives to obtain global integration benefits, local responsiveness and also international learning.

Business and Functional-Level Strategies

The business-level market, operation and product strategies, and the functional-level marketing strategies are expected to evolve from international to global. The development of product and marketing strategies will be examined in the next section from the standardization viewpoint; Table 7.1 describes the development of strategies.

Table 7.1   Evolution of strategies from international to global

Stage of international market involvement	International market penetration (stage 2)	Global alignment (stage 3)
Strategy	• Leverage capabilities • Market expansion • Product-line extension • Product transfer • Product development	• Coordination of marketing tactics and strategy across countries • Globally focused • Globally integrated • Vertical integration along with increased horizontal integration
Key strategic imperatives	• Market responsiveness	• Improved coordination and control • Global restructuring • Strategic flexibility
Market strategy	• Concentration and penetration of the existing base of country markets	• Global rationalization of market activities • Identifying global segments
Standardization of product and marketing strategy	• Non-standardized approach • Product and marketing programme adaptation to country markets	• Both programme and process standardization • Develop standardized product and marketing programmes • Standardize management processes
Typical firms in ICT	• Medium-sized to large diversified firms with country-centred strategies	• Large firms with global strategies

Source: Adapted from Craig and Douglas (1996).

PRODUCT AND MARKETING STRATEGY DIMENSIONS

Global Standardization of Product Strategies

Two approaches to global product standardization will be examined; product content standardization will be discussed first and then process standardization. When discussing content standardization it is beneficial to define different aspects or levels of the product. Kotler (1984, pp. 462–4) argues that a product may be seen on three levels: the core benefit of the product or service, the tangible product and finally the augmented product. Globalizing internationals may standardize the product to some extent at all these levels.

1 *The core product benefit*. In the ICT area, the core product benefit includes issues such as performance, technology and the main functional features. These kinds of benefits are standardized in a high-technology area by developing a common product platform that is then adapted to market requirements through modularity and interchangeability of certain parts. The importance of understanding the product platform-level strategies in the high-technology area has been emphasized by many authors (McGrath, 1995; Sawhney, 1998). Standardization of product platforms has also been one of Nokia Mobile Phones' core targets (Häikiö, 2001).
2 *The tangible product*. This is the tangible product the customer sees and experiences including hardware, software, features, design, packaging and the brand label. The tangible product is often increasingly standardized in many ICT companies. This is common in, for example, electronic component manufacturers.
3 *The augmented product*. This includes additional services, warranty, delivery and installation services. It is rare that all these levels are standardized, but because a product is sold in several countries, there is considerable pressure to standardize, for example, warranty terms.

Product management processes may also be standardized. We may identify a number of different product management processes that may benefit from standardization in globalizing internationals, and some examples are presented below:

1 The process for defining customer input of new product requirements. Gathering a standardized input from markets and customers facilitates the use of information at different levels of the company and has a vital role in a successful global product strategy.
2 The product development process. Companies rationalizing their global businesses benefit from standardizing the product development process as R&D centres are increasingly interlinked across the world.
3 The product launch process may benefit from standardization. Rapid product launches across the globe have become a competitive advantage in

many globalizing ICT industries. Competitive responses from competitors can be minimized by entering multiple markets with new products (Shankar, 1999).

4 Another interesting opportunity is the standardization of product categories (mix) across countries (Yip, 1992). This offers possibilities for globalizing internationals to achieve benefits from standardized marketing material as well as supplying global customers with the same range of products in all markets, nevertheless meeting the technology and standard-related requirements.

Global Standardization of Marketing Strategies

The globalizing internationals also need to consider marketing strategy in addition to product strategy (for example Yip, 1989). The global marketing strategy can be considered in terms of both process and content, and the globalizing companies may either standardize their process across countries, regions or the whole globe. A higher-level integration is achieved through standardizing the content of the marketing mix, or even both the process and the content. In the personal computers (PC) industry, for instance, Fujitsu has standardized its notebook product line and marketing across the globe as part of a rationalization of its global business. The PC-producer Dell has also developed a direct marketing model that it has successfully applied worldwide. The marketing strategies which we discuss are branding and sales and distribution-channel strategies. These can be regarded as critical for gaining global integration benefits and both are closely connected with product strategy. We exclude from the discussion pricing strategy because it is seldom even wise to standardize pricing across countries due to prevailing differences in countries' market capacities (see for example Luostarinen and Gabrielsson, 2001).

Branding strategy is a key element for globalizing internationals and an essential part of communication, and Keegan (1969) suggests that standardization of the communication decision is related to the similarity of the need satisfied. We may identify the following approaches for the globalizing international. First, when the product need is similar in both the domestic and international markets, standardization of the content of the communication is a feasible alternative. Second, if the product function or need satisfied differs, this requires adaptations to the communication. For instance, standard-sized notebooks are only used as standalone PCs in Japanese offices; therefore it is better to emphasize screen size rather than battery duration in marketing communications. Thirdly, if the conditions of product use also differ then the product itself may also have to be adapted. For instance, a preference for smaller notebooks in Japan is partly because they are frequently used in crowded situations; this, then, requires changes in the product specification.

In the international penetration stage, the company adapts communication and the brand to the market to expand to the local markets. As the ICT company starts to globalize its operations, it may often find that it has to rationalize multidomestic brands. Standardization of content would mean that the brand and other communications would be similar in many markets as is often the case in the PC and mobile phones industry.

Aaker and Joachimsthaler (2001) suggested that there are basically two alternatives for global branding: a house of brands or a branded house. First of all, in a house of brands an independent set of product brands is used, each maximizing the impact on the market. Multiple global brands may also be the result of the consolidation of companies, which was the case, for example, when Fujitsu and ICL merged in the PC industry in the 1990s (Gabrielsson, 1999). Secondly, in a branded-house alternative, a single master brand is used to span a set of offerings, although descriptive sub-brands may be used to offer some flexibility to market requirements. The master brand may in some cases be a former successful product name, for instance a Finnish security software company, F-secure, switched its corporate name to match its successful product name. The global brand strategies based on content may be summarized as follows:

1 Single global product or corporate brands (branded house) are replacing local brands. In this strategy, all local brands are collected together by the globalizing international under a principal brand. Possible sub-brands are only treated as descriptive. The global mobile phone producer Nokia has followed the strategy of promoting Nokia as the single brand; the Mobira and Technophone brands have disappeared.
2 Multiple global product brands (house of brands) are replacing local brand portfolios. Here there are many global brands that are communicated consistently to global markets. For Finnish ICT companies this alternative seems too demanding in terms of resources, although it has been used by large US companies such as General Electric.

Standardization of the brand management process would mean that brand management is similar across countries, regions or the whole globe. This would allow for the globalizing company to benefit from brand management systems or brand leadership (Aaker and Joachimsthaler, 1999) when the local circumstances require adaptation to respond to individual needs. This is often the case in the consultation and software industries. Globalizing internationals following brand-management-process standardization would:

1 Switch from local brand-building to support global brand-planning processes and assign global brand responsibilities across markets. This allows both process-related benefits and some market-specific flexibility when needed. For example, Sony allows the modification of some global brand identity elements at the local level based on agreed processes (such as changing a technology leadership slogan to market leadership). IBM nominates global brand

managers and named brand stewards to protect the brand equity (see for example Aaker and Joachimsthaler, 1999).

2 Stimulate sharing of best practices across countries and the distribution of brilliant ideas across subsidiaries. The consumer electronics company Sony and IBM spread their best advertising around the world (*ibid*, 1999).

A sales and distribution-channel strategy is important for globalizing companies, but it is arguably one of the most difficult marketing-mix elements to standardize. Earlier research has found the division of channel design (content) and management (process) useful in dealing with this aspect (Rosenbloom *et al.*, 1997). The following conditions offer opportunities for standardization: first, when the distribution functions performed are similar across countries the channel design can be standardized; and second, when the business culture is similar, standardization of channel management processes is feasible. The design of management processes for sales and distribution channels offers more possibilities for standardization than the content aspects of these channels (Rosenbloom *et al.*, 1997). Gabrielsson (1999) has classified the channel designs as direct, indirect and multiple. Globalizing internationals have the following alternatives:

1 Utilizing the same channel design across countries. For example Dell utilizes a direct sales channel and Compaq an indirect channel across the world.
2 Utilizing certain types of channel members (VARs, dealers and so on) across countries. This would harmonize the channel programmes across markets and respond to the increase in global distributors and resellers, such as Computer 2000 and EDS.

Also, the standardization of processes is expected to be a viable alternative for globalizing internationals, and the following opportunities arise:

1 Channel-member selection procedures and terms and conditions are harmonized across markets as part of global rationalization. Many global companies have developed procedures for channel selection and evaluation, such as Fujitsu ICL.
2 Global management of large chains or customers. Regional or global channel captains have been appointed to PC companies such as Siemens and IBM.

Finally, standardization of both channel process and content would require highly controlled channels, such as direct sales or franchised indirect sales-channel strategies.

The information and communication technology (ICT) companies originating from small and open economies such as Finland faced a tremendous challenge when they globalized their international product and marketing strategies. Yip (1989) and Craig and Douglas, (1996) and the authors of this paper suggest development through two distinct phases – the international penetration stage and

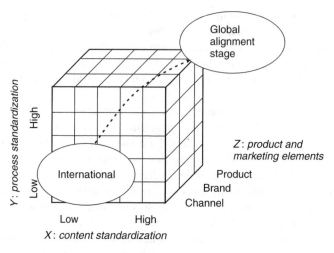

Figure 7.3 Dimensions of standardization

the global alignment stage. The international penetration stage has been well-described by earlier research (Luostarinen, 1970, 1979; Johansson and Vahlne, 1977), but the move towards the global stage has been studied less, in particular with respect to the product and marketing strategies of ICT companies. The standardization of the product and marketing strategies may be seen as a three-dimensional selection on a continuum consisting of the degree of (X) the programme content, (Y) the management process and (Z) the product and marketing elements (see also Walters, 1986; Rosenbloom *et al.*, 1997). We argue that an optimal selection of a position on these dimensions is critical to success in global competition. Successful ICT companies have proactively changed their strategies to match changes in the industry and unfolding environment, thus matching the full globalization potential. As earlier described and illustrated in Figure 7.3, the product, brand or channel strategy may be the object of standardization. The standardization potential is often higher for management processes than for programme content (Walters, 1986), as the convex shape of the dotted line describes. The possibilities for standardization are higher for product strategies than for brands and channels. As regards channels, content standardization is often limited by local conditions but process standardization offers some new possibilities (Rosenbloom *et al.*, 1997). Products have a high potential for both content and process standardization.

Propositions

The conceptual framework presented in Figure 7.2 explains the development of the product and marketing strategies for information and communication technology (ICT) companies as they develop from the international penetration stage towards the global alignment stage. There are mainly three factors explaining the changing product and marketing strategies for globalizing internationals in the ICT field: the ICT industry- and environment-related global drivers, the company-specific strategic levers and resources, the corporate-level business portfolio and main globalization strategy, and the business-level operation and market strategies. We therefore put forward the following proposition:

Proposition 1: The change from international-adaptive product and marketing strategies to globally-standardized strategies is driven by the ICT industry and environment, company-specific strategic levers and resources, corporate-level strategies and also by the business-level operation and market strategies.

In the international penetration stage, the company is penetrating deeper into the existing international market base by utilizing adaptive product and marketing programmes and developing country-specific product lines and variants. Content standardization is therefore low across countries (see Figure 7.3). In this way, the company achieves considerable economies of scope by leveraging existing customer and country-related capabilities. At this point, process standardization is relatively low, as specialized processes are needed to meet the country-specific product and customer requirements. We therefore present proposition 2 as follows:

Proposition 2: In the international penetration stage, the product and marketing programme and the process standardization are low in ICT equipment companies.

The company is then driven on the other hand by the environment and ICT-industry-related globalization drivers and by the proactive strategic decisions (on levers) taken in the global alignment phase, in which the product and marketing programmes are coordinated on global or regional scales and global segments are addressed by standardized products and marketing programmes. Both the product and the marketing programme may be standardized on different levels, enabling the company to adapt to market requirements flexibly when this is required and is financially profitable. Furthermore, the product management processes, brand as well as channel management processes, are standardized giving considerable global benefits. In this way, ICT companies may achieve considerable synergies through global rationalization by transferring product and marketing programme elements across countries and benefiting from economies of scale and scope, which are important sources of competitive advantage in the ICT industry. The focus turns in this global phase to managing the global configuration of the product and markets to sustaining the growth; thus, proposition 3:

Proposition 3: In the global alignment stage, the product and marketing programme and the process standardization are high in ICT equipment companies.

CONCLUSIONS

In this chapter two main theoretical areas have been reviewed: globalization of international businesses (Douglas and Craig, 1989; Yip, 1989), and standardization of product (Quelch and Hoff, 1986) and marketing strategies (Keegan, 1969; Rosenbloom, 1997). Moreover, this study integrates these areas by examining the change in product and marketing strategies for globalizing internationals. This results in an understanding that both content and processes should be standardized to increase global competitiveness (see for example Sorenson and Wiechmann, 1975; Walters, 1986). We next examine the theoretical contribution and managerial implications that the discussion has produced and consider some interesting research avenues.

This study has identified a lack of research on the evolution from international to global product, channel and branding strategies and has described and analysed this phenomenon in the ICT equipment field. Earlier research has treated the topic on a general level; for instance, the internationalization process has been well-described (Luostarinen, 1970, 1979; Johansson and Vahlne, 1977) but the transfer from an international to a global stage has been little researched, especially with respect to product and marketing strategies. We have explored the possibilities for the product, brand and channel dimensions to be standardized by widening the discussion to include management processes as well as programme content. Further, we have divided each of these elements into dimensions and managerial alternatives that are then illustrated by examples from earlier literature or our own experience. We have also developed a tentative framework and a set of propositions to explain the factors influencing the development of product and marketing strategies from the international penetration stage towards the global alignment stage in the ICT field. These tools are beginning to open up possibilities for further empirical research.

The management implications of this study are that, firstly, the cube presenting the product and marketing standardization dimensions in Figure 7.3 can be a useful tool in understanding the strategy alternatives of globalizing internationals in the ICT industry. This can lead to huge economic benefits when properly implemented. Secondly, understanding the impact of the explanatory variables as well as how the global product and marketing strategies change when the company is transferring from the international stage to the global stage is of the utmost importance for ICT companies facing the globalization challenge.

A limitation of this study is that a deeper analysis of specific case companies might have brought a more profound understanding of the area. However, the objective set for this study was to increase our conceptual understanding and prepare the ground for empirical research on globalizing internationals across industry sectors and in the ICT sector in particular.

REFERENCES

Aaker, D.A. and Joachimsthaler, E. (2001) 'The Brand Leadership Spectrum: the key to the brand architecture challenge', *The 67th Conference on Design Management in the Digital Environment*, 29 April–1 May, Pasadena, California, 8–23.

Aaker, D.A. and Joachimsthaler, E. (1999) 'The Lure of Global Branding', *Harvard Business Review*, November–December, 137–44.

Alahuhta, M. (1990) *Global Growth Strategies for High Technology Challengers*, Electrical Engineering series no. 66, thesis for the degree of Doctor of Technology, Helsinki.

Ansoff, I. (1987) *Corporate Strategy*, first published 1965, rev. edn 1987 (London: Penguin).

Bartlett, C.A. and Ghoshal, S. (1987) 'Managing Across Borders: New Strategic Requirements', *Sloan Management Review*, Summer, 7–17.

Bengtsson, L. (2000) 'Corporate strategy in a Small Open Economy: Reducing Product Diversification While Increasing International Diversification', *European Management Journal*, 18 (4), August 2000, 444–53.

Boddewyn, J.J., Soehl R. and Picard, J. (1986) 'Standardisation in International Marketing: Is Ted Levitt in Fact Right?', *Business Horizons*, November–December 1986, 69–75.

Buckley, P.J. and Casson, M.C. (1998) 'Analysing Foreign Market Entry Strategies: Extending the Internationalisation Approach', *Journal of International Business Studies*, 29 (3) (third quarter 1988), 539–62.

Buzzell, R.D. (1968) 'Can You Standardize Multinational Marketing', *Harvard Business Review*, November–December, 102–13.

Chakravarthy, B.S. and Perlmutter, H. (1985) 'Strategic Planning for a Global Business', *Columbia Journal of World Business*, Summer, 3–11.

Chang, T. (1995) 'Formulating Adaptive Marketing Strategies in a Global Industry', *International Marketing Review*, 12 (6), 5–18.

Craig, C.S. and Douglas, S.P. (1996) 'Developing Strategies for Global Markets: An Evolutionary Perspective', *The Columbia Journal of World Business*, Spring, 31 (1), 71–81.

Christensen, C.M. (2001) 'The Past and Future of Competitive advantage', *MIT Sloan Management Review*, Winter, 105–9.

Douglas, S.P. and Craig, C.S. (1989) 'Evolution of Global Marketing Strategy: Scale, Scope and Synergy', *Columbia Journal of World Business*, Fall, 47–59.

Gabrielsson, M. (1999) *Sales Channel Strategies For International Expansion: The Case of Large Companies in the European PC Industry*, Helsinki School Of Economics and Business Administration, A-163, Finland.

Gabrielsson, P. (2002) *Globalising Internationals – Global Product Strategies of the ICT Companies*, Helsinki School of Economics, forthcoming licentiate thesis.

Häikiö, M. (2001) *Nokia Oyj:n historia: Globalisaatio, Telekommukaation maailmanvalloitus 1992–2000* (Helsinki: Edita Oyj).

Hamel, G. and Prahalad, C.K. (1985) 'Do You Really Have a Global Strategy?', *Harvard Business Review*, July–August, 139–48.

Hill, J.S. and Still, R.R. (1984) 'Adapting Products to LDC Tastes', *Harvard Business Review*, March–April, 92–101.

Hout, T., Porter, M.E. and Rudden, E. (1982) 'How Global Companies Win Out', *Harvard Business Review*, September–October, 98–108.

Jain, S.C. (1989) 'Standardization of International Marketing Strategy: Some Research Hypotheses', *Journal of Marketing*, 53, January, 70–9.

Johanson, J. and Vahlne, J.E. (1977) 'The Internationalization Process of the Firm – A Model of Knowledge Development and Increasing Foreign Market Commitments', *Journal of International Business Studies*, 8 (1), Spring/Summer, 23–32.

Keegan, W.J. (1969) 'Multinational Product Planning: Strategic Alternatives', *Journal of Marketing*, 33, January, 58–62.

Keillor, B.D., Hausknecht, R.D. and Parker, R.S. (2001) 'Thinking Global, Acting Local: An attribute Approach to Product Strategy', *Journal of Euromarketing*, 10 (2), 27–48.

Kotler, P. (1984) *Marketing Management: Analysis, Planning and Control*, fifth edn, (Englewar Cliff, NJ: Prentice-Hall, Inc.).

Levitt, T. (1983) 'The Globalisation of Markets', *Harvard Business Review*, May–June, 99–102.

Luostarinen, R. (1970) *Foreign Operations*, first pub. 1970, 4th edn 1982, Helsinki.

Luostarinen, R. (1979) *Internationalisation of the Firm*, Series A: 30, thesis for the degree of Doctor at the Helsinki School of Economics.

Luostarinen, R. (1994) *Internationalisation of Finnish and their Response to Global Challenges*, UNU World Institute for Development Economic Research.

Luostarinen, R. and Gabrielsson, M. (2001) 'Born Globals of SMOPEC – What, Where, When, Why and How', a working paper at *the 27th Annual Conference of the European International Business Academy* in Paris, December 13–15, 1–22.

McGrath, M.E. (1995) *Product Strategy for High-technology Companies: How to Achieve Growth, Competitive Advantage, and Increased Profits* (New York: McGraw-Hill).

Melin, L. (1992) 'Internationalisation as a Strategy Process', *Strategic Management Journal* (13), 99–118.

Moore, G.A., (1998) *Inside the Tornado*, first pub. 1995 (Oxford: Capstone Publishing Limited).

Oviatt, B.M. and McDougall, P.P. (1994) 'Toward a Theory of International New Ventures', *Journal Of International Business Studies*, 1st quarter, 45–64.

Ozsomer, A., Bodur, M. and Cavusgil, S.T. (1991) 'Marketing Standardisation by Multinationals in an Emerging Market', *European Journal of Marketing*, 25 (12), 50–64.

Perlmutter, H.V. (1969) 'The Tortuous Evolution of the Multinational Corporation', *Columbia Journal of World Business*, January–February 1969, 9–18.

Porter, M.E. (1986) 'Changing Patterns of International Competition', *California Management Review*, XXVIII. 2, Winter, 9–40.

Prahalad, C.K. and Doz, Y.L. (1987) *The Multinational Mission: Balancing Local Demands and Global Vision* (New York: Free Press).

Quelch, J.A and Hoff, E.J. (1986) 'Customizing Global Marketing', *Harvard Business Review*, May–June, 59–68.

Rosenblom, B., Larsen, T. and Mehta, R. (1997) 'Global Marketing Channels and the Standardization Controversy', *Journal of Global Marketing*, 11 (1), 49–64.

Sawhney, M.S. (1998) 'Leveraged High-variety Strategies: From Portfolio Thinking to Platform Thinking', *Academy of Marketing Science*, Winter, 54–61.

Shankar, V. (1999) 'New Product Introduction and Incumbent Response Strategies: their Interrelationship and the Role of Multimarket Contact', *Journal of Marketing Research*, 36, August, 327–44.

Simmonds, K. (1985) 'Global Strategy: Achieving the Geocentric Ideal', *International Marketing Review*, Spring, 2 (1), 8–17.

Sorenson, R.Z. and Wiechmann, U.E. (1975) 'Probing Opinions', *Harvard Business Review*, May–June, (53), 38–54, 166–167.

Verhage, B.J., Dahringer, L.D. and Cundiff, E.W. (1989) 'Will a Global Marketing Strategy Work – An Energy Conservation Perspective', *Journal of the Academy of Marketing Science*, Spring, 17 (2), 129–36.

Walters, P.G.P. (1986) 'International Marketing Policy: A Discussion of the Standardisation Construct and its Relevance For Corporate Policy', *Journal of International Business Studies*, 17 (2), Summer, 55–69.

Wernerfelt, B. (1984) 'A Resource-based View of the Firm', *Strategic Management Journal*, (5), 171–80.

Whitelock, J. and Pimblett, C. (1997), 'The Standardisation Debate in International Marketing', *Journal of Global Marketing*, 10 (3), 45–66.

Yip, G.S. (1989) 'Global Strategy . . . In a World of Nations?', *Sloan Management Review*, 29, Fall, 29–41.

Yip, G.S. (1992) *Global Strategy: Managing for Worldwide Competitive Advantage* (Englewar Cliff, NJ Prentice-Hall, Inc.).

8 How Firm-Specific Characteristics Shape Prospective Knowledge-Intensive Alliances in a Large Emerging Economy

Claudio De Mattos and Adam R. Cross

INTRODUCTION

One of the main challenges to global development today is the challenge of inclusion; that is, to promote 'equitable access to the benefits of development regardless of nationality, gender, or race' (Wolfensohn, 1997). Though not without its detractors, modern biotechnology, in particular technology associated with genetic engineering, offers solutions to many of the major developmental problems facing humanity today, especially those relating to malnutrition, disease and pollution. Recent advances in biotechnology may also help to solve the conundrum of how to promote *sustainable* development in the face of natural ambitions for improved national and global economic growth and prosperity (EU White Paper, 1994). But the global biotechnology market is fragmented; the greatest technological advances take place in just a few developed countries (Shan and Song, 1997), whereas humanity's major developmental problems are concentrated mainly in the less-developed economies. Mechanisms are needed so that appropriate biotechnologies created and refined in the 'north' (developed countries) are transferred efficiently and effectively to the 'south' (developing countries) in some mutually beneficial way.

Several recent papers (De Mattos and Sanderson, 2000; Govindarajan and Gupta, 2000; Simos, 2000) highlight the considerable potential for business in the high-technology sectors of large emerging markets (LEMs). Strong growth prospects and first-mover advantages are just two important reasons why developed-country firms should target them. The investment climate is poor in many LEMs; however, some form of alliance with a local concern is one way for developed-country firms to service these markets while circumventing many of the risks and costs associated with majority and wholly-owned modes. Consequently, strategic alliances between biotechnology firms of the developed nations and their counterparts in large emerging markets could prove an important mechanism for bridging the north – south technology gap in this industry, at least while certain impediments to investment prevail.

Barriers to the effective transfer of technology within strategic alliances are well-known, however, especially between developed and developing-country

120

firms. One major barrier concerns the incompatibility of the parties involved (Stopford and Wells, 1972); mismatch is likely to lead to disappointment on the part of one or more of the contracted partners once the alliance is up and running. At best, this may result in the failure by one or more parties to capture the full return on the alliance and hinder the exchange of technology between them; at worst, it may lead to the premature dissolution of the alliance and negligible technology transfer. Therefore, the role of partner compatibility in alliance formation is likely to be a significant determinant of alliance longevity and, it follows, of the quality and quantity of technology transfer within an alliance. Better understanding of the issue of compatibility in the formation of alliances is important, to inform not only managers as they seek and negotiate with potential local partners, but also to host-country policy-makers and other agents concerned with technology transfer who would like to encourage this. In this chapter, we consider one particular, and important, aspect of alliance-partner compatibility; namely, the determinant role of firm-specific factors in the potential formation of alliances with LEM firms.

Alliance-partner compatibility has received some attention in the literature in recent years (for example Brouthers *et al.*, 1995). This literature suggests that the prospects for mismatch are highest when the capabilities of the partners are very different or lack complementarity, and when cultural and geographical distance between the parties is most pronounced. However, the role of firm-specific factors in partner compatibility is poorly understood. We examine those factors internal to the firm that help to shape the congruence (or otherwise) of expectations held by prospective British and German biotechnology companies as they contemplate establishing an alliance with Brazilian counterparts. British and German firms were chosen for this study because many if not most of Europe's leading commercial and research institutions in the biotechnology field are based in those countries (Ernst and Young, 1995). Brazil was chosen as our exemplar LEM because of its large potential market for pharmaceutical products, expected to become the fifth largest in the world by 2010 (CODETEC, 1991). The recent recognition of pharmaceutical patents (including biotechnological products) in Brazil, fully implemented in 1997, is expected to facilitate the internal development of this technology and accelerate its adaptation to the local market. Interest in Brazil's biotechnology markets among developed country firms is therefore likely to be high.

Drawing upon data collected in a larger study (see De Mattos, 1999), we assess the role of firm-specific factors in alliance formation by first distinguishing between two groups of firms from a sample of British and German biotechnology firms that we identify as being either 'most compatible' or 'least compatible' with respect to a sample of biotechnology firms from Brazil. We then examine and compare these two groups of firms in terms of the firm-specific factors that have the potential to contribute most to strategic-alliance success. A variety of statistical techniques is used to aggregate firm-specific variables into variates, and a discriminating analysis of these variates is then conducted to assess which of these most differentiates between the 'most-compatible' and 'least-compatible' developed-country firms. Underpinning our analysis is the premise that the better the fit of prior expectations regarding the partners' respective contributions to the alliance, the more likely that an alliance will be entered into. Standard statistical tests are used in an unconventional way to help inform our understanding of those firm-specific factors that most impact upon the early stages of alliance formation. The study should help both practitioners and policy-makers to better appreciate the characteristics, perceptions and expectations of developed-country firms as they seek to enter into biotechnology alliances with LEM firms.

The chapter is organized as follows. In the first section, we discuss literature on those firm characteristics that determine the propensity to enter into trans-border alliances and joint ventures. In the second section our methodological approach to the data-collection is presented and the analysis is carried out. This involved a questionnaire administered during face-to-face interviews with managers from 71 firms (28 from the UK, 25 from Germany and 18 from Brazil), as well as the use of a variety of statistical techniques and a discriminant analysis. We present our findings in the third section and draw conclusions in the final section.

FIRM-SPECIFIC FACTORS AND ALLIANCE FORMATION

This study takes the definition of Buckley (1996, p. 484) that strategic alliances are 'inter-firm collaborations over a given economic space and time for the attainment of mutually defined goals'. International joint ventures (IJVs) are regarded as a particular type of strategic alliance; one that is cemented by equity participation. Because many, if not most, inter-firm cooperation agreements involve an exchange of technology, know-how and show-how, greater cooperation – especially when formalized within an alliance agreement – between firms from the developed and emerging economies is an important means by which impediments to the international diffusion of technological knowledge can be overcome and the technology gap bridged (Hennart, 1988).

Over the past few decades, strategic alliances have increasingly become viewed as the business approach of the future (Lorange and Roos, 1993). Strategic alliances are now especially evident in emerging industries such as the biotechnology industry (Shan, Walker and Kogut, 1994) and in the international business strategy of smaller firms (Lorange and Roos, 1993). From the early 1980s, cooperative agreements, and in particular joint ventures, have been viewed by both managers and policy-makers as ideal vehicles for taking technological knowledge into the emerging economies (Raveed and Renforth, 1983).

It is known that the success of any strategic alliance is heavily dependent upon the characteristics of the management team of the partner firms involved (Buckley and Casson, 1988). Compatibility between the parties and a congruency in business culture are also often cited as critical to alliance formation and success (Barkema and Vermeulen, 1997). Inkpen (2001), in a recent survey of the major issues and research questions in the study of international alliances, comments that compatibility has multiple dimensions including organizational fit, strategic symmetry, resource complementarities and alliance task-based factors. However, while firm-specific factors could potentially play an important determinant role under each of these headings, they are not identified as a discrete sub-set of issues in this survey. This is in part because the existing literature regarding firms' characteristics and the propensity to internationalize through alliance formation remains limited, particularly in the context of small and medium-sized enterprises (SMEs) and their entry into large emerging economies such as Brazil. Nevertheless, some contributions in this area have been made, especially in regard to joint venture formation, and we survey these briefly below.

International strategic alliances have been associated with firms that have a decentralized decision process in their home market and with those firms with multiple product ranges (Stopford and Wells, 1972). Decentralized decision-making is probably influential because such firms have the managerial structures and attitudes in place to be willing and able to devolve at least an element of control to a foreign partner in the internationalization process. Similarly, the degree of product diversification may be pertinent because this helps to determine the multinational firm's deployment of resources. Firms with few product lines may be less likely to employ joint ventures than those manufacturers of a broad range of products because the negative externalities of technology leakage to the local partner would be that much more profound for them. On the other hand, multinational firms with several product lines may tend to concentrate their resources on development and production rather than on marketing, and, therefore, may seek to access a foreign partner's local knowledge, distribution networks and marketing capacity through a mechanism such as a strategic alliance. This would certainly be the case when the present or projected market size of an emerging market is too small to warrant a wholly-owned operation, and when a capable local partner has the ability to contribute in this direction.

Steinmann *et al.* (1980), in a study of German SMEs, identify three characteristics of firms that commonly employ IJVs in their international strategy. The first is that they own only a limited number of products, technologies and know-how (a finding which contrasts with that of Stopford and Wells reported above). Steinmann *et al.* suggest this is because such firms are particularly concerned with preventing the dissipation of their proprietary technological advantage and therefore opt for higher control modes of market entry, committing more capital to this end. Second, IJVs are used by resource-constrained firms in terms of their physical and financial resources and their limited knowledge about markets and external operations. Three, IJVs are associated with firms in which key managerial positions and property participation belong to a few members of a family. Regarding this latter point, Gunzel (1975) suggests that SMEs, because of their essentially familial characteristics, are more sensitive to the preservation of ownership than larger corporations. Consequently, they tend to prefer the joint venture as a low-risk strategy with regard to resource commitment, certainly compared with wholly-owned operations.

Sales growth and profit are strong motivations for internationalization in SMEs. Several studies show that at higher levels of internationalization, factors external to the firm are less important compared with concerns over profit and sales growth (Douglas and Craig, 1989; Gray, 1997). Dong, Buckley and Mirza (1997), in a study of IJVs involving overseas Chinese partners, show that the local Chinese partner would expect more operational resources such as outward channels of distribution, and quality control techniques in IJVs that are more profit-orientated. A firm's size and age are also constructs deserving attention in the internationalization of firms. However, Reuber and Fischer (1997) demonstrate in their study that these variables seldom establish the internationalization capacity of the firm. Finally, Saxton (1997) in a recent work examined the similarity between partners of an alliance using several factors including those of strategic content such as manufacturing, raw materials, technology (or product), marketing and customers.

METHODOLOGY AND ANALYSIS

In order to explore whether or not it is possible to relate firm-specific factors of a developed economy partner-firm to their compatibility relative to a prospective alliance partner from an emerging economy, we examine the possibility of differentiating between the developed-country firms in terms of the expectations and perceptions of their managers towards the alliance. A pragmatic definition of 'compatibility' is adopted here; that is, it is based on quantifying the match of expectations held by executives regarding their firms' potential contributions to the alliance. From this viewpoint we identify two groups of developed-country firms in our sample – the 'most compatible' and the 'least compatible' – and isolate, define and compare the firm-specific characteristics associated with the firms in each of these groups in the context of a potential alliance with a Brazilian partner.

Data Collection

In order to obtain the developed-country firm perspective, the managers of British and German biotechnology firms were interviewed. The sample comprises firms that are directly developing biotechnology as well as firms supporting that activity as suppliers of reagents, equipment and software. Most of the firms sampled had not established any business contacts in Brazil at the time of the study, although it became clear during the investigation that a number of the managers interviewed were interested in doing so in the future. The British firms were located mainly in the South of England. The German firms come from three regions known to have a greater concentration of firms in the biotechnology sector: Berlin, Düsseldorf and the Munich areas.

The data examined in this study were collected by means of questionnaires completed during face-to-face semi-structured interviews. Two pretest interviews were conducted, which showed that only slight alterations to the survey instrument were necessary. Open and closed questioning were applied, and all interviews were recorded. A six-point Likert scale was used to quantify the respective partners' expected contributions to the potential alliance. This was used as the basis for separating the sampled firms into the most compatible and least compatible groups. Interviews were held with 29 British executives (28 firms), 26 German executives (25 firms) and 19 Brazilian executives (18 firms), making a total of 74 interviews carried out in 71 firms. Most of the interviewed executives held the position of managing director and several of them could be described as 'owner-managers' (Moran, 1998).

Data Analysis

In order to analyse those firm-specific factors most associated with alliance-partner compatibility between the developed country and Brazilian firms it was first necessary to separate the former into two groups – those that were most compatible with the Brazilian firms sampled, and those that were least. This was accomplished by relating each European executive's response to the average of the Brazilian executives' response regarding the importance of potential contributions made by partners to an alliance. Using Spearman rank correlations, 20 firms having the higher coefficients (out of the 53 European firms) were classified as belonging to the 'most compatible' group, and 20 firms having the lower coefficients were classified as belonging to the 'least compatible' group.

The next step was to identify the variates (or factors) that most discriminated between these two groups of firms. First, variables were selected for factor analysis, which is used here as a data-reduction technique. Our aim was to reduce the number of working variables by grouping the initial variables into representative factors or variates. The factor analysis is used only for indicating the variables that could be grouped together; that is, those sharing a substantial common variance. In selecting the appropriate variables the following points were considered: the variable type (metric versus categorical), cross-tabulation results, and the Pearson chi-square. A Pearson chi-square greater than 1 was used to indicate a reasonable potential for differentiation by the individual variable under scrutiny. Then, an exploratory factor analysis was performed to reduce the number of variables under consideration. The Kaiser–Meyer–Olkin measure of sampling adequacy and the Bartlett test of sphericity were applied to confirm the applicability of the factor analysis. By observing the loading of each variable on the factor analysis, variables that share a common variance were identified. These variables were grouped into a number of factors or variates, representing the dimensions underlying the data-set under examination. The variables associated in the variates were then standardized, and the reliability of each set of variables was confirmed using Cronbach alpha and modified, where necessary. A Kolmogorov–Smirnov test was used to test the univariate normality fit for each modified variate. Therefore, factors or variates were built on the basis of equally weighted standardized scales, an adaptation of summated scales deriving from factor analysis proposed by Hair *et al.* (1998, pp. 129–31). Recall that the variates are composed of firm-specific variables or variables connected to characteristics of the firms (refer to Table 8.2 for the specific variables). Finally, a discriminant analysis with the modified factors was performed, and both its significance and its hit ratio were analysed.

Because the statistical approach used in this study is novel, it is worthwhile explaining it in a little more detail (refer also to Appendix). The initial variables relating to the characteristics of the firms are shown in Table 8.1. From the questionnaire results, 49 variables were identified, comprising 24 metric variables and 25 categorical variables. Some of the categorical variables were re-coded as dichotomous, or as dummy variables, whereas some of the metric variables were re-coded into categories. The data-reduction process selected 20 variables (15 metric, 2 dummies and 3 binomial) to take forward to the factor analysis. The sampling adequacy was confirmed by both the Kaiser–Meyer–Olkin measure (in the acceptable range of above 0.50) and the Bartlett test for sphericity ($ = 421$, significance < 0.0001). Using factor analysis, the 20 selected variables were then grouped into seven variates on the basis of equally weighted standard-ized scales, each variate conforming to a minimum eigenvalue of one. Using an interpretative approach, six variates were chosen as meaningful. These are shown in Table 8.2 together with their respective loading in the rotated matrix. The variates were labelled 'size' (*V1*), 'established business' (*V2*), 'production drive and direction' (*V3*), 'degree of specialization' (*V4*), 'expansionist strategy drive' (*V5*) and 'human resources allocated to production' (*V6*).

In order to test for reliability, Cronbach's alpha was applied. An interactive method was used in which the variable that in a particular round test would increase alpha was deleted so reaching the maximum possible alpha for any vari-ate. The highest Cronbach's alpha in each variate is shown in Table 8.2 together with the variables that comprise it. The italicized variables in the second column are those standardized variables that were used to construct the final variates, while the non-italicized variables are those initially selected.

Having built the non-dimensional standardized variates, we then carried out a discriminant analysis. This was used as an exploratory tool in order to identify firm-specific factors that would discriminate between the 'most-compatible' and the 'least-compatible' groups of firms. An intermediate group was used to assess the accuracy of the discriminant function.

Three key assumptions were evaluated prior to the analysis: multivariate nor-mality of the independent variables, equality of covariance matrices for the groups under analysis, and the non-existence of collinearity among variables. The Kolmogorov–Smirnov test was applied to each variate, yielding a 5 per cent level of significance in relation to univariate normality fit. The risk of multi-collinearity was minimized through the use of varimax rotation, due to its ortho-gonality. One of the main validators was the hit ratio. A simultaneous estimation

Table 8.1   Variables associated with firm characteristics

Category	Variable no.	Chi-square	Sign	Degrees of freedom	Type[1]	Description
Time of activity / size / structure	1	1.92	0.38	2	M/C	Period of firm's activities (years)
	2	0.69	0.7	2	M/C	Number of employees
	3	0.48	0.49	1	C	Control by members of one family
	4	0.23	0.63	1	C	More than one family member in executive position
	5	0.13	0.72	1	M/C	Percentage of capital of country's origin
	6	0.63	0.43	1	C	Firm belongs to corporation
	7	0.13	0.72	1	C	Multinational corporation
	8	2.56	0.1	1	C	Substantial change in firm's ownership in last 10 years
	9	0.4	0.52	1	C	Operation in more than one location
	10	0.11	0.74	1	M/C	Number of locations of operations
	11	2.35	0.3	2	M/C	Turnover 1996 (GBP)
	12	3.23	0.19	2	M/C	Percentage turnover increase 1995–96
	13	0.15	0.92	2	M/C	Export revenue (percentage of turnover 1996)
	14	0.46	0.79	2	M/C	Imports revenue (percentage of turnover 1996)
	15	2.13	0.34	2	M/C	Long term debt (percentage of turnover 1996)
	16	0.68	0.87	3	M/C	Estimated expansion 1997–2001
Product / market / distribution	17	4.97	0.08	2	M/C	Percentage of the main product total sales
	18	0.2	0.9	2	M/C	Market share of main product
	19	1.28	0.25	1	C	Permanent channels of distribution
Human resources	20	0.62	0.73	2	C	Difficulty of contracting a marketing manager
	21	0.97	0.62	2	C	Difficulty of contracting a production manager
	22	1.41	0.49	2	C	Difficulty of contracting an R&D manager
	23	1.83	0.4	2	C	Difficulty of contracting specialized technicians
	24	0.21	0.9	2	C	Difficulty of contracting a sales manager

Table 8.1 Continued

Category	Variable no.	Chi-square	Sign	Degrees of freedom	Type[1]	Description
	25	1.17	0.55	2	C	Professionalization of board of directors
	26	0.4	0.52	1	C	Employment of foreign professionals
	27	3.37	0.33	3	M	Number of postgraduate employees
	28	1.07	0.78	3	M/C	Percentage of postgraduate employees
	29	1.76	0.41	2	M	Employees with degree
	30	0	1	2	M	Employees with secondary education
	31	1.9	0.38	2	M	Only R&D postgraduate employees
	32	5.7	0.05	2	M	Only R&D degree employees
	33	8.68	0.01	2	M/C	Percentage of degree R&D employees
	34	0.83	0.65	2	M	Only R&D secondary education employees
	35	0.42	0.51	1	M/C	Percentage of secondary level R&D employees
International strategy	36	0	1	1	C	International operations
	37	0.3	0.85	2	C	Type of international operations
	38	0.4	0.53	1	M/C	Number of target countries in EU
	39	1.9	0.39	2	M/C	Number of target countries outside EU
	40	1.09	0.29	1	C	Difficulties in assessing features of foreign partners
	41	0.9	0.34	1	C	Firm is self-sufficient in international procedures
	42	0.21	0.65	1	C	Advantages from emerging country
	43	0.42	0.52	1	C	Managerial interchange with foreign firms
Legal and political aspects	44	1.9	0.16	1	C	Existence of law department
	45	5.23	0.02	1	C	Existence of lobby
	46	0.48	0.49	1	C	Favouritism to country's firm
	47	4.73	0.03	1	C	Transfer of favouritism in case of an alliance
Strategic Planning	48	2.77	0.09	1	M	Time horizon of strategic planning
	49	0.91	0.82	3	C	Complexity of planning

[1] C = categorical, M = metric and M/C = metric recoded as categoric.

Table 8.2 Modified variates for discriminant analysis

Variate	Standardized variables [1]	Coefficient	Maximum Cronbach's alpha	Final variate designator
V1	Number of employees (0.94) turnover (0.93) etc Number of employees with doctorate (0.90) etc Existence of in-house legal dept. (0.59) etc Number of operational locations (0.63) etc	−0.54	0.98	Size
V2	Growth in turnover (per cent increase 1995–96) (0.88) etc Strategic planning time horizon (0.59) etc Length of time active (−0.43) etc Forecast expansion rate (0.61) etc Proportion of R&D employees with degree (0.44) etc	0.37	0.70	Established business
V3	Proportion of R&D employees without a degree (0.73) etc Number of target countries outside of the EU of strategic interest to the company (0.69) etc Recent substantial change in firm ownership (0.50) etc Lobbying groups close to legislator within sector (−0.31) etc Market share of main product (−0.38) etc	0.16	0.51	Production drive and direction
V4	Difficulty in contracting for an R&D manager (0.82) etc Difficulty in contracting for specialized technicians (0.77) etc	0.63	0.70	Degree of specialization
V5	Sales of main product as a proportion of total sales (−0.58) etc Perception that favouritism would be shown to LEM firm (0.70) etc Perception that alliance would be treated as a local firm by LEM government (−0.79) etc	0.86	0.65	Expansionist strategy drive
V6	Proportion of R&D employees with a degree etc	−0.53	n.a.	Human resources allocated to production
Hit ratio		75 per cent		
Function significance		0.013		

[1] Those variables comprising final variate are italicized. The loading in the rotated matrix is bracketed.

was used; the small number of variates involved, six, does not make stepwise estimation appropriate as data reduction was accomplished previously by factor analysis. The significance associated with the discriminating function responded quickly to an increase in the number of cases under examination. An interactive method was used, and Table 8.2 summarizes the results. The hit ratio (or classification accuracy) of 75 per cent is good. An independent measure of accuracy of the discriminant function is given by the intermediate group of firms. Considering the 12 cases (firms) left out in this group, seven were correctly classified (approximately 60 per cent).

RESULTS AND DISCUSSION

We now discuss our findings in terms of each of the six variates identified by the discriminant analysis, in order of explanatory power.

Expansionism

The variate $V5$, which was labelled 'expansionist strategy drive', has the strongest explanatory power. This finding suggests that, of those sampled, the developed-country firms most compatible with the Brazilian firms are those for which expansion, particularly international expansion, is of the greatest priority. This finding can be explained by considering the three variables that make up this variate: sales of main product as a proportion of total sales, the perception that the Brazilian partner would be favourably treated by its government, and the perception that an alliance would be treated as a local firm by the Brazilian authorities (with the implication that the foreign partner would be advantaged in some way by this favouritism). The similarity in the Pearson chi-squares indicates equivalence in the discriminatory power of these variables. As the variable 'sales of main product as a proportion of total sales' is a proxy measure of the concentration of sales in one product, our study reveals that firms with narrow product ranges are associated with more compatible alliance partners (half of the most compatible firms sampled generated 80 per cent or more of their sales from just a few product lines). This finding confirms the work of Steinmann *et al.* (1980), but is at odds with that of Stopford and Wells (1972). This suggests that large corporations differ from SMEs in this aspect. One possible explanation is that the large corporations examined by Stopford and Wells are able to draw on resources that are not comparable to those available to a SME. The SME will usually experience a resource constraint in their expansionist plans, even when these resources are dedicated to just a few product lines. Larger corporations will tend to be resource-constrained only when they diversify into new product lines or markets.

Firms dependent upon a very small number of product lines may be driven to target a number of national markets as a risk-reducing strategy or to minimize dependence on any one market. Indeed, this expansionist pressure is likely to be felt most acutely by companies that own just a few biotechnology patents, because they have only a limited time period in which to exploit their technological advantage. More managers (70 per cent) of the most compatible firms in our study also seem to place a high degree of importance on the benefits they think they would secure from the Brazilian government or local authorities through the alliance, the local alliance partner, or both, relative to entering that market alone. Of course, local government and other agencies have an important role to play in setting the rules for market access, the regulatory regime and other aspects of the local operating environment, especially in the biotechnology sectors of an LEM such as Brazil (Beamish, 1987). Of particular concern to technology owners will be the protection and enforcement of their intellectual property (IP) rights (especially patents and trademarks) in the LEM. It is common for developing countries to be weak in this regard, particularly in respect of judicial enforcement. Managers from developed-country firms may be especially keen to receive preferential treatment that might lead to a strengthening in the protection of their IP, such as, for example, a commitment by government to resolve disputes speedily or to uphold IP-related decisions by the courts. This role would be of particular concern to companies seeking market access for a single product line upon which its survival and future growth plans depend. This reinforces the influence of the product range variable in this study. Moreover, it is reasonable to assume that the most compatible firms may well already be investigating market possibilities in LEMs, including Brazil, and therefore may already be aware of the importance of preferential treatment that LEM governments tend to confer on alliances involving local parties.

Regarding the least compatible firms, our findings bolster our assertions regarding the characteristics of the most compatible firms. The least compatible firms show a tendency to offer a broader range of product lines than their more compatible counterparts, and are generally less aware of the importance of preferential treatment on the part of Brazilian agencies in shaping the local business environment for biotechnology-related activities.

Degree of Specialization

The second most important variate is termed the 'degree of specialization' (*V4*), and this refers to the ownership advantages and specialized knowledge within the firm. The importance of this variate is shown by its high coefficient in the discriminant analysis, although an independent cross-tabulation indicates a less than strong significance (0.19). This variate is made up of two variables relating to recruitment; the perceived difficulty in recruiting R&D managers and the perceived difficulty in recruiting specialized technicians. The most-compatible firms report less difficulty in recruiting such individuals than the least-compatible firms. Considered separately, the discriminatory power of these two variables is not strong, but their effect is much more evident when considered in combination. Initially, this finding appears counter-intuitive; one might expect companies that concentrate on a narrower range of products (as part of the discussion of variate *V5* above reveals) to find it less easy to recruit scientists with the requisite expertise in relevant or related areas.

However, two possible explanations can be envisaged. First, highly-specialized companies may be more likely than product-diversified companies to have developed deeper and more extensive personal and professional relationships with academics and researchers in universities and other research centres working in similar fields of activity. These personal networks can be used to identify pools of new and appropriately skilled R&D personnel. Second, because specialized companies are likely to follow more expansionist growth strategies, they may have to provide more attractive remuneration packages and prospects than companies offering a broader range of products. This may contribute to the comparative ease such firms experience when recruiting technical staff. Unfortunately, existing literature offers little guidance in this area. However, these results should be regarded as being of medium discriminatory power and are indicative only of a possible pattern to be verified by further research.

Firm Size

The variate 'size' (*V1*) consists of those variables that may be interpreted as relating to the managerial and financial resources of the sampled British and German firms, namely the number of employees, annual turnover (in 1996) and the number of employees educated to postgraduate level. Although this variate is associated with a high internal reliability (0.98), it presents only moderate explanation of the discriminant function variance, which is associated with a small loading (-0.22). The comprising variables *per se* do not present significant discriminant power. The analysis suggests that 'smaller' SME firms are more likely to be 'most compatible' than larger ones, and trends within each constituent variable strengthen this assertion. For instance, 30 per cent of the 'most-compatible' firms employ more than four postgraduate employees compared with 40 per cent of the 'least-compatible' firms, while 70 per cent of the 'most-compatible' firms employ less than three postgraduate employees compared to 60 per cent of the 'least-compatible' firms. Finally, 45 per cent of the 'most-compatible' firms had a turnover in 1996 of between £0.6 and £3.5 million compared with just 25 per cent for the 'least-compatible' firms. This finding can be interpreted as a resource-constraint issue. Smaller companies (within the category of SME), in terms of both their financial and managerial capacity, are less likely to have the capability to enter and develop foreign markets alone and, it follows, are more likely to wish to ally themselves with foreign partners in order to accomplish this. Nevertheless, the fact that this variate provides only weak explanatory power seems to confirm other research in this area, for example that of Reuber and Fischer (1997) who established that size is seldom associated with the internationalization capacity of the firm. A partial explanation for our finding may be that all the firms sampled could be classified as small and medium-sized and are therefore difficult to distinguish between in our analysis.

Production Human Resources

The variate *V6* was seen as representing 'human resources allocated to production'. It is composed of only one variable, namely the 'proportion of R&D employees with a degree'. This variable was considered by itself because of its high single discriminant power relative to other variables. However, in the discriminating function it has only weak discriminating power, suggesting that most of its variance is already explained by other variates. Within the 'least-compatible' group was a strong concentration of firms (over 75 per cent) reporting that the proportion of their R&D employees with a degree was in the range 11 to 40 per cent. For the 'most-compatible' firms this proportion was either below 10 per cent (in 9 out of 14 firms) or above 41 per cent (in 7 out of 9 firms). This finding is difficult to interpret from the perspective of the 'most-compatible' firms, but could indicate the existence of at least two subgroups in this category. Once again, the literature provides little direction regarding this point, and further investigation is required.

Production Drive and Established Business

We now turn our attention to two variates that have only weak explanatory power, namely 'production drive and direction' (*V3*) and 'established business' (*V2*). Regarding the first, this consists of four variables: the proportion of R&D employees without a degree, the number of countries outside the EU of strategic interest to the company, the occurrence of a recent substantial change in firm ownership, and the presence of lobbying groups close to the legislating agencies within a sector with which the respondent has had appreciable involvement. Of these, the most important discriminator between most and least-compatible firms is the latter variable, which is significant at the 5 per cent level. One possible explanation for this is as follows. Firms that proactively seek to engage with legislating agencies at home, either directly or indirectly, are likely to understand the importance of this activity in the foreign market where they will probably try to replicate this behaviour. Should this be the case, such firms will prefer to enter into an alliance that will take advantage of the stronger lobbying position of the local partner than would be possible if they developed that market alone.

The occurrence of a substantial change of ownership in the previous 10 years is also an important discriminator for the 'most-compatible' firms sampled (significant at the 10 per cent level). The reasons for this are unclear, although a change in ownership often brings with it a change in corporate culture, a change in the management team, or both. The new management team, or its surviving members, may exhibit a higher tolerance to the risks commonly associated with major strategic undertakings, as opposed to those managers who have operated within the same organizational structure or mindset for much longer periods of time. The two remaining variables that make up this variate, the proportion of R&D employees without a degree and the number of countries outside of the EU of strategic interest to the company, have only weak discriminatory power, and in effect seem to dilute the explanatory power of the two aforementioned variables contained within this variate. Nevertheless, the number of target countries outside the EU of strategic interest to the responding firms merits passing comment, being greater, as one might expect, for those firms that are 'most-compatible'.

Finally, the variate 'established business' ($V2$) has only poor explanatory power. This seems again to be corroborated, even if indirectly, by Reuber and Fischer (1997) who suggest that a firm's size and age (which are indicators of business establishment) do not influence a firm's internationalization capability. This variate comprises the variables 'growth in turnover' (the year-on-year increase from 1995 to 1996), and 'the time-horizon used by management in their strategic planning'. We find that firms with lower turnover growth rates and shorter time horizons belong to the 'most-compatible' group. This could be because firms experiencing low or declining turnover may have reached market saturation at home, or may be facing other domestic difficulties that necessitate a more outward-looking expansion strategy, for reactive reasons. Similarly, such firms may have a short time horizon in their strategic planning because they have to respond quickly to the volatility and dynamism of their operating environment, which itself is probably becoming more international in character, among other things. However, these are only tentative interpretations. As the variables are statistically not significant at the 10 per cent level, further research is needed in order to resolve the role of these variables in discriminating between more and least-compatible firms to an international strategic alliance.

CONCLUSIONS

Central to this chapter is the notion that one essential determinant of the future success of a strategic alliance lies in the match of expectations that participating firms have prior to entering into the agreement. It has been demonstrated that certain firm-specific characteristics can be linked to the potential for these expectations to be met. In other words, we find that firm-specific characteristics can indeed be associated with the degree to which potential alliance partners are compatible. Using factor analysis and discriminant analysis, this study identifies certain firm-specific characteristics that distinguish between most compatible and least compatible British and German biotechnology companies in the context of forging possible strategic alliances with LEM firms. We make this distinction by identifying and comparing variates – or groups of variables – and by using Brazil as an exemplar LEM country.

Of those sampled, firms that are identified as having a strong expansionist strategy, in general, are found to be more compatible with the Brazilian firms than those which did not. The same is found for companies that we identify as being more specialized, although this finding is not as strong. The size of the firm is also an important determinant of compatibility, although our findings are contrary to expectations. Our data suggests that smaller SMEs are more likely to be compatible with firms from LEMs than larger firms. The role of human resources allocated to production is also found to be a determinant, although its effect is unclear. This points to the need for further research. In our sample, the variates concerning production drive and direction and the role of the established business have only weak explanatory power. These findings confirm that firm-specific characteristics do seem to have non-trivial impacts upon the compatibility of the developed country firms with firms from a large emerging market when a strategic alliance is contemplated. In turn, this suggests that firm-specific characteristics will also impact on the viability of the strategic alliance once initiated, and certainly in the early stages of the arrangement.

Of course, the methodological approach adopted here is exploratory, and it would benefit from further refinement and testing, particularly in the context of other industries and countries. In particular, the relatively small number of firms surveyed could be a possible cause for the comparatively low number of significant results recorded. However, this study sets a path for future confirmatory research which, it is hoped, will lead to valuable results. Both the strong and the not so strong results could be quantitatively tested by further research on this topic. Nevertheless, this chapter introduces a novel approach to evaluating firm-specific factors and these are found, *ex-ante*, to contribute to the potential formation of viable strategic alliances.

Certain policy implications also arise from this study. In order to increase the likelihood that successful strategic alliances with developed-country firms in the biotechnology sector will be entered into, and to improve the chances that greater flows of technology through the alliance will then follow, our study suggests that LEM policy-makers should take into account firm-specific issues. In particular, they would be wise to design policies and promotion activity that is targeted at developed-country firms that are smaller, more specialized and, perhaps, more entrepreneurial, rather than, or in addition to, those that are larger and more established. This is because such firms are likely to be more compatible alliance partners for local companies than their larger counterparts, and are therefore more likely to enter into a viable arrangement, other things being equal. Strategic alliances, once established, will play an increasingly important role in facilitating the integration of LEMs such as Brazil into global commercial biotechnology markets, and will assist in promoting indigenous capabilities in this area. Policy-makers need to be more aware of the role and function that firm-specific characteristics play in determining whether or not partner expectations will be met. This in turn will help to determine the long-term prospects of the alliance and the volume of technology transferred from 'north' to 'south' through the alliance arrangement.

Appendix

Statistical procedure or test	Explanation
Spearman rank correlation	This test generates a coefficient that shows the association of two independent rankings (in our case rankings of the importance of potential partners' contributions to an alliance)
Cross tabulation	The main purpose of this is to visualize the variable potential for differentiating between the groups being compared
Pearson chi-square	A measure of the degree to which two variables are independent. In this analysis it is an indication of the discrimination potential of a variable; it compares observed and expected values in the cross tabulation's cells
Kaiser–Meyer–Olkin Measure of sampling adequacy	This tests the adequacy of the data to perform a factor analysis (a minimum value of 0.50 is recommended)
Bartlett test of sphericity	Tests the overall significance of all correlations within a correlation matrix
Data reduction through factor analysis	This is used here in an exploratory perspective in order to reduce the number of variables in the analysis; at the same time it indicates underlying dimensions through the grouping of highly correlated variables
Reliability testing through Cronbach's alpha	Tests the reliability of a set of two or more variables
Kolmogorov–Smirnov normality fit test	A univariate test of normality used in the modified factors or variates
Discriminant analysis	This is used here as an indicative tool to assess the discriminant potential of the variates deriving from the factor analysis

REFERENCES

Barkema, H.G. and Vermeulen, F. (1997) 'What Differences in the Cultural Backgrounds of Partners are Detrimental for International Ventures?', *Journal of International Business Studies*, 28 (4), 845–64.

Beamish, P.W. (1987) 'Strategic Alliances in LDCs: Partner Selection and Performance', *Management International Review*, 27 (1), 23–37.

Brouthers, K.D., Brouthers, L.E. and Wilkinson, T.J. (1995) 'Strategic Alliances: Choose your Partners', *Long Range Planning*, 28 (3), 18–25.

Buckley, P. and Casson, M. (1988) 'The Theory of Cooperation in International Business', in Contractor, F. and Lorange P. (eds), *Cooperative Strategies in International Business*, (Lexington, MA: Lexington Books) 31–4.

Buckley, P.J. (1996) 'Cooperative Forms of Transnational Corporation Activity', in United Nations, *Transnational Corporations and World Development* (London and Boston: ITBP on behalf of the UNCTAD Division on Transnational Corporations and Investment).

CODETEC-Companhia de Desenvolvimento Tecnológico (1991) *Patentes Farmacuticas*, (Campinas: Codetec), July, 74.

De Mattos, C. (1999) 'Biotechnology Alliances in Emerging Economies', University of Bradford, unpublished PhD dissertation.

De Mattos, C. and Sanderson, S. (2000) 'Expected Importance of Partners' Contributions to Alliances in Emerging Economies: a Review', University of Bradford Working Paper Series, (Working Paper 0004).

Dong, H., Buckley, P.J. and Mirza, H. (1997) 'International Joint Ventures in China from a Managerial Perspective: a comparison between Different Sources of Investment', in Chryssochoidis, G. Millar, C. and Clegg, J. (1997) *Internationalisation Strategies* (ch. 9), (New York: St Martin's Press).

Douglas, S.P. and Craig, C.S. (1989) 'Evolution of Global Marketing Strategy: Scale, Scope and Synergy', *The Columbia Journal of World Business*, 24 (3), 47–59.

Ernst Young, (1995) *European Biotech 95 – Gathering momentum*, industry annual report.

EU (1994) *Growth, Competitiveness, Employment – the challenges and ways forward into the 21st century*, White Paper.

Govindarajan, V. and Gupta, A. (2000) 'Analysis of the Emerging Global Arena', *European Management Journal*, 9, 361–74.

Gray, B.J. (1997) 'Profiling Managers to Improve Export Promotion Targeting', *Journal of International Business Studies*, 28 (2), 387–420.

Gunzel, D. (1975) *Das betriebswirtschaftliche Grossenproblem kleiner und mittlerer industrieller Unternehmen*, Gottingen, 106, cited in Steinmann *et al.* (1980).

'Conceptualizing the Internationalization process of Medium-sized firms: some preliminary considerations for a research design', 60.

Hair, J.F. *et al.*, (1998) *Multivariate Data Analysis* (5th edn) (New Jersey: Prentice Hall).

Hennart, J.F. (1988) 'A Transaction Costs Theory of Equity Joint Ventures', *Strategic Management Journal*, (9), 361–74.

Inkpen, A.C. (2001) 'Strategic Alliances', in Rugman, A. and Brewer, T.L. (eds), *The Oxford Handbook of International Business* (Oxford: Oxford University Press) (ch. 15).

Lorange, P. and Roos, J. (1993) *Strategic Alliances: Formation, Implementation and Evolution* (Oxford: Blackwell).

Moran, P. (1988) 'Personality Characteristics and Growth-orientation of the Small Business Owner-manager', *International Small Business Journal*, 16 (3), 17–38.

Raveed, S.R. and Renforth, W. (1983) 'State Enterprise – Multinational Corporation Strategic Alliances: How Well Do They Meet Both Partners' Needs?', *Management International Review*, 1.

Reuber, A.R. and Fischer, E. (1997) 'The Influence of the Management Team's International Experience on the Internationalization Behaviors of SMEs', *Journal of International Business Studies*, 28 (4), 807–25.

Saxton, T. (1997) 'The Effects of Partner and Relationship Characteristics on Alliance Outcomes', *Academy of Management Journal*, 40 (2), 443–61.

Shan, W. and Song, J. (1997) 'Foreign Direct Investment and the Sourcing of Technological Advantage: Evidence from the Biotechnology Industry', *Journal of International Business Studies*, 28 (2), 267–84.

Shan, W., Walker, G. and Kogut, B. (1994) 'Interfirm Cooperation and Startup Innovation in the Biotechnology Industry', *Strategic Management Journal*, 15, 387–94.

Simos, E.O. (2000) 'International Economic Outlook: The World Economy in 2009', *The Journal of Business Forecasting Methods and Systems*, 19 (3), 31–5.

Steinmann, H., Kumar, B. and Wasner, A. (1980) 'Conceptualizing the Internationalization Process of Medium-sized firms: Some Preliminary Considerations for a Research Design', *Management International Review*, 20 (1), 50–66.

Stopford, J.M. and Wells Jr., L.T. (1972) *Managing the Multinational Enterprise: Organization of the Firm and Ownership of the Subsidiaries* (New York: Basic Books).

Wolfensohn, J.D. (1997) 'The Challenge of Inclusion', President of the World Bank's address to the Board of Governors – 23 September, Hong Kong, China, mimeo.

9 Management of Internationalization Ventures: Should International Partners be 'Agents' or 'Stewards'?

Pavlos Dimitratos *

INTRODUCTION

In spite of the large number of studies in international business, the question of how firms can achieve superior performance in the international market-place is far from resolved. Many variables in a firm's internal and external environment may affect its international performance. The objective of the present study is also related to international performance since it concentrates on the features associated with effective management of internationalization ventures.

Numerous studies in the international business literature have dealt with relevant management aspects. However, researchers and practitioners may be bewildered by the findings of these studies. Apart from the fact that these findings are to a large extent contradictory (for example Geringer and Hebert, 1989; Leonidou, 1998; Delany, 2000), researchers have examined features related to international management by focusing on each international expansion mode category separately. International business scholars tend to disregard the fact that effective management of internationalization ventures may present some common success features, *regardless of whether the firm employs exporting, joint ventures or subsidiaries in its foreign markets.*

This study examines firms which employ any of the aforementioned categories of expansion modes. 'Best management practice' in internationalization ventures constitutes the focus of enquiry of this study. Specifically, the research objective in this chapter is to apply two theoretical frameworks of organization theory to the international management characteristics of successful firms, irrespective of the expansion mode employed. Towards this objective, this study employs a multi-perspective approach that embraces the agency and stewardship theories. The contribution of this research is the use of the two theories to explore a particular international business theme.

---

* The author would like to thank Stephen Young, Spyros Lioukas and Neil Hood for their constructive comments on earlier versions of this paper. The usual disclaimer applies.

Successfully internationalized Greek firms are investigated in this research. This examination offers some evidence on the theme of international management for firms based in a small country with a dynamic economy. Greece is a member of the EU, and has recently joined the Economic and Monetary Union (EMU) and entered the Eurozone. Boosted by the 2004 Olympic Games to be held in Athens, Greece's dynamic economy is expected to continue to grow at rates higher than the EU average (OECD, 2001).

The chapter is organized as follows. In the next section the theoretical foundations of the study are discussed, and in the third section the methodological aspects of the research are examined. In the fourth section information on the investigated firms is set out. In the fifth section, based on the evidence obtained, the findings related to the use of the agency and stewardship theories in the theme of effective management of internationalization ventures are analysed. This is accomplished by examining the interaction of the two theoretical frameworks in each of four recurring characteristics that distinguish effective management of internationalization ventures. In the concluding section, a synopsis is provided along with implications for researchers and practitioners.

LITERATURE REVIEW

The international business literature does not appear to provide a coherent account of what constitutes effective international management, regardless of the expansion mode employed. Specifically, the exporting literature commonly acknowledges that planning intensity and procedures (Samiee and Walters, 1990; Zou and Stan, 1998; Shoham, 1999), and control systems (Madsen, 1989; Bello and Gilliland, 1997) are positively related to export performance. A significant degree of attention has been paid to behavioural aspects affecting management of export enterprises, and it is generally accepted that smooth relations between the exporting firm and its agents or distributors, and provision of motivation and support to the partners, is a prerequisite of superior export performance (Styles and Ambler, 1994; Leonidou, 1998; Zou and Stan, 1998).

Numerous studies dealing with international joint ventures have examined various aspects associated with management of these partnerships. Choosing an appropriate partner is key to the venture's success (Harrigan, 1985; Devlin and Bleakley, 1988; Geringer, 1991). The joint-venture collaboration works best when the partner offers complementary resources (Killing, 1983; Harrigan, 1985; Geringer, 1991), and superior joint venture performance is connected with commitment to the collaboration and a minimal level of conflict between the partners (Blodgett, 1992; Hyder and Ghauri, 1993). Contradictory findings are obtained on the optimal decision-making discretion that should be given to foreign partners and the types of control to use while collaborating with them (Killing, 1983; Lee and Beamish, 1995; *cf.* Glaister and Buckley, 1998).

The literature on multinationals does not provide an unambiguous viewpoint on the role of subsidiaries in the management of international operations by the multinational firm (Birkinshaw and Hood, 1998; Delany, 2000). Customarily it was presumed that the headquarters of a multinational is the strategic centre in which decision-making authority is located and the subsidiaries are essentially subordinate entities which follow orders from the headquarters (Vernon, 1966; White and Poynter, 1984). Nevertheless, increasingly researchers have been questioning this leading role of the headquarters. It is acknowledged that subsidiaries may implement their own 'subsidiary strategy' (Prahalad and Doz, 1981) in an internationally 'interorganizational network' (Ghoshal and Bartlett, 1991), in which they may also serve as 'centres of excellence' (Forsgren and Pedersen, 1998; Holm and Fratocchi, 1998). Nevertheless, multinationals share different philosophies and cultures, and pursue global or multidomestic strategies in industries with varying levels of customer and competitor demands. Taking this into consideration, it not surprising that there is no accord in the related literature on how much decision-making authority should rest with the subsidiaries.

In order to illuminate success features in the management patterns of all types of internationalized firms, a theoretical background is required which can potentially have an all-embracing applicability. Towards this objective, two theoretical frameworks of organization theory, namely the agency and stewardship theories are employed. The use of *agency theory* is dictated by the consideration that in order to achieve its goals in the foreign market, the internationalized firm (the principal) has to delegate responsibilities to export agents, export intermediaries, joint-venture partners or subsidiaries (the agents). This theory posits that because of these partners' differing goals and attitudes towards risk, the collaborating parties may prefer dissimilar courses of action. Consequently, the principal has to make sure that the agent behaves in the principal's best interests (Jensen and Meckling, 1976; Eisenhardt, 1989a). The agency theory has been used to explain collaborative patterns of behaviour in firms which employ exporting (for example Karunaratna and Johnson, 1997), joint ventures (see Peng, 2000) and subsidiaries (see Roth and O' Donnell, 1996) to expand abroad.

Stewardship theory is used because it assumes that partners can act like stewards rather than agents. Stewards may act for the benefit of the collaboration rather than their own organizational objectives, which presupposes that stewards place greater utility in cooperative rather than self-serving behaviour (Davis *et al.*, 1997). The stewardship theory does not appear to have been implemented in any empirical study in international business. Although Davis *et al.* (1997) admit that this theoretical framework has received little empirical verification, it can potentially help understand the management of internationalization ventures in conjunction with agency theory. This can be especially true since in the international marketplace firms are involved in a web of networks where various principal–agent or principal–steward relations can evolve, depending on which dyad is considered (see O' Donnell, 2000).

In short, the agency and stewardship theories may provide useful tools to identify success features in the planning, implementation and control processes of internationalized firms. These two theories have not been used collectively so far in any study of international management, and this chapter explores whether this multi-perspective approach can provide an effective avenue of research in international business.

METHODOLOGY

Case studies across 12 successfully internationalized Greek firms were undertaken in this study, a methodology which provides a dynamic and holistic view of the phenomenon under investigation (Yin, 1989). The data-collection methods used were comprehensive interviews with knowledgeable managers of these firms, and examination of company documents and archival data. The collected data were content-analysed.

The firms had to meet the following four criteria in order to be included in the study: (a) they should be independent Greek firms; (b) they should be manufacturing firms since internationalized Greek firms are normally manufacturers of goods rather than service providers; (c) they should have outward international activities, that is market their products abroad, for at least the last six years (1993–98); the year 1993 was selected as it was considered to be a turning point for the international operations of many Greek firms for two main reasons: the opening of Southeast European markets and the increasing unification of the European market in the early 1990s, two events which set off numerous internationalization ventures for many Greek firms in the last decade; and (d) they should have achieved superior international performance for the last four years (1995–98). Superior international performance was determined by: growth of at least 30 per cent in (the absolute volume of) international sales during this period; and an international sales ratio of at least 50 per cent in each of the four years during this period. The international sales ratio is expressed as the percentage of international company sales over total company sales.

Since the present study sought to examine firms with superior international performance, international sales growth of 30 per cent was believed to be a reliable cut-off point for the inclusion of companies. This is due to the fact that the growth of international sales of Greek firms during the 1994–96 period was reported to be 21.5 per cent (Athens University of Economics and Business, 2000). As far as the international sales ratio is concerned, a 50 per cent cut-off point was selected in order to investigate firms that assigned primary significance to international markets. No profit measures were used to capture international performance, because firms were either unable or reluctant to provide information on the profitability of their internationalization ventures.

After applying the above four criteria, 12 firms were randomly selected and agreed to cooperate in the study by providing interview time and releasing required information. Twelve cases were used for reasons of cost, time and theoretical saturation. Theoretical saturation is reached when no additional learning from the research is acquired (Eisenhardt, 1989b).

Data collection was carried out in four stages. In the first stage, an in-depth interview was conducted with the best-informed manager of the firm's international operations. All interviews were transcripted. To ensure that no misinterpretation took place, the transcript of each interview was returned to the manager a few days after the meeting. In the second stage, a second interview with the same respondent was organized to illuminate the points that were unclear during the first interview. In addition, this respondent was asked to identify another manager of the firm who was also involved in the management of international operations. This was considered essential because management of internationalization ventures is typically the responsibility of more than one person. Therefore, in the third stage, a second interviewee was asked to answer the same questions, and this interview was again transcripted. Each of the interviews lasted between one-and-a-half and two hours. In the fourth stage, investigation of company documents and archival data occurred.

The interviews were based on a semi-structured questionnaire addressing key issues related to planning, implementation and control processes of internationalization ventures. Managers were asked to comment on their perceived satisfaction with the internationalization ventures as well as on their perception of the impact that management styles, methods and systems used had on international performance. They were also asked to recollect past successful and unsuccessful events in the management of the internationalization ventures. The search for 'best management practice' in internationalization ventures was largely directed at themes and key issues extracted from the relevant literature. Research studies outlined in the previous section of this paper were instrumental in formulating questions concerning planning, implementation and control between international partners and/or subsidiaries as well as locus of decision-making authority. The agency and stewardship theories provided the conceptual underpinnings of the questionnaire.

THE FIRMS EXAMINED

The investigated firms belong to the food, beverages, garments, textiles, metal products, plastics, and chemical sectors. The level of sales ranged from 0.5 to 46 million euros and the number of employees from 30 to 440. All examined firms perceive international markets as very important to their business operations. They have at least nine years international experience and market their products in up to 20 foreign countries. Their international sales have increased at a rate of at least 34 per cent during the four-year period 1995–98, while their average annual international sales ratio ranges from 55 per cent to 100 per cent in the same time.

All managers in this research were convinced that, *ceteris paribus*, their management styles, methods and systems had a major contribution to their superior international performance. In relation to the modes of international expansion, the firms use exporting through agents or intermediaries, majority equity joint ventures as well as wholly-owned subsidiaries. Nevertheless, even if they use joint ventures or subsidiaries to achieve market presence abroad, exports from Greece continue to supplement their international sales.

In the remaining part of this chapter, 'focal companies' are defined as the internationalized firms which are based in the home country and expand in foreign markets through any kind of international expansion mode. Furthermore, 'partners' are defined as the firms or business entities that cooperate in the internationalization ventures. Therefore, partners may be: the focal company and its export agents; the focal company and its export intermediaries; the focal company and its joint venture partners; or, the focal company and its subsidiaries.

DISCUSSION OF FINDINGS

The exploratory evidence from this study suggests that four features associated with the application of agency and stewardship theories emerge as key characteristics of effective management of internationalization ventures. These four features are: (a) consensus on the objectives and strategy of the internationalization venture between partners; (b) a 'situational' decision-making approach which allows the most knowledgeable partner to carry out the decision at each instance; (c) provision of appropriate incentives to partners; and (d) suitable measurement of performance achieved by partners.

These four features transcend the planning, implementation and control processes associated with management of internationalization ventures. It appears that these characteristics are strongly interrelated dimensions which firms have to work upon and nurture in order to achieve superior performance when managing their internationalization ventures. The extent to which all characteristics reinforce each other appears to be a critical dimension of success. Both theoretical frameworks, namely the agency and stewardship theories can illuminate the four features of effective management with varying degrees of success.

Consensus on Objectives and Strategy

Partners in different countries have to agree on the specific goals and strategy that will be pursued in the foreign market. This proposition is compatible with findings of studies examining associations between specific goal-setting and performance (Locke and Latham, 1990; Terpstra and Rozell, 1994). Implementation of this feature also presupposes that firms from different countries learn each other's cultural modes of business thinking and communication (Hamel *et al.*, 1989; Parkhe, 1991), which is an argument that emerges repeatedly from the findings of this study. In essence, consensus on specific objectives and strategy would make international management easier. This is why arriving at such a consensus appears to be a *sine qua non* of effective management of internationalization ventures.

Reaching an agreement on objectives and strategy applies also to the internationalization ventures of firms which use their own subsidiaries to expand abroad. As the findings of this research suggest, even when a firm employs its own subsidiary in a foreign country, diffusion of the headquarters' objectives and strategy is not free of problems. This is associated with the proposition that power struggles within organizations is a ubiquitous phenomenon (Pfeffer, 1981).

The findings of this study also suggest that partners favour agreement on the approved goals and strategy with a view to collaboration in the long run. This is compatible with the contention that effective collaboration between partners in international business is based on long-term relations and continuity (Dyer and Chu, 2000). Partners may better understand each other's patterns of behaviour through such long-term interactions (Sohn, 1994). *The existence of this characteristic appears to be at odds with agency theory* that would posit that an opportunistic behaviour could have rendered a long-run harmonious relationship between the focal company and its partners abroad impossible.

In contrast, stewardship theory argues that such behaviour is expected because international partners are long-term, rather than short-term-oriented, and favour trust rather than monitoring mechanisms. This is especially true given the fact that success in the international market is likely to be accomplished in the long run (see for example Karafakioglu, 1986; Zahra *et al.*, 2001). Therefore, *the presence of this success feature is in accord with stewardship theory*.

'Situational' Decision-Making Approach

Neither the focal company nor its partners have perfect knowledge on all issues regarding the venture abroad. The findings from the study suggest that ultimate decision-making discretion has to rest with the partner who possesses the best and most specific knowledge on the particular problem or situation concerning the internationalization venture. This appears to be the case not only for operational decisions, but also for decisions which are more strategic in nature within the context of agreed objectives. Therefore, it seems that the Greek firms investigated in this study follow neither a centralized nor a decentralized decision-making mode in their internationalization ventures. This can be at odds with a widespread belief in the management literature which argues in favour of a decentralised mode of decision-making (see Pfeffer, 1998).

With agency theory it is expected that the decision-making authority would always be with the principal, that is the focal company. Viewed in this light, *this finding seems to contradict the underlying principle of agency theory* that the role of the principal is central in controlling the agent's opportunistic behaviour. *This finding appears to be compatible with the rationale of stewardship theory* which argues that the partner can be a steward of the goals of the collaboration and look for utility in collective behaviour rather than maximisation of its own benefit (Davis *et al.*, 1997). It seems that the partner in the foreign market may have such a strong interest in pursuing the agreed common objectives that it can use unreservedly all its specific knowledge to attain these objectives. In essence, the motives and behaviours of the steward may be strongly aligned with those of the principal.

Provision of Incentives to Partners

The third interrelated success characteristic of the management of internationalization ventures is provision of suitable motivation mechanisms to encourage partners to implement the agreed course of action. The evidence from this study suggests that incentive schemes appear to provide significant motivation to the partners involved as long as they are tailor-made to their individual demands across foreign countries.

In addition, most interviewed managers admit that both fixed (for example a 'flat' remuneration scheme) and pay-for-performance schemes (such as bonuses achieved for additional sales abroad) employed to influence action are important, but the latter appear to be mostly valued by international partners. *This pattern of behaviour seems to contradict the stewardship theory and is consistent with agency theory.* Well-designed and clearly communicated incentives are used to guard against opportunistic behaviour and are primary control mechanisms in agency theory. Also, this theory proposes that pay-for-performance or 'outcome-based' incentives are likely to make the agent behave in the interests of the principal (Eisenhardt, 1989a), in line with the partner behaviour observed in this study.

Suitable Measurement of Partner Performance

The evidence from this study suggests that on a systematic and timely basis focal companies have to be informed how their partners perform; that is, what are the partners' contributions towards the objectives of the internationalization venture. Along with the other success features, performance measurement is key to effective management of internationalization ventures. The evidence from this study also suggests that supporting information and communication systems are vital to suitable performance measurement associated with internationalization ventures.

Inasmuch as suitable measurement of partner performance can serve as a monitoring mechanism, *its existence essentially validates the rationale of the agency theory* which suggests that scrutiny of behaviour is significant in ensuring that the international partner behaves in the focal company's best interests. *The presence of this feature appears to weaken the predictive power of stewardship theory.* In fact, such a controlling mechanism can be counterproductive since it may weaken the pro-partnership behaviour of the steward by lessening its motivation (Argyris, 1964).

In addition, the evidence from the study suggests that Greek focal companies do not measure performance based only on aspects that are easy to gauge (such as contribution to sales) without taking non-quantifiable dimensions (for example contribution to networking gains) into consideration. Compatible with agency theory, the principal would use different types of performance measurement depending on how measurable the expected outcome is. Focusing solely on quantifiable indicators to gauge performance can lead to erroneous conclusions as far as the contribution of partners to the goals of the internationalization venture is concerned. This argument also emphasises that appropriate performance measurement of partners in foreign countries is a difficult task to achieve.

CONCLUSIONS

This research based on 12 successfully internationalized Greek firms has provided some tentative evidence related to characteristics of effective management of internationalization ventures. Unlike past studies, the present research examined aspects of planning, implementation and control processes seeking commonalities across international expansion modes. Four recurring and interrelated success features relevant to the employed multi-perspective approach were identified and discussed. These are: (a) consensus on specific objectives and long-term strategy; (b) a 'situational' decision-making approach, depending on which partner has the best and most specialized knowledge on the particular issue; (c) provision of appropriate pay-for-performance and fixed schemes for those that make the decisions; and (d) suitable measurement of performance in order to ensure that those who implement the decisions are properly awarded. *Ceteris paribus*, the firms consider these features as aspects that considerably affect international performance.

The study's contribution for researchers is that it uses the agency and stewardship theories to show that their synthesis in a multi-perspective approach can provide valuable insights into the management of internationalization ventures and that this offers a promising avenue of research in international business. To a significant extent, the existence of the first two characteristics corroborates the rationale of the stewardship theory whereas the presence of the last two characteristics strengthens the logic of the agency theory. Consequently, this study provides some evidence that the agency and stewardship theories can effectively coexist and complement one another. This argument is consistent with the reasoning of proponents of stewardship theory (Donaldson and Davis, 1994; Davis *et al.*, 1997). The inclusion of stewardship theory appears essential in the examination of increasingly interconnected networks in the international marketplace. Nevertheless, it should be noted that the 'coexistence' of the two theoretical frameworks may be restricted to the particular type of firms investigated. In other words, firms that are less successful in their internationalization ventures may follow an international management pattern that would be better explained by different 'combinations' of agency and stewardship theories.

The study's contribution for practitioners is that it offers some 'best practice' evidence on how to manage a firm's internationalization ventures. International partners should be both 'agents' and 'stewards' in order for superior performance to be attained. Focal companies can view the four characteristics as constituents of a success framework in which each one relies on the existence and strengthening of the others. Internationalized firms have to consider that a holistic treatment of this framework may require continuing efforts and emphasis on lasting processes and long-term results. In order for firms to develop and strengthen concomitantly the four success characteristics and effectively manage their internationalization ventures, they may have to devise novel ways to reconfigure their business processes and decision-making modes.

REFERENCES

Argyris, C. (1964) *Integrating the Individual and the Organization* (New York: Wiley).

Athens University of Economics and Business (2000) '*Export and Internationalization Strategies of Greek Firms*', Unpublished research report (in Greek) (Athens, Greece: Research Centre).

Bello, D.C. and Gilliland, D.I. (1997) 'The Effect of Output Controls, Process Controls, and Flexibility on Export Channel Performance', *Journal of Marketing*, 61 (1), 22–38.

Birkinshaw, J. and Hood, N. (1998) 'Multinational Subsidiary Evolution: Capability and Charter Change in Foreign-owned Subsidiary Companies', *Academy of Management Review*, 23, 773–95.

Blodgett, L.L. (1992) 'Factors in the Instability of International Joint Ventures: An Event History Analysis', *Strategic Management Journal*, 13, 475–81.

Davis, J.H., Schoorman, F.D. and Donaldson, L. (1997) 'Toward a Stewardship Theory of Management', *Academy of Management Review*, 22, 20–47.

Delany, E. (2000) 'Strategic Development of the Multinational Subsidiary through Subsidiary initiative-taking', *Long Range Planning*, 33, 220–44.

Devlin, G. and Bleakley, M. (1988) 'Strategic Alliances – Guidelines for Success', *Long Range Planning*, 21, 18–23.

Donaldson, L. and Davis, J.H. (1994) 'Boards and Company Performance – Research Challenges the Conventional Wisdom', *Corporate Governance: An International Review*, 2, 151–60.

Dyer, J.H. and Chu, W. (2000) 'The Determinants of Trust in Supplier-Automaker Relationships in the U.S., Japan, and Korea', *Journal of International Business Studies*, 31, 259–85.

Eisenhardt, K.M. (1989a) 'Agency Theory: An Assessment and Review', *Academy of Management Review*, 14, 57–74.

Eisenhardt, K.M. (1989b) 'Building Theories from Case Study Research', *Academy of Management Review*, 14, 532–50.

Forsgren, M. and Pedersen, T. (1998) 'Are there any Centres of Excellence among Foreign Owned firms in Denmark?', in Birkinshaw J. and Hood N. (eds), *Multinational Evolution and Subsidiary Development* (London: Macmillan).

Geringer, J.M. (1991) 'Strategic Determinants of Partner Selection Criteria in International Joint Ventures', *Journal of International Business Studies*, 22, 41–62.

Geringer, J.M. and Hebert, L. (1989) 'Control and Performance of International Joint Ventures', *Journal of International Business Studies*, 20, 235–54.

Ghoshal, S. and Bartlett, C.A. (1991) 'The Multinational Corporation as an Interorganizational Network', *Academy of Management Review*, 15, 603–25.

Glaister, K.W. and Buckley, P.J. (1998) 'Management–Performance Relationships in UK Joint Ventures', *International Business Review*, 7, 235–57.

Hamel, G., Doz, Y.L. and Prahalad, C.K. (1989) 'Collaborate with your Competitors – and Win', *Harvard Business Review*, 67 (1), 133–39.

Harrigan, K.R. (1985) *Strategies for Joint Venture Success* (Lexington, MA: Lexington Books).

Holm, U. and Fratocchi, L. (1998) 'Centres of Excellence in the International Firm', in Birkinshaw, J. and Hood, N. (eds), *Multinational Evolution and Subsidiary Development* (London: Macmillan).

Hyder, S.A. and Ghauri, P.N. (1993) 'Joint Venture Relationship between Swedish Firms and Developing Countries: A Longitudinal Study', in Buckley, P.J. and Ghauri, P.N. (eds), *The Internationalization of the Firm: A Reader* (London: Academic Press).

Jensen, M.C. and Meckling, W. (1976) 'Theory of the Firm: Managerial Behaviour, Agency Costs and Ownership Structure', *Journal of Financial Economics*, 3, 305–60.

Karafakioglu, M. (1986) 'Export Activities of Turkish Manufacturers', *International Marketing Review*, 3 (4), 34–43.

Karunaratna, A.R and Johnson, L.W. (1997) 'Initiating and Maintaining Export Channel Intermediary Relationships', *Journal of International Marketing*, 5 (2), 11–32.

Killing, J.P. (1983) *Strategies for Joint Venture Success* (New York: Praeger).

Lee, C. and Beamish, P.W. (1995) 'The Characteristics and Performance of Korean Joint Ventures in LDCs', *Journal of International Business Studies*, 26, 637–54.

Leonidou, L.C. (1998) 'Organizational Determinants of Exporting: Conceptual, Methodological, and Empirical Insights', *Management International Review*, 38 (1), special issue, 7–52.

Locke, E.A. and Latham, G.P. (1990) *A Theory of Goal Setting and Task Performance* (Englewood Cliffs, NJ: Prentice Hall).

Madsen, T.K. (1989) 'Successful Export Marketing Management: Some Empirical Evidence', *International Marketing Review*, 6 (4), 41–57.

O' Donnell, S.W. (2000) 'Managing Foreign Subsidiaries: Agents of Headquarters, or an Independent Network?', *Strategic Management Journal*, 21, 525–48.

OECD (Organization for Economic Co-operation and Development) (2001) *Economic Surveys – Greece*.

Parkhe, A. (1991) 'Interfirm Diversity, Organizational Learning, and Longevity in Global Strategic Alliances', *Journal of International Business Studies*, 22, 579–601.

Peng, M.W. (2000) 'Controlling the Foreign Agent: How Governments Deal with Multinationals in a Transition Economy', *Management International Review*, 40 (2), 141–65.

Pfeffer, J. (1981) *Power in Organizations* (Marshfield, MA: Pitman).

Pfeffer, J. (1998) 'Seven Practices of Successful Organizations', *California Management Review*, 40 (2), 96–124.

Prahalad, C.K. and Doz, Y.L. (1981) 'An Approach to Strategic Control in MNCs', *Sloan Management Review*, 22 (4), 5–13.

Roth, K. and O' Donnell, S. (1996) 'Foreign Subsidiary Compensation Strategy: An Agency Theory Perspective', *Academy of Management Journal*, 39, 678–703.

Samiee, S. and Walters, P.G.P. (1990) 'Influence of Firm Size on Export Planning and Performance', *Journal of Business Research*, 20, 235–48.

Shoham, A. (1999) 'Bounded Rationality, Planning, Standardization of International Strategy, and Export Performance: A Structural Model Examination', *Journal of International Marketing*, 7 (2), 24–50.

Sohn, J.H.D. (1994) 'Social Knowledge as a Control System: A Proposition of Evidence from the Japanese FDI Behaviour', *Journal of International Business Studies*, 25, 295–324.

Styles, C. and Ambler, T. (1994) 'Successful Export Practice: The U.K. Experience', *International Marketing Review*, 11 (6), 23–47.

Terpstra, D.E. and Rozell, E.J. (1994) 'The Relationship of Goal Setting to Organizational Profitability', *Group and Organization Management*, 19, 285–94.

Vernon, R. (1966) 'International Investments and International Trade in the Product Cycle', *Quarterly Journal of Economics*, 80, 190–207.

White, R.E. and Poynter, T.A. (1984) 'Strategies for Foreign-owned Subsidiaries in Canada', *Business Quarterly*, 49 (2), 59–69.

Yin, R.K. (1989) *Case Study Research – Design and Methods* (Newbury Park, CA: Sage).

Zahra, S., Hayton J., Marcel, J. and O' Neill, H. (2001) 'Fostering Entrepreneurship during International Expansion: Managing Key Challenges', *European Management Journal*, 19 (4), 359–69.

Zou, S. and Stan, S. (1998) 'The Determinants of Export Performance: A Review of the Empirical Literature between 1987 and 1997', *International Marketing Review*, 15 (5), 333–56.

10 The De-Internationalization Process: A Case Study of Marks and Spencer

Kamel Mellahi

INTRODUCTION

The increased internationalization of business has made internationalization an important research topic. However, by and large, theories of the internationalization of the firm have focused on one side of the coin – the internationalization process – and have tended to ignore the de-internationalization process (Caves, 1995; Hadjikhani and Johanson, 1996; Benito and Welch, 1997; Matthyssens and Pauwels, 2000; Burt *et al.*, 2002). The lack of research into the de-internationalization process may be attributed to three factors; the stigma of failure associated with de-internationalization (Bower, 1970; Caves, 1995, p. 20); international firms themselves wipe failed international activities from their record books or public memory (Burt *et al.*, 2002); and personnel in the host country often move after de-internationalization and neither they nor the artifacts remain to inform researchers (Burt *et al.*, 2002). Consequently, we know remarkably little about how firms de-internationalize, particularly the management of the de-internationalization process. This study deals with the process of de-internationalization in response to crisis at home and abroad.

This chapter helps address the gap in the de-internationalization literature by investigating the *process* of de-internationalization. Using the case of Marks and Spencer's (M&S) withdrawal from continental Europe, this study seeks to first understand the process, and second to explore the interaction between the organization and its wider operating environment.

De-internationalization is a 'significant phenomenon' in international business (Boddewyn, 1979, p. 22), and is arguably more complicated than the internationalization process (Nees, 1978–79). It involves numerous variables at multiple levels of analysis (Boddewyn, 1983; Ghertman, 1987) including hostile political actors (Hadjikhani and Johanson, 1996). Research on divestment by international firms (Nees, 1978–79; Boddewyn, 1983; Ghertman, 1987) shows that choosing the wrong strategy, or implementing the correct strategy poorly can increase the cost of exit or jeopardize the whole strategy. As such, improved understanding of the de-internationalization process will not only provide theoretical contributions towards a more complete theory of the internationalization of the firm, but will also have practical implications for firms aiming to de-internationalize.

THE MEANING OF 'DE-INTERNATIONALIZATION'?

At the very outset, there are clearly definitional issues to be resolved. Different terms have been used in the literature, for example international divestment and closure (Boddewyn, 1983; Ghertman, 1987), and de-internationalization (Benito and Welch, 1997; Burt *et al.*, 2002). Benito and Welch (1997, p. 8) note that 'de-internationalization refers to any voluntary or forced actions that reduce a company's engagement in or exposure to current cross-border activities'. A short-coming of this definition is that it focuses specifically on the initial decision-making stage and does not take into account the implementation process after the decision has been taken. As a result, it ignores the influence of the institutional actors and the environment on the de-internationalization process. It is argued that any working definition should encompass the latter, and also that de-internationalization is an intentional, proactive management strategy to cut back international activities. This voluntary de-internationalization could be caused by a search for productivity and efficiency, whether in response to organizational decline at home or abroad, or as a means of enhancing corporate profitability under non-decline conditions. Thus, we propose that de-internationalization is the voluntary *process* of decreasing involvement in international operations in response to organizational decline at home or abroad, or as a means of enhancing corporate profitability under non-crisis conditions.

LITERATURE REVIEW

Over the last three decades, some attempts have been made to study de-inter-nationalization and some progress has been made. However, as far as the de-internationalization *process* is concerned, this body of research suffers from three limitations. First, explicitly or implicitly, in much of the research on de-internationalization, researchers have adopted a rational economic perspec-tive, to model, predict and explain the *occurrence* of a firm's exit from inter-national arenas (Shapiro, 1993). This is particularly true in the research stream which attempts to link modes of entry and post-entry strategies with the like-lihood of exit (Li, 1995; Benito, 1997; Chang and Singh, 1999; and Mata and Portugal, 2000). Second, the small number of recent studies that have attempted to examine the de-internationalization phenomenon itself have focused on the causes and motives of de-internationalization (Benito and Welch, 1997; Richbell and Watts, 2000; and Burt *et al.*, 2002), de-internationalization barriers (Karakaya, 2000), forced withdrawal from international markets (Akhtar and Choudhry, 1993), exit due to turbulence in the home market (Hadjikhani and Johanson, 1996) and the psychological phenomenon and process of international market-exit (Matthyssens and Pauwels, 2000). Although much in the above-cited research stresses the importance of studying the de-internationalization *process*, the latter is described only occasionally. Third, most attempts that seek to investigate the de-internationalization process (*Business International*, 1976; Marois and Jourde, 1977; Nees, 1978–79; Grunberg, 1981; Boddewyn, 1983; Ghertman, 1987), are dated, and one could argue that during the last 20 years international managers and consultants have learned a great deal about the de-internationalization process. Further, although this body of research provides much needed information and insights about the de-internationalization process during the 1970s and early 1980s, it did not study the de-internationalization process by firms under crisis (Ghertman, 1987).

More relevant to the present research are the factors influencing international divestment and exit. While the process of within-country divestment and exit has been explored in some depth in the literature (see for example Porter, 1976; Nargundkar *et al.*, 1996), the dynamics and effects of different and complex contexts and different national cultures on international exit as a field of study are not fully understood. By ignoring the spatial context within which a firm operates, generalization of findings from the 'within-country' exit and divestment literature are hard to justify, and they are even tougher to uphold across international, institutional and cultural borders. For instance, past research showed that foreign barriers to exit are lower than national barriers (Boddewyn, 1983), and Boddewyn argues that there is a 'distance of psychological detachment' when executing a divestment decision abroad. The findings of past research are summarized in four points: first, economic factors, and more particularly financial factors, predominate when it comes to explaining divestment (*Business International*, 1976; Boddewyn, 1979); second, several studies emphasize the importance of the 'new man' in initiating the process (for example Gilmour, 1973; Tornneden, 1975); third, foreign divestment review is usually conducted at the behest of the parent company unknown to the foreign subsidiary (Boddewyn, 1979); and fourth, attempts were also made to examine the impact of advance notice in international closures and suggest that while advance notice could reduce resistance by employees and other interest groups to the closure, it could also shake the confidence of financial institutions, precipitating a spiral of decline in production (McDermott, 1989, p. 15).

RESEARCH METHOD

This research uses a case-study approach to examine an individual situation, with the intention of gaining insights into the process of de-internationalization. The study is based on textual analysis of a large set of publicly available secondary data: the secondary sources of data include interviews with a variety of actors including top management, union representatives, government officials and employees during and after the start of the process; the company's press releases, national and professional newspaper articles and studies, and court cases against the company. This was not a small task since the M&S withdrawal from continental Europe was highly publicized and chronicled in detail by popular and professional press. Bevan (2001, p. 186) reported that since 1988 M&S has been mentioned in the UK press more than 1000 times a month, and during the first 10 days after the announcement of the de-internationalization process M&S were mentioned 60 times in the *Financial Times* alone.

THE CASE STUDY

The trajectory of the de-internationalization process of M&S from launch to closure is set out in the case study.

The Context and Planning Stage

In 1998, M&S faced a crisis that threatened its very survival. Prior to the crisis, M&S had been one of the most successful British retailing companies; by 1998 the business had retail sales of almost £8 billion, traded from almost 500 M&S stores around the world, and owned Brooks Brothers and King's Supermarkets in the United States. In 1998, M&S hit a crisis when the previously continuous growth of the company stopped and subsequently went into decline (for a review of the causes of the crisis see Bevan, 2001 and Mellahi *et al.*, 2002). Between 1998 and 2001, there was a massive decline in pre-tax profits from £1.15 billion to £0.14 billion. Mellahi *et al.*'s (2002) study of the causes of M&S crisis reported that during the early stage of the crisis the internal culture, the personality, values and characteristics of the decision-maker(s) left a strong imprint on its strategic behaviour towards the crisis. After the crisis in 1998, the company's history and its embedded management culture restricted management capacity to enact strategic change (Bevan 2001; Mellahi *et al.*, 2002). Mellahi *et al.* (2002) argue that because top management helped design the strategies that caused the failure, it made them reluctant to admit openly their failure. Additionally, M&S stuck to its previous routine procedures and commitment to international expansion as evidenced by large-scale modernization of its European branches in the late 1990s.

In an attempt to turn around the company, M&S in January 2000 appointed a new chief executive, Luc Vandevelde, who had previously worked for Promodes, a French multinational with stores in 13 countries. A condition of the new Chairman's contract was that the company would be turned around in two years. During early 2000, top management was composed of both new 'outsiders' focusing on internal processes and promoting radical change and willing to question the company's international ambitions, and 'old insiders' promoting continuity and commitment to international activities. The new Chairman described the recovery plan that emerged during this period as

> not good enough to address the real problems of the company...the plan was like feeding a tree that was already overgrown and unhealthy. What it really needed was serious pruning back. Having reached this conclusion, my next step was to appoint a new team (Vandevelde, 2001).

This was a turning point in the company's history; the concept of international retrenchment started taking over from international expansion.

Differences between new 'external' top managers and longer-tenured 'internal' top managers resulted in divergent perceptions of the causes of organizational decline and therefore the best way to deal with them (Bevan, 2001). In particular, internal managers attributed failure to external, uncontrollable and temporary causes (Mellahi *et al.*, 2002), whereas new managers saw the cause of decline as controllable. The focus of the dominant coalition hampered management trying to initiate large-scale change in the firm's strategic orientation, including withdrawal from international markets. The continued poor performance of the company's international activities served a signal to the shareholders that the alignment with the external environment was not occurring at the desirable speed, and that the 'coalition' did not have the characteristics necessary to initiate and manage a radical strategic change (Bevan, 2001). The latter triggered a legitimacy crisis, 'new outside' managers withdrew support and loyalty to old key figures and replaced them with 'new outside' managers who were prepared to consider radical change. Thus, the new management team was able to criticize openly the old strategy and initiate radical change without the embarrassment of associated failure. In brief, changes in leadership at the top created an opportunity for redirecting the course of M&S ambition to be the first truly international British retailing company.

On 18 September 2000, the Chairman ousted three executive directors. It was the fifth management shake-up in two years and by far the biggest in M&S's 116-year history (*Business Week*, October 2000). By October 2000, M&S had put a new management team in place and started the process of a strategic review of its business activities. The aim of the review was to 'stop the bleeding' by closing down loss-making operations and focus on the UK business. On 29 March 2001, M&S announced a fundamental overhaul of its business, described by Luc Vandevelde as an 'urgent' plan for recovery based on the UK business. The measures announced included the closure of all 39 company-owned stores in continental Europe in Belgium, France, Germany, Luxembourg, the Netherlands, Portugal and Spain, and the sale of American chains Brooks Brothers and Kings Supermarkets. The company reported that it was losing £34 million a year in Europe. Bevan (2001, p. 236) described the international exit decision as '[M&S management] made the decision that only an outsider free of the emotional baggage of the past could make: they had to go'. The de-internationalization process was initiated by the new management team led by Luc Vandevelde, and M&S budgeted £250–300 million as the cost of withdrawing from continental Europe. By the end of December 2001, M&S completed its exit from Europe after 26 years of trading in the region.

The initial de-internationalization strategy was dominated by overconcentration on finance affairs to safeguard the survival of M&S in the UK (Bevan, 2001, p. 237). Because of the crisis at home and abroad, management decisions were driven by economic rationality seeking primarily to optimize economic utility from the closure (Bevan, 2001, p. 237).

We concentrate on the exit from France, because we believe it plays a crucial role in explaining the de-internationalization process and in particular helps explore some unanticipated consequences of the M&S strategy (see Table 10.1 for the different modes of exit from Europe).

The De-Internationalization Process: The Implementation Stage

The description that follows is a summary of the events that occurred from M&S's announcement of the closure to the final exit of M&S from France. Although this summary is incomplete because of space limitations, it does include the major elements of the story.

The analysis of the case study was carried out using a temporal bracketing strategy, which involves decomposing the chronological data into successive discrete time periods, or phases. Phases are defined so that there is continuity in the context and actions being pursued within them, but discontinuities at their frontiers. In this case, the boundaries of the chosen periods were defined either by changes in the key people involved, or by a major change in the company's or other interest groupings' policy towards the de-internationalization of M&S. It is important to understand that these phases do not represent 'stages' in the sense of a predictable sequential process; however, they are more than just a descriptive convenience. Specifically, they permit the constitution of clear phases that permits analysis for the exploration and replication of theoretical ideas generated from this research.

First Phase
On 29 March 2001, M&S sent a message by e-mail to its management in European branches informing them of the plan to close its operations in Europe. Shortly after receiving the information, the company's closure plan was presented to the central Works Council of the French subsidiary at an extraordinary meeting. The communication took place a few minutes before the London stock exchange opened. The M&S share price rose by 7 per cent on the day of the announcement. Following the announcement, workers organized a demonstration

Table 10.1   Modes of exit from Europe

Country	Mode of exit	Profile*	Resistance
France	Sold to Galeries Lafayette	Very high	Very high
Spain	Sold to El Corte Ingles	Low	Low
Belgium	Closed	Moderate	Moderate
Germany	Closed	Low	Low
Portugal	Sold to El Corte Ingles	Low	Low

* Attention given to the case in the local media, political interference and resistance by trade unions to the exit.

outside M&S stores in Paris against the closure plan and the way it was announced. The demonstration marked the start of undesirable and unanticipated consequences for M&S. The demonstrations soon spread, as other French institutions were called upon to stop the closure.

Although M&S were a foreign company this was not necessarily a disadvantage because the Chairman Luc Vandevelde was a Belgian, and had extensive managerial experience in France as a former head of the French retail chain Promodes. Nevertheless, M&S management misjudged not only the legal obligations but also the extent to which France's unions, media and political class would unite in condemning the way the company handled the closure. While the decision to close the branches in France made sense in business terms to M&S managers, interest groups in France looked beyond business measures to question the rationality of the decision. Interest groups in France were concerned about job losses and the legality of M&S decision.

Three days after the announcement, French trade unions launched a legal action against M&S to forestall the planned closure. They challenged the closure procedures, and claimed M&S failed to give due warning to employees' representatives when it made its announcement to close its French branches. Under European law, local and multinational firms must hold annual meetings with employee-elected works councils. Further, the works council must be informed and consulted about business relocation or closure proposals as they arise.

Complying with local laws and regulations when announcing closure is not straightforward; laws governing plant closure differ from one country to another. Further, host-country laws and regulations sometimes clash with those of the home country. For instance, M&S had to take into consideration several factors before making the announcement. M&S's management argued that M&S tried to balance the need of reporting the announcement to the London stockmarket, according to stock exchange regulations, with the French legal requirement for consultation and information. Bevan (2001, p. 238) notes that 'Pulling out of Europe was price-sensitive information that needed to be reported to the Stock Exchange first – failure to do so would have been a breach of Financial Exchange Act'. Similarly, Alan Juillet, the manager in charge of the closure of French operations, noted that

> Marks & Spencer never wanted to exceed the French laws. The true problem, in fact, is the absence of [a coherent] European regulation. When you make such a strategic decision on a global level, you are subjected to all kinds of constraints: there are the various national laws, but also the stock exchange regulation. Marks & Spencer sought to find a solution which takes into account all the different constraints. (*Nouvel Observateur*, 2001)

The above procedural error – not consulting employees about the closure – ignited a strong movement to reverse the whole de-internationalization process. The dispute started first by workers' and unions' complaints about the 'the method of communication', then escalated very quickly into media coverage. As a result, a negative spiral of intensifying hostility was set in motion.

The hostility with unions and workers was exacerbated by negative media coverage and political interference. The media in France condemned M&S's action and the closure dominated national news for several weeks. Editorials focused on four controversial topics: (1) the closure and the expected Chairman's annual bonus of £650 000, (2) the strategic reasons for the closure – mainly to satisfy UK shareholders and the City of London supported by the positive reaction of the market to the closure, (3) the 'un-human and brutal' method of closure – 'licencies par e.mail', and (4) the export of brutal Anglo-Saxon management practices to France (*L'Humanite*, 26 July 2001; 5 April 2001; *Le Monde*, 14 April 2001). Further, the political class united against M&S. The Jospin government called for the pro-secution of M&S managers, and the French Prime Minister Lionel Jospin noted 'The workers who give life to this group and who enrich this group should be treated in a different way... Such behaviour deserves to be punished'. The French labour ministry, led by Elisabeth Guigou, called upon the state prosecutor to launch an investigation under penal law that could impose a prison sentence of up to one year on M&S's senior French management, as well as another FF25 000 fine. A French judge subsequently found that, in failing to consult its workforce about the proposed closures, M&S breached French and EU law. The judge ordered M&S to suspend its closure plans while it undertook a proper consultation process.

Another factor that affected the reaction of French workers, trade unions and other groupings was the timing of the closure. First, the closure was announced during a heated political debate over workers' rights and work conditions in France (*Economist*, 16 June 2001). A 'social modernization' bill was passed by the French parliament on 11 January 2001, the core of which was to strengthen the right to work, improve redundancy prevention and tackle precarious employment.

Second, on the same day that M&S announced its plan to exit from France – 29 March 2001 – Danone, the French-based food multinational and the world's second-largest food-processing group, also announced a reorganization of its biscuits division. The plan involved the reorganization of five plants in Europe and the closure of six others, with a net loss of around 1800 jobs. The closure was planned to start in early 2002 and to last until mid-2004. Danone announced wideranging measures to minimize the effect on employees and communities, including redeployment, outplacement assistance, retraining and advice. As a result, the response of the trade union was markedly different to that of M&S, though several demonstrations called for the boycott of Danone products, and strikes took place at the affected plants. The media and French unions contrasted the two-to-three-year timetable for the Danone closure with the announcement of virtually immediate closure of M&S. In an interview with *Le Monde*, the Chairman of M&S defended his actions by noting that 'if it was possible for me to communicate directly with all employees all over the country, and make the announcement myself I would have done so' (*Le Monde*, 7 April, 2001). He added that it is unfair to compare Danone with M&S 'When we are losing money in France, we don't have a choice' (*ibid.*).

Second Phase: A New Manager, a New Approach to Closure

The disputes were costing significant amounts of time, energy and money and creating frustration. Further, conflict of this magnitude would damage the organization's reputation. As a result, the strategic decision-making process which was predominately based on an 'economic rationale', began to view the closure decision through the 'institutional' lens. The change in the perceptions of management were, perhaps, constructed from the interactions with the institutionally-advocated modes of behaviour. As a result, the company needed a new strategy.

On 2 May 2001, M&S appointed a new manager, Alain Juillet, who had extensive experience in restructuring companies in France, to head the closure operation. He added a new perspective to the M&S closure strategy. Though the objective remained the same – to manage the closure of all French branches by the end of year 2001, the new manager's aim was to carry out the process in a 'socially responsible' manner. During the process, Mr Juillet repeatedly stressed that M&S would apply the legal requirements and particularly the '*code du travail*', especially Article 122-12. He reported that '*Un salarié ne se jette pas comme un Kleenex* [– employees should not be disposed of like a Kleenex]' (*Nouvel Observateur*, 17 May 2001). He outlined a new 'social' scheme and proposed that (a) there would be no dismissals, (b) all employees would be offered another job and a new social plan similar to that of Danone, and (c) the transfer of the stores would be accompanied by the best possible protection of employees by offering current employees the chance to continue in their job (*Nouvel Observateur*, 2001).

Third Phase: From Closure to Selling

On 3 April 2001, M&S initiated a consultation process with its European works council (EWC). Again, the legality of the process was challenged by three French unions and referred to court. According to three French unions – the CFDT, CFTC and CGC-FE – the M&S European council is not a genuine EWC but a unilateral management initiative aimed at avoiding the requirements of the EWCs. The unions claimed that, although the company informed and consulted the European council about the closures on 3 April 2001, this did not constitute information and consultation as required by the Directive. CFDT alleged that M&S's EWC was established by M&S management in violation of the French legislation, and the three French trade unions launched legal action against M&S on 3 April 2001 to forestall the planned closure.

Because the unions had been successful in exerting so much pressure during the initial stage of the dispute, they sought to escalate the conflict. Thus, the closure plans in France soon ran into trouble again after a demonstration against the closure and specifically the way M&S had been handling the closure, organized in London on 17 May 2001 by Union Network International (UNI), which represents retail workers from around the world, and the UK Trade Union Congress

(TUC). According to different estimates, around 2000 protesters including M&S employees from France, Belgium, Spain and Ireland attended the protest rally. The demonstration fuelled the crisis and more institutions such as the British TUC joined the 'stop the closure' movement.

In July, M&S once again changed its strategy and decided to 'sell' rather than 'close' its European branches. In September, the French court dismissed the case brought by the CFDT, CFTC and CGC-FE against M&S and confirmed the validity of the agreement under which the works council was set up. Further, Galeries Lafayette made an offer to buy M&S's stores in France. The deal was approved by M&S management but was subject to an agreement with the unions. On 30 November 2001 the workers' council at the French division announced that it would not contest the plans of M&S to sell its stores to the French retail chain Galeries Lafayette. Galeries Lafayette required the council's consent for the deal as a condition of its offer to take over 19 sites and 1500 employees from M&S. The Lafayette plan was to exploit 60 per cent of M&S's French sales space, spread over 10 different sites, and employ 60 per cent of M&S's staff.

On 11 December 2001, the employees' committee of M&S France approved the takeover plan offered by Galeries Lafayette, and M&S made it clear that it was to close its operations in France by 31 December regardless of the outcome of the negotiations. The 1500 M&S employees in France had three options: (1) accept the offer by the new employer and keep their jobs, (2) be given help to obtain another job with the new employer, GL, and its partners Hennes & Mauritz, Virgin Megastore, Franc and Andaska at another site, or (3) accept redundancy with compensation. Only 20 per cent took the last option.

DISCUSSION AND CONCLUSIONS

Certain conclusions can be drawn from the preceding analysis of the case study. First, the study provides evidence for those who argue that de-internationalization is often initiated by a new manager or, as in this case, a new management team. This study shows that top management motivation to de-internationalize is crucial for initiating the process. The case study reveals that crisis at home and abroad and the struggle for survival alone are not sufficient to cause organizational de-internationalization. The latter is perhaps necessary but not sufficient to bring about de-internationalization. The old management team did not consider de-internationalization, but escalated its commitment to internationalization by investing more money in international activities despite financial problems exacerbated by failed overseas operations. The case study demonstrates that while the external environment exhibited was an important stimulus for the company to review its international activities, the effect of external stimuli varies in accordance with the management team in place. While the old management team sought to escalate their commitment to international activities, the new management team decided to de-internationalize.

Second, despite variations in institutional contexts in different countries, managers adopted a standard approach, especially regarding consultation with local employees and unions. This typifies the perceived power of multinationals to override local variations. The de-internationalization process started with decisions and actions based on a logical, 'economic rationale' and communicated in a similar way to all foreign branches. Nevertheless, the course of action gradually but progressively took French institutional pressures and constraints into consideration, ending with a compromise of both rational economic decisions and institutionally constrained actions.

Third, the research shows that it is more difficult to exit in certain EU countries than in others. The ease with which a multinational can exit a country is perhaps determined by the legal framework of employment relations, the nature of labour-market institutions and the attitudinal and behavioural norms that characterize employment relations in a particular country. The case study showed that the process of exiting from France was based on serious misunderstandings of the political and legal contexts, and prevailing values and norms of conducting business in France. As a result, the procedures were transformed considerably when they were introduced in the host country.

Fourth, once strategy is considered, the case study shows that managers encounter several dilemmas and paradoxes. These include, informing openly and broadly versus shielding interested parties from information, even information that is required by law to be divulged, and dealing with different incompatible international laws and regulations.

Because accepted business culture and practices are not shared by established local law, international firms cannot justify their actions on the grounds of business rationale. Put simply, international disputes cannot be resolved on business ideological grounds. The case of M&S's exit from France shows that what is accepted as right and proper in the UK was not only unacceptable practice in France but illegal. Further, management saw the survival of M&S in the UK as sacrosanct, whereas unions in France saw limitations on such rights.

REFERENCES

Akhtar, S.H. and Choudhry, Y.A. (1993) 'Forced Withdrawal from a Country Market: Managing Political Risk', *Business Horizons*, 36 (3), 47–55.

Benito, G.R.G. (1997) 'Divestment of Foreign Production Operations', *Applied Economics*, 29 (10), 1365–77.

Benito, G. and Welch, L. (1997) 'De-internationalization', *Management International Review*, 37 (2), 7–25.

Bevan, J. (2001) *The Rise and Fall of Marks and Spencer* (Profile Books: London).

Boddewyn, J.J. (1979) 'Foreign Divestment: Magnitude and Factors', *Journal of International Business Studies*, (10), 21–6.

Boddewyn, J.J. (1983) 'Foreign and Domestic Divestment and Investment Decisions: Like or Unlike?', *Journal of International Business Studies*, Winter, 23–35.

Bower, J.L. (1970) *Managing the Resource Allocation Process* (Boston: Harvard University Graduate School of Business Administration, Division of Research Publication).

Burt, S., Mellahi, K., Jackson, P. and Sparks, L. (2002) 'Retail Internationalization and Retail Failure: Issues from the Case of Marks and Spencer', *International Review of Retail, Distribution, and Customer Research*, 12 (2), 191–219.

Business International (1976) *International Divestment: A Survey of Corporate Experience* (Geneva and New York).

Business Week (Online October, 2000) *Lighting a Fire under Marks & Sparks. Can a management shake-up revive the troubled retailer?*

Caves, R. (1995) Growth and Decline in Multinational Enterprises: From Equilibrium to Turnover Processes, in Cheung, Stephen (ed.) *Corporate Links and Foreign Direct Investment in Asia and the Pacific* (Pymble: Harper Educational).

Chang, S. and Singh, H. (1999) 'The Impact of Modes of Entry and Resources Fit on Modes of Exit by Multinational Firms', *Strategic Management Journal*, (20), 1019–35.

Davies, G. (1999) 'The Evolution of Marks and Spencer', *The Service Industries Journal*, 19 (3), 60–73.

Ghertman, M. (1987) 'Foreign Subsidiary and Parent Roles During Strategic Investment and Divestment Decisions', *Journal of International Business Studies*, Spring, 47–67.

Gilmour, S.C. (1973) *The Divestment Decision Process*, Unpublished DBA Dissertation (Boston, MA: Harvard University, Graduate School of Business Administration).

Grunberg, L. (1981) *Failed Multinationals Ventures: The Political of International Divestments* (Lexington, MA: Lexington Books).

Hadjikhani, H. and Johanson, J. (1996) 'Facing Foreign Market Turbulence: Three Swedish Multinationals in Iran', *Journal of International Marketing*, 4 (4), 53–74.

Karakaya, F. (2000) 'Market Exit and Barriers to Exit: Theory and Practice', *Psychology and Marketing*, 17 (8), pp. 651–668.

Le Monde (7 April 2001) Entretien avec le président de Marks and Spencer: 'La fermeture de tous les magasins est la seule décision qui avait du sens', 18.

Le Monde (14 April 2001) 'Un beau 'cadeau' pour le PDG du Marks and Spencer', 18.

Le Monde (1 December 2001) 'Marks and Spencer s'en va, les Galeries Lafayette se développement', 19.

L'Humanité (5 April, 2001) Le Riboud, editorial by Calude Cabanes.

L'Humanité (26 July 2001) 'La mobilisation des "licencies par e.mail"'.

Li, J. (1995) 'Foreign Entry and Survival: Effects of Strategic Choices on Performance in International Markets', *Strategic Management Journal*, 16 (5), 333–51.

Marois, B. and Jourde, J.E. (1977) 'Le désinvestissement des firmes françaises à l'étranger', *Banque*, April, 405–11.

Mata, J. and Portugal, P. (2000) 'Closure and Divestiture by Foreign Entrants: The Impact of Entry and Post-entry Strategies', *Strategic Management Journal*, (21), 549–62.

Matthyssens, P. and Pauwels, P. (2000) 'Uncovering International Market-exit Processes: A Comparative Case Study', *Psychology and Marketing*, 17 (8), 697–719.

McDermott, C.M. (1989) *Multinationals: Foreign Divestment and Disclosure* (London: McGraw-Hill).

Mellahi, K., Jackson, T.P. and Sparks, L. (2002) 'An Exploratory Study into Failure in Successful Organizations: The Case of Marks and Spencer', *British Journal of Management*, 13 (2), 15–29.

Nargundkar, S.V., Karakaya, F. and Stahl, M.J. (1996) 'Barriers to Market Exit', *Journal of Managerial Issues*, 8 (2), 239–59.

Nees, D.B. (1978–79) 'The Divestment Decision Process in Large and Medium-sized Diversified Companies: A Descriptive Model Based on Clinical Studies', *International Studies of Management and Organisation*, Winter, 67–95.

Nouvel Observateur (17 May, 2001) 'Marks & Spencer: Il n'y aura pas de licenciements with Alain Juillet', 1908.

Porter, M.E. (1976) 'Please Note Location of Nearest Exit – Exit Barriers and Planning', *California Management Review*, 19 (2), 21–33.

Richbell, S.M. and Watts, H.D. (2000) 'Plant Closures in Multiplant Manufacturing Firms: Adding an International Perspective', *Management Decision*, 38 (2), 80–8.

Shapiro, D.M. (1993) 'Entry, Exit, and the Theory of Multinational Corporation', in Kindleberger, Charles P. and Audretsch, David B. (eds), *The Multinational Corporation in the 1980s* (Boston, MA: MIT Press).

The Economist (Jun 16, 2001) 'Europe: Don't Sack your Workers', 359 (8226), 52.

Tornedon, R.L. (1975) *Foreign Disinvestment by US Multinational Corporations: With Eight Case Studies* (New York: Praeger).

Vandevelde, L. (11 July, 2001) Chairman's Presentation, Marks and Spencer, Annual General Meeting.

Whitehead, M. (1991) 'International Franchising – Marks and Spencer: A Case Study', *International Journal of Retail and Distribution Management*, 19 (2), 10–12.

11 Small and Medium-Sized Northern Irish Design Exporters: Their International Sales-Channel Strategies

Sharon Loane, Jim Bell, Mika Gabrielsson and Zuhair Al-Obaidi

INTRODUCTION

Small and medium-sized enterprises (SMEs) make valuable contributions to national economies in general (OECD, 1997), and to small open economies like Finland and Ireland in particular where they constitute 99.7 per cent of all firms. Irish design is well-known and valued around the world, and the 'Irishness' of offerings confers many benefits. Although Northern Irish design firms undoubtedly benefit from this 'Irishness', the domestic market is small, therefore in order to grow and prosper they must sell on world markets competing with the worlds finest design firms, although their own resources and marketing skills may be limited. Our research is essentially interested in how they achieve this aim.

This research attempts to achieve this objective by following and replicating the original research design of a study by Gabrielsson and Al-Obaidi (2002). Previous research on export sales channels draws on both the internationalization process literature (Luostarinen, 1970; Johanson and Vahlne, 1977; Leonidou and Katsikeas, 1996) and domestic channel marketing literature (Stern and Reve, 1980). This earlier research tended to investigate sales-channel choice from a single-channel approach, and as Gabrielsson and Al-Obaidi (2002) observed, multiple sales channels as a means of international expansion has been largely underresearched. They investigated four Finnish design companies and found that multiple sales channels were used by all of the case companies, although only in selected markets. They also found evidence to support the contention that the rationale underlying the stages approach to internationalization also applies to sales channels. Finnish design firms exported in the first instance through indirect sales channels, expanding into direct sales channels later after experience had been gained. Evidence also emerged that as the case firms became more internationalized, they tended to use multiple channels. This is not restricted to design firms; Turnbull and Ellwood (1986) obtained similar evidence among European IT companies, as did Gabrielsson (1999) in the personal computer industry. This suggests that multiple sales channels are now increasingly used by companies in many industries as a means of international expansion.

This leads to our research question – *Do small and medium-sized Irish design companies use different international sales channel structures, and if so, why?* In order to address this issue, a number of sub questions are pertinent:

- What kind of sales-channel structures do SME design companies use and how have they developed over time?
- What are the motives and reasons for using the various channel structures and what factors have been influential in their development?
- How have recent technological and environmental changes impacted sales-channel structure strategies of small and medium-sized design companies?
- How adequate are current sales-channel theories for predicting small and medium-sized companies' sales-channel behaviour?

RESEARCH BACKGROUND AND DEFINITIONS

Distinct definitions with regard to sales-channel structures have been developed in both the international business (IB) and marketing literatures, although some confusion is found. The IB literature views these structures from an internationalization-stage perspective (Luostarinen, 1970, 1979; Johanson and Vahlne, 1977) and the marketing literature from a domestic or single-market perspective (Mallen, 1977; Hardy and Magrath, 1988; Rosenbloom, 1995). The correct international sales-channel strategies for Irish design companies are central to success, as mistakes at this level are costly to correct and many of the relationships may be contractual and of a relatively long-standing nature. The internationalization process literature recognizes two main types of marketing operations forming the basis for sales-channel strategies (Luostarinen, 1970, 1979; Johanson and Vahlne, 1977):

- *Export operations*, part of the non-direct investment marketing operation modes (indirect export mode, direct export mode and own export mode).
- *Sales and marketing subsidiary operations*, part of the direct investment marketing operation modes.

The received wisdom regarding the internationalization trajectories of SMEs located in small open economies is that they will internationalize in the first instance via indirect, direct or own export modes. In indirect exporting mode, the firm deals with another firm located in the home market, who then exports. With the direct exporting mode the firm will deal with one or more intermediaries located in the target market. In the case of own-export mode, no intermediaries are involved and the firm will export directly to end-users (Luostarinen, 1979).

As the firm expands and grows, gathering experience in foreign activities, it may then establish a sales or marketing subsidiary. A sales subsidiary may be regarded as a middleman in the chain, whose activities may be compared to an importer or an exporter (Hentola, 1994). Firms may use direct or indirect sales-channel structures, dependant on the nature of the goods involved and the characteristics of the target market. In the marketing literature Stern *et al.*(1989) comment:

> Marketing channels can be viewed as sets of interdependent organisations involved in the process of making a product or service available for use or consumption. Not only do the marketing channels satisfy demand…they also stimulate demand by the promotional activities by the units composing them.

International sales channels can be further sub-divided into (Gabrielsson, 1999):

- *direct sales channels* – where the exporter sells directly to the end customer; or
- *indirect sales channels* – where firms do not enter directly into sales activities with the end customers or consumers, instead independent middlemen located in the target markets are used as intermediaries. There can be a one-level structure or a two-level structure (see Figure 11.1). Level one refers to resellers or retailers selling to the end customer, whereas the two-level structure has an additional level in which distributors are present between the exporter and the resellers or retailers.

However, firms are not just limited to these two choices, they may use multiple sales channels simultaneously (Hardy and Magrath, 1988) in the form of either a dual sales channel or a hybrid sales channel (Gabrielsson, 1999); see Figures 11.2 and 11.3.

Dual sales channels will contain at the same time both direct and indirect sales channels in the same target market, and may be viewed as adversarial in nature. The *hybrid sales channel* strategy is different in that the responsibility for sales and promotion are shared between the participant members, and this channel is more cooperation-based than the dual sales channel (Gabrielsson, 1999). Indeed, there may exist a third type where the exporter may enter a particular target market via two or more indirect sales-channel members; we refer to them as *dual indirect sales channels*, as they do not consist of an indirect and a direct sales channel, rather this structure has two indirect sales channels used in parallel. Additionally, Irish design firms have to make choices with regard to the numerous types of middlemen available to them at each channel level.

These may be distributors, agents, resellers or retailers. Distributors by their very nature do not sell directly to the end customer, rather they sell to either the retailer (handling consumer goods) or reseller (handling industrial goods). Agents may differ in that they can either sell on to the resellers or retailers, or directly to the end customer (this being the case, they are usually termed sales

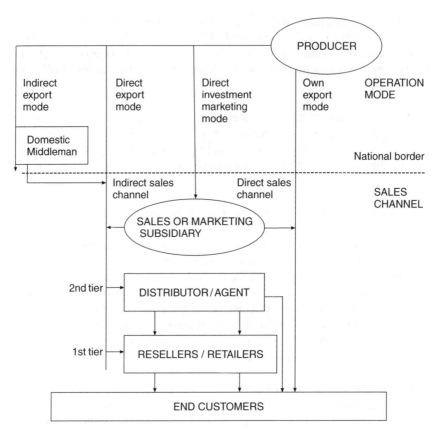

Figure 11.1 Sales channels for international expansion

Source: Gabrielsson and Al-Obaidi (2002), adapted from Gabrielsson (1999).

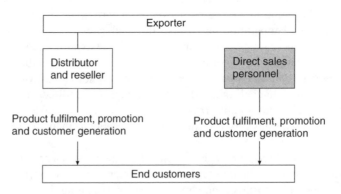

Figure 11.2 Dual sales channel

Source: Gabrielsson and Al-Obaidi (2002), adapted from Gabrielsson (1999).

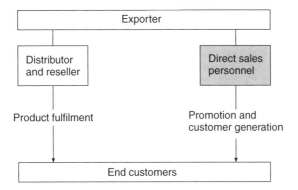

Figure 11.3   Hybrid sales channel

Source: Gabrielsson and Al-Obaidi (2002), adapted from Gabrielsson (1999).

agents). However, the name or label given to them is less important than the functions they perform (Rosenbloom, 1995).

THEORETICAL FRAMEWORK

Four approaches to explain the sales-channel strategy choices and development of the Irish design firms studied are utilized:

- Internationalization processes (Luostarinen, 1970, 1979; Johanson and Vahlne, 1977).
- Sales-channel economic structure (transaction-cost analysis) (Williamson, 1975, 1985).
- Product life-cycles (Rogers, 1962).
- Long-term relations (Dwyer *et al*., 1987).

The internationalization process literature centres around explaining the pattern of stages companies move through as they gradually move towards more demanding products, operations and international markets at both company (Luostarinen, 1979) and country levels (Luostarinen, 1970; Johanson and Vahlne, 1977). Therefore each company has a unique product, operational and market mix that will affect the sales-channel choices they make. International process literature is rooted in Cyert and March's (1963) behavioural theory, and Penrose's (1959) growth of the firm theory. The underpinning sentiment of the internationalization process theory is that the laterally rigid (Vaivio, 1963) behaviour of the companies' decision-makers can be overcome as they learn and have more experience of international markets (Luostarinen, 1970).

This rationale may be applied to the sales-channel selections for exporting. In this case, Irish design companies would be expected to export through indirect sales channels in the first instance. As firms learn about international markets, direct sales channels would be established. Gabrielsson and Al-Obaidi (2002) further comment that, 'however, the companies positive experiences of a particular channel strategy either domestically or in an international market increases the chances that the company will choose a similar strategy for a new market entry'.

The sales-channel economic structure literature aims to explain channel choices based on both cost and efficiency factors. The transaction-cost approach (TCA) is widely used (Williamson, 1975, 1985) and posits that the level of vertical integration (market or hierarchical control) will be based on the efficiency of the transactions involved. Such costs are naturally not easy to measure; therefore proxies are used, and these are asset specificity, external uncertainty, internal uncertainty and transaction volume. TCA is not just based on economic factors, there is also a socio-political element. Therefore, when asset specificity is high, a direct sales channel makes sense when the transaction volumes are large. Furthermore, multiple (dual or hybrid) channels are the most optimal for increasing sales volume in highly diversified markets due to the economies of scale and scope in handling a large number of transactions, and also in managing the external uncertainty created by such diversity.

The product life-cycle (plc) literature describes and explains the various stages a product will pass through in its life-cycle. Rogers's (1962) theory of diffusion and adoption of innovation provides the underpinnings for this theory. It is suggested that in the introduction phase, a single sales channel (direct sales force or indirect specialized) structure is used. In the growth phase, dual sales-channel structures, and in the maturity phase multiple, that is dual and hybrid, sales channels are used. In the last stage, decline, hybrid or direct marketing channels are used.

Long-term channel relationship literature examines the development of relationships over time (Dwyer *et al.*, 1987). The nature of relationships in sales channels can lead to partnership advantages (Sethuraman *et al.*, 1988) or to internal conflicts (Moriarty and Moran, 1990). Several relationship variables such as power, trust and commitment come into play in such sales-channel relationships. The nature of these relationships would appear to be extremely useful in explaining, for example, the adoption of hybrid sales-channel structures which Gabrielsson and Al-Obaidi (2002) contend are not adversarial, but embody cooperation and trust and therefore partnership advantages may be achieved. In the dual-channel structure Irish design companies would be, relatively speaking, more powerful, therefore any channel conflicts which may arise could be resolved and overcome.

From the four approaches outlined above, the framework shown in Figure 11.4 has been used to guide and focus the empirical work.

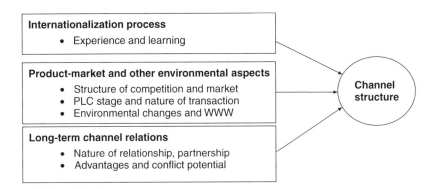

Figure 11.4   Framework for sales-channel structure choice

Source: Gabrielsson and Al-Obaidi (2002), adapted from Gabrielsson (1999).

METHODOLOGY

Following the original research design, multiple case studies were used facilitating the inductive building of theory (Eisenhardt, 1989). Case research adequately answers the 'How' and 'Why' questions with regard to sales-channel structure choices. In multiple cases the evidence produced is often regarded as more impressive and assuring and there is also the opportunity to replicate the findings across cases (Yin, 1989), with a more in-depth understanding of the processes and outcomes involved being provided.

Four firms were studied: Belleek, Parian china giftware manufacturers; Tyrone Crystal, producers of fine lead crystal tableware and giftware; Magee and Co., textile manufacturers; and Consarc, professional services providers (architecture, quantity surveying and project management). These companies were selected from the researchers' knowledge of local companies and are all considered to be leading design companies in Ireland. Due care and diligence were observed in order to adequately establish cross-cultural equivalence following principles laid down by Cavusgil and Das (1997).

Theoretical sampling logic was used (Yin, 1989), and cases for inclusion were checked against the following criteria: that they were exporters of design products or a service; and that they were SMEs. The original study had Avarte, which designs and manufactures furniture, as part of the sample, but no such 'design' firm exporting design products or services could be located in Northern Ireland; therefore, as an interesting alternative, a firm of architects working in international markets was chosen for inclusion.

Multiple data-collection methods were used to triangulate findings (Miles and Hubermann, 1994), and primary data collection was by means of in-depth interviews with the export managers. Secondary sources such as company websites, published information and statistical data were also used. The interviews were recorded and transcribed onto a preprepared template, which both guided the interviewer to follow the interview schedule used in the Finnish research, and aided in recording the outputs thus enhancing reliability.

The next step was careful analysis, utilizing techniques suggested by Yin (1989) and developed by Miles and Hubermann (1994). Evidence for each construct was examined and the underlying reasons – the 'Why' question – searched for. The main analysis method therefore was explanation-building (Yin, 1989). Eisenhardt's (1989) last two steps are (1) comparing findings with the literature for similarities and differences, and (2) 'reaching closure' as theoretical saturation is reached. The motives and reasons for the companies using the various sales channels, and the factors influential in their development, are examined in the next section. This is achieved through cross-case analysis following the framework above (Figure 11.4), and three sections are presented:

- The internationalization process.
- Product-market and other environmental aspects.
- Long-term channel relations.

The Internationalization Process of the Case Firms

Belleek (www.belleek.ie)

Belleek, established in 1857, is Ireland's top-selling china giftware brand, with a worldwide reputation for design, artistry and handcraftsmanship. It is a substantial operation, employing 220 people with an annual turnover of £7 million per annum. It supplies retail and mail-order giftware markets worldwide, with key export markets being the USA, the Caribbean, Canada, Europe, the Far East and Australia. Interestingly Belleek supplied the US market virtually from inception, with Mark Twain among its first collectors. At this time companies sought business and prestige through patronage, and influential collectors furthered Belleek's reputation. They were also extremely active in bringing the Belleek brand onto the world stage as the following list of early trade shows demonstrates:

Dublin Exposition 1865 (Gold Medal)   Dublin Exposition 1872
Adelaide Exposition 1887 (Gold Medal)   Chicago Trade Fair 1898
Paris Exhibition 1900 (Gold Medal)   Wembley Exhibition 1926

Export sales were £1.8 million in 1993, but by 1998 this had risen to £4 million. This remarkable export sales growth was recognized in 1999 when it was awarded the prestigious Queen's Award for Export Achievement. Belleek has expanded in recent years through a number of acquisitions, strengthening resources across the member companies as well as opening up significant new distribution channels. In all export markets except the USA, it uses a network of agents and distributors. In the USA a dual-indirect sales-channel structure exists, as it supplies one of their major

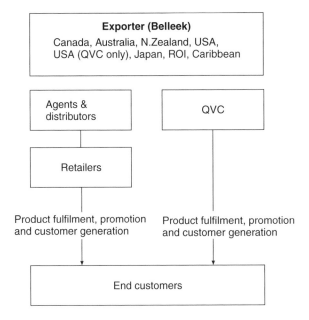

Figure 11.5   Belleek's export sales-channel structure (dual indirect)

customers, the QVC shopping channel, through direct export mode. Belleek's actual export market sales-channel structure is shown diagrammatically in Figure 11.5.

Tyrone Crystal (www.tyronecrystal.com)

Tyrone Crystal was established in 1971, employs 100 people, has an annual turnover of approximately £5 million, and has an international reputation for producing the finest quality crystal. The Tyrone collection is wide-ranging and the company claims design excellence and quality throughout production, whilst still using traditional hand-cut processes pioneered 200 years ago. Tyrone possesses the coveted BS5750/ISO 9000 award. It exports to a number of international markets, including the USA, the United Arab Emirates and Japan.

Tyrone has enjoyed considerable export success since going to the USA in 1982, and its crystal is increasingly popular as commissioned sports trophies. Since 1997, when it introduced the Golf Collection, it has successfully built a strong relationship with the PGA in America and continues to develop golf partners across Europe. In the US market, agents are used who have two functions. Firstly to service Tyrone's needs with the retailers and wholesalers, and secondly and more importantly (two-thirds of US business is from the corporate golf market), to service the corporate channel for trophies. Once the agent gets the order, these are commissioned and Tyrone takes it from the design stage right through to shipping. In all other export markets Tyrone uses a network of agents and distributors. This sales-channel structure is shown in Figure 11.6.

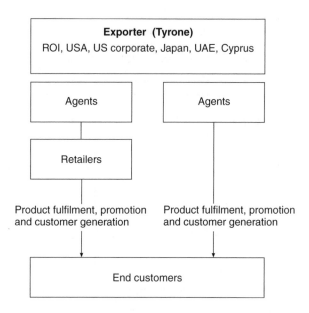

Figure 11.6   Tyrone's export sales-channel structure (dual indirect)

Magee and Co. Ltd (http://www.magee.com)

Magee, founded in 1866, employs 200 people with annual sales of £13.5 million. Since 1990 it has developed significant business in the UK, Germany, Belgium, France and the Netherlands. It designs, manufactures and markets quality modern 'classic' men's clothing with a strong design element aimed at the top end of the market.

Magee uses sales agents in each export market, and the sales channel structure is identical across all export markets. The export manager states that 'this is the only satisfactory structure for the business as we cannot afford high distributors' margins'. Magee is also presently offering a selection of their menswear for sale online direct to the end customer, therefore evolving to the dual sales-channel structure shown in Figure 11.7.

Consarc Design Group Ltd

Consarc, founded in 1911, employs 80 people with an annual turnover of £3 million. It provides professional architectural services, quantity surveying and project management services. It experienced rapid international growth during the 1950s and 1960s when it built sports cities in Libya, Yemen and Jordan. The opportunity to tender for these developments came via an ex-partner in the colonial service in Uganda. This partner eased its passage through the many cultural and technical specification barriers encountered in each

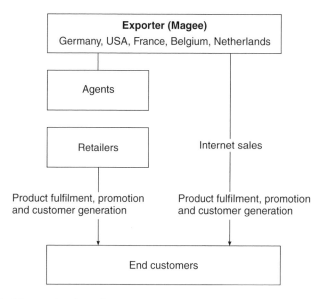

Figure 11.7 Magee sales-channel structure (dual)

location. In the 1970s, international business was quiet and projects were mainly in the UK and the Republic of Ireland (ROI). In the late 1970s, requests were received from the original sports cities to update the facilities and to add swimming pools.

In the 1990s, Consarc provided the design element for international marine, residential and commercial projects in Libya, Yemen, Uganda, Egypt and Thailand. Political events in the Middle East changed the firm's focus, and this, coupled with the emergence of the Celtic Tiger, meant that it found more profitable opportunities in the Republic of Ireland, closer to home.

Consarc places great emphasis on formal and informal networks, as sources of business at home and abroad, claiming not to indulge in any other promotional activity. It also claims that its innovative work draws in clients, as most are aware of the 'state' of the architectural design industry. Without an actual product to distribute, Figure 11.8 is a representation of how the sales process works.

CROSS-CASE SUMMARY

In this summary we are comparing the channel structure of the case companies and its development along the following dimensions: degree of internationalization, product market and other environmental aspects, and long-term channel relations. Table 11.1 provides a summary of the details.

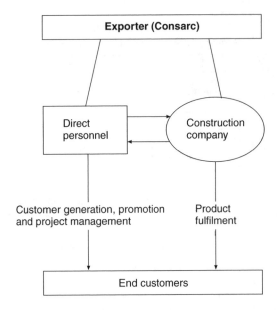

Figure 11.8   Consarc's service sales-channel (hybrid)

Degree of Internationalization

The manufacturing case companies vary in their degree of internationalization. Although they all started exporting by using single indirect channels, their sales-channel structures have subsequently evolved in some markets (for example, Belleek and Tyrone now use dual-indirect sales channels in the USA). Until very recently Magee used a single indirect sales-channel structure in every export market; with the addition of online sales transactions, their sales-channel structure has now become dual in nature (with an indirect and a direct approach in every export market). Consarc has always used a hybrid export sales-channel structure and their degree of internationalization varies according to its current client base. None of the companies have progressed to the 'stage' where they establish foreign sales subsidiaries or retail outlets in foreign locations. They are all actively exporting, but have expressed no wish to expand via foreign sales subsidiaries or foreign manufacturing operations, or to expand their current client base.

Product-Market and Other Environmental Aspects

All firms have in common the fact that both the quality and elegance of product/service are central to the business model. Tyrone and Belleek products are not mass-produced, instead they use traditional manufacturing processes. Magee uses methods well-established in the textile industry, with extensive hand finishing. All three manufacturing companies' processes are labour-intensive with high

Table 11.1   Cross-case summary

	Belleek	Magee	Tyrone	Consarc
Activity	Parian China	Menswear	Lead crystal	Construction
Established	1857	1866	1971	1911
No. employees	220	200	100	80
Turnover £ stg (m)	7	13.5	5	3
Year 1st exported	1860	1990	1982	1957
Present export markets	USA Caribbean Canada Europe Far East Australia	USA Germany Belgium France Netherlands	USA Republic of Ireland UAE Japan Cyprus	Republic of Ireland
Sales-channel structure	Dual-indirect	Dual	Dual-indirect	Hybrid
Individual transaction cost	Low	Low	Low	Extremely high
Online sales offered	No	Yes	Limited	No

176

Table 11.1 Continued

	Belleek	Magee	Tyrone	Consarc
Internet impact	Improved communications	Improved communications Increased sales of selected products	Improved communications	Sophisticated web technology aids international project management
Other environmental factors	Off-shore competitors	Weather patterns and different fabric weights, off-shore competitors	Off-shore competitors	Political events make some markets unavailable/risky
Design element	Handcrafted	Hand-finished	Handcrafted	Innovative design
Plc stage	Original pieces and newer shorter-lived pieces (2 yrs)	Seasonal collections	Original pieces and newer shorter-lived pieces (3/5 yrs)	One-off designs, location-specific
Long-term channel relations	Long-term contractual, new contracts are short-term; No competing products to be carried by channel members	Long-term contractual, new contracts are short-term; No competing products to be carried by channel members	Long-term contractual, new contracts are short-term; No competing products to be carried by channel members	Contract duration only,but networks are important but and longstanding; Confiden- tiality between players

raw materials costs, making production expensive. All three are also in direct competition with larger firms who have off-shore, low-labour-cost production facilities (see Table 11.1), and therefore they assiduously build their brand offering in an attempt to counter lower-cost rivals.

The characteristics of design products mean that the companies must carefully design and select their sales-channel structures and target-market locations. Communicating the uniqueness of design products is not only the manufacturer's responsibility, it is also incumbent upon the other channel partners to convey these elements to the consumer. Magee's export manager commented that, 'the agent has the responsibility to find the "right" retailer, it has to be top-end, and the retailer must be capable of positioning and promoting our brand correctly in his/her shop'. The manufacturers also takes joint responsibility for promotion. For example, Magee provides point-of-sale materials, sends a weaver out on a 'road-show', and attends overseas trade fairs.

All of the companies are aware of the changing dynamic nature of their environment and monitor any potential threats, and also monitor sales-channel effectiveness. Consarc, which exports knowledge via a consulting service, is particularly aware of environmental shifts. It has withdrawn from Middle Eastern markets due to the political developments of recent times, and it has also been obliged to follow market trends in the construction industry and concentrate on areas of major activity. Interestingly, changing climatic patterns, with hotter summers and warmer autumns, have affected Magee's business. The window of opportunity for sales of traditional wool-based heavy menswear is shorter, and therefore Magee has had to introduce looser, lighter garments in an attempt to maximize sales.

Product Life-cycles
In the earliest stages of their product life-cycles the firms were immune from imitators, but once they appeared on the international stage, this changed. Many of their direct competitors use cheaper raw materials, or manufacture in lower labour-cost locations. In order to compete, the Irish design firms have worked diligently to create their brands, continuously upgrading their design offerings.

Belleek and Tyrone are unusual with regard to the product life-cycles of their products. At Belleek some of the early designs, for example, are still sold extensively over a century after their launch, and Tyrone still make the Antrim suite (produced from 1971). Running alongside these lines are others which are updated regularly. The newer more design-oriented pieces are usually only in production for a few years, are fashion-led, and therefore have to 'fit' with current trends in both customer taste and home decor trends. The life-cycles of these particular products are getting shorter each year, and the onus is on the designers to come up with more innovative and creative designs whilst still using the traditional handcrafted manufacturing process. Magee's product life-cycles are seasonal and relatively short, therefore the company is always engaged in designing a new collection whilst the current range is in the stores. Consarc's projects are unique and demanding in terms of design, and it is unlikely that a design could be reused in another location for many reasons. The type of project, however, has changed from the sports facilities in the early international market activities to the contemporary retail and leisure spaces currently in demand.

Product-Market

Clearly the foreign markets that were entered influenced the choice of sales-channel structure, as did previous positive experience of using the particular sales channel. For Magee and Tyrone, the USA represents a lead market. Both the Tyrone corporate channel and the Belleek-QVC direct export mode have evolved into new forms, to serve new types of business there, facilitating growth. Magee's product dictates the markets, as the continental buyer demands this 'look'. Consarc, on the other hand, follows lead markets and clients around the world. It currently works in an export market close to home, thereby reducing risk and the potential effects of turbulent political regimes. Their 'channel' structure depends heavily upon informal long-term relations and network partnerships.

Environmental Changes and the WWW

The Internet operates as both a commercial medium and as a market (Hoffman *et al.*, 1995; Alhadeff and Cohen, 1997; Indermaaur, 1997; Seeley, 1997), allowing people and firms in different locations to interact, resolve problems, reach consensus and work together online (Miller, 2001). It is particularly interesting to examine how the design companies in this study viewed the Internet, bearing in mind the sensate, tactile nature of design products.

Belleek has discounted an online sales facility, as it feels that the potential sales volume would not be significant. It provides historic, company and some product information on the home page. The Internet and the advent of e-mail communications with export customers has helped to improve the speed and ease of operations, particularly across time zones. However, the export manager observes:

> on-line sales have the potential to depress prices and to introduce conflict into existing channels, and damage the good relationships presently in place with existing distributors. However, we will move with the times, the distributors may work on-line if they wish, but we will not. Instead we will concentrate on designing and offering a quality product which is desirable in our chosen markets, at the right price.

Magee is engaging in online sales and has positioned the website to reflect their emphasis on quality, although there is only a limited product range available on-line. The export manager commented:

> it has difficulties at present, but it will eventually work out, but there is potential for introducing conflict into the channels, and we will not aggressively sell

on-line, as this could damage the sales volume especially from the small top-end independents.

The agents were kept informed of all online activities pre-launch, and price points had been discussed with them. He also stated that potential online customers would probably have already experienced the Magee product, as it really had to be seen and touched to appreciate the beauty and fabric quality. Internet e-mail communications now eased the day-to-day running of the business, and aided off-shore sourcing and buying procedures. Again Magee was happy to let the agents use Internet technology if they wished. If any agents did choose this route Magee felt that it would have to monitor both the relevant sites and the results carefully as they did not wish their garments to be positioned as anything less than top-end.

Tyrone has a limited online order facility, which is insignificant at present in overall terms. It does not aggressively promote this online facility, and feels it will not upset consumers at all. Tyrone also commented that as its brand presence worldwide is less than that of major competitors, it could afford some online sales. Its online customer database is built by capturing the e-mail addresses of tourists when they visit the factory. Potential customers will have already experienced Tyrone Crystal, so that the difficulties of promoting a design product online are reduced. The managing director commented that small-scale online sales would not affect the agents in any way, and that channel conflict would not be a problem. Again Internet technologies had impacted upon Tyrone positively, as communications with foreign agents and customers was easier now, particularly the commissioned trophy end of the business where drawings and specifications could be received quickly and easily, speeding up the process from design to manufacture.

Consarc has sophisticated communications and web technologies, facilitating the interaction of various people, government agencies and firms in different locations. Internet communications have speeded up the design process, as it is easy to send imagery and drawings online. Online conferencing can also take the place of site meetings, and therefore the time-efficiency of expensive professional architects is maximized. Consarc's website is not intended as a promotional or advertising tool, which is hardly surprising as the nature of the industry means that single transactions can cost many thousands of pounds. Consarc's products must be experienced in a holistic manner to appreciate their innovativeness, therefore, in general, the customers for such complexes tend to visit similar sites and then enquire which architectural firm was involved or who does similar work.

Although some of the literature claims that the Internet can give companies global reach and facilitate rapid foreign market entry (Hamill and Gregory, 1997), there is evidence of difficulties in operationalizing online selling. The Belleek case supports the findings of other research (Al-Obaidi *et al.*, 2000) regarding the problems that may arise when online activities are not well coordinated with channel members.

Long-Term Channel Relations

Channel membership is usually characterized as a sensitive personal business, where long-term relationships become extremely important. Relationships nurtured through mutual trust and commitment can confer many advantages. Magee, Belleek and Tyrone Crystal are all locked into relatively long-term contractual relationships, which although difficult to change are working well. However, new channel partners are introduced on a short-term basis only until the relationship is proven and trust is established. Magee in particular commented that contractual arrangements of a long-term nature are difficult and expensive to revoke, therefore it exercises extreme caution in choosing new partners. All stated that sales-channel partners must not carry competing products, only complimentary items. Dual sales channels have potential for conflict, but the relative power of the design company appears to have reduced the incidence in these particular company cases.

Consarc, as a knowledge and service-intensive firm, points to the fact that long-term embedded relationships are vital in its operations. These provide the networks, formal and informal which both provide business and also ease the operational difficulties such firms experience when dealing in markets away from home.

DISCUSSION AND CONCLUSIONS

After reviewing the sales-channel structures used by the case companies from Northern Ireland, we are still left with an interesting question: 'How adequate are the current sales channel theories for predicting small and medium-sized companies' sales-channel behaviour?'

The internationalization process literature focuses on explaining the pattern of stages undertaken as companies gradually proceed towards more demanding products (P), operations (O), and markets (M) (Johanson and Vahlne, 1977; Luostarinen, 1979). It was stated previously that design companies would be expected to commence exporting via indirect channels, and when more experience has been gained direct channels would be established. This study confirms this pattern, in the main, as Tyrone and Magee both commenced exporting this way. Belleek, however, provides a slightly different case, as it has exported to the USA practically right from inception. None of the case firms established foreign sales subsidiaries or foreign production facilities, nor have they plans to do so. It would be expected that the more internationalized the firm, the greater use would be made of multiple sales channels, and Tyrone and Belleek do conform as they both now have a dual-indirect sales-channel structure. Magee has now evolved to a dual sales-channel structure from the simpler single sales-channel structure previously favoured. Evidence was also found to support the fact that a positive experience with a sales channel would increase the probability of that structure being used for a new foreign market entry.

The sales-channel economic structure literature views sales-channel structure selection as based on cost and efficiency considerations (Coase, 1937; Williamson 1975, 1985). Based on this, it would appear that a direct sales-channel structure would be optimal when transaction volume is large. Belleek and Tyrone have adopted a dual-indirect sales-channel approach in the USA. However, the suggestion that multiple (dual or hybrid) channels are optimal for highly diversified markets received only limited support.

The long-term channel relationship literature explains the development of relationships over time (Dwyer *et al.*, 1987), and this helps explain why companies chose either a dual or a hybrid structure. It would appear that hybrid sales channels would be chosen as partnership advantages would be achieved through trustworthy and committed relationships (Consarc), whereas a dual sales channel would seem to indicate that the design companies would be relatively powerful (Magee). The case firms did state that they expected to be powerful in the channel relationships and seemed happy to bear with their existing structures as channel conflicts could be resolved.

Rogers' (1962) plc model describes the stages through which a product passes. The assertion that different channel structures would be used at different stages of the product life-cycle has proved difficult to establish and results are inconclusive. However, when looking at the more internationalized companies, Belleek and Tyrone, they do use dual-indirect sales-channel structures and both run 'traditional' older designs alongside the newer more innovative pieces, with the traditional giftware appealing to a broader segment.

The use of multiple channels is by and large an underresearched area, and the Finnish precursor of this study (Gabrielsson, 1999; Gabrielsson and Al-Obaidi, 2002) identified this research gap. Usually sales-channel decisions are viewed from a single-channel perspective, but the case companies in this research use multiple sales-channel structures in selected markets, supporting Gabrielsson and Al-Obaidi (2002).

Sales-channel decisions are of paramount importance to managers, and incorrect and inappropriate structures may be detrimental to sales volume and impact on long-term organizational performance. Inappropriate structures may be expensive to change and time-consuming in resolving contractual arrangements, therefore further study is merited.

FUTURE RESEARCH

Although some support is found in this work for the 'staged' sequential process approach to small-firm internationalization, Belleek does not really conform. Arguably they were 'Born Global', in 1857, long before the term was coined by contemporary researchers (McKinsey and Co, 1993; Madsen and Servais, 1997), supporting Knight, Bell and McNaughton (2001), who posit that the Born Global phenomenon is really a rebirth of an old concept. It would be interesting to research these old 'born globals' further, to explore the factors that influenced their internationalization strategies.

The results of this research may apply to other industries (Turnbull and Ellwood, 1986; Anderson and Coughlan, 1987; Corey *et al.*, 1989; Gabrielsson, 1999; Gabrielsson and Al-Obaidi, 2002). There is a need for further research within other sectors to establish what sales-channel structures are being utilized by companies and how are these changing, particularly in the knowledge-and service-intensive sectors. Further exploratory studies in other countries with a view to undertaking a larger-scale study in the future would also be desirable.

Another avenue for future research may be to return to the particular case companies and to carry out a longitudinal study, examining how their sales-channel decisions change over time, and in relation to their degree of internationalization. Also, to explore the impact of new communications technology and e-commerce on sales-channel structures and whether increased Internet adoption promotes the use of more hybrid channels, with cooperation built in, or leads to greater channel conflict and damage to long-term relationships.

REFERENCES

Alhadeff, J. and Cohen, R. (1997) 'Assembling the Right Internet Business Model', *DB2 Magazine*, Winter, 11–16.

Al-Obaidi, Z. (1999) 'International Technology Transfer Control: A Case Study of Joint Ventures in Developing Countries', Helsinki School of Economics, series A–151 (doctoral thesis).

Al-Obaidi, Z., Nathar, N. and Huda, N. (2000) 'A Framework for the Analysis of Barriers in IT Enabled Exporting of High-tech Firms', In R. Hackey (Ed.), *Proceedings of the Business Information Technology Management: E-futures* (on CD-ROM), 10th Annual BIT Conference, 1–2 November 2000, Manchester.

Anderson, E. and Coughlan, A. (1987) 'International Market Entry and Expansion via Independent or Integrated Channels of Distribution', *International Market Entry and Expansion*, 51 (Jan.), 71–82.

Cavusgil, T. and Das, A. (1997) 'Methodological Issues in Empirical Cross-cultural Research: A Survey of the Management Literature and a Framework', *Management International Review*, 71–97.

Coase, R.H. (1937) 'The Nature of the Firm', *Economica N.S*, 47, 386–405.

Corey, R.E., Cespedes, F.V. and Rangan, K.V. (1989) *Going to Market: Distribution Systems for Industrial Product* (Boston: Harvard Business School).

Cyert, R. and March, J. (1963) *A Behavioural Theory of the Firm*, 2nd edn 1992 (New York: Blackwell Publishers).

Dwyer, R., Schurr, P. and Oh Sejo (1987) 'Developing Buyer–Seller Relationships', *Journal of Marketing*, 51 (April), 11–27.

Eisenhardt, K. (1989) 'Building Theories from Case Study Research', *Academy of Management Review*, 14 (4), 532–50.

Gabrielsson, M. (1999) 'Sales Channel Strategies for International Expansion: The case of large companies in the European PC industry', *Helsinki School of Economics*, series A–163 (doctoral thesis).

Gabrielsson, M. and Al-Obaidi, Z. (2002) 'Multiple Sales Channel Strategies in Export Marketing of Small and Medium Sized Design Companies', in *International Business:*

Adjusting to New Challenges and Opportunities, McDonald, F., Tüselmann, H. and Wheeler, C. (eds) (Basingstoke: Palgrave).

Hamill, J. and Gregory, K. (1997) 'Internet Marketing in the Internationalization of UK SME's', *Journal of Marketing Management*, 13 (1), 9–28.

Hardy, K. and Magrath, A. (1988) *Marketing Channel management: Strategic Planning and Tactics* (New York: Scott, Foresman and Company).

Hentola, H. (1994) *Foreign Sales Subsidiaries and Their Role within the Internationalization Process of a Company: A Study of the Finnish Manufacturing Firms* (Helsinki: Helsinki School of Economics and Business Administration, CIBR research reports, series X–2).

Hoffman, D., Novak, T. and Chatterjee (1995) Commercial Scenarios for the Web: Opportunities and Challenges, 4.11.01 *http://www.usc.edu/dept/annenberg/issue3/hoffman.html*.

Indermaaur, K. (1997) 'Behind the Lines', *Internet Systems*, July, pp. S4–S8.

Johanson, J. and Vahlne, L. (1977) 'The Internationalization Process of the Firm: A Model of Knowledge Development on Increasing Foreign Commitments', *Journal of International Business Studies*, Spring/Summer, 23–32, in Buckley, Peter and Ghauri, Pervez, *The Internationalization of the Firm*, (London: Dryden Press, 1993), 32–45.

Knight, G., Bell, J.D. and McNaughton, R. (2001) 'The "Born Global Phenomenon": A Rebirth of an Old Concept', *Proceedings of the 4th McGill International Entrepreneurship Conference*, September (Glasgow).

Leonidou, L.C. and Katsikeas, C.S. (1996) 'The Export Development Process: An Integrative Review on Empirical Models', *Journal of International Business Studies*, 27, 3.

Luostarinen, R. (1970) 'Foreign Operations of the Firm', 1st edn, Helsinki School of Economics, licensiate thesis.

Luostarinen, R. (1979) 'Internationalization of the Firm: An Empirical Study of the Internationalization of Firms with Small and Open Domestic Markets with Special Emphasis on Lateral Rigidity as a Behavioural Characteristic in Strategic Decision-making', Helsinki School of Economics, series A–30 (doctoral thesis).

Madsen, T. and Servais, P. (1997) 'The Internationalization of Born Globals: An Evolutionary Process', *International Business Review*, 6 (6), 561–83.

Mallen, B. (1977) *Principles of Marketing Channel Management, Interorganisational Distribution Design and Relations* (Toronto: Lexington Books/D.C. Heath & Company).

McKinsey & Co. (1993) 'Emerging Exporters: Australia's High Value-added Manufacturing Exporters' (Canberra, Australian Manufacturing Council).

Miles, M. and Hubermann, A.M. (1994) *Qualitative Data Analysis: An Expanded Source Book* (2nd edn) (Newbury Park CA: Sage Publications).

Miller, E. (2001) 'Using the Web to go Global', *Computer-Aided Engineering*, 20 (3), 44–7.

Moriarty, R.T. and Moran, U. (1990) 'Managing Hybrid Marketing Systems', *Harvard Business Review*, November–December (1990).

OECD (1997) *Globalization and Small and Medium (SMEs) Enterprises*, 1: Synthesis report and 2: Country Studies (Paris).

Penrose, E. (1968) *The Growth of the Firm*, 1st pub. 1959 (Oxford: Basil Blackwell).

Rogers, E. (1962) *Diffusion of Innovations* (New York: Free Press of Glencoe).

Rosenbloom, B. (1995) *Marketing Channels: A Management View*, 1st edn 1978 (London: Dryden Press).

Seeley, R. (1997) 'Internet Commerce Emerges', *Application Development Trends*, June, 38–48.

Sethuraman, R., Anderson, J.C. and Narus, J.A. (1988) 'Partnership Advantage and Its Determinants in Distributor and Manufacturer Working Relationships', *Journal of Business Research*, 17, 327–47.

Stern, L. and Reve, T. (1980) 'Distribution Channels as Political Economies: A Framework for Comparative Analysis', *Journal of Marketing*, 44 (Summer), 52–64.

Stern, L., El-Ansary, A. and Brown, J. (1989) *Management in Marketing Channels* (Englewood Cliff, NJ: Prentice Hall).

Turnbull, P.W. and Ellwood, S. (1986) 'Internationalization in the Information Technology Industry', in Turnbull, Peter W. and Paliwoda, Stanley J. (eds), *Research in International Marketing* (Sidney: Croom Helm).

Vaivio, F. (1963) 'Rigid Adherence to Plans as an Element of Business Behaviour', *Finnish Journal of Business Economics*, 1963/III.

Williamson, O. (1975) *Markets and Hierarchies: Analysis and Antitrust Implications* (New York: Free Press).

Williamson, O. (1985) *The Economic Institutions of Capitalism* (New York: Free Press).

Yin, R. (1989) *Case Study Research: Design and Methods* (Newbury Park, CA: Sage Publications).

Part Three

The Internationalization of the Small Firm

12 The Role of Resources/Capabilities in the Internationalization and Performance of High-Technology Small Firms: Mode Choice and Performance

Luis Bernardino and Marian V. Jones

INTRODUCTION, AIMS AND OBJECTIVES

Over the last decade or so, small and medium-sized enterprises (SMEs) have become increasingly active in international markets (Bonaccorsi, 1992; Oviatt and McDougall, 1994, 1995). The internationalization of SMEs is widely recognized as driven by the increasing globalization of the world economy with the decline in trade barriers imposed by governments and parallel advances in telecommunications, informatics and lower transportation costs. Such changes have opened the doors to international market opportunities for SMEs.

As SMEs are acknowledged as vital to a country's development and well-being (Reynolds, 1997), any movement of their goods, services, resources or business interests in general across borders is likely to be of some interest to government policy-makers, and to the competing firms themselves. Of particular concern is the important role played by SMEs in high-technology sectors, in creating opportunities for new and skilled employment, and in contributing to economic growth and development (Coviello and McAuley, 1999). However, high-technology small firms (HTSF) compete in markets characterized by short and shortening life-cycles, in which technologies fast become obsolete. They face high technological risks and operate in industries subject to dramatic structural changes (Coviello and Munro, 1995). Domestic technology markets may be too small to accommodate the technology-based niche strategies typically pursued by small firms, and consequently small high-tech firms need to be active abroad, practically from the outset (Coviello and Munro, 1995).

Conventionally, the main focus of research on small-firm internationalization has been on issues relating to exports and the development of export sales (for a comprehensive review see Leonidou and Katsikeas, 1996). However, in recent years a growing number of studies have been carried out using one or several theoretical frameworks, looking in detail to the antecedents, processes and decisions taken during the internationalization processes of SMEs. This body of work is distinct from the conventional literature on small-firm internationalization and is generally known as the emerging field of international entrepreneurship

187

(see Jones and Coviello, 2002a for a review). This study is positioned within that body of work.

A few studies, emerging within the field of international entrepreneurship, have focused on the firm's resource base as being of particular importance in relation to internationalization (McDougall *et al.*, 1994; Vatne, 1995; Steensma *et al.*, 2000). This focus emerged within a gap in the traditional literature on internationalization which did not adequately address the effects of the small-firm internal resource base, particularly in technology-intensive sectors, on its international performance (McDougall and Oviatt, 1996; Coviello and McAuley, 1999). Although the literature on small firms acknowledges shortages of resources such as financial, managerial, organizational and so forth, the inter-nationalization literature has traditionally tended to examine small firms as a homogeneous sector within which resource shortages were seen as having the aggregate effect of acting as barriers or inhibitors to foreign market entry (Miesenbock, 1988; Buckley, 1989). However, within the general body of litera-ture on small firms, there are a number of studies that indicate that in order to overcome the above mentioned shortages, small firms may develop cooperative linkages with partners in order to pursue their growth strategies irrespective of whether they are domestic or international (Jones, 1998, 1999). Establishing link-ages with other firms allows small high-technology firms to gain access to resources and capabilities that would otherwise require considerable time and money, that currently they could not afford (McDougall *et al.*, 1994; Oviatt and McDougall, 1994; Zacharakis, 1997; Lu and Beamish, 2001).

In this context, our research focuses on the internal resource base of the firm, and the opportunity to access externally-held resources through cooperation with other firms in relation to the foreign market entry mode utilized, and their ultimate impact on international performance. More specifically, the main aim of this study is *to explore the relationship between the firm's internal resources and entry-mode choice, distinguished as cooperative versus independent modes. The central proposition is that the firm's internal resources will influence foreign entry-mode choice and ultimately its performance.* Therefore this study aims to develop a conceptual model for future empirical work with the following objectives:

1   To enhance understanding of the role that resources play in the international-ization of HTSFs

   * to identify the internal resources/capabilities which underpin sources of competitive advantage amongst HTSFs, and
   * to anticipate the likely impact that those internal very often intangible resources/capabilities have on the international performance of high-technology small firms.

2   To investigate the influence of internal resources/capabilities on the foreign market entry-mode utilization of HTSFs

- to determine the extent to which internal resources/capabilities possessed by small high-technology firms are associated with entry-mode utilization,
- to determine whether differences in resources/capabilities of small high-technology firms are associated with independent versus cooperative mode utilization, and
- to determine the impact of independent versus cooperative entry-mode utilization on a firm's international performance.

THEORETICAL FRAMEWORK

In the context of the research questions and objectives stated above, a research framework was developed as shown in Figure 12.1. This framework, inherently dynamic, tries to capture the linkage between the firm's internal resources/capabilities, foreign entry-mode utilization and international performance. In the framework, the firm is depicted as a bundle of resources and capabilities, with essentially two options for foreign market entry, shown by the bold arrows, either directly through independent entry modes or in cooperation with a partner. In the latter option, the firm is likely to participate in a process of discussion, negotiation and other interaction, summarized here as 'cooperation' with a partner. This process of cooperation may result in the exchange of resources between partners, exposure to the partner's capabilities, expertise and so forth, which will result in an adjustment of the focal firm's resource base, which is anticipated to impact the entry mode utilized and, ultimately, the firm's international performance. The process is seen as iterative and hence performance will feed back into the

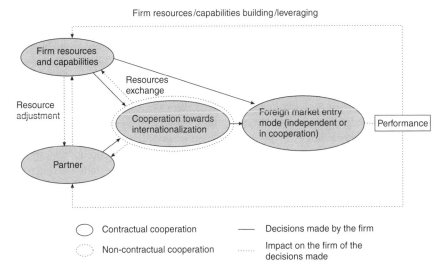

Figure12.1   A dynamic framework for international small-firm cooperation

resource base in the form of enhanced knowledge, financial resources, capabilities etc. which will effect future entry mode utilization and future performance and so on. It is proposed that differences in the firms' endowment of resources will influence their entry mode utilization.

Types of entry modes which can be defined as cooperative include licensing, joint ventures and other cooperative modes since they involve collaboration with partners (Root, 1994; Shrader, 2001). By contrast, export sales and wholly-owned subsidiaries can be considered independent entry modes since they do not involve cooperation with other partners (Root, 1994; Shrader, 2001).

Depending on the endowment of internal resources, the HTSF will internationalize through utilization of predominantly independent or predominantly cooperative entry modes. In the former instance, for example, it is likely that the HTSF will conduct its overseas business independently of a partner if it has, broadly speaking, all the required resources/capabilities to enable it to do so (Shrader, 2001). Furthermore, the literature suggests that if an HTSF wants to protect all its core competencies against any opportunistic behaviour from a potential partner, it will utilize independent modes, or internalized channels (Hill *et al.*, 1990; Agarwall and Ramaswami, 1992). As indicated, such modes include wholly-owned subsidiaries and direct exports to end customers. In the latter instance, for example, it is likely that firms which do not have all the required resources/capabilities to conduct business abroad are more likely to establish cooperation with partners in order to compensate for any resource deficiencies, and in so doing may augment their own resource base with their partner's resources/capabilities. In this context, although not explicit in the literature, there would seem to be an exchange or pooling of complementary resources/capabilities with the selected partner.

Cooperation may be the preferred mode for firms involved in very specialized activities, or those which play a specialized role in an industry's value chain. There is some indication in the literature on flexible specialization in small-firm sectors (Brock, 2000; Jones, 2001) that if an HTSF specializes in a specific part of a product or industry value-chain, it may try to find partners with capabilities or resources that will help link the firm more firmly into that value-chain activity (Jones, 2001; Jones and Tagg, 2001). This is the case, for example, for HTSFs that have developed an exploitable technology but do not have the necessary marketing and sales resources to produce, market or distribute it internationally. In this situation, a local partner may provide knowledge about the foreign country in terms of political and economic conditions, market potential, market segments, competition, distribution channels and other factors on how to conduct business. Currently, these kinds of partnerships are even more important in high-technology sectors considering that the geographical scope in which technology can be exploited is much wider than the firm's marketing expertise (Buckley and Casson, 1996). Under these conditions the firm can expand its activities to more geographical areas faster with lower costs, risks and market uncertainty (Contractor and Lorange, 1988; Aulakh *et al.*, 1996; Buckley and Casson, 1996).

Theoretically at least, cooperation can allow firms and particularly HTSFs to concentrate on a few core capabilities, very often protected by knowledge barriers, and which may not require important financial investments. In addition, HTSFs can simultaneously leverage complementary capabilities from other firms in order to achieve competitive advantage in international markets. In this situation it is proposed that the HTSF may adjust its resource base from its initial internal resources position to draw on potential synergetic resources from a selected partner. Thus, it is further proposed that the new venture, utilizing cooperative modes of foreign market entry, will have a broader resource and capabilities base and consequently, overtime, will achieve higher performance in a foreign market.

THE INTERNAL RESOURCE-BASE OF FIRMS

Firms have been described as a bundle of heterogeneous resources (Barney, 1991; Grant, 1991). Indeed the literature in economics acknowledges different categories of resources such as financial, physical, human, technological and organizational. However, the resource-based view (RBV) gives special emphasis to the firm's idiosyncratic resources, that is those specific and very often intangible resources which reside within the organization (Barney, 1986, 1991; Peteraf, 1993; Wernerfelt, 1984). These include, for example, technological knowledge, trade secrets, know-how generated by R&D activities and managerial, marketing or production skills that are valuable and difficult to imitate by competitors (Dollinger, 1995).

However, not all the firm's resources can be seen as holding the potential for competitive advantage, rather only those resources that are: (1) valuable, that is those which exploit market opportunities or render market threats ineffective; (2) scarce, among current and potential competitors; (3) imperfectly imitable, that is competitors do not possess then, and are unable to obtain these resources; and (4) non-substitutability for other resources (Barney, 1991; Dierickx and Cool, 1989; Peteraf, 1993). Currently, the RBV considers that a firm holds competitive advantage when it pursues a strategy not implemented by any other of its current and potential competitors (Barney, 1991). Furthermore, the competitive advantage is considered sustained when competitors are unable to replicate a firm's current strategy. In sum, the RBV points out:

1   firms within an industry possess different strategic resources which may have a strong influence in its competitiveness and consequently in performance; and

2   these resources may be hard to imitate and imperfectly tradable.

Consequently, heterogeneity in terms of endowment of resources between firms is clearly assumed. In these circumstances the RBV examines the link between idiosyncratic resources held by the firm and market performance. However, very often small firms only cover part of the production/industry value-chain activities and consequently their strategy is not only dependent on their internal resources but also upon contacts with other firms. In this situation firms are limited by their resource endowment, and consequently they need to establish business contacts with other firms having complementary resources (Borch and Arthur, 1995; Lee *et al.*, 2001). These external contacts play a very important role not only to the procurement of those complementary resources/assets, but also in the exploitation of market opportunities both national and international. In this context, cooperation with other firms seems to be critical in the search for market opportunities, to the testing of new ideas, or getting access to external resources. In conclusion, small firms establish linkages with other firms in which partners make available and obtain resources through long-lasting relationships. In addition, these relationships evolve explicitly in two-way exchanges of resources (Lee *et al.*, 2001).

In this chapter we examine the link between idiosyncratic intangible resources possessed by small high-technology firms as sources of competitive advantage and international performance. *Furthermore*, it is proposed that firms possessing higher levels of idiosyncratic resources are more entrepreneurial, that is more innovative, proactive and risk-seeking in their entry mode utilization, since they have higher levels of expertise in creating or seizing foreign market opportunities and pursuing them regardless of the resources that they currently control (Timmons, 1994). Under these circumstances they are more likely to favour cooperative modes that better enable them to adjust their resource and capabilities base through the establishment of external links with other firms, consequently enhancing international performance.

MODEL COMPONENTS

As already indicated, the study explores the relationship between internal idiosyncratic/intangible resources possessed by small high-technology firms, acknowledging the potential need for cooperation with other firms to access external resources, and international performance. Internal resources, in general, include all assets, capabilities, organizational processes, firm attributes, knowledge and so forth controlled by the firm which enable the firm to create, develop and implement its strategy and improve its efficiency (Daft, 1983). In this context, the RBV suggests that capabilities, organizational processes, firm attributes and knowledge might be considered as providing competitive advantage since they are valuable, scarce, imperfectly-tradable and non-substitutable. By contrast, tangible assets, as they can be obtained on the market, do not represent a source of competitive advantage (Barney, 1986).

In sum, all the resources – tangible and idiosyncratic/intangible – are deployed with the intent of their transformation into final products and services through managerial processes. The capacity of a firm in effectively and efficiently deploying resources and transforming them into products and services which fulfil the needs of end customers are, in some studies, termed *capabilities* (Grant, 1991; Amit and Schoemaker, 1993). In this study and as Foss (1997) points out, *capabilities* and *idiosyncratic resources* embedded in organizational routines have the same meaning and can be used interchangeably. One of the challenges faced in the development of the research design for this study is to identify and separate out the idiosyncratic resources that may contribute to the international performance of the small high-technology firm. This task is particularly challenging since management information systems tend to show only a partial and fragmented base of a firm's resources. Formal accounting systems are clearly inadequate in this matter because balance sheets in particular do not take into account the great majority of intangible assets (a notorious exception are software packages) and human resources. Indeed, this situation is mainly due to the difficulty of evaluating intangible assets.

The heterogeneity and imperfect transferability of the great majority of intangible assets make the use of valuation systems such as market prices, stockmarket values and so on difficult, if not impossible. In this context a possible approach to appraise intangible assets is to do the calculation of the difference between the stockmarket value and the replacement value of its tangible assets (Cockburn and Griliches, 1988). Nevertheless this type of reasoning is not applicable to the great majority of small high-technology firms since most of them are not quoted on the stockmarket.

More important for researchers in the field of international entrepreneurship is the challenge to develop measures of value in relation to idiosyncratic resources. The extant literature provides some useful categorizations and insights; for example, five different types of resources have been suggested. These are physical, financial, human, technological and organizational. However, not all of them are potential sources of competitive advantage. In this context, based on the RBV and entrepreneurship literatures combined with preliminary interviews with experts and academics on small high-technology firms, it is suggested here that four different types of resources/capabilities which represent potential sources of competitive advantage can be identified, and it is also suggested that these are likely to potentially influence a firm's international performance. The four types include organizational, technological, financial and human resources and will be discussed in the following sections.

Organizational Resources

Organizational resources are particularly idiosyncratic. They have been examined as composite variables that are said to indicate a firm's level of *entrepreneurial orientation* (Lee *et al.*, 2001). Entrepreneurial orientation (EO) attempts to capture organizational/management processes, methods and styles (Miller, 1983; Lumpkin and Dess, 1996). Organizational resources can be considered as providing competitive advantage since they are embedded in organizational routines; they are intangible and dispersed across teams and individuals within the company and not available on the market (Lumpkin and Dess, 1996; Lee *et al.*, 2001).

As suggested by Miller (1983) and further developed in other studies (Covin and Slevin, 1989; Lumpkin and Dess, 1996; Lee *et al.*, 2001), EO is characterized by three dimensions – innovativeness, risk-taking propensity and proactiveness. Innovativene*ss* refers to a firm's propensity to engage in the generation and development of new ideas through R&D activities to the introduction of new products/services and/or technological processes. More particularly, innovation is very important for HTSFs since otherwise they would rely on traditional ways of doing business and consequently would have less chance to be successful in the market (Covin and Slevin, 1989; Lumpkin and Dess, 1996).

Indeed, without innovations HTSFs would deliver to the market traditional products and services through traditional distribution channels. Under these circumstances HTSFs would be disadvantaged in relation to established competitors since HTSFs could be characterized by shortages of resources, limited awareness and brand reputation coupled with less-competitive cost structures. In sum, the introduction of new products, processes and marketing innovations are very important for HTSFs in order to differentiate them from competitors (Lumpkin and Dess, 1996; Lee *et al.*, 2001). Bruderl and Preisendorfer (2000) in a recent empirical study of a sample of German start-ups, found innovation as the most important predictor of firm growth. Innovativeness is measured by the emphasis that the HTSF gives to R&D activities, technical leadership and innovations, through the continuous introduction of new products or services reflecting dramatic technological changes from one product generation to the next.

Another dimension of EO is *risk-taking behaviour* that is characterized by the large commitment of resources to high-risk uncertain business in order to achieve high returns by identifying opportunities in the market. Examples of high-risk actions are, for instance, to borrow heavily, investing in new technologies or launching new products in new markets (Lumpkin and Dess, 1996; Lee *et al.*, 2001). In this context, internationalization might be considered part of the risk-taking behaviour of the entrepreneur. Risk-taking behaviour is measured, as suggested by Miller (1983), by the degree of adoption of risky R&D projects, as well as by the capital expenditures on those projects. It is considered a risky R&D project when the return of the project is not certain, which is the case for those projects that deal with the commercialization of brand new technologies or new product concepts never used before.

Finally, another dimension of EO is proactiveness. *Proactiveness* refers to the seeking of market opportunities that may or may not be related to the firm's current activities. Examples of these opportunities include the introduction of new products, systems and services ahead of the competition as well as through the streamlining of operations/processes which are in mature or declining life-cycles. Proactive firms may be considered pioneers in their domain of activities by their first-mover actions, influencing market trends, creating new market segments or replacing existing firms by the introduction of new products and services.

Proactiveness is operationalized, as suggested by Covin and Slevin (1989) and Miller (1983), by the firm's tendency to lead rather than to follow, in terms of projects that develop new technologies, procedures and processes and the introduction of new products and services.

Technological Capabilities

According to the RBV, technological capabilities represent sources of sustainable competitive advantages since they are currently valuable and difficult to imitate by competitors. Technological resources/capabilities include technological knowledge generated by R&D activities and other technology-specific intellectual capital, patents protected by law and intellectual property rights. In addition, if these skills are tacit and complex, as is very often the case with technological capabilities, they are very hard to imitate considering that they remain embedded in a firm's organizational routines (Winter, 1987; Barney, 1991; Kogut and Zander, 1995). However, not all-technological resources/capabilities are protected by patent law, some are protected only by knowledge barriers. Indeed, although knowledge barriers appear to provide weak protection against the potential opportunistic action held by competitors, it is important to bear in mind that very often competitors are not able to imitate a firm's skills, processes and capabilities (Miller and Shamsie, 1996).

Nevertheless, competitors may develop their skills to achieve the foreseen talent and knowledge of the focal firm. However, this is a process which currently takes time while the firm develops its skills, further maintaining the gap between its current and potential competitors. In sum, technological capabilities depend to a great extent on the technological knowledge and know-how developed within the firm through R&D activities required for the successful market introduction of state-of-the-art products or services. In such situations, technological capabilities may be measured by R&D intensity, that is by the number of equivalent R&D full-time employees, expenses in R&D, and by the degree of technological complexity and innovation in the products/services developed within the firm.

Financial Resources

Financial resources represent a medium of exchange for other productive resources (Chatterjee, 1990), and offer flexibility to managers in their deployment. Financial resources generated through business activity could be distributed in the form of dividends or other payments to shareholders/venture capitalists, or instead could be redeployed in further business activities. These business activities may include R&D for the development of new products and processes, new manufacturing plants or expansion to new geographical areas (Elango, 2000). In fact HTSFs may invest a high proportion of their available financial capital in product and market development (Lee *et al.*, 2001). Nevertheless, they very often lack the financial resources necessary to develop other critical activities such as technology development, marketing research and marketing communications because they do not usually have the borrowing capacity or the cash available to larger or longer established firms (*ibid.*). Indeed, since their fixed assets are not very significant, the firms are seen as risky and consequently must pay a premium for cash or other credit lines obtained from banks, suppliers or other firms. In this situation compared with bigger and more established firms HTSFs are charged higher interest rates by financial institutions and must pay higher prices with unfavourable credit conditions from suppliers and other firms.

By contrast, firms with greater amounts of financial capital are in a situation of more resource-independence for the firm (Dollinger, 1995). Furthermore, in order to overcome liabilities of newness (Brock, 2000) HTSF's with sufficient financial capital can afford to hire highly skilled personnel in areas critical to the firm's future development. Empirical evidence lends support to the observation that, other conditions being equal, *underfinanced* firms perform worse than firms with *adequate* financial resources (Schoonhoven *et al.*, 1990; Roberts and Hauptman, 1987). In this context, a firm is considered *underfinanced* when it does not have the financial capital to successfully develop the business according to market requirements.

According to the RBV, financial resources do not provide sustained competitive advantage since they are not rare, imitable or tradable. Nonetheless, it is reasonable to expect that those firms which invest more financial resources in their business will accumulate larger stocks of strategic assets compared with other firms which lack financial resources for the development of their businesses (Dierickx and Cool, 1989). Although financial resources can be indicated by the financial capital available to the firm, we prefer, similarly to Lee *et al.* (2001), to use the relative amount of cash deployed in technology development (R&D), market research and marketing communications, since these are critical activities to the growth and international performance of the HTSF.

Human Resources

Human resources may be the most critical resource to a firm's competitive advantage (Barney, 1991). Human resources perform different activities such as (1) productive tasks towards generation of a firm's products and services; (2) technical expertise within the knowledge of products and services; (3) organizational skills for decision-making in different functional areas (for example operations and marketing and sales); (4) provision of business services (such as accounting, law); (5) communication to different publics (for example customers, suppliers, banks, investors); and (6) leadership skills through the definition of the vision/ mission, overall business strategy and further implementation (Wickham, 2001).

Of some importance is the idiosyncratic or intangible component of human resources and, most particularly, the role of the entrepreneur/founding team (Jones and Coviello, 2002b). Indeed the entrepreneur could be considered the most valuable resource within the firm (Bruderl *et al.*, 1992; Bruderl and Preisendorfer, 2000). The role of the entrepreneur is even more critical in the case of small firms since he/she is simultaneously in charge of creating and developing the vision, strategy and leadership for the firm, and often performs some functional and administrative tasks towards the venture's success (Jones and Coviello, 2002a). At a personal level the entrepreneur must have a sense of achievement with high motivation, high skills and capabilities, and possess a network of personal contacts based on his/her own previous experience (Jones and Coviello, 2002b). Very often these networks of contacts represent the firm's initial customer base (Grieve-Smith and Fleck, 1987).

Human capital theory provides insight into the characteristics of founders' entrepreneurs' education, careers, histories and previous experience of business performance. From a review of the literature, Jones and Coviello (2002b) identify a distinction between general and specific human capital. The former refers to years of schooling and years of work experience, while the latter is related to the entrepreneur's industry-specific experience and specific human capital. The entrepreneur's industry-specific experience refers to his or her prior experience in the industry before starting the business, and its dimensions include prior self-employment experience; leadership experience in managing and directing employees; and parental self-employment (Becker, 1975). Reuber and Fischer (1997) define another aspect of human capital as the entrepreneur's international orientation which they measure as a composite of working experience abroad, international marketing and sales experience.

Human capital is likely to be an important component in internationalization since some empirical literature has identified a positive association between human capital and profitability (Bates, 1985; Bruderl *et al.*, 1992). In this context, even before the establishment of the firm, people with higher levels of human capital may be able to identify profitable market niches not yet exploited by other competitors (Bates, 1985). Moreover, entrepreneurs who currently have higher levels of human capital are likely to better deploy their knowledge of how to start a business successfully through the assessment of all relevant information and consequently all opportunities and threats. Industry-specific experience is an important predictor of specific capital because it enhances knowledge about attractive niches in order to develop business activity. On the other hand, entrepreneur-specific human capital may represent to the entrepreneur the best preparation, in terms of knowledge acquired, for the future entrepreneurial venture.

This section has identified and discussed four types of internal resources/capabilities held by the HTSF which may be sources of competitive advantage. The next section will focus on the foreign entry-mode choice by the HTSF.

Small High-Technology Firms and Entry Mode

Traditionally, foreign market entry modes are seen as methods employed by firms to gain access to international markets (Young *et al.*, 1989; Root, 1994). Currently there are a wide range of options available to firms which include exporting, licensing, franchising, management contracts, other cooperative agreements, joint ventures and wholly-owned subsidiaries (Young *et al.*, 1989). Each entry mode determines, to some extent, the degree of control that the firm has over foreign business activities (Anderson and Gatignon, 1986; Root, 1994), the level of risk and resource commitment to the foreign market (Hill *et al.*, 1990), the level of fixed and variable costs and the return on investment (Buckley and Casson, 1985), and the level of organizational commitment and market involvement (Johanson and Vahlne, 1977; Welch and Luostarinen, 1988; Erramilli and Rao, 1990; Burgel and Murray, 2000).

In addition, the traditional view of foreign market entry mode indicates that initial entry-mode choices may be changed only with considerable investment of time and money (Hill *et al.*, 1990; Root, 1994). Therefore, the selection of the appropriate entry mode is a strategic, and potentially long-term decision for the internationalizing firm (Agarwall and Ramaswami, 1992). However, this classification of modes using the above-mentioned criteria has tended to emerge from analysis and comparison between individual entry-mode types mainly from research on multinational manufacturing firms (Jones, 2001). The scope and scale of entry-mode activity, and especially FDI made by small and micro-firms, merits further investigation in light of changing cost structures, the downsizing of technology, the development of the software industry, and of a wide range of service and information-based industries.

The effects of such developments are implicit in recent studies on the internationalization of small firms which tend to view entry modes as firm-specific ways to conduct business abroad rather than merely as access to international markets (Bell *et al.*, 1998; Jones, 1998, 1999, 2001). In fact, recent empirical studies (Jones, 1998, 1999) on the internationalization of small firms provide evidence that certain entry modes could be combined in the early stages of internationalization even though firms generally have a limited resource base (Jones, 1999).

Although facing shortages of different types of resources, small high-technology firms may have the flexibility to choose between different modes based on their determination of the best way to conduct business abroad. In addition, it has been found that small firms do not always approach internationalization as an incremental process of increasing knowledge, commitment and investments in international markets. The process of internationalization may evolve very quickly and simultaneously to different foreign markets through the use of single or combinations of entry modes, relating to one or several value-chain activities (Jones, 1999, 2001). Indeed, small high-technology firms may specialize in one or several value-chain activities and consequently their process of internationalization may reflect the characteristics of the businesses they are in as well as their industry positions (Jones, 2001).

Returning to the RBV, firms are inherently heterogeneous in terms of resources and capabilities. In this context, the foreign market entry mode may reflect the firm's endowment of resources and capabilities which have been adjusted over time in accordance with the evolution of their own internationalization process. In this situation, small high-technology firms might have the choice to internationalize through independent rather than cooperative entry modes.

Based on research developed by Shrader (2001) and Root (1994), the main cooperative and independent foreign market entry modes which could be utilized by the HTSF are accommodated in the research model section presented above.

International Performance

To date, although there is a prolific and well-developed literature on export performance, much less is known about the more general effect of internationalization on SME performance (McDougall and Oviatt, 1996; Coviello and McAuley, 1999). This is a very important issue since internationalization is important to a firm's market performance and long-term profitability. Indeed, profitability and performance are two closely linked concepts since they represent the return that a firm gets from its international involvement. It may be presumed that firms which internationalize their businesses have certain performance targets in mind in relation to their international activities. The extant literature has, for the most part, focused on internationalization performance in relation to the scope and growth of sales overseas (Antoncic and Hisrich, 2000). Accordingly, the great majority of studies present export intensity, that is the percentage of a firm's overall sales accounted for by exports and export sales growth as the main criteria to measure export performance (Aaby and Slater, 1989).

Some studies suggest other criteria to measure export performance such as sales profitability in comparison with domestic sales profitability (Nakos *et al.*, 1998), geographic scope of foreign sales (Reuber and Fisher, 1997), or return on sales (Elango, 2000; Shrader, 2001). These are objective financial measures of export performance. Nonetheless, it has been suggested that subjective measures of performance and profitability should be used in studies of SMEs (Spanos and Lioukas, 2001). Indeed, although managers' responses in survey research may be problematic due to the subjectivity of their perceptions, the alternative of collecting 'objective' data has its owns drawbacks. In fact, very often, financial data for SMEs is unavailable or unreliable due to differences in accounting procedures or managerial manipulation (Dess and Robinson, 1984). In addition, the heterogeneity of small firms, and of their industries, raises questions of equivalence in the use of performance measures and in such situations it is may be necessary to introduce some kind of normalization of the considered variable (such as performance) in relation to the industry average in order that the comparison will be meaningful (Jones and Coviello, 2002b). In addition, one can argue that industry boundaries are quite fuzzy and ill-defined and therefore, the validity of such comparisons will be questionable.

In sum, although the subjectivity of perceptual measures has attracted some criticism, in practice they may provide more meaningful comparators than 'objective' data and 'absolute' measures (Spanos and Lioukas, 2001).

THEORETICAL BACKGROUND AND DEVELOPMENT OF PROPOSITIONS

The research model proposed here (Figure 12.1) uses the resource-based view as the dominant theoretical approach. However, as noted by Coviello and McAuley (1999), the complexity of the field of internationalization as it applies to small and to entrepreneurial firms, merits complementary interpretation from multiple theoretical perspectives. As indicated throughout our discussion, concepts and constructs from internalization, transaction-cost, network and social-capital approaches have been employed in the development of the main arguments and constructs of the model and, equally, will be used in the interpretation and analysis of results from future empirical stages of the research.

Returning to the alternative entry-mode options proposed in the conceptual model, certain trade-offs and paradoxes emerge from theory-based interpretation. The transaction-cost approach suggests that firms with a higher endowment of internal capabilities will try to protect their know-how against potential opportunistic behaviour of any partners, and are more likely to pursue independent entry modes or rapidly internalize their partnerships (Williamson, 1988). Any form of cooperation, contractual or non-contractual, is likely to be pursued cautiously and on an *ad hoc* basis. The potential benefits of cooperation for such firms are likely to lie in the potential exchange of knowledge, a form of idiosyncratic resource, between partners (Lawless and Price, 1992). However, classic transaction-cost interpretation suggests that the transfer of knowledge to outside partners may be inhibited by bounded rationality and fear of opportunism (Williamson, 1988; Seth and Thomas, 1994). Bounded rationality refers to the fact that individuals do not have access to all critical information to make decisions, neither do they have full comprehension of the information made available to them. Fear of opportunism is related to the opportunistic behaviour of individuals pursuing their own personal goals. Information or resource exchange between partners may be inefficient due to such factors.

Also, some forms of knowledge are more difficult to transfer than others. For example tacit knowledge, knowledge that is ill-codified or embedded in organizational routines is very hard to transfer across firm boundaries (Anderson and Gatignon, 1986; Buckley and Casson, 1996). Anecdotal evidence suggests that the risk of opportunism increases where knowledge is transferred to external partners. In other words, it increases the dissemination risk (Agarwall and Ramaswamy, 1992). Dissemination risk is related to the risk that some of a firm's capabilities, which might be sources of competitive advantage, may be appropriated by the partners with whom the firm cooperates. This is a very important issue since often knowledge constitutes the basis for competitive advantage for firms.

However, the transaction-cost approach also acknowledges the benefits of cooperation. This is the case, for example, when an internationalizing firm establishes a partnership with a local firm to enter a foreign market. In this situation, the local partner might provide relevant knowledge about the host market such as market potential, market segments, competition and market trends. The foreign market entrant, on the other hand, may provide knowledge about its products, systems, services and business practices in order to extend and exploit its competitive advantages without significant additional costs in the foreign country (Dunning, 1983; Makino and Delios, 1996). In this way the internationalizing firm may reduce the investment and the risk in doing business in an unknown environment whilst simultaneously leveraging its competitive advantage and facilitating the speed and scope of its internationalization process. While much of the research on transaction costs and foreign market entry modes has been concerned with large or well-established MNCs, it has relevance also for small entrepreneurial firms (Zacharakis, 1997).

To summarize, decisions relating to cooperation versus independent modes incorporate both advantages and disadvantages. According to the transaction-cost approach, both independent modes and cooperation involve substantial transaction costs. The former include costs related to the hiring of additional personnel, overheads, added costs on plant and equipment, and opportunity costs with the ownership of specific assets to internal transactions (Shrader, 2001), while the latter include the costs associated with the bureaucracy involved in establishing contracts/agreements with other firms, training, technology and management assistance and potential conflict due to different and opposed goals of the alliance partners (Buckley and Casson, 1996; Lyles and Salk, 1996). Furthermore, potential conflict may arise between partners due to conflicting goals, self-interest and managerial incompetence *inter alia* (Buckley and Casson, 1996). Nonetheless, the most important costs of cooperation, as already mentioned above, are associated with bounded rationality and opportunism. In short there are significant tradeoffs between independent modes and cooperation, particularly for those HTSFs with innovations or innovative potential.

In fast-moving technology markets, the most pressing danger is probably that HTSFs may miss important foreign market opportunities if they do not move quickly into foreign markets. Furthermore, they may also lose foreign market opportunities if they lack the necessary resources/capabilities to internationalize and find themselves on the horns of a dilemma where potentially they develop their ideas internally but miss important market opportunities, or collaborate with partners and risk losing either intellectual property or their competitive advantage where it resides in the idiosyncratic resources of their organization.

Empirical studies based on the internationalization of HTSFs provide evidence that competitive advantage is often based on the ability to offer innovative and differentiated products and services (Oviatt and McDougall, 1994, 1995; Coviello and Munro, 1995). Moreover, these studies suggest that HTSFs may enter foreign markets in order to recover expenditures on R&D too significant to recoup fully from their home markets (Oviatt and McDougall, 1994, 1995). Furthermore, because such products have short life-cycles, continuous investment in R&D is required in order to maintain competitive advantage. Although proprietary and knowledge-based resources, gained from R&D, can be transferred to partners against the payment of royalties or other fees, it seems unlikely that formal transfer will occur where knowledge-based resources are idiosyncratic by nature, ill-codified, complex and characterized by uncertainty. Very often this knowledge may be so complex, or so embedded in routines, that even a firm's personnel do not comprehend it and consequently it cannot be easily communicated to an external partner (Buckley and Casson, 1996).

As discussed, significant challenges associated with transaction costs and dissemination risk emerge when transfer of organizational/entrepreneurial orientation and technological capabilities to external partners is considered. Apparently, there is a preference for firms to transfer marketing-based advantages to local partners through brand reputation and product differentiation (Shrader, 2001). Such advantages generally require an in-depth knowledge about local market demand, customer preferences and tastes. It is this type of knowledge that local partners are well-suited to provide. Under these circumstances, pragmatism suggests that the firm cooperate with local partners in order to obtain from the outset competitive advantage, for example by establishing their products or services as industry standards ahead of competition (Jolly *et al.*, 1992; Oviatt and McDougall, 1995).

In short, HTSFs may not possess all the required resources and capabilities to establish business activities abroad and consequently face the paradox of trying to protect their core competencies (for example technology knowledge, trade secrets, manufacturing skills) whilst simultaneously trying to establish linkages with other firms to get access to external resources. Paradoxically, also, the higher the endowment of the firm's idiosyncratic resources/capabilities the more likely it is that it will proactively seek potential partners in order to expand abroad more quickly and to more locations (Shrader, 2001). Firms that are less well-endowed, particularly in respect of entrepreneurial resources and orientation, are less likely to seek partnership. In addition the greater the endowment of firm's tangible internal resources the more likely the firm is to be seen as a suitable partner by other firms.

These arguments lead to the following main propositions:

- *Proposition 1*: The greater the endowment of technological capabilities, the more likely is the HTSF to use independent modes of foreign market entry.
- *Proposition 2*: The greater the endowment of entrepreneurial orientation, and specific aspects of human capital, the more likely is the HTSF to use cooperative modes of foreign market entry.
- *Proposition 3*: Cooperative modes of foreign market entry utilized by HTSFs are associated with higher levels of international performance in those foreign markets where firms have adjusted their resource base through cooperative entry.
- *Proposition 4*: Entrepreneurial orientation, in particular, is associated with cooperative modes of market entry, and subsequently higher levels of international performance.

- ***Proposition 5***: The greater the endowment of overall idiosyncratic resources/ capabilities, the more likely is the HTSF to use cooperative modes of foreign market entry, and subsequently higher levels of international performance.

CONCLUSIONS AND RECOMMENDATIONS

The study described in this chapter is concerned primarily with the relationships between a firm's resources, its utilization of either cooperative, or independent entry modes, and international performance. It highlights the central role of the entrepreneur/founding team to the international success of the small high-technology firm (HTSF). This role is recognized as including the creation of a vision/mission for the firm, developing and implementing the strategy and running the business on a daily basis. Due to limited human resources in HTSFs, the entrepreneur may also perform marketing, sales and administration tasks but may have a technical or scientific, rather than a business background.

The study also emphasizes the importance of a firm's idiosyncratic and intangible resources that can be sources of competitive advantage. These include entrepreneurial orientation, technological capabilities, human and financial resources. As suggested in the literature (Miller, 1983), entrepreneurial orientation includes innovativeness, risk-taking and proactiveness. Financial resources are critical to a firm's current business activity and fundamental to tasks such as the development of technological knowledge, market research and marketing communications – for example advertising, symposiums, trade fairs and public relations (Lee *et al.*, 2001) – but are not in themselves proxy measures for the resource base of the firm.

Implicit in the theoretical framework developed in this chapter is the firm's external network of informal cross-border links. By establishing linkages with foreign partners, the HTSF can minimize the risks and resources required for foreign market expansion (Shrader, 2001).

In short, in order to create value from its international activities, the HTSF may need to achieve a balance between the accumulation of internal resources/capabilities and the development of cooperative linkages with other firms to gain access to complementary resources. In fact, as suggested above, if the entrepreneur prioritizes the development of internal capabilities, it may be at the expense of missing important market opportunities. Conversely, if emphasis is placed on the development of networks of external partners, the trade-off may be in the internal development of the firm. In this case external partners may not find the firm attractive enough, in terms of its internal capabilities and resources, to risk investment in a cooperative arrangement (Chung *et al.*, 2000).

The choice between cooperative versus independent entry modes appears to be very much one of balance. The firm's internal resource-base and the composition and balance of its resources are indicated in the extant literature to be of some importance. The critical factor, however, is likely to be the entrepreneur and the creativity with which the entrepreneur enters the foreign market and assimilates that process and experience into the adjustment of the firm's resource base, and towards performance.

REFERENCES

Aaby, N. and Slater, S.F. (1989) 'Management Influences on Export Performance: A Review of the Empirical Literature 1978–1988', *International Marketing Review*, 6, 7–23.

Agarwal, S. and Ramaswami, S.N. (1992) 'Choice of Foreign Market Entry Mode: Impact of Ownership, Location and Internalization Factors', *Journal of International Business Studies*, 23 (1), 1–27.

Amit, R. and Schoemaker, P.J. (1993) 'Strategic Assets and Organizational Rent', *Strategic Management Journal*, 14 (1), 33–46.

Anderson, E. and Gatignon, H. (1986) 'Modes of Foreign Entry: A Transaction Cost Analysis and Propositions', *Journal of International Business Studies*, 17 (3), 1–26.

Antoncic, B. and Hisrich, R.D. (2000) 'Global Marketing Co-operation and Networks', *Journal of Euromarketing*, 9 (2), 17–35.

Aulakh, P.S., Kotabe, M. and Sahay, A. (1996) 'Trust and Performance in Cross-Border Marketing Partnerships: A Behavioural Approach', *Journal of International Business Studies*, 27 (5), 1005–32.

Barney, J.B. (1991) 'Firm Resources and Sustained Competitive Advantage', *Journal of Management* 17, 99–120.

Barney, J.B. (1986) 'Strategic Factor Markets: Expectations, Luck and Business Strategy', Management Science, 42, 1231–41.

Bates, T. (1985) 'Entrepreneur Human Capital Endowments and Minority Business Validity', *Journal of Human Resources*, 20 (4), 540–54.

Becker, G.S. (1975) *Human Capital* (Chicago: University of Chicago Press).

Bell, J., Crick, D. and Young, S. (1998) 'A Holistic Perspective on Small Firm Growth and Internationalisation' (City University Business School).

Bonaccorsi, A. (1992) 'On the Relationship between Firm Size and Export Intensity', *Journal of International Business Studies*, 23 (4), 605–35.

Brock, J.K.U. (2000) 'Virtual Globals: Marketspace and the Internationalisation of Small Technology-Based Firms', PhD thesis (University of Strathclyde).

Borch, O.J. and Arthur, M.B. (1995) 'Strategic Networks Among Small Firms: Implications for Strategy Research Methodology', *Journal of Management Studies*, 32 (4), 419–41.

Bruderl, J. and Preisendorfer, P. (2000) 'Fast-Growing Businesses', *International Journal of Sociology*, 30, 45–70.

Bruderl, J., Preisendorfer, P. and Ziegler, R. (1992) 'Survival Chances of Newly Funded Business Organizations', *American Sociological Review*, 57 (2), 227–42.

Buckley, P.J. (1989) Foreign Direct Investment by Small and Medium-Sized Enterprises: The Theoretical Background, *Small Business Economics*, 1, 89–100.

Buckley, P. and Casson, M. (1996) 'An Economic Model of International Joint Venture Strategy', *Journal of International Business Studies*, 27 (5), 849–76.

Buckley, P.J. and Casson, M. (1985) *The Economic Theory of the Multinational Enterprise* (London: Macmillan).

Burgel, O. and Murray, G.C. (2000) 'The International Market Entry Choices of Start-Up Companies in High Technology Industries', *Journal of International Marketing*, 8 (2), 33–62.

Chatterjee, S. (1990) 'Excess Resources Utilization Costs and Mode of Entry', *Academy of Management Journal*, 33 (4), 780–800.

Chung, S., Singh, H. and Lee, K. (2000) 'Complementary, Status Similarity, and Social Capital as Drivers of Alliance Formation', *Strategic Management Journal*, 21 (1), 1–22.

Cockburn, I. and Griliches, Z. (1988) 'Industry Effects and the Appropriability Measures in the Stock Market's Valuation of R&D and Patents', *American Economic Review*, 78 (2), 419–23.

Contractor, F.J. and Lorange, P. (1988) *Cooperative Strategies in International Business* (Lexington: Lexington Books).

Coviello, N.E. and McAuley, A. (1999) 'Internationalisation and the Smaller Firm: A Review of Contemporary Literature', *Management International Review*, 39 (3), 223–56.

Coviello, N.E. and Munro, H. (1995) 'Growing the Entrepreneurial Firm: Networking for International Market Development', *European Journal of Marketing*, 29 (7), 49–61.

Covin, J.G. and Slevin, D.P. (1989) 'Strategic Management of Small Firms in Hostile and Benign Environments', *Strategic Management Journal*, 10 (1), 75–87.

Daft, R. (1983) *Organization Theory and Design* (New York: West).

Dess, G. and Robinson, R.B. (1984) 'Measuring Organisational Performance in the Absence of Objective Measures', *Strategic Management Journal*, 5, 265–73.

Dierickx, I. and Cool, K. (1989) 'Asset Stock Accumulation and Sustainability of Competitive Advantage', *Management Science*, 35 (12), 1504–14.

Dollinger, M.J. (1995) *Entrepreneurship: Strategies and Resources* (Boston, MA: Irwin).

Dunning, J.H. (1983) 'Market Power of the Firm and International Transfer of Technology: An Historical Excursion', *International Journal of Industrial Organization*, 1 (3), 333–53.

Elango, B. (2000) 'An Exploratory Study into the Linkages Between Corporate Resources and the Extent and Form of Internationalization of U.S. Firms', *American Business Review*, 18 (2), 12–26.

Erramilli, M.K. and Rao, C.P. (1990) 'Choice of Foreign Market Entry Modes by Service Firms: Role of Market Knowledge', *Management International Review*, 30, 135–50.

Foss, N.J. (1997) 'Resources and Strategy: Problems, Open Issues and Ways Ahead', in *Resources, Firms and Strategies*, Foss, Nicolai J. (ed.), (Oxford: Oxford University Press) 345–65.

Grant, R.M. (1991) 'The Resource-Based Theory of Competitive Advantage: Implications for Strategy Formulation', *California Management Review*, 114–35.

Grieve-Smith, J. and Fleck, V. (1987) 'Business Strategies in Small High-Technology Companies', *Long Range Planning*, 20 (2), 61–9.

Hill, C.W., Hwang, P. and Kim, W.C. (1990) 'An Eclectic Theory of the Choice of International Entry Mode', *Strategic Management Journal*, 11 (2), 117–28.

Johanson, J. and Vahlne, J.-E. (1977) 'The Internationalization Process of the Firm: A Model of Knowledge Development and Increasing Foreign Market Commitments', *Journal of International Business Studies*, 8 (1), 23–32.

Jolly, V.K., Alahuta, M. and Jeannet, J.-P. (1992) 'Challenging the Incumbents: How High Technology Start-Ups Compete Globally', *Journal of Strategic Change*, 1, 71–82.

Jones, M.V. (1998) 'International Expansion of Small High Technology Based Firms: The Role of External Linkages in International Growth and Development', PhD thesis (University of Strathclyde).

Jones, M.V. (1999) 'The Internationalisation of Small UK High Technology Firms', *Journal of International Marketing*, 7 (4), 15–41.

Jones, M.V. (2001) 'First Steps in Internationalisation: Concepts and Evidence from a Sample of Small High Technology Firms', *Journal of International Management*, 7, 191–210.

Jones, M.V. and Tagg, S.K. (2001) 'A Value Chain Analysis of UK High Technology Based Firms' Internationalisation', in, *4th McGill Conference on* International Entrepreneurship, Researching New Frontiers Proceedings, 2, 85–112 (Glasgow: University of Strathclyde).

Jones, M.V. and Coviello, N.E. (2002a) 'Methodologies for Understanding International Entrepreneurship', The 2002 Small Business and Entrepreneurship Conference Proceedings, 15–16 April (University of Nottingham, UK), 251–60.

Jones, M.V. and Coviello, N.E. (2002b) 'A Time-Based Contingency Model of Entrepreneurial Internationalisation Behaviour', working paper 2002–12 (University of Calgary: Haskayne School of Business).

Kogut, B. and Zander, U. (1995) 'What Firms Do? Coordination, Identity and Learning', *Organization Science*, 7, 502–18.

Lawless, M.W. and Price, L.L. (1992) 'An Agency Perspective on New Technology Champions', *Organization Science*, 3 (3), 342–55.

Lee, C., Lee, K. and Pennings, J.M. (2001) 'Internal Capabilities, External Networks, and Performance: A Study on Technology-Based Ventures', *Strategic Management Journal*, 22 (6,7), 615–40.

Leonidou, L.C. and Katsikeas, C.S. (1996) 'The Export Development Process: An Integrative Review of Empirical Models', *Journal of International Business Studies*, 6 (2), 517–51.

Lu, J.W. and Beamish, P.W. (2001) 'The Internationalization and Performance of SMEs', *Strategic Management Journal*, 22 (6,7), 565–86.

Lumpkin, G.T. and Dess, G.G. (1996) 'Clarifying the Entrepreneurial Orientation Construct and Linking it to Performance', *Academy of Management Review*, 21 (1), 135–72.

Lyles, M.A. and Salk, J.E. (1996) 'Knowledge Acquisition from Foreign Parents in International Joint Ventures: An Empirical Examination in the Hungarian Context', *Journal of International Business Studies*, 27 (5), 877–904.

Makino, S. and Delios, A. (1996) 'Local Knowledge Transfer and Performance: Implications for Alliance Formation in Asia', *Journal of International Business Studies*, 27 (5), 905–28.

McDougall, P.P., Shane, S. and Oviatt, B.M. (1994) 'Explaining the Formation of International New Ventures: The Limits of Theories from International Business Research', *Journal of Business Venturing*, 9, 469–87.

McDougall, P.P. and Oviatt, B.M. (1996) 'New Venture Internationalization, Strategic Change, and Performance: A Follow-up Study', *Journal of Business Venturing*, 11, 23–40.

Miesenbock, K.J. (1988) 'Small Businesses and Exporting: A Literature Review', *International Small Business Journal*, 6 (2), 42–61.

Miller, D. (1983) 'The Correlates of Entrepreneurship in Three Types of Firms', *Management Science*, 29, 770–91.

Miller, D. and Shamsie, J. (1996) 'The Resource-Based View of the Firm in Two Environments: The Hollywood Film Studios from 1936 to 1965', *Academy of Management Journal*, 39 (3), 519–43.

Nakos, G., Brouthers, K.D. and Brouthers, L.E. (1998) 'The Impact of Firm and Managerial Characteristics on Small and Medium-Sized Greek Firms' Export Performance', *Journal of Global Marketing*, 11 (4), 23–47.

Oviatt, B.M. and McDougall, P.P. (1995) 'Global Start-Ups: Entrepreneurs on a Worldwide Stage', *Academy of Management Executive*, 9 (2), 30–44.

Oviatt, B.M. and McDougall, P.P. (1994) 'Towards a Theory of International New Ventures', *Journal of International Business Studies*, 25 (1), 45–64.

Peteraf, M.A. (1993) 'The Cornerstones of Competitive Advantage', *Strategic Management Journal*, 14 (3), 179–91.

Reuber, A.R and Fischer, E. (1997) 'The Influence of the Management Team's International Experience on Internationalization Behavior', *Journal of International Business Studies*, 28 (4), 807–25.

Reynolds, P.D. (1997) 'New and Small Firms in Expanding Markets', *Small Business Economics*, 9 (1), 79–84.

Roberts, E.B. and Hauptman, O. (1987) 'The Financing Threshold Effect on Success and Failure of Biomedical and Pharmaceutical Start-Ups', *Management Science*, 33, 381–94.

Root, F.R. (1994) *Entry Strategies for International Markets* (Lexington, MA: Lexington Books).

Schoonhoven, C.B., Eisenhardt, K.M. and Lyman, K. (1990) 'Speeding Products to Market: Waiting Time to First Product Introduction in New Firms', *Administrative Science Quarterly*, 35 (1), 177–207.

Seth, A. and Thomas, H. (1994) 'Theories of the Firm: Implications for Strategy Research', *Journal of Management Studies*, 31 (2), 165–91.

Shrader, R.C. (2001) 'Collaboration and Performance in Foreign Markets: The Case of Young High-Technology Manufacturing Firms', *Academy of Management Journal*, 44 (1), 45–60.

Spanos, Yiannis E. and Lioukas, Spyros (2001) 'An Examination into the Causal Logic of Rent Generation: Contrasting Porter's Competitive Strategy Framework and the Resource-Based Perspective', *Strategic Management Journal*, 22 (10), 907–34.

Steensma, H.K., Marino, L., Weaver, K. and Dickson, P.H. (2000) 'The Influence of National Culture on the Formation of Technology Alliances by Entrepreneurial Firms', *Academy of Management Journal*, 43 (5), 951–73.

Timmons, J.A. (1994) *New Venture Creation*, 4th edn (Burr Ridge, IL: Irwin).

Vatne, E. (1995) 'Local Resource Mobilisation and Internationalisation Strategies in Small and Medium-Sized Enterprises', *Environment and Planning*, 27, 63–80.

Welch, L.S. and Luostarinen, R.K. (1988) 'Internationalization: Evolution of a Concept', *Journal of General Management*, 14 (2), 34–55.

Wernerfelt, B. (1984) 'A Resource-Based View of the Firm', *Strategic Management Journal*, 5 (2), 171–80.

Wickham, Philip A. (2001) *Strategic Entrepreneurship: A Decision Making Approach to New Venture Creation and Management* (Harlow: Financial Times/Prentice Hall).

Williamson, O.E. (1988) 'Corporate Finance and Corporate Governance', *Journal of Finance*, 43 (3), 567–91.

Winter, S.G. (1987) 'Knowledge and Competence as Strategic Assets', in *The Competitive Challenge*, Teece, D.J. (ed.) (Cambridge, MA: Ballinger), 159–84.

Young, S., Hamill, J., Wheeler, C. and Davies, J.R. (1989) *International Market Entry and Development: Strategies and Management* (Hemel Hempstead: Harvester Wheatsheaf).

Zacharakis, A.L. (1997) 'Entrepreneurial Entry Into Foreign Markets: A Transaction Costs Perspective', *Entrepreneurship Theory and Practice*, 21 (3), 23–39.

13 De-Internationalization and the Small Firm

Romeo V. Turcan

INTRODUCTION

The last decade of the twentieth century has contributed most to the body of knowledge about the internationalization of small firms. During that period, the focus was primarily on the growth – or positive development – of international business operations (Benito and Welch, 1997). The problem with the growth of the firm, however, is simply that most firms do not experience growth (Penrose, 1959). This is particularly true not so much at the initial internationalization stage, when firms start exporting, but at the next stage of real international commitment, for example making an international investment (Yip *et al.*, 2000). In such situations, trying to manage the firm's portfolio proactively (Douglas and Craig, 1996), managers may decide to reduce international engagement or leave the foreign market completely (Pauwels and Matthyssens, 1999). To date, the research on the withdrawal of small firms from cross-border activities (totally or partially) is relatively scarce (Benito and Welch, 1997; Pauwels and Matthyssens, 1999; Matthyssens and Pauwels, 2000; Crick, 2002). This chapter aims to further the understanding of cross-border activities of small firms by exploring the nature of the de-internationalization processes in small firms. To do this, literature from several disciplinary areas will be brought together and a conceptual framework of small firms' withdrawal processes will be developed.

A PERSPECTIVE ON INTERNATIONALIZATION

Processes of Internationalization

Two theoretical approaches dominate contemporary research on the internationalization of small firms (for a comprehensive review see Coviello and McAuley, 1999). They are (1) the stage approach initiated by Cavusgil (1980), Johanson and Vahlne (1977), Johanson and Wiedersheim-Paul (1975), and (2) the network approach initiated by Johanson and Mattsson (1988, 1992), Johanson and Vahlne (1977).

Known also as the Uppsala model, the stage approach suggests that each stage of internationalization involves an increased commitment to international activities and that the process of internationalization is the consequence of the acquisition of experiential knowledge, in particular market-specific knowledge. Commitment increases as firms learn more and therefore become less uncertain about foreign markets (Johanson and Vahlne, 1977; Cavusgil, 1984). However, the stage approach was widely criticized (for a comprehensive review see Andersen, 1993, 1997), and widely challenged in the literature (for example Sullivan and Bauerschmidt, 1990; Bell, 1995; Bell *et al.*, 2001; Jones 2001; Knight *et al.*, 2001). The major limitation of the stage approach is in its use of linear models to try to explain complex, dynamic, interactive and frequently non-linear behaviour (Bell, 1995). Also, it does not include cooperative modes of entry and does not permit mode changes involving decreasing foreign commitment (Andersen, 1997). In this respect, internationalization can be viewed as a barrier to de-internationalization (Benito and Welch, 1997).

At the same time, the network approach has received a lot of attention and recognition in the process of explaining the internationalization of small firms (recent examples include Anderson *et al.*, 1994; Coviello and Munro, 1995, 1997; Coviello, 1996; Elg and Johansson, 1996; Tikkanen, 1998; Coviello and Martin, 1999; Dennis, 2000). The network approach is based on theories of social exchange and resource dependency, and focuses on firm behaviour in the context of a network of interorganizational and interpersonal relationships (Axelsson and Easton, 1992). It has been suggested that success in new foreign market development is rooted in a firm's relationships in current markets, whether these be domestic or foreign, rather than in the identification and analysis of foreign market characteristics and the development of tailored market strategies (Johanson and Mattsson, 1988). Also, the network approach provides for reciprocity between inward and outward activities (Crick and Jones, 2000), and recognizes the importance of the networking role on inward international activities as part of the growing research on networks and internationalization (Johanson and Mattsson, 1988; Johanson and Vahlne, 1990). The firms' propensities to influence their exchange conditions and form new linkages while terminating others (Elg and Johansson, 1996) might explain the process of reduction of international involvement.

Patterns of Internationalization

However, the empirical literature on internationalization has tended to focus on the outward rather than inward patterns, while inward-outward patterns of internationalization have received limited coverage (Korhonen *et al.*, 1996). As a result a holistic approach towards internationalization of small (high-technology) firms has been called for (see for example Jones, 1999, 2001; Bell *et al.*, 2001; Fletcher, 2001), where both inward and outward patterns of internationalization are emphasized and described (recent examples include Welch and Luostarinen, 1993; Oviatt and McDougall, 1994; Bell, 1995; Korhonen *et al.*, 1996; Jones, 1999, 2001; Crick and Jones, 2000; Jones and Tagg, 2001).

The issue of inward–outward activities is crucial not only from an academic point of view, but also from a policy-making standpoint. As government organizations tend to encourage only outward operations (mainly exports that contribute positively to the balance of payments), and to some extent inward investment (which makes a positive contribution to the local economy and ultimately stimulates exports), many inward activities by foreign firms may be overlooked as internationalization opportunities for domestic enterprises. In their study, Korhonen *et al.* (1996) found that for a majority of Finnish SMEs the inward operations were their first internationalization stage, whereas the outward operations played a secondary role. Crick and Jones (2000) criticize the view of internationalization of small firms evident in the provision of trade assistance programmes and suggest that international expansion strategies other than pure exporting may better represent internationalization processes.

From the point of view of withdrawing from international activity, an understanding of inward–outward patterns of internationalization is pivotal as it allows the interrelation and integration of (such) decisions and (such) processes that identify a firm's individual pattern(s) of internationalization (Jones, 1999). In this context, the next section will bring together relevant strands of literature from several disciplinary areas in order to discuss and analyse the phenomenon of de-internationalization.

A PERSPECTIVE ON DE-INTERNATIONALIZATION

Why De-Internationalization?

To date, most of the literature on the internationalization of firms has focused on the growth – or positive development – of international business operations (Benito and Welch, 1997). The problem with the growth of the firm, however, is simply that most firms do not experience growth (Penrose, 1959). As argued earlier this is particularly true not only during initial internationalization, but also when there is real international commitment.

In an attempt to explain and understand how and why companies decrease their international involvement, it has been suggested that firms may experience 'epochs' of internationalization, followed by periods of consolidation or retrenchment, or they may be involved in particular 'episodes' that lead to rapid international expansion or de-internationalization (Kutschker *et al.*, 1997; Jones, 1999, 2001). Also the existence of different internationalization 'pathways', 'trajectories' and non linear 'patterns' and 'profiles' has been acknowledged and explored (Jones, 1999, 2001; Bell *et al.*, 2001; Jones and Tagg, 2001; Knight *et al.*, 2001). However, to date the research on the reduction of internationalization engagement is far less common (Benito and Welch, 1997; Pauwels and Matthyssens, 1999; Matthyssens and Pauwels, 2000; Crick, 2002), probably due to the seemingly negative and undesirable features associated with these phenomena (Benito and Welch, 1997) – for example human nature having a tendency to suppress admission of failure (Clarke and Gall, 1987), or difficulty in getting longitudinal data (Benito, 1997). Also, the managers' decisions to either reduce the international engagement or leave the foreign market completely should not, *a priori*, be viewed as a failure (Pauwels and Matthyssens, 1999; Crick, 2002). For example, this issue becomes important when determining the trade support that might be required by managers (Crick, 2002), as trade support can be used to encourage withdrawal from foreign operations which may then allow the firm to maximize domestic market opportunities. Thus, investigating the underlying drivers of why and how small firms might reduce or even withdraw from their international engagement may lead to a better understanding of a more holistic internationalization process of the small firm (Pauwels and Matthyssens, 1999).

How De-Internationalization is Defined

Welch and Luostarinen (1988, p. 37) introduced the term 'de-internationalization' arguing that 'once a firm has embarked on the process [of internationalization], there is no inevitability about its continuance'. Benito and Welch (1997) who made one of the first attempts to define de-internationalization, defined the concept as '. . . any voluntary or forced actions that *reduce* a company's *engagement in* or *exposure to* current cross-border activities' (emphasis added, p. 9). They also recognized the importance of differentiating between partial and full de-internationalization. The three constructs emphasized above require further investigation in order to improve the definition of de-internationalization. For example, when a company changes the foreign market servicing mode from investment to franchising (see Alexander and Quinn, 2002), partial de-internationalization, the company's *engagement in* and *exposure to* cross-border activities might still *increase* (see Hadjikhani, 1997). Thus, it might be argued (see also Kutschker *et al.*, 1997) that despite decreasing the level of internationalization, as represented by type of entry mode, the overall growth of the firm will be towards an increased level of cross-border activity.

However, the above definition of de-internationalization acknowledges that the cross-border activities of a firm can be (and must be) investigated holistically by understanding the hows and whys of both (inward–outward) internationalization and (inward–outward) de-internationalization decisions and processes. Thus, the process of cross-border activity of the firm can be defined as a cause – effect relationship between internationalization and de-internationalization, whereby a firm can not de-internationalize (the effect) without having internationalized (cause). If this statement is true, the cross-border activity paradigm (see Figure 13.1) evolves, whereby the firm de-internationalizes in the same way as it has internationalized by demonstrating the same but reverse behaviour.[1]

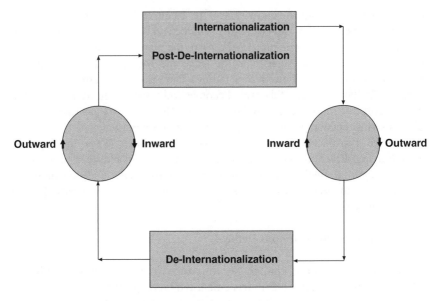

Figure 13.1   A model of cross-border activity

How De-Internationalization is Conceptualized

Despite the recent attempts to develop a holistic approach towards international-ization (for example Jones, 1999, 2001; Bell *et al.*, 2001; Fletcher, 2001), the concept of de-internationalization has not been fully developed and integrated within the cross-border literature. Benito and Welch (1997) undertook the first step towards developing a conceptual framework of the de-internationalization process and suggested that the probability of withdrawal from international oper-ations declines as the commitment to these operations increases. They argued that de-internationalization, like advanced internationalization, should be seen as part of the broader perspective of the overall [cross-border] strategy of a firm. However, they also concluded that 'it takes us a limited distance in terms of pro-viding an appropriate conceptual setting for de-internationalization moves and in seeking to explain them' (p. 19), and opted for further research that would follow de-internationalization moves by a number of firms through an extended period of time, and internationalization stages in order to clarify the circumstances and influences on decisions to withdraw.

Another area of research that has been concerned with withdrawal from for-eign operations is the literature on divestment, and, to a lesser extent, on export withdrawal. The conceptual framework that emerged from the divestment research (for a review see Chow and Hamilton, 1993) has been based primarily on two streams of literature, one from economics (Buckley and Casson, 1976; Dunning, 1980; Williamson, 1985) that focuses on asset specificity (see Porter,

1976) as a barrier to exit (Nargundkar *et al.*, 1996; Karakaya, 2000), and the second from strategic management that approaches divestment from the product life-cycle perspective (Harrigan, 1980; Harrigan and Porter, 1983) and the product portfolio perspective (Porter, 1987) with the main theme being strategic change and strategic fit (Kelly and Amburgey, 1991; Zajac *et al.*, 2000). In an attempt to understand the determinants of de-investment (for example Haynes *et al.*, 2000), it was found that divestment was systematically related to leverage, corporate governance, strategy and – to a limited extent – market structure characteristics.

However, despite the fact that de-investment has been viewed as the end result of strategic decisions regarding: (1) reallocation or concentration of productive resources at a national, regional or global level; (2) change of foreign market servicing mode, for example from local production to export; or (3) complete withdrawal from a host country (Benito, 1997), and that there is a large amount of empirical research on de-investment (for example Hoskisson *et al.*, 1994; Chang and Singh, 1999; Haynes *et al.*, 2000; Mata and Portugal, 2000; Shin, 2000; Tegarden *et al.*, 2000), the focus of the research has been on product and business exits rather than on exits from international markets (Matthyssens and Pauwels, 2000). This makes it difficult, or impossible, to make any inferences about how and why a (small) firm might change its foreign market serving mode.

Recent exploratory studies (Wheeler *et al.*, 1996; Pauwels and Matthyssens, 1999; Matthyssens and Pauwels, 2000; Alexander and Quinn, 2002) try to minimize this problem by employing inductive qualitative research. For example, in a cross-case analysis, Alexander and Quinn (2002) focused on decisions, processes, effects and response phases of the divestment process in the retail industry. They found that divestment had an impact on subsequent market-entry mode; that is, initially the firms established subsidiaries through a high-control mode of entry, then they switched to partnerships, concessions and franchising as the favoured entry mode. Wheeler *et al.* (1996) studied the structural dynamics in the distribution of foreign-produced machine tools in the UK, and suggested, *inter alia*, cyclical influences on intermediary choice in importing whereby a firm may switch, say, from sales subsidiary to independent agent/distributor. Although Matthyssens and Pauwels (2000) and Pauwels and Matthyssens (1999) did not focus on switching between entry modes, they performed a retrospective strategy process study of export withdrawals, focusing primarily on cognitive and behavioural processes in the decision-making and implementation processes. In their attempt to build middle-range theories, three processes were uncovered: (a) escalation of commitment; (b) creation of strategic flexibility; and (c) confrontation between processes (a) and (b). To the above, Crick (2002), in his research on the withdrawal of small firms from exporting, indirectly proposed a comprehensive list of reasons for discontinuing export activities.

As can be seen from the above review, a theoretical understanding of the process of de-internationalization, especially within small firms, is in its infancy. The question arises how to apply the existing research to the study of the de-internationalization process in small firms. The next section discusses this issue and presents a conceptual model of de-internationalization in small firms.

DE-INTERNATIONALIZATION OF THE SMALL FIRM: A CONCEPTUAL MODEL

De-Internationalization: Emerging Themes

While the research to date on de-internationalization has focused on large corporations, some issues might form the core constructs of research on de-internationalization of the small firm. These constructs are (1) commitment, (2) strategic change, and (3) time (see Figure 13.2).

Commitment
When conditions deteriorate, decision-makers may be faced with a dilemma over whether to risk continuing or withdraw (Drummond, 1995). In such circumstances, decision-makers may compound the problem by continuing to act irrationally (Staw and Ross, 1987; Brockner, 1992). Brockner (1992) defined the tendency for decision-makers to persist with the failing courses of action as escalating commitment, where a decision to persevere might only escalate the risks. It is argued that several factors encourage decision-makers to become locked into failing courses of action (Staw and Ross, 1987). These are psychological, social, structural and project-related (for a review see Brockner, 1992; Drummond,

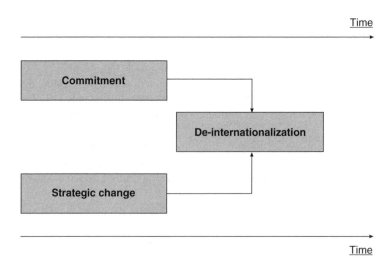

Figure 13.2   Small firms' context of de-internationalization

1994). Based on these factors, Bowen (1987) developed a model that suggests that withdrawal is more likely to occur in conditions opposite to those believed to favour persistence, that is low commitment and low equivocal information. Drummond (1995) corroborated Bowen's model and extended it by arguing that the escalation is a function of commitment and power with information as an important component of power.

From the perspective of the small firm, it is the founding entrepreneur that makes a unique contribution to the firm's development (Hill and Wright, 2001), and it is entrepreneurial commitment, determination, vision, energy, tolerance of risk and ambition that makes the entrepreneurial process happen in these firms (Hill and McGowan, 1999). Hence, according to Drummond's model (1995), the entrepreneur would be viewed as being highly committed and having high perceived power, thus making the withdrawal less possible. Therefore, there will be a challenge for researchers to study both tacit and explicit entrepreneurs' decisions to de-internationalize in order to identify and estimate the salience of the factors which finally prompt withdrawal (Drummond, 1995). The most difficult task, however, is how to operationalize and measure the commitment in a dynamic way – a task that remains a challenge (Pauwels and Matthyssens, 1999). In addition, there will be a need to define and operationalize the perceived failing course of action[2] and to account for cognitive bias in investigating the de-internationalization decision process (Watson and Everett, 1993, 1999; Das and Teng, 1999).

Strategic Change

Planning for adversity is well worth the effort (Porter, 1976), so decision-making processes not only need to allow for the possibility of failure, but also need to facilitate withdrawal where appropriate (for example Drummond, 1995; Crick, 2002). However, strategic changes like divestiture, diversification and replacement of the manager available to large corporations (Porter, 1976; Harrigan and Porter, 1983; Staw and Ross, 1987; Brockner, 1992; Hoskisson *et al.*, 1994; Nargundkar *et al.*, 1996; Benito, 1997; Benito and Welch, 1997; Pauwels and Matthyssens, 1999; Haynes *et al.*, 2000; Mata and Portugal, 2000) are not generally available to small firms.

Alternatively, decisions to de-internationalize might be viewed in the context of change in the business networks, especially in the dyadic networks (for example Anderson *et al.*, 1994; Halinen *et al.*, 1999). For example, Halinen *et al.* (1999) emphasized the central role of business-relationship dyads for understanding the mechanism of network change and for the purpose of understanding dyadic network dynamics, introduced the term 'critical event' as an incident that triggers radical change in a business dyad and/or network. According to them, the start of a radical change depends on the actions and intentions of dyadic partners. Thus there will be a need to develop a longitudinal approach in order to understand fully and anticipate the change in the dyadic network (see for example Welch and Welch, 1996) – that is, actions and intentions that will help understand the de-internationalization process of small firms.

Time

Although all phenomena exist in and through time, researchers often ignore, treat implicitly, or treat explicitly but in an inadequate manner the duration and rates of time (George and Jones, 2000). Further, George and Jones (2000) argue that time can and should play a much more important and significant role in theory and theory-building because time directly impacts the what, how and why elements of a theory (see also Welge and Holtbrugge, 1999; Hurmerinta-Peltomaki, 2001; Jones and Coviello, 2002). Thus, it is time that makes it possible to consider four phenomena which are of crucial importance to internationalization and de-internationalization strategies: timing, duration, chronological sequence and velocity of different cross-border moves (Kutschker and Baurle, 1997).

Hence, fundamental to the entrepreneurs' experience of time in the present is the knowledge he/she has of the past and how he/she uses this knowledge to envision the future (Butler, 1995); that is, how the present is determined depends roughly on entrepreneurs' subjective perceptions and experiences, even if there is objectivity[3] behind it (for example Chapman, 1982), paying special attention to decision-makers' personal and social idiosyncrasies (Macharzina and Engelhard, 1991) in order to get insights into how and why small firms (see Scott and Rosa, 1996) might de-internationalize. Accordingly, attention must be paid to the way a phenomenon is created subjectively out of a person's ongoing experience, and constructs must be defined so as to reflect the dimension of time (George and Jones, 2000) – that is, (1) codes and memories; (2) congruence and horizons; and (3) present experience (Butler, 1995).

De-Internationalization: A Conceptual Framework

As the above discussion suggests, the conceptual framework of de-internationalization process research (see Figure 13.3) is based on three constructs (1) the commitment of *entrepreneurs* which is influenced by project, psychological, social and structural factors; (2) change in dyadic networks, that is triggered by a critical event, and depends on the actions and intentions of dyadic partners (*entrepreneurs*); and (3) time, that is experienced in the present by *entrepreneurs* by relating

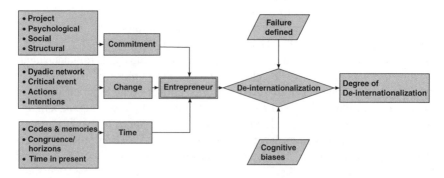

Figure 13.3   A conceptual framework of de-internationalization

themselves to codes and memories (past), and congruence and horizons (future). As control variables, failures have to be defined and cognitive biases accounted for.

Building De-Internationalization Theory

The previous discussion clearly suggests that in order to develop an understanding of the process of de-internationalization of small firms, there is a need for a paradigm shift from positivism towards realism (Guba and Lincoln; 1994), the ontology of which assumes that there is a 'real' world out there to discover even if it is only imperfectly and probabilistically apprehensible (Godfrey and Hill, 1995), and that the research deals with complex social phenomena involving reflective people (Healy and Perry, 2000) particularly when studying networks relationships (Hill *et al.*, 1999). By employing the realism paradigm in de-internationalization process research, the researcher understands the need to minimize the distance between the researcher and the entrepreneur (Hill and Wright, 2001). This epistemology suggests that the research methodology must be inductive in nature based on case studies (Eisenhardt, 1989; Yin, 1994), longitudinal (Pettigrew, 1995), and should use mainly in-depth interviews and observations in order to clarify the circumstances and influences on decisions which are made (Benito and Welch, 1997).

CONCLUSIONS

While the extant literature has emphasized the role of domestic and foreign country factors on the initial choice of foreign market entry modes, less is documented on the effect of changes in the external environment, or indeed internal changes within the firm on the continuance of internationalization beyond selected decisions. Perhaps the questions that most need to be addressed by firms, policymakers and researchers are, 'To what extent is this mode of operation continuing to deliver returns and positive performance and, if less than optimal, what change would better effect attainment of projected targets?'

Thus, the importance of the proposed conceptual framework for the study of the process of de-internationalization is twofold. First, it may help to develop a better theoretical understanding of small-firm internationalization. Second, if there is a better understanding of the factors that are likely to influence de-internationalization and post-de-internationalization decisions, this will help policymakers develop trade-support strategies.

Notes

1. It has been argued elsewhere (for example Boddewyn, 1985; Casson, 1986) that it is possible to see divestment of international operations as the reverse of the investment process. Or, as Benito and Welch (1997) question whether these forces (that move a firm forward internationally over time) operate in reverse, perpetuating a withdrawal process.

2. For example, in the USA the buy-out of a small firm by a large corporation is viewed as an exit strategy (Westphal, 1999), whereas in Germany a merger with another company is perceived as failure (Achtenhagen, 2002).
3. As Halinen *et al.* (1999) argue, they (environmental forces) are always transmitted within the network through individual relationships; or as Macharzina and Engelhard (1991) point out, internationalizing firms adjust to their environments through their decision-makers.

REFERENCES

Achtenhagen, L. (2002) 'Entrepreneurial Failure in Germany – Stigma or Enigma?', paper presented at the Babson–Kauffman Entrepreneurship Research Conference, University of Colorado, Boulder, CO.

Alexander, N. and Quinn, B. (2002) 'International Retail Divestment', *International Journal of Retail and Distribution Management*, 30 (2), 112–25.

Andersen, O. (1993) 'On the Internationalization Process of Firms: A Critical Analysis', *Journal of International Business Studies*, 24 (2), 209–31.

Andersen, O. (1997) 'Internationalization and Market Entry Mode: A Review of Theories and Conceptual Frameworks', *Management International Review*, 37 (2), 27–42.

Anderson, J., Hakansson, H. and Johanson, J. (1994) 'Dyadic Business Relationships within a Business Network Context', *Journal of Marketing*, 58 (4), 1–15.

Axelsson, B. and Easton, G. (1992) (eds), *Industrial Networks: A New View of Reality* (London: Routledge).

Bell, J. (1995) 'The Internationalization of Small Computer Software Firms – a Further Challenge to "Stage" Theories', *European Journal of Marketing*, 29 (8), 60–75.

Bell, J., McNaughton, R., Young, S., and Crick, D. (2001) 'Towards an Eclectic Model of Small Firm Internationalization', 4th McGill Conference on International Entrepreneurship (University of Strathclyde, Glasgow); 1, 95–110.

Benito, G. (1997) 'Divestment of Foreign Production Operations', *Applied Economics*, 29, 1365–77.

Benito, G. and Welch, L. (1997) 'De-Internationalization', *Management International Review*, 37 (2), 7–25.

Boddewyn, J. (1985) 'Theories of Foreign Direct Investment and Divestment: A Classificatory Note', *Management International Review*, 25 (1), 57–65.

Bonaccorsi, A. (1992) 'On the Relationship between Firm Size and Export Intensity', *Journal of International Business Studies*, 23 (4), 605–35.

Bowen, M. (1987) 'The Escalation Phenomenon Reconsidered: Design Dilemmas or Decision Errors?', *Academy of Management Review*, 12 (1), 52–66.

Brockner, J. (1992) 'The Escalation of Commitment to a Failing Course of Action: Toward Theoretical Progress', *Academy of Management: The Academy of Management Review*, 17 (1), 39–62.

Buckley, P. and Casson, M. (1976) *The Future of the Multinational Enterprise* (London: Holmes & Meier).

Butler, R. (1995) 'Time in Organizations: Its Experience, Explanations and Effects', *Organization Studies*, 16 (6), 925–50.

Casson, M. (1986) 'International Divestment and Restructuring Decisions (with special reference to the motor industry)', *International Labour Organization*, working paper 40 (Geneva: ILO).

Cavusgil, S. (1980) 'On the Internationalization Process of Firms', *European Research*, 8, 273–81.

Cavusgil, S. (1984) 'Differences Among Exporting Firms based on their Degree of Internationalization', *Journal of Business Research*, 12, 195–208.

Chang, S. and Singh, H. (1999) 'The Impact of Modes of Entry and Resource Fit on Modes of Exit by Multibusiness Firms', *Strategic Management Journal*, 20 (11), 1019–35.

Chapman, T. (1982) *Time: A Philosophical Analysis* (Holland: Reidel Publishing Company).

Chow, Y. and Hamilton, R. (1993) 'Corporate Divestment: An Overview', *Journal of Managerial Psychology*, 8 (5), 9–13.

Clarke, C. and Gall, F. (1987) 'Planned Divestment – a Five Step Approach', *Long Range Planning*, 20 (10), 17–24.

Coviello, N. (1996) 'Foreign Market Entry and Internationalization: The Case of Datacom Software Research', *Entrepreneurship Theory and Practice*, 20 (4), 95–109.

Coviello, N. and Martin, K. (1999) 'Internationalization of Service SMEs: An Integrated Perspective from the Engineering Consulting Sector', *Journal of International Marketing*, 7 (4), 42–66.

Coviello, N. and McAuley, A. (1999) 'Internationalization and the Smaller Firm: A Review of Contemporary Empirical Research', *Management International Review*, 39 (3), 223–56.

Coviello, N. and Munro, H. (1995) 'Growing the Entrepreneurial Firm: Networking for International Market Development', *European Journal of Marketing*, 29 (7), 49–61.

Coviello, N. and Munro, H. (1997) 'Network Relationships and the Internationalization Process of Small Software Firms', *International Business Review*, 69 (4), 1–26.

Crick, D. (2002) 'The Decision to Discontinue Exporting: SMEs in Two U.K. Trade Sectors', *Journal of Small Business Management*, 40 (1), 66–77.

Crick, D. and Jones, M. (2000) 'Small High-Technology Firms and International High-Technology Markets', *Journal of International Marketing*, 8 (2), 63–85.

Das, T. and Teng, B.-S. (1999) 'Cognitive Biases and Strategic Decision Processes: An Integrative Perspective', *Journal of Management Studies*, 36 (6), 757–78.

Dennis, C., (2000) 'Networking for Marketing Advantage', *Management Decision*, 38 (4), 41–7.

Douglas, S. and Craig, S. (1996) 'Executive Insights: Global Portfolio Planning and Market Interconnectedness', *Journal of International Marketing*, 4 (1), 93–110.

Drummond, H. (1994) 'Too Little Too Late: A Case Study of Escalation in Decision Making', *Organization Studies*, 15 (4), 591–607.

Drummond, H. (1995) 'De-Escalation in Decision Making: A Case of a Disastrous Partnership', *Journal of Management Studies*, 32 (3), 265–81.

Dunning, J. (1980) 'Toward an Eclectic Theory of International Production: Some Empirical Tests', *Journal of International Business Studies*, 11 (1), 9–31.

Eisenhardt, K. (1989) 'Building Theories from Case Study Research', *Academy of Management Review*, 14 (4), 532–50.

Elg, U. and Johansson, U. (1996) 'Networking when national boundaries dissolve: the Swedish food sector. (Nordic Perspective on Relationship Marketing)', *European Journal of Marketing*, 2, 61–75.

Fletcher, R. (2001) 'A Holistic Approach to Internationalization', *International Business Review*, 10, 25–49.

George, J. and Jones, G. (2000) 'The Role of Time in Theory and Theory Building', *Journal of Management*, 26 (4), 657–84.

Godfrey, P. and Hill, C. (1995) 'The Problem of Unobservable in Strategic Management Research', *Strategic Management Journal*, 16 (7), 519–33.

Guba, E. and Lincoln, Y. (1994) 'Competing Paradigms in Qualitative Research', in Denzin, N. and Lincoln, Y. (eds) *Handbook of Qualitative Research* (Newbury Park, CA: Sage Publications).

Hadjikhani, A. (1997) 'A Note on the Criticisms Against the Internationalization Process Model', *Management International Review*, 37 (2), 43–66.

Halinen, A., Salmi, A. and Havila, V. (1999) 'From Dyadic Change to Changing business Networks: An Analytical Framework', *Journal of Management Studies*, 36 (6), 779–94.

Harrigan, K. and Porter, M. (1983) 'End-Game Strategies for Declining Industries', *Harvard Business Review*, 61 (4), 111–19.

Harrigan, K. (1980) *Strategies for Declining Industries* (Lexington, MA and Toronto, ONT: Lexington Books).

Haynes, M., Thompson, S. and Wright, M. (2000) 'The Determinants of Corporate Divestment in the UK', *International Journal of Industrial Organization*, 18, 1201–22.

Healy, M. and Perry, C. (2000) 'Comprehensive Criteria to Judge Validity and Reliability of Qualitative Research within the Realism Paradigm', *Qualitative Market Research: An International Journal*, 3 (2), 118–26.

Hill, J. and McGowan, P. (1999) 'Small Business and Enterprise Development: Questions about Research Methodology', *International Journal of Entrepreneurial Behavior & Research*, 51, 5–18.

Hill, J. and Wright, L. (2001) 'A Qualitative Research Agenda for Small to Medium-Sized Enterprises', *Marketing Inelegance & Planning*, 19 (6), 432–43.

Hill, J., McGowan, P. and Drummond, P. (1999) 'The Development and Application of a Qualitative Approach to Researching the Marketing Networks of Small Firm Entrepreneurs', *Qualitative Market Research: An International Journal*, 2 (2), 71–81.

Hoskisson, R., Johnson, R. and Moesel, D. (1994), 'Corporate Divestiture Intensity in Restructuring Firms: Effects of Governance, Strategy, and Performance', *Academy of Management Journal*, 37 (5), 1207–51.

Hurmerinta-Peltomaki, L. (2001) 'Time and Internationalization: Theoretical Challenges Set by Rapid Internationalization', paper presented at the 4th McGill Conference on International Entrepreneurship (Glasgow: University of Strathclyde).

Johanson, J. and Mattsson, L.G. (1988) 'Internationalization in Industrial Systems – a Network Approach', in Hood, N. and Vahlne, J.E. (eds), *Strategies in Global Competition* (London: Croom Helm), 287–314.

Johanson, J. and Mattsson, L.-G., (1992) 'Network Positions and Strategic Action – An Analytical Framework', in Axelsson, B. and Easton, G. (eds), *Industrial Networks: A New View of Reality* (London: Routledge), 205–17.

Johanson, J. and Vahlne, J.-E. (1977) 'The Internationalization Process of the Firm – A Model of Knowledge Development and Increasing Foreign Market Commitments', *Journal of International Business Studies*, Spring/Summer, 23–32.

Johanson, J. and Vahlne, J.-E. (1990) 'The Mechanism of Internationalization', *International Marketing Review*, 7 (4), 11–24.

Johanson, J. and Wiedersheim-Paul, F. (1975) 'The Internationalization of the Firm – Four Swedish Cases', *Journal of Management Studies*, October, 305–22.

Jones, M.V. (1999) 'The Internationalization of Small High-Technology Firms', *Journal of International Marketing*, 7 (4), 15–41.

Jones, M.V. (2001) 'First Steps in Internationalization: Concepts and Evidence from a Sample of Small High Technology Firms', *Journal of International Management*, 7, 191–210.

Jones, M.V. and Coviello, N.E. (2002) 'A Time-Based Contingency Model of Entrepreneurial Internationalisation Behaviour', working paper 2002–12, University of Calgary, Haskayne School of Business.

Jones, M.V. and Tagg, S.K. (2001) 'Profiling Internationalization Behavior: Patterns of Start-Up and Development', 4th McGill Conference on International Entrepreneurship, (Glasgow: University of Strathclyde), 2, 58–84.

Karakaya, F. (2000) 'Market Exit and Barriers to Exit: Theory and Practice', *Psychology & Marketing*, 17 (8), 651–68.

Kelly, D. and Amburgey, T. (1991) 'Organizational Inertia and Momentum: A Dynamic Model of Strategic Change', *Academy of Management Journal*, 34 (3), 591–612.

Knight, J., Bell, J. and McNaughton, R. (2001) 'The "Born Global" Phenomenon: A Re-birth of an Old Concept?', 4th McGill Conference on International Entrepreneurship, (Glasgow: University of Strathclyde), 2, 113–25.

Korhonen, H., Luostarinen, R. and Welch, L. (1996) 'Internationalization of SMEs: Inward – Outward Patterns and Government Policy', *Management International Review*, 36 (4), 315–29.

Kutschker, M. and Baurle, I. (1997) 'Three + One: Multidimensional Strategy on Internationalization', *Management International Review*, 37 (2), 103–25.

Kutschker, M., Baurle, I. and Schmid, S. (1997) 'International Evolution, International Episodes, and International Epochs – Implications for Managing Internationalization', *Management International Review*, 37 (2), 101–24.

Macharzina, K. and Engelhard, J. (1991) 'Paradigm Shift in International Business Research: From Partist and Eclectic Approaches to the GAINS Paradigm', *Management International Review*, 31 (special issue), 23–43.

Mata, J. and Portugal, P. (2000) 'Closure and Divestiture by Foreign Entrants: The Impact of Entry and Post-Entry Strategies', *Strategic Management Journal*, 21 (5), 549–62.

Matthyssens, P. and Pauwels, P. (2000) 'Uncovering International Market-Exit Processes: A Comparative Case Study', *Psychology and Marketing*, 17 (8), 697–719.

Nargundkar, S., Karakaya, F. and Stahl, M. (1996) 'Barriers to Market Exit', *Journal of Managerial Issues*, 8 (2), 239–58.

Oviatt, B. and McDougall, P. (1994) 'Toward a Theory of International New Ventures', *Journal of International Business Studies*, 24 (1), 45–64.

Pauwels, P. and Matthyssens, P. (1999) 'A Strategy Process Perspective on Export Withdrawal', *Journal of International Marketing*, 7 (3), 10–37.

Penrose, E. (1959) *The Theory of the Growth of the Firm* (Oxford: Basil Blackwell).

Pettigrew, A. (1995) 'Longitudinal Field Research on Change: Theory and Practice', in Huber, G. and Van de Van, A. (eds) *Longitudinal Field Research Methods: Studying Processes of Organizational Change* (California: Sage Publications).

Porter, M. (1976) 'Please Note Location of Nearest Exit', *California Management Review*, 19 (2), 21–33.

Porter, M. (1987) 'From Competitive Advantage to Corporate Strategy', *Harvard Business Review*, 65 (3), 43–59.

Scott, M. and Rosa, P. (1996) 'Opinion: Has Firm Level Analysis Reached its Limits/ Time for a Rethink', *International Small Business Journal*, 14 (4), 81–9.

Shin, S.-H. (2000) 'The Foreign Divestment Factors in South Korea: An Analysis of the Trading Sector', *Multinational Business Review*, 8 (2), 98–103.

Staw, B. and Ross, J. (1987) 'Knowing When to Pull the Plug', *Harvard Business Review*, 65 (2), 68–74.

Sullivan, D. and Bauerschmidt, A. (1990) 'Incremental Internationalization: A Test of Johanson and Vahlne's Thesis', *Management International Review*, 30 (1), 19–30.

Tegarden, L., Echols, A. and Hatfield, D. (2000) 'The Value of Patience and Start-up Firms: A Re-Examination of Entry Timing for Emerging Markets', *Entrepreneurship Theory and Practice*, 24 (4), 41–58.

Tikkanen, H. (1998) 'The Network Approach in Analyzing International Marketing and Purchasing Operations: A Case Study of a European SME's Focal Net', *Journal of Business and Industrial Marketing*, 13 (2), 109–30.

Turcan, R. and Jones, M. (2002) 'Internationalization Patterns of Small High Technology Firms: Keep On, Step Back, or Withdraw', 29th AIB Conference on International Business in the Global Knowledge Economy (Preston: University of Central Lancashire), 498–527.

Watson, J. and Everett, J. (1993) 'Defining Small Business Failure', *International Small Business Journal*, 11 (3), 35–48.

Watson, J. and Everett, J. (1999) 'Small Business Failure Rates: Choice of Definition and Industry Effects', *International Small Business Journal*, 17 (2), 31–45.

Welch, D. and Welch, L. (1996) 'The Internationalization Process and Networks: A Strategic Management Perspective', *Journal of International Marketing*, 4 (3), 11–28.

Welch, L. and Luostarinen, R. (1988) 'Internationalization: Evolution of a Concept', *Journal of General Management*, 14 (2), 34–55.

Welch, L. and Luostarinen, R. (1993) 'Inward–Outward Connections in Internationalization', *Journal of International Marketing*, 1 (1), 44–56.

Welge, M. and Holtbrugge, D. (1999) 'International Management under Postmodern Conditions', *Management International Review*, 39 (4), 305–22.

Westphal, L. (1999) 'Entrepreneurs in Wireless Industry Realize Exit Strategy', *Direct Marketing*, 62 (8), 56–61.

Wheeler, C., Jones, M. and Young, S. (1996) 'Market entry modes and channels of distribution in the UK machine tool industry', *European Journal of Marketing*, 30 (4), 40–58.

Williamson, O. (1985) *The Economic Institutions of Capitalism* (New York: Free Press).

Yin, R. (1994) *Case Study Research: Design and Methods* (London: Sage Publications).

Yip, G.S., Biscarri, G. and Monti, J.A. (2000) 'The Role of the Internationalization Process in the Performance of Newly Internationalizing Firms', *Journal of International Marketing*, 8 (3), 10–35.

Zajac, E., Kraatz, M. and Bresser, R. (2000) 'Modeling the Dynamics of Strategic Fit: A Normative Approach to Strategic Change', *Strategic Management Journal*, 21 (4), 429–53.

14 Satisfaction with Paying for Government Export Assistance

John Knight, Jim Bell and Rod McNaughton

INTRODUCTION

How should governments assist exporters most effectively? This question has vexed export researchers over two decades, and a definitive answer remains elusive. Most governments have trade-promotion programmes in recognition of the need to assist small firms in various areas. The motives of such programmes include a desire to stimulate export-led economic growth, increase the international competitiveness of firms, and reduce the trade deficits affecting many nations in recent decades (Leonidou and Katsikeas, 1996; Czinkota and Ronkainen, 1998; Moini, 1998). A continuing problem is that the effectiveness of government assistance programmes is difficult to measure (Seringhaus, 1986; Seringhaus and Rosson, 1990; Diamantopoulos *et al.*, 1993), and there is doubt as to whether governments deliver what firms require. A further problem is that such government assistance programmes fly in the face of emerging attitudes towards free trade and the removal of subsidies and tariffs. A response of some governments is to introduce commercial charges for services. It becomes important to know whether firms consider they receive value for money, and whether providing such commercial consultancy services is the business that governments should be in.

New Zealand has, since the mid-1980s, conducted one of the most radical economic reforms seen in any modern economy. Prior to 1984, import-substitution policies maintained 'Fortress NZ' as one of the most highly protected economies in the OECD (Winkelman and Winkelman, 1998). Subsidies were rife and non-tariff barriers were widespread. In fact the proportion of New Zealand imports subject to non-tariff barriers far exceeded that of any other OECD country (Laird and Yates, 1990). An extreme example was that in the 1970s margarine was only available on a doctor's prescription, a measure to protect the highly important dairy industry. Since 1984 successive governments have instituted a programme of radical unilateral reforms of New Zealand's trade policy in a manner that is unique in the developed world. The removal of import licensing and reductions in tariff levels have 'turned the economy into one of the most open, market-oriented and lightly regulated in the OECD' (OECD, 1999). In line with its free-market philosophy, the New Zealand government has instituted 'user pays' principles into virtually every aspect of export services. Until 1997, government grants provided 50 per cent of the cost of many services purchased from Trade New Zealand. Abolition of such grants coincided with charges for virtually every service being raised substantially, and in particular charges for provision of specific export information.

This study investigates perceptions of exporters in the New Zealand seafood sector concerning the impact that these changes in charging practices have had. The sector was chosen as the focal industry for this study because it represents an important and well-demarcated export sector, accounting for approximately 6 per cent of New Zealand's exports. Furthermore, unlike some of New Zealand's primary sectors like dairy, kiwifruit and apples (which all have single-desk sellers), or meat and forestry (which are dominated by large companies), it comprises many small and medium-sized firms. The New Zealand experience seems likely to be highly relevant to export-promotion organizations in other countries that may be contemplating a move towards 'user pays' philosophies in export promotion.

In New Zealand the principal export promotion organization (EPO) is the New Zealand Trade Development Board (Trade New Zealand). Its range of services is broadly similar to those offered in other advanced nations (Bell, *et al.*, 2000), and includes provision of general market information, as well as client-specific intelligence needs. Trade New Zealand's funding was derived 93.2 per cent from direct government grant and 4.7 per cent from client payment for services in the year ended 30 June 2000 (New Zealand Trade Development Board, *Annual Report*, 2000). Trade New Zealand's mission as reported in this annual report is to 'use our global network to enhance the ability of New Zealand businesses to convert opportunities into sustainable and profitable foreign exchange earnings'. In 1998, a new charging regime was introduced in a bid to apply 'user pays' philosophy to exporting firms and to reinforce New Zealand's position as an exporting country that aims to be free of any kind of subsidy or trade-distorting mechanism.

We provide a brief overview of literature dealing with the efficacy and nature of government export-assistance programmes, and with firms' perceptions of such programmes. The objective of this study was to provide understanding of the interface between government agencies and exporting firms, to determine how firms go about obtaining export information, and how useful or otherwise they perceive government services to be in this area – particularly services that firms pay for. Because the object was not to determine how many firms use particular methods or encounter particular problems, but to determine why they favour particular methods, we deemed it more appropriate to use qualitative rather than quantitative methods. In-depth personal interviews were used to identify both the nature and intensity of problems, and resulted in a richness of material that would be unlikely to result from a quantitative approach (Bell, 1997). Exporters in this study perceived that Trade New Zealand had moved away from the type of service that they (and the extant literature) identify as the most useful: facilitation of experiential knowledge. Instead, the organization appears to be moving further towards the type of service that is identified in the literature as the least useful (provision of institutional information). A view expressed by several firms was that payment for information-gathering services would be fine provided there was a direct connection between the outcome of such market research (as measured by new export orders) and the cost – essentially a 'payment for results' philosophy. We are not aware of previous work suggesting such a mechanism for government export assistance, and consider that it may have significant implications for EPOs in other countries.

THE EFFICACY OF GOVERNMENT ASSISTANCE PROGRAMMES

Despite conventional wisdom that government export-assistance programmes are both necessary and beneficial, the efficacy of such programmes in meeting government objectives has frequently been questioned and attempts to quantify the benefits have generally failed (Seringhaus, 1986; Seringhaus and Rosson, 1990). Czinkota (1992) has pointed out a fundamental flaw in the design of government programmes that have responded to desires of exporters without ensuring that help in those areas will in fact lead to greater export performance. 'Of course everybody is for programs that enhance profitability and make life easier. However, the real question is whether or not these programs will result in more exports' (Czinkota, 1992, p. vii).

According to Miesenbock (1988) the use of export-stimulation measures increases export success 'but most firms would not even reduce marginally their export activities if they [export stimulation measures] did not exist'. Diamantopoulos *et al.* (1993) drew attention to the 'notable lack of objective indicators of the impact of export assistance [for example effect on export sales] as well as a tendency to prefer global measures of export assistance'. They argued that 'the crucial point appears to be the assessment of the impact that export assistance has on export behavior'. Bannock and Peacock (1989) have gone further, and argued that such schemes are in fact detrimental to the international competitiveness of firms. They suggest that the link between profitability and efficiency is broken if profitability depends on bargaining skill in the interface with government officials rather than with satisfying domestic and international consumers. According to Seringhaus and Rosson (1998) 'the sink-or-swim approach may produce fitter exporters'.

In addition to uncertainty about the impact of government assistance programmes on export sales, evidence of the success of governments in stimulating export behaviour seems equivocal. For example, in Bannock's UK survey, only 1.18 per cent of respondents indicated that they began exporting as a result of government encouragement (Bannock and Peacock, 1989). Pleas to begin exporting made by government or private organizations had a low motivating effect on participants in Leonidou's (1995) study in Cyprus. Katsikeas and Piercy (1993) found that the role of the Greek government in stimulating internationalization and facilitating a long-term export strategy was perceived to be negligible. Weaver and Pak (1990) found that in South Korea the second most important factor influencing a firm's decision to sell abroad was a 'patriotic duty to contribute to national economic development', but this appears to have as much to do with the New Confucian ethic as with government action specifically.

The Focus of Government Assistance Programmes

Designers of government programmes tend to concentrate resources on the area of information provision, which is understandable in view of the critical importance of knowledge of international markets to any would-be exporter. However, many studies over the last 30 years have shown that experiential knowledge gained from visiting the foreign market and from actually carrying out the business of exporting is without peer in the longer term (Cunningham and Spigel, 1971; Johanson and Vahlne, 1977; Seringhaus, 1987; Bell, 1997). Indeed, Thirkell and Dau (1998), who studied export success determinants for New Zealand manufacturing exporters, found that 'the most controllable element is the commitment to sending people offshore'.

Despite this New Zealand study, Trade New Zealand (like similar organizations in other countries) still concentrates on providing information-gathering services for firms rather than facilitating gathering of information by firms themselves. Institutional information sources have been found to be the least used by small firms, even though well-meaning designers of government programmes invest large amounts of public money on establishing and expanding such resources (Reid, 1984; McDowell and Rowlands, 1995). Diamantopoulos and Souchon, (1996) note that information originating from personal and internal sources tends to be used much more extensively than that stemming from external sources because it is trusted to a larger extent. Information provided by government export assistance organizations was seldom used because it was 'too general', 'irrelevant' and 'outdated'. Information generated in-house was considered superior in terms of both relevance and timeliness, and thus more likely to be used effectively. Furthermore, the more experience a decision-maker had of his/her industry and exporting activity, the more they would rely on intuition as a basis for making export decisions, perhaps using information 'symbolically' to support a decision already made on intuition (Diamantopoulos and Souchon, 1996).

Attitudes Towards Export Assistance Programmes

Diamantopoulos *et al.* (1993) consider that inexperienced firms tend to perceive export information assistance as more beneficial than do experienced exporters, an observation similar to that of Czinkota (1982). Is this because such programmes are carefully tailored towards the needs of beginning exporters, or is it that more experienced exporters have learned to their cost that such programmes are of limited usefulness? The provision of export information has been widely criticized (see Pointon, 1978; Buckley, 1982; Walters, 1983).

There is also a general acceptance that experiential information and knowledge is preferable to information from secondary sources (Cunningham and Spigel, 1971; Johanson and Vahlne, 1977; Reid, 1984; Seringhaus, 1987). Research indicates that firms do not have high regard for information provided by export-promotion organizations, and prefer services that provide financial support for export activities and require a high degree of involvement on the user's part (Seringhaus, 1987; Kotabe and Czinkota, 1992). Trade fairs and trade missions, which enable firms to obtain market knowledge and experience first-hand, are generally highly regarded by firms (Walters, 1983; Seringhaus and Rosson, 1990; Seringhaus and Rosson, 1998).

Gray (1997) suggested that a solution to the problem of poor targeting of government export-promotion schemes could lie in developing a better understanding of the needs of managers who make export marketing decisions. He noted (p. 415):

It appears that promotion organizations and business researchers have overlooked the obvious: that to be more effective, promotion programs should target the needs of the individuals who make market entry and penetration decisions, rather than the apparent needs of the organizations who employ these managers.

A logical extension of this 'customer orientation' line of reasoning is that government programmes should offer training and facilitation of managers obtaining their own export information, rather than providing information services (whether subsidized or not) as seems widespread at present.

In view of the continuing uncertainty in the literature as to whether government programmes deliver what they are supposed to deliver, the New Zealand experiment in 'user pays' philosophy seems highly relevant to other countries.

RESEARCH APPROACH AND METHODOLOGY

In-depth focused interviews were conducted with export-marketing decision-makers in order to gain insights into how government initiatives help or hinder their activities. According to Kamath *et al.* (1987), the dominant use of logical-empiricist methodology has 'bedevilled' export research by providing partial – and in some cases misleading – perspectives on the phenomena under investigation. Because our objective was to determine why firms use the methods they do, how useful they find various methods, and what deficiencies they perceive, a qualitative approach seemed most appropriate.

A complete listing of New Zealand seafood exporters is available on the Seafood Industry (SEAFIC) website. Following the classification used by Thirkell and Dau (1998), the 125 firms listed were classified as large (over NZ$50 million annual turnover), medium ($10–50 million), and small (under

Table 14.1　Size of firms in the New Zealand seafood export sector on the basis of turnover

North Island firms (68)			South Island firms (57)			Total
Large	Med	Small	Large	Med	Small	
6	18	44	5	14	38	125
9%	26%	65%	9%	25%	67%	

Note:　Large – greater than NZ$50 million p.a.; medium – $10–50 million p.a.; small – less than $10 million p.a.

$10 million) based on the personal knowledge of a key informant from within the seafood industry (see Table 14.1).

A stratified sample of two large, six medium and 16 small firms, divided equally between the North Island and the South Island, was deemed representative of the industry in terms of both size and geographical location. These 24 firms ranged in turnover from NZ$200 000 to several hundred million New Zealand dollars. While the original intention was to select two firms with turnover in excess of $50 million, it became apparent during interviews that four of the selected firms were in this category. Six of the firms reported turnover in the $10–50 million range, whereas 14 of the firms had turnover of less than $10 million.

Companies ranged from one-person operations sharing office facilities with unrelated companies, to a company with 1500 employees operating a substantial fleet of fishing vessels and several processing factories (Table 14.2). Considerable diversity of activity was encountered among the companies sampled. Seven firms were long-established operators of in-shore fishing boats, and had diversified into processing and exporting as the industry matured. One of these companies has grown to be very large by New Zealand standards, and has expanded into production and export of frozen vegetables and ice cream in addition to seafood. Twenty-one of the 24 firms reported that 80 per cent or more of their turnover was exported, and in 18 of these firms the export ratio exceeded 90 per cent. This reflects the high degree of export focus existing within the New Zealand seafood sector. The company with the lowest export ratio was an industrial company involved in importation and manufacture of steel and steel products in addition to acting as a seafood purchaser for a major Japanese conglomerate.

Firms selected according to size and geographical location were contacted by telephone in the order in which they appeared in the SEAFIC directory. For example, if there were six small firms listed in the city of Wellington, and the appropriate sample was deemed to be two small firms from Wellington, then firms were contacted in order until two were found where (a) someone answered the phone, (b) the company was still solvent and in the seafood business, and (c) an appropriate informant was available. One firm was bankrupt, one was no longer in the seafood business, one was a duplicate listing under another name, and in one case the export manager was overseas. In all other cases, once the

Table 14.2 Demographic profile of companies in sample

Company	Interviewees	Years company estab.	Activities	Export turnover $ million	No. of employees	Export ratio %	Product range	Country markets (number)	Geographic spread
A	Owner-operator	11	Export–Import	1–10	0	90	Seashells, speciality marine	10	Asia, EU
B	Export manager	49	Export–Import, agent	20+	8	25	Seafood, steel, wool	1	Japan
C	Owner-operator	4	Ex-Im, broker	20–30	1	90	Frozen seafood	20+	Asia, EU, North America
D	CEO	22	Exporter, broker	1–10	9*	85	Eels	15	Au, Asia, EU
E	Export manager	30	Fishing, processor, export	5	20	65	Fresh-chilled; frozen fish	20+	Au, Asia, EU
F	Export manager	25	Fishing, processor, export	20	60	90	Frozen fish 90%, fresh chilled 10%	20+	Au, Asia, EU, USA
G	Export manager	30	Fishing, processor, export	50+	300	90	Frozen scampi, orange roughy, fresh chilled fish 10%	20+	Au, Asia, EU, USA
H	Owner-operator	7	Exporter, broker	1–10	0	100	Frozen fish 90%, fresh chilled fish 10%	20+	Asia, EU

Table 14.2 Continued

Company	Interviewees	Years company estab.	Activities	Export turnover $ million	No. of employees	Export ratio %	Product range	Country markets (number)	Geographic spread
I	CEO	11	Exporter, broker	15–18	4	99	Live crayfish, eels, mussels, fresh chilled & frozen fish	10+	Asia, USA
J	Export manager	4	Fishing, processor, export	20–30	50	95	Sea-frozen & land-frozen fish	20+	Asia, EU, USA
K	CEO	11	Exporter	1–10	3	100	Fresh-chilled fish; mussels	10+	Asia, EU
L	CEO	40	Fishing, processor, export	1–10	30	40	Fresh chilled fish 60%, frozen fish 40%	10+	Au, Asia, EU
M	CEO	7	Processor, exporter	1–10	25	80	Dietary supplements & therapeutic goods	20+	Asia, EU, USA
N	CEO	6	Processor, exporter	2–3	70*	100	Scallops	1	France
O	CEO	16	Processor, exporter	1–10	12	100	Dried fish products	5	Asia
P	Export manager	64	Fishing, processor, export	100+	1500	80	Fish, shellfish, frozen, fresh-chilled, frozen vegetables ice cream	20+	Au, Asia, EU, USA

Q	CEO	13	Harvesting, processor, export	3	30	100	Clams	1	USA
R	Export manager	15	Aquaculture, processor, exporter	10–50	120	90	Mussels	20+	Au, Asia, EU, USA
S	Owner-operator	15	Processor, exporter	<1	0	95	Shark liver oil, skin cream	1	Au
T	Export manager	15	Fishing, processor, export	100+	130	97	Live crayfish, frozen fish 80%, fresh-chilled fish	20+	Au, Japan, EU
U	Export manager	25	Fishing, processor, export	50+	200	95	Fish frozen 90%, fresh-chilled 10%	10–20	Au, Asia, USA
V	CEO	14	Harvesting, processor, export	1–10	12	95	Clams Fresh-chilled fish	10+	Asia, EU, USA
W	CEO	20	Processor, exporter	1–10	10	95	Live crayfish, frozen fish	?	Indirect Export
X	CEO	4	Exporter	5	0**	100	Live crayfish	5	Asia

Note: * Seasonal labour; ** All labour contracted; Au-Australia.

purpose and nature of the study was explained and assurances of confidentiality and anonymity given, the contact person agreed to be interviewed (a response rate of 100 per cent of available firms).

In-depth interviews took between an hour and 90 minutes, and took the form of a 'focused interview' based on an interview schedule that set forth the major areas of inquiry (Merton 1956). Semi-structured questions were used to elicit the views of the interviewee as uncoloured as possible by the preconceptions of the inter-viewer. Topics included: how firms meet their export information requirements; why firms adopt the information-gathering techniques they use; what difficulties firms encounter in their exporting activities; how firms go about selecting and entering new markets; how government initiatives help or hinder their exporting activities; why government initiatives have the effects identified; and what improvements firms believe could be made. Only the material dealing with provi-sion and effectiveness of government assistance is dealt with in this study.

All except two interviewees agreed to the interview being tape-recorded. Tapes were transcribed, themes were delineated, and each interview was analysed theme by theme. The end result of this process was a rich resource of experiences and opinions relating to each area covered. An attempt was made to quantify the numbers of firms reporting particular viewpoints but it quickly became apparent that this would not result in valid estimates of frequency of response. With the exception of certain areas that represented a universal experience (for example 'initiation of exporting'), the material did not lend itself well to *post hoc* treat-ment. For example, when analysing 'usefulness of trade fairs', it would be haz-ardous to conclude that because six of the 24 firms mentioned trade fairs, that was the number that had attended them, or even that this was the number that had found them useful. The subject of 'trade fairs' was not asked about specifically, but was raised by some firms in response to open-ended questioning about meth-ods they had used to build relationships with overseas customers.

According to Merton (1956), 'An unstructured question is, so to speak, a blank page to be filled in by the interviewee'. Patton (1990) points out that a strength of the 'interview guide' approach, such as was adopted in our study, is that it permits the interviewer to pursue topics or issues that were not anticipated when the interview was planned. In accord with this type of approach, experiences and opinions were summarized without any attempt to ascribe weight based on numbers of responses.

RESULTS

Usefulness of Government Export Assistance

Several firms spoke warmly of the role that Trade New Zealand had filled in the past, acting as 'the facilitator, the greaser of wheels' in foreign markets. Positive views were expressed concerning the informal support role that the organization used to play, providing a base to visit in foreign cities, providing informal advice, providing useful moral support – described by one firm as 'the government holding your hand'. Firms perceived that with a change in charging policy in 1998, Trade New Zealand had moved away from this rather comforting 'warm, fuzzy' approach to a commercial cost-recovery approach, which they found much less appealing.

Areas of previous activity that firms particularly valued included:

- provision of meeting facilities where firms could invite business contacts to meet with them in an environment that implied support from the home government;
- provision of interpreters and drivers that firms felt were 'on our side';
- access to Trade Commissioners by telephone or personal visit in order to gain an informal opinion on market conditions;
- accompaniment by home-country officials when meeting with potential business contacts in the foreign market (signalling endorsement and support from the home government);
- trade fairs and trade missions, which Trade New Zealand used to provide substantial support for, but has largely withdrawn from supporting in recent years.

Six firms felt that Trade New Zealand were 'not relevant to us', with three of these firms presuming that Trade New Zealand must be doing something useful for other companies. Interestingly, two small firms felt that Trade New Zealand must be helping 'the big boys' or 'big business', whereas a large firm felt that they must be helping 'the little guy' because they were of no use to him. One company mentioned that they were satisfied with information provided even though no business resulted.

Three companies were strongly dissatisfied with the information provided. Comments included: 'We sent them into Spain to give us price information. They came back with price of product that was so far out from what we knew to be prices there – we couldn't even ship it for that price.' 'They are OK with general stuff that people can do from a desk, but for hard commercial information they are not that much use.' 'They've given us names, and we've spoken to them on the phone, and they've been . . . hopeless. Nothing ever came of it and you pay a fortune for it.'

Four firms questioned the practicality of expecting a government agency like Trade New Zealand 'doing your business for you'. One firm commented that you could not expect government officials to have an intimate knowledge of your product. Another felt that anyone who is any good at seeking out specific market opportunities would get headhunted by companies, or they would pick up work as a high-performing broker.

Firms reported little difficulty in obtaining information about agents and distributors, or about prospective customers. Many relied on generally known information that came from a lifetime of trading. A rather typical comment was: 'The bulk of fish traded out of New Zealand go to a small number of customers. Mostly those customers come to you. They are very hard to replace.' Another company commented 'It doesn't matter which country New Zealand companies export to, we all know the same people.' Price information, also, seems to be a 'generally known thing'. As one company expressed it: 'We all talk. Traders talk. We're talking offshore all the time. You verify your information by going to 3 or 4 sources. It's very much trading – seat of the pants stuff.' A second company noted: 'We've grown up as traders all our lives. We know the value of each species of fish, and it is a generally known thing. Everyone in the fishing industry knows what flounders are worth. It diffuses throughout.' A third company expressed skepticism that government officials could help in such matters: 'We talk among ourselves. Prices for lobsters change by the hour. We talk to customers by telephone on a daily basis. No government agency could help you with that.'

As a means of gaining experience of a foreign market, meeting with secondary customers, and indeed meeting with other New Zealand seafood exporters, trade fairs and trade missions were seen in a very favourable light. One firm commented: 'Going to food fairs is good because it opens your eyes as to what is happening.' A second firm noted that there is a low return for effort but still considered the effort worth it:

> The hit rate at a seafood show is about 2 per cent for anyone. Of 100 people that talk to you, only 2 or 3 are going to be any good. It's tough going, but being at seafood fair can be a good way to get a new client. I got company Z at the Boston Seafood Fair – the first client we hadn't robbed off some other (New Zealand) company.

One firm spoke of value other than gaining orders: 'At the Brussels Seafood Fair you meet a lot of other New Zealand exporters – maybe that is actually its main value.' Another regretted that Trade New Zealand does very little to help at seafood shows now.

On the subject of trade missions, five firms reported that they had found this to be a highly useful mechanism for gaining confidence in a previously unfamiliar foreign market. A typical comment was:

> We used to get assistance with things like trade missions to China etc. Those were great, not only from the point of view of going up and seeing these markets yourself, but also because you'd get in there with a bunch of people similar to yourself. No business came of it at the time but it gave me a lot of confidence to be able to phone people in China and see what's going on there. I don't think there are many of these anymore.

A confirmatory view was:

> I got on a mini-trade mission to China, look and learn, and subsequently developed business from it. The Trade New Zealand offices in Beijing and Shanghai

were very, very helpful. That's the way the government should be heading. Keeping a presence out there, very politically aware, so that opportunities can be grasped, and translate that into trade.

Perceptions of Cost-Effectiveness

Fifteen of the 24 firms (including three of the 'not relevant to us' firms and five of the 'formerly useful' firms) were critical of the cost-effectiveness of Trade New Zealand services. Considerable depth of feeling was revealed during the interviews, to the extent that two firms revealed that they were currently in the process of disputing Trade New Zealand invoices, and in one case flatly refusing to pay for information that was regarded as worthless. Dissatisfaction with cost-effectiveness was not confined to firms lacking financial resources, but included large, medium and small firms. Firms were not asked specifically about the cost-effectiveness of Trade New Zealand services. Instead they were asked open-ended questions along the lines of had they used such services and how did they find them?

Every one of the 15 firms that raised the issue of cost-effectiveness appeared to have a strong opinion that such services were now very expensive and poor value for money. Firms that had enlisted Trade New Zealand help in providing interpreters, drivers, and other basic services in overseas countries were particularly irate to find that they were charged more than they believed such services would cost them if they had made their own arrangements.
One firm commented:

I found that in recent years Trade New Zealand have got very expensive, and may have priced themselves off the market. Last year in China for a seafood show we had a stand, and Trade New Zealand offered their services as interpreters for us on the stand. They were about three times as expensive as somebody we ended up getting ourselves.

Another firm asked: 'Is it just another form of government-run enterprise? In my view we don't need state-owned enterprises in the marketplace.'

Firms Favoured Payment for Results

Eight firms favoured payment for results, in particular favouring payment of a commission on the first shipment resulting, or alternatively an agreed fee for an agreed result (Table 14.3). This possibility was not raised with each firm specifically; it was either raised by the firms themselves in response to a general question concerning how they found the services and what changes could they suggest, or it was raised by the interviewer in response to strong expressions of dissatisfaction with the cost-effectiveness of current services. However, one firm expressed scepticism that such a system would be workable.

Table 14.3   Companies favouring payment-for-results for Trade New Zealand services

---

'We need people with industry expertise, experience and contacts to source opportunities in overseas markets where New Zealand companies could be getting higher returns. If you paid someone like me a retainer, and they then worked on commission, that could make a real difference. There's no use having bureaucrats who lack that kind of personal experience.'

'They should be working on a commission basis – I don't mind paying for results.'

'I feel that it should be payment on results. I'd be happy to pay for performance.'

'There are a lot of times I just find it's a waste of space. I have no problems spending money on Trade New Zealand, but I'd like there to be some relationship between the money I spend and the money I earn. They give me a report. I don't want to pay by the inch – I want to pay by the dollar. I'd be happy to pay a percentage . . . I'd find it really useful if Trade New Zealand came to me with specific opportunities. I'd be happy to treat them as a business partner and pay a commission.'

'I want a result for my money. If they could sell a container, I'd be happy to pay a commission.'

'A commission-based system would be better.'

Favoured by two firms was the possibility of Trade New Zealand changing from being reactive to being proactive – seeking out opportunities in overseas markets and making them known to firms who indicated willingness to pay a commission on business resulting from identification of such opportunities.

CONCLUSIONS

Acquiring and using adequate export information can minimize risk and uncertainty associated with export transactions and lessen the chances of costly mistakes and wasted opportunities (Ricks, 1983; McAuley, 1993; Diamantopoulos and Souchon, 1996). Availability of information did not pose a particular problem among seafood exporters in the present study. Informational barriers were identified as a major hurdle in several studies reviewed by Seringhaus and Rosson (1991), but not in Bell's study of exporters of computer software (Bell, 1997). Perhaps the fact that both Bell's study and the present study focused on experienced exporters resulted in respondents who have learned, one way or another, how to solve any informational problems.

Seafood exporters in our study typically exuded an indomitable spirit and a 'can-do' attitude, no doubt the result of what one company termed 'cut and thrust' negotiations with overseas customers, and also bureaucratic officials. Those who would find obtaining information a major problem have presumably quit the industry long since.

Diamantopoulos and Souchon (1996) found that the more experience a decision-maker had of their industry and of exporting activity, the more they relied on intuition as a basis for making export decisions. Information was sometimes used 'symbolically' to support decisions already made on the basis of intuition. An example we encountered was: 'We have used Trade New Zealand for an overview of the market in various countries, and they reinforced what the company was getting into.'

Bannock and Peacock (1989) commented on the disdain which experienced exporters generally have for official sources of information, and the scepticism which they have for advice given by banks and professional advisors. Institutional information sources have been found to be the least used by small firms, even though government programmes tend to focus on small firms and invest large amounts of public money on providing information services for them (Reid, 1984; McDowell and Rowlands, 1995). The attitudes expressed by respondents in our sample certainly confirm this well-documented disdain for institutional information.

There is general agreement in the literature that experiential knowledge gained from visiting foreign markets and from actually carrying out the export business cannot be replaced by programmes designed by well-meaning government agencies (Cunningham and Spigel, 1971; Johanson and Vahlne, 1977; Reid, 1984; Seringhaus, 1987; Bell, 1997). Nor can advice from consultants, either governmental or commercial (Brooks and Rosson, 1982; Joynt, 1982; McAuley, 1993), provide an adequate substitute. Trade fairs and trade missions, which enable firms to obtain market knowledge and experience first-hand, are considerably more highly regarded than objective information provided by export-promotion organizations (Walters, 1983; Seringhaus and Rosson, 1990, 1998). Thirkell and Dau (1998) in their study of export success determinants for New Zealand manufacturing exporters, concluded that 'nothing appears to substitute for time spent in the marketplace'. Thus, it seems ironic that in recent years Trade New Zealand appears to have moved away from mechanisms that facilitate this gaining of experiential knowledge by spending time in the marketplace – lauded by both the exporters in this sample and by the international literature.

Depending on whether the principal aim of government EPOs is to assist non-exporters to become exporters, or to maximize export returns gained by firms no matter whether they are new or existing exporters, the findings reported in this study may have significant implications for government export assistance policy. Trade New Zealand, in its 2000 *Annual Report*, defines its vision as: 'We champion New Zealand export businesses to be world leaders.' The intended focus would appear to be on empowering and enhancing the strengths of existing successful exporters, but this does not seem borne out by the reality of the information provision services offered. In this regard, Trade New Zealand appears to have moved towards the type of service that the literature shows is least useful and least trusted, and away from the type of service that is most highly regarded both in the literature and by exporters in this study.

The attitudes of firms towards paying for information services have implications for designers of export assistance programmes in New Zealand and elsewhere.

Our sample of exporters very much favoured a return to the supportive 'helping-hand' type of philosophy that they used to encounter rather than the 'I'll get you a quote' type of approach encountered now. Strong dissatisfaction with paying commercial rates for services that have no guarantee of resulting in successful outcomes was expressed by the majority of exporters in the present study. The unsolicited suggestion from some of these exporters that a 'payment for results' system might be preferable seems worthy of serious consideration by EPOs.

In a broader context, the cost-recovery approaches to export assistance that are now being pursued by export promotion organizations in many countries need to be questioned. In effect, the charges for services appear to be an attempt to provide some proxy measure of the value of such assistance, in the absence of other satisfactory measures of efficacy. Unfortunately, the perception among many exporters is that these agencies are now much more interested in generating revenues rather than providing the types of support their remits mandate. A second and valid grievance is the view that firms are actually being charged twice, firstly through general corporate taxation and then through additional fees. Thirdly, the accuracy and utility of some of the information provided appears to be questionable and service quality issues need to be considered carefully if 'user-pays' approaches are to be accepted, otherwise firms will simply stop using provisions. Such a situation would undoubtedly impact negatively on the credibility of these export promotion agencies among the very firms they purport to assist and on their ability to fulfil their remits.

A limitation of this study is that this particular sample of exporters may not necessarily be representative of exporters in general within New Zealand, let alone in other countries. New Zealand seafood is in high international demand, so the information requirements of the exporters in this industry may be rather specialized and indeed less intense than those of exporters in other sectors. In particular, seafood exporters frequently expressed the view that the last thing they needed was more customers, as they had trouble supplying the ones they already had. So it might be expected that services based on locating potential customers in foreign markets might not be valued by this industry sector. Uncertainty concerning the generalizability of the findings reported here points to the need for further research on this subject, both in New Zealand and in other countries. In order to address this issue, the authors are currently undertaking research within the fishing industry in Ireland and Australia. A future direction will also be to broaden the scope of the study to include firms in various industry sectors in these and other locations.

REFERENCES

Bannock, G. and Peacock, A. (1989) *Governments and Small Business* (London: Paul Chapman Publishing).

Bell, J., McNaughton, R. and Bennett, S. (2000) 'Export Assistance the New Zealand Way', in McNaughton, R.B. (ed.), *Developments in Australasian Marketing*, Advances in International Marketing (Stanford, CT: JAI Press).

Bell, J. (1997) 'A Comparative Study of the Export Problems of Small Computer Exporters in Finland, Ireland and Norway', *International Business Review*, 6 (6), 585–604.

Brooks, M.R. and Rosson, P.J. (1982) 'A Study of Export Behaviour of Small and Medium-sized Manufacturing Firms in Three Canadian Provinces', in Czinkota M. and Tesar G. (eds), *Export Management: An International Context* (New York: Praeger) 39–54.

Buckley, P. (1982) 'The Role of Exporting in the Market Servicing Policies of Multinational Manufacturing Enterprises', in Czinkota, M. and Tesar, G. (eds), *Export Management* (New York: Praeger) 89–109.

Cunningham, M.T. and Spigel, R.I. (1971) 'A Study in Successful Exporting', *British Journal of Marketing*, 5 (1), 2–12.

Czinkota, M.R. (1982) 'An Evaluation of the Effectiveness of US Export Promotion Efforts', in Czinkota M. and Tesar G. (eds), *Export Policy: A Global Assessment* (New York: Praeger).

Czinkota, M.R. (1992) 'Export Promotion and Competitiveness: The Case of Small- and Mid-sized US Firms', in: *How To Manage for International Competitiveness* (New York: International Business Press).

Czinkota, M.R. and Ronkainen, I.A. (1998) *International Marketing* (New York: Harcourt Brace).

Diamantopoulos, A., Schlegelmilch, B. and Tse, K.Y. (1993) 'Understanding the Role of Export Marketing Assistance: Empirical Evidence and Research Needs', *European Journal of Marketing*, 27 (4), 5–18.

Diamantopoulos, A. and Souchon, A.L. (1996) 'Instrumental, Conceptual and Symbolic Use of Export Information: An Exploratory Study of UK Firms', *Advances in International Marketing*, 8, 117–44.

Gray, B.J. (1997) 'Profiling Managers to Improve Export Promotion Targeting', *Journal of International Business Studies*, 28 (2), 387–420.

Johanson, J. and Vahlne, J.E. (1977) 'The Internationalization Process of the Firm – a Model of Knowledge Development and Increasing Foreign Commitments', *Journal of International Business Studies*, 8 (1), 23–32.

Joynt, P. (1982) 'An Empirical Study of Norwegian Export Behaviour', in Czinkota, M. and Tesar, G. (eds), *Export Management: An International Context* (New York: Praeger) 55–69.

Kamath, S., Rosson, P.J., Patton, D. and Brooks, M. (1987) 'Research on Success in Exporting: Past Present and Future', in Rosson, P.J. and Reid, S.D. (eds) *Managing Export Entry and Expansion* (New York: Praeger) 398–421.

Katsikeas, C.S. and Piercy, N.F. (1993) 'Long-term Export Stimuli and Firm Characteristics in a European LDC', *Journal of International Marketing*, 1 (3), 23–47.

Kotabe, M. and Czinkota, M.R. (1992) 'State Government Promotion of Manufacturing Exports: A Gap Analysis', *Journal of International Business Studies*, 23 (4), 637–58.

Laird, S. and Yates, A. (1990) *Quantitative Methods for Trade Barrier Analysis* (New York: New York University Press).

Leonidou, L.C. (1995) 'Export Stimulation: A Non-exporter's Perspective', *European Journal of Marketing*, 29 (8), 17–36.

Leonidou, L.C. and Katsikeas, C.S. (1996) 'The Export Development Process: An Integrative Review of Empirical Models', *Journal of International Business Studies*, 27 (3), 517–51.

McAuley, A. (1993) 'The Perceived Usefulness of Export Information Sources', *European Journal of Marketing*, 27 (10), 52–64.

McDowell, D. and Rowlands, I. (1995) 'Export Information: A Case Study of SMEs in Northern Ireland', *Business Information Review*, 11 (4), 45–53.

Merton, R. (1956). *The Focused Interview: A Manual of Problems and Procedures* (Glencoe, IL: Free Press).

Miesenbock, K.J. (1988) 'Small Businesses and Exporting: A Literature Review', *International Small Business Journal*, 6 (1), 42–61.

Moini, A.H. (1998) 'Small Firms Exporting: How Effective are Government Export Assistance Programs?', *Journal of Small Business Management*, 36 (1), 1–15.

New Zealand Trade Development Board (2000) *Annual Report*.

OECD (1999) *OECD Economic Surveys: New Zealand*.

Patton, M.Q. (1990) *Qualitative Evaluation and Research Methods* (Newbury Park, CA: Sage Publications).

Pointon, T. (1978) 'Measuring the Gains from Government Export Promotion', *European Journal of Marketing*, 12 (6), 451–62.

Reid, S. (1984) 'Information Acquisition and Export Entry Decisions in Small Firms', *Journal of Business Research*, 12, 141–57.

Ricks, D.A. (1983) *Big Business Blunders* (Homewood, IL: Dow-Jones Irwin).

SEAFIC, New Zealand Seafood Industry Council, (1999) *Exporter Directory*. *www.seafood.co.nz/ExportDirect.html*

Seringhaus, F.H.R. (1986). 'The Impact of Government Export Assistance', *International Marketing Review*, 3 (2), 55–65.

Seringhaus, F.H.R. (1987) 'Export Promotion: The Role and Impact of Government services', *Irish Marketing Review*, 2, 106–16.

Seringhaus, F.H.R. and Rosson, P.J. (1990) *Government Export Promotion: A Global Perspective* (London: Routledge).

Seringhaus, F.H.R. and Rosson, P.J. (1991) 'Export Promotion and Public Organizations: State of the Art', in Seringhaus, F. and Rosson, P. (eds). *Export Development and Promotion: The Role of Public Organizations* (Norwell, MA: Kluwer) 3–18.

Seringhaus, F.H.R. and Rosson, P.J. (1998) 'Management and Performance of International Trade Fair Exhibitors: Government Stands vs Independent Stands', *International Marketing Review*, 15 (5), 398–412.

Thirkell, P. and Dau, R. (1998) 'Export Performance: Success Determinants for New Zealand Manufacturing Exporters', *European Journal of Marketing*, 32 (9/10), 813–29.

Walters, P. (1983) 'Export Information Sources – a Study of their Usage and Utility', *International Marketing Review*, Winter, 34–43.

Weaver, K.M. and Pak, J. (1990) 'Export Behaviour and Attitudes of Small and Medium-sized Korean Manufacturing Firms', *International Small Business Journal*, 8 (4), 59–70.

Winkelman, L. and Winkelman, R. (1998) 'Tariffs, Quotas and Terms-of-trade: The Case of New Zealand', *Journal of International Economics*, 46, 313–32.

Part Four

The Internet and E-Commerce

15 A Network Analysis of the Internet's Impact on Internationalization: The Case of Hong Kong SMEs

Helen Chen, Sue Bridgewater and Shan Pan

INTRODUCTION

Despite suggestions that the Internet will bring about a global marketing revolution (Berthon *et al.*, 1999; Lazer and Shaw, 2000), there has been, to date, little empirical research into the precise nature of the Internet's impact. Valuable work has been produced in the areas of the Internet and its impact on exporters (Bennett, 1997; Hamill and Gregory, 1998) and on service firms (Berthon *et al.*, 1999; Lituchy and Rail, 2000). Yet the impact of the Internet on the ongoing process of internationalization remains underresearched.

Research does suggest that 'fundamental reasons for the slow, gradual and evolutionary internationalization of companies [will be] no longer relevant' (Bennett, 1997, p. 328). Moreover, authors suggest that the Internet will reduce a number of the barriers that inhibit internationalization, such as psychic distance (Benjamin and Wigland, 1995; Hamill and Gregory, 1998) or geographic and time distances (Quelch and Klein, 1996).

There is also general consensus that the Internet will reduce the resource requirements needed to internationalize, particularly for firms whose product or service can be digitized and delivered via the Internet (Berthon *et al.*, 1999; Arnott and Bridgewater, 2002). For all firms, the Internet provides access to market research and communication at reduced cost and is proposed as a facilitator of international expansion (Sterne, 1995; Hamill and Gregory, 1998).

Beyond the question of reducing costs of internationalization, however, research has paid little attention to the questions of whether and to what extent the Internet will increase the scope and effectiveness of international activity. Nor does it address the question of what challenges firms face in using the Internet in their internationalization strategies.

This chapter offers preliminary insights into these questions. Firstly, it identifies the challenges of operation in the global Internet marketspace (referred to hereafter as the e-marketspace). Secondly, the rationale for using network theory to explore the Internet's impact on internationalization is presented and finally the network approach is applied to three cases of Hong Kong SMEs to offer insights into the impact of the Internet on the internationalization process.

243

CHARACTERISTICS OF E-MARKETSPACE

The e-marketspace has a number of distinctive characteristics, namely that it is global, real time, open and dynamic.

Global

The Internet's value lies in the connections that it creates between consumers and businesses on a global scale (Hamill and Gregory, 1998). Together with the lower resource requirements offered by the technology, this might be expected to favour the international expansion of firms. In particular, small firms might find an increased level of opportunities for low-cost expansion on a global scale (Bakos and Brynolffson, 1993).

Real-Time

One of the biggest promises of the Internet is that marketers can communicate with their customers anywhere in the world regardless of time-zone differences (Quelch and Klein, 1996). Even if data are updated when it is midnight in the target country, the messages and product or service offer will be available whenever required and orders can be processed automatically online regardless of the time in the home country of the firm.

Real-time accessing and processing of data are not, however, free from problems. The diminishing time lags of order processing build corresponding expectations from customers of rapid order fulfilment. Unless the product or service can be digitized and communicated electronically, then this expectation is unrealistic (Berthon *et al.*, 1999). Global scope, especially for smaller less-experienced firms, may bring associated difficulties in living up to the physical distribution challenges raised by the Internet.

Open

Although global connectivity offers immense opportunities, firms are connected not only to those with whom they wish to have relationships, but, once information is put into the e-marketspace, this is freely accessible by competitors and also customers (Evans and Wurster, 2000) who may be from markets where the firm charges higher prices. Moreover, it may prompt unsolicited approaches from customers. A number of firms have become 'unintentional internationalists' through the open nature of the technology.

Dynamic

The nature and constituency of the Internet is ever-changing. Customers may click on a site once and not return. Links to other websites may be created but then later broken.

LITERATURE REVIEW

Network Perspectives on Marketing and Strategy

Research into networks within the marketing and strategy fields belongs to two main schools. Firstly, the 'networks as a hybrid mode' school considers the network as a type of operation to be used where it confers benefits. These include access to scarce resources (Jarillo, 1988), flexibility in turbulent market conditions (Miles and Snow, 1986) or to allow clusters of small firms to compete against larger rivals (Lorenzoni and Ornati, 1988). To this school belongs Thorelli's seminal view of the network as a hybrid mode between markets and hierarchy:

> In some ways these distinctions are analogous to Williamson's (1975) markets and hierarchies, although he would likely include as part of 'markets' a number of in-between forms where we would rather apply the generic term networks. (Thorelli, 1986, p. 37)

The second school, known as 'markets as networks' can be differentiated from the above on the basis of a number of distinctive characteristics (Johanson and Mattsson 1987):

- *Interdependence*. Firms are viewed as interdependent. The firm's use of assets is influenced by its relationships: 'The markets are characterised by interaction between firms in relationships where the parties have some control over each other and the organizations are not "pure" hierarchies' (Johanson and Mattsson, 1987, p. 12). In this situation, firms do not create sustainable advantages alone, but their actions are favoured or constrained by those of other actors with whom they are directly or indirectly connected.

    Interdependence also makes it difficult to establish where the boundary of control over resources lies. The smallest unit of analysis is not the firm, but a relationship between two actors (dyadic relationship). Network theorists, however, argue that simplification of a network to a dyad 'ignores other significant relationships that the actors involved may have (Easton and Håkansson, 1996, p. 408). Accordingly, they argue that an understanding of networks requires analysis of a larger web of relationships (Johanson and Mattsson, 1987). This argument is based on the idea that positions within networks are influenced not only by the direct relationships of each actor but by the impacts of a broader set of firms with whom the actor may only be indirectly connected.

    Critics argue, however, that this holistic study of the network results in a tendency to describe complexity, rather than to analyse critical issues. A common compromise is to study the focal network around the firm. This is defined as the 'relations above a certain minimum degree of closeness to a focal or "hub" firm' (Cunningham and Culligan 1991, p. 254).

- *Dynamic Structures*. Networks may be both stable and changing. Relationships may become stable and institutionalized as trust and commitment build and mutual adaptations are made (Easton and Lundgren, 1992; Håkansson, 1992). However, they are also subject to both continuous and discontinuous change (Lundgren, 1992) when relationships dissolve or new relationships are formed.

Markets as Networks as an Approach for Studying the Internet

Both of the above characteristics of the markets-as-networks approach seem appropriate to the Internet. The Internet has parallels with markets as networks in terms of its changing constituency. The growing popularity of 'portals' where firms may cooperate to provide products and services to customers, of e-procurement and e-supply chains mean that firms using the Internet often have to work cooperatively. They may be interdependent, in the sense that both need to be consulted about resource commitment decisions. Whilst the Internet does have market-based transactions (such as e-auctions), this chapter focuses on the cooperative nature of many Internet interactions. Likewise, the Internet is dynamic in its connectivity and the changing nature of its links resembles network structures.

Key Strategic Challenges from a 'Markets as Networks' Perspective

The major strategic challenge from a markets-as-networks perspective is that of how firms should build strong positions from which they can gain strategic advantage. One of the most frequently cited models of network analysis is that of Håkansson and Johanson (1992). This identifies the role of actors, activities and resources in understanding how network positions are built, these categories are used in the remainder of this section to identify the issues firms face in building network positions.

Actors

Networks consist of actors, who occupy positions that can be more or less 'structured'. Tightly structured networks tend to have long-established and stable relationships (Kinch, 1992; Seyed-Mohamed and Bolte, 1992). Actors have created well-defined positions and have clear 'recipes' for serving the market. Loosely structured networks, in contrast, are dynamic and rapidly changing. The composition of the network may be subject to change, with new actors coming in, and old ones leaving the network. Positions may change and are not always clear to those attempting to understand the network (Seyed-Mohamed and Bolte, 1995).

At first sight it may appear that it is easier to build positions in loosely structured networks, as there may be more gaps in the market. Conversely, however, it may be difficult to identify what will ultimately constitute a successful position in the market (Seyed Mohammed and Bolte, 1995). Hence, although they are highly

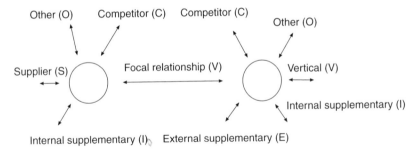

Figure 15.1   Five kinds of network connection of a focal dyadic relationship

competitive, it may be easier to understand the rules of a tightly structured net-work and to achieve success by exploiting the weaknesses of one of the existing positioning strategies of a competitor.

The nature of the actors that might play a role in building network positions has also been explored. Lee (1993) identifies three levels of network relation-ships, macro-, interorganizational and intraorganizational. Blankenburg (1995), however, simplifies this to 'external' and 'internal' relationships, although she further identifies the category of relationship as shown in Figure 15.1 (Holm *et al.*, 1997).

Activities

When building network positions, actors engage in a dynamic process. In the internationalization process, Blankenburg (1995) describes the process of market entry as a set of activities happening over time and identifies the external/internal nature of the influences on this process (see Figure 15.2). The new activities that firms may have to engage in include breaking relationships in old networks and building positions in new 'nets'.

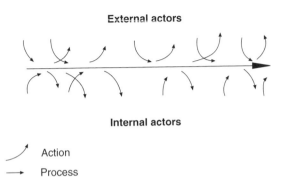

Figure 15.2   Internal/external actors

To become established in a new market, that is, a network which is new to the firm, it has to build relationships which are new both to itself and its counter-parts. This is sometimes done by breaking old, existing relationships, and sometimes by adding a relationship to already existing ones. (Johanson and Mattsson, 1988, p. 306)

Some of the activities in which the firm engages will be proactive, whilst others will be initiated by other actors with whom the firm is connected:

A Swedish firm might increase its penetration in a South American market because of its relationship in Japan with an internationalizing Japanese firm. Other examples of such international interdependence are 'big projects' in which design, equipment, supply, construction, ownership and operation can all be allocated to firms of different national origin. (Johanson and Mattsson, 1988, p. 315)

Resources
The process of building positions may involve the firm in resource-commitment decisions. As previously identified, actors in a network do not have sole control over their resources, but may be involved in joint projects, or be influenced in their decisions by others with whom they are connected. Mattsson (1989) classi-fies the resource commitments of network actors as being either external (market) or internal (marketing) investments.

A Network Theoretical Analysis of the Internet and Internationalization

Actors
The e-marketspace has been modelled as a network or 'hyperarchy'. The most significant difference between this and any other network is that the relationships or links between the firms are virtual (often via hyperlinks – hence hyperarchy). The hyperarchy is extremely loose in structure – the number and positions of actors are subject to rapid change and there are no clearly defined recipes for success.

Activities
Given the open nature of the Internet, firms may not even actively seek to enter networks in a particular market, but once they have a website, automatically occupy a position in a global network. In consequence, their market data is accessible to customers from all countries. The key activities facing firms in this global hyperar-chy is that they will have to be able to do business effectively with customers across this broad geographic scope. Research into the Internet points to the importance of interaction as a means of building these virtual relationships (Hoffman and Novak, 1996; Dutta and Segev, 1999). Activities within the firm may then revolve around use of and integration of the Internet into the firm's capabilities and developing competence in virtual relationships with actors on a global scale.

Resources

Given the geographic distances that may exist between firms and their customers, a key challenge is that of achieving rapid, or even real-time, order fulfilment on a global scale. This may require the creation of new physical distribution channels to market. Moreover, resource commitment will also be required to build the interactive capacity of the web interface with customers. Hence firms will need to make the market and marketing investments identified by Johanson and Mattsson (1988).

From a resources perspective, a key characteristic of the Internet is that firms are globally accessible as soon as they post a website. To meet customers' needs effectively, firms may need to build stronger positions – in physical distribution and marketing interface terms – very rapidly. This will mean high early resource commitment to the Internet operation. To understand fully the implications of these aspects of Internet internationalization, this chapter explores the cases of three Hong Kong-based SMEs using the actors–activities–resources framework.

METHODOLOGY

Choice of Research Method

The methodology used in this research meets a number of challenges. The Internet is a relatively new area of research, and given its 'theory-building' nature (Deshpandé, 1983; Harrigan, 1983; Bonoma, 1985) this research is most suited to a fine-grained qualitative research technique. Secondly, as there are possible interrelationships between the decisions of each firm and those of its competitors, customers and other stakeholders, methods which use statistical inference may be invalid as they make assumptions of independence of the unit of analysis (Easton, 1995). For both of these reasons, a case-study methodology is preferred as this allows the market-entry decisions to be seen in context and can capture the richness of the data. Yin (1983) proposes the use of a case-study method for the study of contemporary issues in their social context. The rich data yielded by the case-study method is used to formulate research propositions for further studies in this area.

Selection of Cases

A survey undertaken by the Hong Kong Productivity Council and IBM China/Hong Kong Ltd classifies e-commerce use into five levels:

1 *Shows intention.* Companies at level 1 currently have no e-mail account but intended to open one within the next six months.
2 *Basic adoption.* Companies have an e-mail account.

3   *Prospecting*. e-mail account and website with basic information on products/ services.
4   *Business integration*. Web page is interactive and becomes a meeting place for current and potential customers. Companies either have online transactions, that is allowing payment on the net, or basic integration and internal integration of e-commerce with in-company databases (such as material requirement planning (MRP) or customer relationship management (CRM).
5   *Business transformation*. New business generated through e-business and traditional businesses migrate to the Internet. Back-office functions become electronic and are streamlined.

To study the issues relating to the impact of the Internet the case studies focus on one firm each from stages 3–5 of this classification. The stage-3 firm has its own web page with an e-mail account as a new communication tool. The stage-4 firm uses the web page as a way to collect and process customer information. The stage-5 firm is creating new business from the Internet and is also shifting its traditional business to the new technology.

The cases are selected from sectors where the Internet is important. A *Financial Times* report (1999) ranks computer products (with sales of $196.2m), books and magazines ($38.3m) and music and entertainment ($35m) as the biggest sellers on the Internet. Accordingly, the cases in this study are selected from these sectors. Although differences in the way these sectors use the Internet might result in different impacts on internationalization, research suggests (Zafarulan *et al.*, 1998; Coviello and Martin, 1999) that sectoral differences do not significantly influence the internationalization behaviour of small firms. The characteristics of the firms are shown in the Appendix.

Multiple sources of evidence were used to develop the case studies. These included internal documents from the companies and face-to-face interviews with respondents from the firms including the general manager, the managing director, the marketing manager and the IT manager from each firm. Each interview lasted around two hours. A semi-structured research instrument was used with open questions relating to the pattern of internationalization, subsequent internationalization, market selection and mode of operation (Coviello and Martin, 1999) and the impact of the Internet.

FINDINGS

Case A

Actors

Firm A was already international before it began to use the Internet. It is a manufacturer and exporter of CDs, and 50 per cent of its sales came from international markets. Although its sales growth was healthy during the 1980s it was looking for new ways to communicate with its customers:

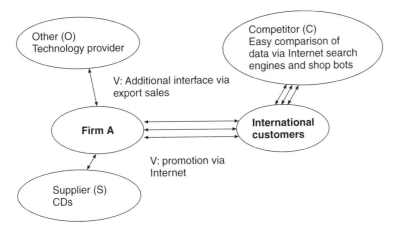

Figure 15.3   The network connections of firm A

We noticed in the mid-1990s that a number of large firms used a web page to promote sales. We had heard that firms like Amazon.com benefited from the Internet. Nevertheless, we were not sure at that moment whether launching a web page would work in our case.

Firm A's network is shown in Figure 15.3.

Activities
Despite its uncertainty as to the value of the new technology, firm A decided to set up a web page to broaden its exposure. The web page was launched in November 1999. In explaining their decision, firm A's marketing director said:

> The birth of the Internet brought a big change to the way people obtain information. They can read on the Internet everything, which used to be found in newspapers, brochures, catalogues, etc. Hence, we decided to set up our own web page and upload some information onto the Internet. By doing this more and more potential customers can get information about our firm. The best thing is that we can contact international customers via email at very, very low cost.

Firm A's website served effectively as an online brochure, containing information about the firm, products, contact e-mail address and contact persons. Alongside the web interface, firm A continued to export using telephone, fax or e-mail and delivering products from the Hong Kong base. Despite its simple website, firm A attracted a great number of foreign customers. 'We could not believe that such a simple web site would have such a great effect. We got a lot of enquiries every day about our products, price and even about why we didn't have an on-line transaction facility.'

External activities

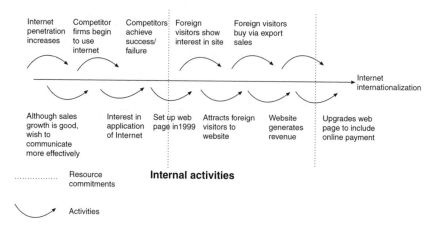

Figure 15.4   The international expansion of firm A

Encouraged by this response from customers, firm A decided to upgrade the web page to provide an online payment system. This was expected to have a dramatic effect on the firm:

> Providing an on-line payment system is not costly at all. We won't lose anything by doing so as our traditional way of doing business is still there. If the provision can bring more customers order and payment on line, we will consider it a bonus.

Resources

The cost implications of setting up an Internet site played a role in firm A's decisions. As it was initially unsure how much benefit it would gain from its Internet site, it limited the sophistication of the website and decided for an online brochure. Only after it became apparent that the Internet was generating revenue did firm A decide to make the additional internal resource investment to set up online order processing. Firm A's process of using the Internet in its international activities is summarized in Figure 15.4.

Case B

Actors

Firm B was set up as a facilitator between leisure users and providers in Hong Kong. As the directing manager said: 'Hong Kong is full of people, many of whom do not know what to do in their leisure time. So its is very important for us to "introduce" these activities to them.'

The actors in its network include not only firm B and its customers, but also the providers of the leisure activities that it promotes. Firm B was not international

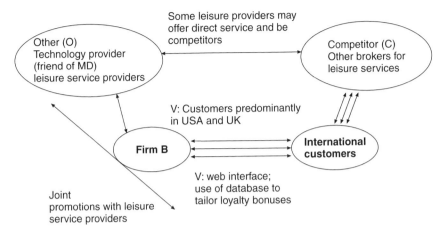

Figure 15.5   The network connections of firm B

until the advent of the Internet; its customers are predominantly located in the USA and the UK:

> Our foreign customers are tourists coming to Hong Kong. Before they came, they, particularly Americans and Brits, would browse the Internet to see what they could do in Hong Kong . . . Listed in *www.yahoo.com* and *www.yahoo.com.hk*, we could be easily found. If they were interested in the activities we provide, they would try every means to contact us, by phone, fax or email.

The network of actors surrounding firm B is shown in Figure 15.5.

Activities
In its early days, firm B used printed brochures to promote its services. Several months later it launched a website with the help of the managing director's (MD) friend. The MD said of the benefit of the website:

> We were going to do most of the promotion with hard-copy information, but it is very expensive. We would have done this if the Internet hadn't existed . . . What the Internet does for us is it makes getting information about our customers very cheap, extremely cheap, to get lots of information, and lots of customers. That's the main benefit for us, if we would do this in hard copy, the company would have been fouled now because we would not have enough return to cover the cost.

Firm B's success is not only based on the Internet. It also relies heavily on building trust in customers. To help to build this trust, firm B set up a customer database with information obtained from the Internet and other kinds of enquiries and orders. The database is used to structure all kinds of promotions, such as

External activities

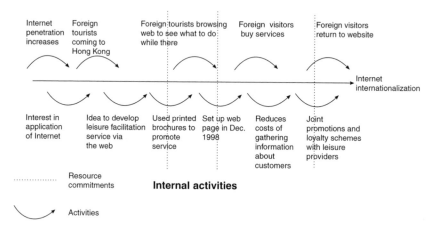

Figure 15.6   The international expansion of firm B

loyalty bonuses for customers who order twice. To this extent, relationship-building is an important activity for firm B.

Resources
When it first decided to use the Internet, firm B was also uncertain about the potential value of the technology. To limit the initial outlay, the first website was designed by a friend of the managing director. This investment has been repaid by the low-cost access to customer information provided by the website.

Firm B's proactive use of the Internet to access international customers has proved a good way to reduce the costs of internationalization: 'It's amazing that our advertising cost last year was almost zero due to lots of co-advertising programmes. This is very good for such a small firm like us.' The resource outlay of internationalization is reduced, therefore, also by joint initiatives with the firms that it is promoting.

The internationalization process of firm B is shown in Figure 15.6.

Case C

Actors
Firm C is the Hong Kong regional office of a UK-based e-retailer. A month after the e-retailer launched its UK website, selling a broad range of goods, many customers were attracted, a third of them from the European Union (EU), particularly Germany. Given that one of the biggest attractions of the Internet lies in the speed of order fulfilment, the managing director decided to set up the first off-shore office in Germany. This acted as a European hub, fulfilling orders for Germany and continental Europe. The favourable location of the German operation within Europe contrasts with the UK operation:

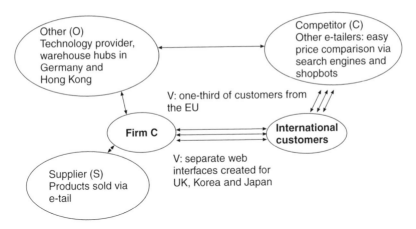

Figure 15.7 The network connections of firm C

It might, for example, be cheaper for a German customer to buy a fax machine in the UK. But if you add the shipping cost and the VAT, at 17.5 per cent, then the price is comparable. Although you might save, say, £5, you could be losing one week in shipment. Then it's a trade-off.

The success of the German website stimulated the firm's internationalization process. Hong Kong was selected as the next location for a website, with the idea that this would act as a hub for the Asia-Pacific region:

Having only one off shore web site is not enough for us. We perceive that on-line sales can save customers' time and money. If a customer in Asia buys something on the Germany or UK site, he has to pay the shipping all the way to where he is living, plus he has to wait longer for the goods to arrive. So both the convenience and price disappear. If there is a web site in Hong Kong, we can obtain Asian customers.

The expanding network of actors surrounding firm C is shown in Figure 15.7.

Activities
Firm C has engaged in a process of 'learning by doing' in its use of the Internet. Depending on the origin of its orders, it has altered the network surrounding the firm in order to serve these markets more effectively. As the German market became important, a warehouse was set up to improve order fulfilment time. After the German operation proved a success, firm C set up a similar operation to serve the Asia-Pacific hub and used this as a springboard for increased activity in new Asia-Pacific markets.

As Korea and Japan became important, a specific web interface tailored to the needs of each market was introduced. The process of internationalization of firm C is shown in Figure 15.8.

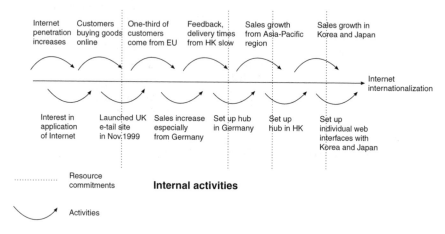

External activities

Internet | Customers | One-third of | Feedback, | Sales growth | Sales growth in
penetration | buying goods | customers | delivery times | from Asia-Pacific | Korea and Japan
increases | online | come from EU | from HK slow | region

Internet
internationalization

Interest in | Launched UK | Sales increase | Set up hub | Set up | Set up
application | e-tail site | especially | in Germany | hub in HK | individual web
of Internet | in Nov.1999 | from Germany | | | interfaces with
| | | | | Korea and Japan

.... Resource
                commitments   **Internal activities**

          Activities

Figure 15.8   The international expansion of firm C

Resources

Firm C has made both marketing (internal) and market (external) investments in
its Internet internationalization. The internal investments are in setting up new
web interfaces with different markets; the external investments involve establishing physical distribution hubs in different markets. Whilst connectivity was provided at low cost via the Internet, the process of internationalization and building
effective network positions has required additional resource commitment and the
introduction of new actors (for example German and Asia-Pacific distributors) in
the network.

DISCUSSION

The advent of the Internet has provided connectivity for each of the firms at low
cost. The ability to interact with customers on an international scale has proved to
be valuable in each case, and the experiences of these firms supports the research
expectation that low-cost communication is one of the most valuable opportunities
provided by the new technology (Sterne, 1995; Quelch and Klein, 1996). As each
firm was unsure of the scale of potential benefits, initial resource commitment
to the technology was limited. Firm B made use of personal networks to build
a low-cost website, whilst firms A and C both introduced additional Internet
functions over time.

From a network perspective, internationalization via the Internet is revealed as
a dynamic process of interaction between actors. When using the Internet, firm A
begins to build relationships with new actors in other markets. It finds that there
is marketing potential in new markets and begins to commit resources to internal

activities such as additional web functions – order processing – and export order fulfillment to serve these markets.

One dimension of the Internet as a 'virtual network' is that once a website is posted on the web, interest is generated on a global scale and the information is accessible across the entire network. The Internet is extremely loose in structure (Seyed-Mohamed and Bolte, 1992). The precise nature of its connections are not clear to the actors posting websites, and therefore the level and locus of interest are difficult to anticipate. This may explain the initial reluctance of all three firms to commit high levels of resources to the Internet.

Whilst this loose structure may make the Internet difficult to understand and to anticipate, the positive responses to the internal marketing investments (Johanson and Mattsson, 1985) prompts each firm to make additional investments in building successful network positions. Further investment in internal capabilities – order processing for firm A, joint promotions with leisure providers for firm B, and new market-specific web interfaces for firm C – are needed to build these. Firm C, which has the most developed network position, has also invested externally in new activities such as warehouse hubs.

Viewing the Internet as a loosely structured network offers insights into some of the questions that are vexing international marketers. How great an investment should they make in this technology if they already have channels to international markets? What are successful recipes for Internet operation? Axelsson and Johanson (1992) suggest that if networks are loosely structured, one of the issues facing firms is that they tend to be 'opaque' and it may be difficult to understand remote parts of the network. In the case of the Internet, few of the relationships, especially those with customers, are face-to-face, so the challenges revolve around understanding relationships with an extremely opaque network of actors.

The virtual nature of these relationships may complicate the creation of trust – which *the markets as networks view* suggests is the 'glue' that creates stable and longstanding relationships. Worries about Internet security and the remote nature of interactions raise questions for international marketers about whether virtual relationships can replicate the social interaction that tends to underpin the creation of trust (Balabanis and Vassileiou, 1999). Internet literature suggests that the creation of virtual communities (McWilliam, 2000) may be the nearest proxy for social interaction and may increase customers' propensities to return to websites. On this basis, the loyalty schemes and use of customer data by firm B seem likely to contribute to successful relationship-creation.

Without the creation of long-term stable relationships, one of the principal challenges for the Internet and internationalization is that firms are making resource-commitment decisions on the basis of potentially transient customer interactions. Firm C sets up a hub in Germany given that there is a large volume of activity from the market. Given the loose structure of the network, lags in the timing of investments may mean that firms fail to capitalize on initial interest in a website.

Firm C does appear to have succeeded in building on the interest in Germany by improving the speed of its order fulfillment to the market. This kind of flexible response may be necessary for the creation of successful network positions. A common thread in each case is that the firms 'learn by doing'. None of the firms have a clear picture of the Internet's potential, of the actors with whom they may need to build relationships, or of the scale and nature of investments that may be required. They do, however, learn from initial successes what may constitute effective network positions, and alter the composition of the network, activities and resource commitment to develop these positions.

PRACTITIONER IMPLICATIONS

The case studies in this chapter suggest that the Internet raises a number of issues for small firms. Firstly, how much should they invest in an initial foray into the Internet? The firms in this study reflect the uncertainty of how great the advantages of the Internet will be. Their initial investment tends to be low and often uses the technical skills of those who they already know. This allows them to 'put a toe in the water' without too great an expense, although the costs of adding additional functionality later and the professional impact of the initial website should be taken into account in opting for this 'stepwise' approach.

Secondly, small firms should be aware of the possible scale of international interest and should consider strategies for dealing with customers who they either cannot, or do not want to, serve. It is better to have a politely negative response prepared – or even to look at passing business to an associate or related site rather than to fail to respond. At some point you may be in a position to do business with these customers.

Finally, small firms should consider the possible negative features of the Internet as a replacement for face-to-face dealing with international customers. The Internet involves remote interaction; written words, symbols, and the use of colours may all be perceived differently by customers of different nationalities. The initial 'hits' should be analysed to find out more about the nationalities of those using the site, and the cultural preferences of the main nationalities might be considered to avoid negative 'signals'.

CONCLUSIONS

In its global connectivity and the importance of interactive relationships, the Internet seems to have parallels with network theoretical views of markets. Consequently, the actors, activities and resources framework is applied to understand the challenges for firms in building positions in the international e-marketspace.

In terms of the actors, the e-marketspace is rapidly changing and loosely structured, and it is difficult for firms to understand what will constitute successful market positions. Perhaps as a result of this uncertainty there is initial reluctance to commit high levels of resources to the technology, and this may also relate to the size of the firms and their relative resource constraints.

Resources are committed both externally – for example firm C's warehouse hubs – and internally – as with the same firm's tailored interfaces with different markets, the loyalty and promotional activities of firm B and in the increased functionality of adding e-payment systems to firm B.

In creating successful positions, network theory points to the importance of stable, trusting relationships. Research suggests that interaction is essential to the creation of loyalty and to strong positions, and without stable relationships firms may be committing resources to transient business opportunities. The possibility that business is transient – given the current uncertainty in ascertaining what are the successful positions – seems to explain the emphasis on 'learning by doing' and on committing resources incrementally.

Appendix: Characteristics of Case Firms

Case	Sector	Original country	Firm size (employees)	Time of firm's set-up	Time of the web-site's set-up	First time serving foreign customers	Total foreign sales (%)	Foreign sales obtained online (%)
1	CD manufacturer	HK	35	June 1988	Nov. 1999	July 1988	60%	10%
2	Leisure activity provider	HK	5	May 1998	Dec. 1998	Jan. 2000	5%	5%
3	Department store	UK	85	Jan. 1999	Nov. 1999	Feb. 1999	35%	35%

REFERENCES

Arnott, D.C. and Bridgewater, S. (2002) 'Internet, Interaction and Implications for Marketing', *Marketing Intelligence and Planning*, 20 (2), 86–95.

Axelsson, B. and Johanson, J. (1992) 'Foreign Market Entry – The Textbook vs. The Network View', in G. Easton and B. Axelsson (eds), *Industrial Networks – A New View of Reality* (London: Routledge), 218–32.

Bakos, J.Y. and Brynolffson, E. (1993) 'Information Technology, Incentives and the optimal number of suppliers', *Journal of Management Information Systems*, 10 (2), 37–47.

Balabanis, G. and Vassileiou, S. (1999) 'Some Attitudinal Predictors of Home-Shopping through the Internet', *Journal of Marketing Management*, 15, 361–85.

Benjamin, R. and Wigland, R. (1995) 'Electronic Markets and Virtual Value Chains on the Information Superhighway', *Sloan Management Review*, 36, Winter, 72.

Bennett, R. (1997) 'Export Marketing and the Internet: Experiences of Web Site Use and Perceptions of Export Barriers among UK businesses', *International Marketing Review*, 14 (5), 324–44.

Berthon, P., Pitt, L., Katsikeas, C. and Berthon, P. (1999) 'Executive Insights: Virtual Services Go International: International Services in the Marketspace', *Journal of International Marketing*, 7 (3), 84–105.

Blankenburg, D. (1995) 'A Network Approach to Foreign Market Entry', in Möller, K. and Wilson, D. (eds) *Business Marketing: An Interaction and Network Perspective* (Berlin: Kluwer) 375–410.

Bonoma, T. (1985) 'Case Research in Marketing: Opportunities, Problems and a process', *Journal of Marketing Research*, 12, 199–208.

Coviello, N. and Martin, K.A.M. (1999) 'Internationalization of Service SMEs: An Integrated Perspective from the Engineering Consulting Sector', *Journal of International Marketing*, 7 (4), 42–63.

Cunningham, M. and Culligan, K. (1991) 'Competitiveness Through Networks of Relationships in Information Technology Product Markets', in Paliwoda, S. (ed.) *New Perspectives on International Marketing*, (London: Routledge) 251–75.

Desphande, R. (1983) 'Paradigms Lost': On the Theory and Method in Research in Marketing', *Journal of Marketing*, 47, Fall, 101–10.

Dutta, S. and Segev, A. (1999) 'Business Transformation on the Internet', *European Management Journal*, 17 (5), 466–76.

Easton, G. (1992) 'Industrial Networks: A Review, in Easton, G. and Axelsson, B. (eds) *Industrial Networks: A New View of Reality* (London: Routledge).

Easton, G. (1995) 'Methodology and Industrial Networks', in Wilson, D.T. and Möller, K. (eds) *Relationships and Networks: Theory and Application* (Kent: PWS).

Easton, G. and Håkansson, H. (1996) 'Markets as Networks: Editorial Introduction', *International Journal of Research in Marketing, Special Issue on Markets as Networks*, 13 (5), 407–13.

Easton, G. and Lundgren, A. (1992) 'Changes in Industrial Networks as Flow through Nodes' in Easton, G. and Axelsson, B. (eds) *Industrial Networks: A New View of Reality* (London: Routledge).

Evans, P. and Wurster, T.S. (2000) *Blown to Bits* (Harvard Business School Press).

Håkansson, H. (1992) 'Evolution Processes in Industrial Networks', in Axelsson, B. and Easton, G. (eds) *Industrial Networks: A New View of Reality* (London: Routledge) 129–42.

Håkansson, H. and Johanson, J. (1992) 'A Model of Industrial Networks', in Axelsson, B. and Easton, G. (eds) *Industrial Networks: A New View of Reality* (London: Routledge).

Hamill, J. and Gregory, K. (1998) 'Internet Marketing and the Internationalization of UK SMEs', *Journal of Marketing Management*, 14, 9–29.

Harrigan, K. (1983) 'Research Methodologies for Contingency Approaches to Business Strategy', in *Academy of Management Review*, 8 (3), 398–405.

Hoffman, D.L. and Novak, T.P. (1996) 'Marketing in Hypermedia Computer-Mediated Environments: Conceptual Foundations', *Journal of Marketing*, 60, 50–68.

Holm, D. Blankenburg and Johanson, J. (1997) 'Business Network Connections and the Atmosphere of International Business Relationships', in Björkman, I. and Forsgren, M. (eds) *The Nature of the International Firm* (Copenhagen Business School Press).

Jarillo, J.C. (1988) 'On Strategic Networks', *Strategic Management Review*, 11, 479–99.

Johanson, J. and Mattsson, L.G. (1985) 'Marketing Investments and Market Investments in Industrial Networks', *International Journal of Research in Marketing*, 2, 185–95.

Johanson, J. and Mattsson, L.G. (1987) 'Interorganisational Relationships in Industrial Systems – A Network Approach compared with the Transaction Cost Approach', *International Journal of Management and Organisation*, 17 (1), 34–48.

Johanson, J. and Mattsson, L.G. (1988) 'Internationalisation in Industrial Systems – A Network Approach', in Hood, N. and Vahlne, J.E. (eds) *Strategies in Global Competition*, reproduced in Buckley, P.J. and Ghauri, P. (eds) *The Internationalisation of the Firm: A Reader* (London: Academic Press).

Kinch, N. (1992) 'Entering a Tightly Structured Network – Strategic Visions or Network Realities', in Forsgren, M. and Johanson, J. (eds) *Managing Networks in International Business* (New York: Gordon & Breach).

Lee, J.W. (1993) 'The Development of Strategic Position in the Korean Industrial Turbines Market', Uppsala Working Paper Series 1993/8 (University of Uppsala).

Lazer, W. and Shaw, E.H. (2000) 'Executive Insights: Global Marketing Management: At the Dawn of the New Millennium', *Journal of International Marketing*, 8 (1), 65–77.

Lituchy, T.R. and Rail, A. (2000) 'Bed and Breakfasts, Small Inns and the Internet: The Impact of Technology on the Globalization of Small Businesses', *Journal of International Marketing*, 8 (2), 86–97.

Lorenzoni, G. and Ornati, O.A. (1988) 'Constellations of Firms and New Ventures', *Journal of Business Venturing*, 4 (2), March, 133–47.

Lundgren, A. (1992) 'Co-ordination and Mobilization Processes in Industrial Networks', in Axelsson, B. and Easton, G. (eds) *Industrial Networks: A New View of Reality* (London: Routledge).

Mattsson, L.G. (1989) 'Development of Firms in Networks: Positions and Investments', in Cavusgil, S.T. (ed.) *Advances in International Marketing*, 3, JAI Press, 121–39.

McWilliam, G. (2000) 'Building Stronger Brands Through Online Communities', *Sloan Management Review*, Spring, 43–54.

Miles, R.E. and Snow, C. (1986) 'Organisations: New Concepts for New Forms', *California Management Review*, 28, 62–73.

Quelch, J.A. and Klein, L. (1996) 'The Internet and International Marketing', *Sloan Management Review*, Spring, 60–75.

Seyed-Mohamed, N. and Bolte, M. (1992) 'Taking a Position in a Structured Business Network', in Forsgren, M. and Johanson, J. (eds) *Managing Networks in International Business* (New York: Gordon & Breach).

Sterne, J. (1995) *World Wide Web Marketing: Integrating the Internet into your Marketing Budget* (New York: John Wiley).

Thorelli, H.B. (1986) 'Networks: Between Markets and Hierarchies', *Strategic Management Review*, 7, 37–51.

Williamson, O.E. (1975) *Between Markets and Hierarchies: Analysis and Antitrust Implications* (Macmillan).

Yin, R. (1983) *Case Study Research: Design and Methods* (Newbury Park, CA: Sage).

Zafarullan, M., Mujahid, A. and Young, S. (1998) 'The Internationalization of The Small Firm in Developing Countries: Exploratory Research from Pakistan', *Journal of Global Marketing*, 3 (11), 21–40.

16 Internet Usage and Marketing Relationships in the Real-Estate Sector: Some Preliminary Insights from Canada and the UK

Dennis Sakalauskas and Kevin I.N. Ibeh

INTRODUCTION

During the past few years, the real-estate industry, like most other sectors, has witnessed increased Internet-based marketing activities (De la Torre and Moxon, 2001). This is evident in the emergence of online realtors and real-estate websites in the USA, where 98 per cent of properties are reportedly marketed online (*e-first*, July 2000), and most other industrialized economies, including Canada (for example, www.reic.ca, OttawaHomes.com, www.ottawarealestate.org) and the UK (for example, propertyfind.co.uk, asserta.co.uk).

Notwithstanding some demographic distinctions, notably geographical space, population size and average age of real-estate products (MacDonald, 2000), the Canadian and UK's real-estate markets share a number of important similarities. They both have very active and growing real-estate markets (Bell, 2000; Klump, 2000; Young *et al.*, 2000), have comparable institutional environments for Internet usage and e-commerce readiness (Oxley and Yeung, 2001), and are witnessing significant reduction in the number of real-estate agents. It is arguable that these falling numbers could have resulted, at least in part, from the emergence of online realty operations. Fuelled by improvements in full-time employment and disposable incomes, the Canadian real-estate market has been growing since 1996. A record number of homes were sold in 1997, and sales in 1999 increased by a further 7 per cent (Klump, 2000). Available figures also suggest significant growth in the UK's real-estate market, for example between 1981 and 1996 the number of Scottish households increased from 1 854 000 to 2 136 000 (Young *et al.*, 2000). Moreover, Scottish Homes expects these figures to reach 2 233 000 by 2001 and 2 346 000 by 2013 (Young *et al.*, 2000).

Although the above trends have attracted some research interest (Canadian Mortgage and Housing Corporation, 1999; NDP Online Research, 1999; Ernst & Young, 2000), very few studies have explored the views of property buyers on the importance of Internet sources in the property purchase decision. Moreover, no previous research has directly compared developments within this industry in Canada and the UK.

262

This chapter contributes towards redressing the research gap identified above. It reports the findings of an exploratory investigation into the relative impact of Internet usage on the real-estate markets in Canada and the UK. Also, given the widely observed importance of relationships in influencing purchase decisions for high involvement, service-oriented items (Gummesson, 1994; Lyons, 1994; Peck *et al.*, 1999) such as real estate, this chapter examines the effect of the technological capabilities/opportunities associated with the Internet on the strength of the relationships within the real-estate sector (particularly between real-estate agents and property buyers). Other specific objectives of the chapter include providing some insights into the online real-estate markets in Canada and the UK, and assessing the prospects of electronic commerce in these two markets.

CONCEPTUALIZATIONS AND PROPOSITIONS

Four key conceptual factors connected to the use of the Internet for real-estate purposes are outlined and propositions are determined from these and then assessed by a comparative study of Canada and the UK.

Internet Usage and Perceived Importance

The literature suggests that the Internet could assist real-estate agents in their normal role of developing relationships with customers and delivering the ultimate transaction (Ernst and Young, 2000; Fox, 2000). This could take a number of forms, including facilitating the task of tracking information about their clientele; enabling more accurate monitoring of competitors' movements; offering a more diversified portfolio of services (on a massive number of properties) at a faster rate, 24 hours a day, seven days a week; and communicating more easily with prospects, including international ones (Hamill, 1997). There exists some evidence that property buyers are utilizing the Internet in their purchase decision-making process. For example, a web-based survey conducted by NDP Online Research (1999) found that 64 per cent of the 2355 respondents indicated having searched for real-estate information online. More importantly, 19 per cent confirmed that their online search resulted in an actual meeting with a realtor. Among the most influential motivations identified in the study for customers' use of the Internet in property search were convenience, time-saving and a huge property assortment, in that order (Kyle, 2000); this suggests that such service elements could beneficially be integrated into online realty operations.

Given the very high levels of Internet adoption in both Canada (Canadian users incur the lowest Internet access costs among G7 countries, and their economy generated an estimated total Internet revenue of $28.5 billion or 1.5 per cent of GDP in 1998 – BCG Canada, 2000) and the UK, it should be expected that a majority of property buyers in Canada and the UK would employ the Internet at some stage during their property decision process. Hence:

P1:   A majority of property buyers in Canada and the UK are likely to use the Internet for realty purposes.

Also, given that Canada has higher Internet penetration levels than the UK (nearly one in three Canadians, 29.7 per cent or 9.2 million, use the Internet compared to 18.3 per cent, or 10.8 million, in the UK – Kyle, 2000; Lynch and Beck, 2001; Oxley and Yeung, 2001), it should be expected that a higher proportion of property buyers in Canada would utilize Internet-based sources. Hence:

P1a: A higher proportion of property buyers in Canada would utilise the Internet for realty purposes relative to their UK counterparts.

Breadth and Depth of Online Services

The proliferation of real-estate websites is making it increasingly difficult to distinguish one online operator from another (Ward and Lee, 2000). This increased competitiveness has meant that it is no longer enough merely to maintain an online presence with communication and information provision functions (Quelch and Klein, 1996; Hamill, 1997), or to compete solely on the basis of price (Segner, 2000). Reflecting Peck *et al.*'s (1999) call on service providers (including realtors) to determine and focus on 'superior value delivery', strategy-oriented virtual realtors have increasingly emphasized service quality, and have invested effort towards strengthening their service mix with value-adding contents, including mortgage advice and finance-related services. These realtors have, thus, positioned themselves to serve not only as virtual facilitators or liaisons between buyers and sellers, but as organizers of a multi-package of activities such as mortgage, prices and finance, all of which are facilitated by the Internet (Wilford, 2000). Virtual tours which showcase rooms in advertised houses 24 hours a day, seven days a week, thus making prospective buyers feel as close to the property as possible without physically seeing it (Fox, 2000), and paperless transactions, are also increasingly becoming popular.

Furthermore, reflecting the now established trend in online marketing (Poon and Jevons, 1997; Lettl and Schlegelmilch, 1999), many real-estate operators are linking up with, or are being absorbed by, other bigger online players that offer real-estate information as part of their portfolio of online services. Considering the earlier discussed levels of e-business development in Canada and the UK, it should be expected that:

P2:   Real estate businesses in Canada and the UK are likely to offer a wide variety of complementary online services.

P2a: Property buyers in Canada are likely to make greater use of complementary online services than their UK counterparts.

E-Commerce Applications

The recent shake-out in the Internet economy and the continuing lack of profitability of some of its best-known brands would suggest that the Internet, for all its many benefits, improved productivity, better service quality, superior customer relationships, new services development, and flexibility/adaptability to customer needs (Mang and Stauss, 1999), does not guarantee competitive advantage. The recent reports (January 2002) regarding Amazon.com fourth-quarter (2001) profits and Yahoo's minimal loss figures may indicate that steps to improve profitability are beginning to work for some of the dot.com companies. It may be argued, however, that businesses that fail to leverage Internet capabilities, including e-commerce applications, could be putting themselves at some disadvantage (De la Torre, 2001; Porter, 2001). This is particularly so in view of some recent evidence that real-estate products have been purchased directly online (Wilford, 2000) by certain kinds of clientele (for example, celebrities) with enough disposable income to make such high-value purchases online without going through all stages in the property purchase decision-making process (Berkowitz, 1994).

Considering that Canada and the UK have their fair share of the category of property buyers described (and given Ernst and Young's, 2000, finding that 6 per cent of the 186 EU companies surveyed had implemented e-commerce applications), it is proposed that:

P3:   Direct online purchase is likely to be a significant feature of the real estate markets in Canada and the UK.

The Internet and Relationship Management

The strategic implementation of the Internet could assist realtors to establish and maintain more effective online (and offline) relationships with both property buyers and sellers. Zineldin (2000), for example, highlighted the importance of '*techno-logicalship marketing*' (that is, marketing based on the use of technology tools such as the Internet and Extranets) in managing customer (particularly one-to-one) relationships and enabling technological partnerships and formation of alliances (Quelch and Klein, 1996; Poon and Jevons, 1997; Lettl and Schlegelmilch, 2001). Griffith (2000) has also remarked that, 'coherence in online marketing can make all the difference in the brave new world of one-to-one customer relationships'.

This is because by analysing relevant electronic database(s) on current and prospective customers' buying habits and needs (or initiating online dialogue with them), realtors could provide a better-targeted, more tailored service (for example, property lists reflecting an individual client's specific requirements on price, size of property, location and so on). This effort toward minimizing the gap between clients' expectations and actual experience (Berkowitz, 1994) could affect the overall perception of the online realtor's service – since a customer's perception of service quality is often associated with the extent to which expectations are met. The literature also suggests that clients who experience such (Internet-enabled) customized service often return to continue the already initiated online relationship (Sterne, 1996). Based on the foregoing, it should be expected that:

> **P4**: Canadian and UK property buyers who used the Internet during the property decision-making process will be more likely to have strong relationships with their real estate agents.

THE STUDY

The primary data for this study was collected in two phases. In the first phase, a number of in-depth interviews were conducted with real-estate professionals linked to the relevant industry associations in both Canada and the UK. Based on insights from these preliminary interviews, and having proper regard to the relevant best practices, for example avoiding technical Internet jargon and adjusting real-estate terms as necessary to ensure consistency of meanings between Canadian and UK responses (Easterby-Smith *et al.*, 1991), two separate questionnaires were designed and pretested among the appropriate study populations. It should be noted that in addition to providing constructive comments towards improving the quality and effectiveness of the data-collection instruments, the above-mentioned experts assisted with the distribution through their respective organizations.

The relevant study population were identified as recent property buyers, that is those who purchased property within the 12-month period, 1 July 1999 to 30 June 2000. This is because such recent buyers were considered more likely to have an accurate recall of their purchasing experience. They also had a greater likelihood of being exposed to online real-estate services, which, after all, is a relatively new phenomenon.

To obtain an adequate number of recent property buyers, the present researchers solicited the assistance of various organizations with an existing clientele database, including property agencies, house-builders and surveyors. This study's sample frame was, thus, drawn from relevant databases supplied by real-estate organizations in Toronto and Ottawa (Canada), and Glasgow and Edinburgh (Scotland). These locations were chosen as they are the largest and most urbanized centres in Canada and Scotland; it was also thought that they would offer a large sample of recent property purchasers and real-estate organizations. Furthermore, the four cities appeared to be experiencing growth at levels broadly similar to their overall national markets (Klump, 2000; Young *et al.*, 2000).

Overall, 700 recent property purchasers – 400 from the UK and 300 from Canada – were identified as comprising the sample frame for the study. The relative distribution reflects the UK's larger population and the greater flexibility of its real-estate organizations in providing property-buyer databases. The number of questionnaires returned at the final cut-off date was 135. Further screening revealed that all 135 questionnaires were suitable for inclusion in the analysis. Considering the overall trend towards lower response rates in survey research (Baldauf *et al.*, 1999; Ibeh *et al.*, 2001), the combined response rate of 19 per cent from the Canadian and UK recipients is deemed sufficient to support the simple statistical analysis intended. It should also be indicated that the response rates from all four cities are within a similar range, between 17.3 per cent and 20.5 per cent, further suggesting that the respondents' sample is broadly representative of recent property purchasers in Canada and the UK.

FINDINGS

The findings from the study were used to assess the propositions that were determined from the four conceptual factors outlined above.

The Importance and Perceived Usefulness of the Internet among Property Buyers

To generate relevant data for testing Proposition 1, respondents were asked to indicate whether they used the Internet at any point during property search or purchase. The result, presented in Table 16.1, suggests a reasonably high level of Internet usage for realty purpose among Canadian and UK respondents (64.8 and 43.2 per cent respectively). These figures suggest some support for P1; they also approximate the Internet usage rate observed in the earlier-cited NDP online real-estate survey (NDP Online Research, 1999).

Support also seems to exist for P1a that Internet sources are more likely to be adopted for realty purposes in Canada than in the UK. Apart from the markedly different Internet usage figures indicated above, it also emerged that whilst online sources (websites) ranked third among communication methods employed by Canadian property purchasers, they were placed fifth in the UK. Further analysis revealed that the percentage of Canadian respondents that considered the Internet to be useful exceeded their UK counterparts by a 2:1 ratio (that is, 50 per cent to

Table 16.1   Internet usage for realty purposes in Canada and the UK

	Canada (n = 54)	UK (n = 81)
Internet usage and perceived usefulness		
Usage of the Internet for realty purposes	64.8%	43.2%
Realty websites were useful/very useful	50%	24.6%
E-commerce opportunities and prospects		
Offered a chance to buy property online	7.4%	0%
Likely to purchase property online	7.4%	2.5%
Undecided about buying property online	22.2%	6.2%

24.6 per cent). This may be explained by a greater appreciation of the Internet by Canadians, or could suggest the need for UK websites to enhance their overall effectiveness (Ahola, 2000).

Online Services Provided by Canadian and UK Realtors

To obtain relevant insights on the issues raised by P2 and P2a, those respondents with some online realty experience were asked to indicate the services offered online by realtors in Canada and the UK. It would appear from the analysis that property listing, customized search facilities, virtual tours, mortgage and financial services, in that order, are among the most popular services provided online by Canadian and UK realtors.

Sixty and 62.5 per cent respectively of the Canadian and UK respondents (who employed the Internet in their property search) indicated using a customized search facility. In addition to reflecting the varying levels of customer needs in a rapidly evolving market (Sterne, 1996), this widespread provision of customized search facilities indicates some appreciation that customization helps create one-to-one marketing relationships and may generate greater customer value (Peck *et al.*, 1999). A substantial proportion of respondents (47.5 per cent in the UK and 27.5 per cent in Canada) also reported undertaking virtual property tours (an emerging trend in the industry with significant knowledge/value-adding and relationship-enhancing elements – see Fox, 2000), and taking benefit of the mortgage (31 per cent in the UK) and financial packages (31 per cent in the UK and 27.5 per cent in Canada) linked to the realtor's website.

The foregoing suggests some support for P2 (that is, real-estate businesses in Canada and the UK are likely to offer a wide variety of complementary online services), and reflects the trend among online businesses to offer an enlarged portfolio of services, usually through the formation of strategic alliances and reciprocal links (Dodds, 1999; Fox, 2000; Porter, 2001). Support was not found, however, for P2a, which suggests that property buyers in Canada are likely to make greater use of complementary online services than their UK counterparts. This result is somewhat surprising given that the Canadian markets are thought to approximate developments in the USA to a greater extent than UK markets.

The Potential for E-Commerce Applications

The opportunity to undertake property purchase online, that is e-commerce, appears to be minimally offered among Canadian and UK realtors. While none of the UK respondents had had the opportunity to purchase online, only four (or 7 per cent) of the Canadian respondents reported having been offered such an opportunity (see Table 16.1). This suggests a lack of support for P3, that direct online purchase is likely to be a significant feature of the real-estate markets in Canada and the UK.

What strongly emerges from the study is that the physical appreciation of property, and some face-to-face contact (Leamer and Storper, 2001), are still very important. Asked if they would undertake online purchase without prior physical view or inspection of the property, the bulk of UK and Canadian respondents indicated that they were either 'unlikely' or 'most unlikely' to do so. This reflects the increasingly accepted view that the Internet is best seen as a complement to traditional channels (Porter, 2001) rather than as a synonym for disintermediation (Turban, 2000).

Internet Usage and Perceived Strength of Buyer–Realtor Relationships

Chi-square analysis results presented in Table 16.2 suggest that Internet usage is significantly linked to having a strong relationship with real-estate represent-atives (see $\chi^2$9.84, significance 0.007 for the UK sample). (Also 37 and 29 per cent of Internet-user Canadian and UK respondents, respectively, reported having strong business relationships with their realtors, as against 23 per cent and 18 per cent of non-Internet-user respondents who indicated so).

These results support P4, and underline the importance of the online channel in strengthening marketing relationships in the real-estate sector (Dodds, 1999; Gummesson, 1999; Griffith, 2000). This is understandable given that the Internet has beneficial implications for various types of buyer–realtor relationships, including the service-encounter relationship, the knowledge relationship and the electronic relationship (Gummesson, 1999).

The strength of the online relationship may have been enhanced via effective service customization, for example online customized property searching. This, as previously mentioned, seems well-suited to the needs of the property buyer, at least in the two countries studied. What is more, it represents a successful merger of Internet and relationship marketing practices in furthering online business relationships.

Table 16.2 Internet usage and relationship strength

Use of internet	Strength of relationship		
	Strong	*Neutral*	*Weak*
Canada (n = 51)			
Yes	19 (37%)	12 (23%)	2 (4%)
No	12 (23%)	6 (12%)	0 (0%)
UK (n = 80)			
Yes	23 (29%)	11 (14%)	1 (1%)
No	14 (18%)	26 (32%)	5 (6%)

[UK: $\chi^2$9.841; significance level = 0.007   Canada: $\chi^2$1.280; significance level = 0.527]

CONCLUSIONS AND IMPLICATIONS

This chapter has reported some interesting findings on the relative level of Internet and e-commerce adoption among Canadian and UK property buyers, including the effect of Internet usage on buyers' perceptions of service quality and relationship strength. It suggests an appreciably high degree of Internet usage for realty purposes among the surveyed Canadian and UK property buyers (in Canada to a greater extent); these real-estate clients are, increasingly, exposed to a range of complementary online services, which perhaps explains the positive association observed between online realty experience and buyer–realtor relationship strength. Opportunities (or prospects) for e-commerce were, however, found to be minimal.

These findings have a number of important implications. First, given the observed widespread use of the Internet for realty purposes, realtors should invest necessary resources to orchestrate and manage strategically their online effort. A crucial step in this direction could be to draw, albeit selectively, from the growing body of literature on e-business and web-management best practices (Ahola, 2000; Morath, 2000). Among the more important headline points would be: adopting a customer-centred approach rather than a selling mentality; developing a distinctive online brand identity that delivers on its promises (Wonnacot, 2000); focusing on more specialised or even localised services (Bell, 2000); and offering access to value-adding complementary services through well-considered alliances with appropriate e-marketplaces and specialist providers (Dodds, 1999; Fox, 2000). Real-estate operations in Canada and the UK (and beyond) could benefit from benchmarking themselves against these competitive standards, given that only a half and a quarter, respectively, of the responding property buyers rated their websites as either useful or very useful.

Secondly, the findings of the present study seem to reinforce the increasingly accepted view that companies' Internet-enabled capabilities ought to be employed in ways that complement and support their existing (or traditional) channels (Leamer and Storper, 2001; Porter, 2001). For all its widespread use, the Internet ranked no higher than third and fifth among the communication methods used in obtaining initial property-related information in Canada and the UK respectively. It is therefore important that the other channels, notably 'word of mouth' (most preferred in Canada) and newspapers (highest ranked in the UK), are not neglected. Rather, realty firms should strive to integrate and deploy all the communication avenues available to them in a mutually reinforcing manner; for example, positive word of mouth communications could be furthered through online newsgroups; also the popularity of newspapers and outdoor property signs could be utilized to publicize the realtor's web address (Hamill, 1997).

The general lack of e-commerce applications and the minimal prospects for direct online purchase of property observed in this study further underline the importance of appreciating the limits of the Internet, while taking advantage of its complementary benefits. What this set of findings suggests is that the physical view of the property is still important to property buyers and that some offline contact with the real-estate company (or its representative) is necessary prior to purchase. This reflects the predominant reality for high-value, less standardized products such as real estate in the so-called 'Internet economy' (Globerman *et al.*, 2001; Leamer and Storper, 2001), and suggests that click and mortar realty operations, (rather than dot.coms and their implied disintermediation (Turban, 2000) are the sustainable way forward. Effective integration of the realtor's online and offline activities could assist the realtor in emphasizing the best of both worlds, in terms of leveraging the communication, relationship and efficiency-enhancing features of the Internet, while optimizing the higher-contact, negotiation-based approaches that have traditionally served the industry well.

Further research is needed to explore the extent to which the present study's conclusions would apply to countries at markedly different levels of economic and socio-infrastructural development, including Internet access costs/usage, government Internet policies and cultural characteristics (for example, countries such as Spain, Greece, Hungary, the Czech Republic and Poland all have less than 20 Internet hosts per 1000 inhabitants (OECD, 2001) compared to over 120 and 60 for Canada and the UK respectively; also per capita PC penetration in Eastern and Southern Europe is generally less than 10 per cent (Mikus, 2001) and 20 per cent (Bauer *et al.*). It could also be useful for future studies to employ more robust statistical techniques (for example, Logit regression) in hypotheses tests, in order to strengthen the reliability of the findings and the resulting managerial policy recommendations.

REFERENCES

Ahola, H. (2000) 'Internet Marketing – Literature Review and Research Agenda', http://www.netties.net/2000/papers/InternetMarketing_Ahola.html.

Baldauf, A., Reisinger, H. and Moucrief, W.C. (1999) 'Examining Motivations to Refuse in Industrial Mail Surveys', *Journal of the Market Research Society*, 41 (3), 345–53.

Bauer, J.M., Berne, M. and Maitland, C. (2000) 'Regulating the Internet: EU and US Perspectives', presentation at the University of Washington, Seattle 27–29 April, http://jsis.artsci.washington.edu/programs/europe/Netconference/BernePaper.htm

Bell, K. (2000) 'Teamwork: Searching for More Time and Profits, Residential Real Estate Agents are Creating Brokerages within Brokerages', *Ottawa Business Journal*, 15–18.

Berkowitz, E.N. (1994) *Marketing: The Second Edition* (Toronto: Times Mirror Professional Publishing Ltd).

BCG (Boston Consulting Group) Canada, (2000) 'Fast Forward: Accelerating Canada's Leadership in the Internet Economy', www.bcg.com

CMHC Canadian Mortgage and Housing Centre (1999) *The Future of Internet Marketing in the Housing Sector*.

De la Torre, J. and Moxon, R.W. (2001) 'E-commerce and Global Business: The Impact of the Information and Communication Technology Revolution on the Conduct of International Business', *Journal of International Business Studies*, 32 (4), 617–39.

Dodds, J. (1999) *Virtual Advisor for Young House buyers*, www.scot-homes.gov.uk

Easterby-Smith, M., Thorpe, R. and Lowe, A. (1991) *Management Research: An Introduction* (London: Sage Publications).

E-First Media Ltd, (2000) *e-commerce for Business Leaders* (Somerset: E-First Media Ltd).

Ernst & Young (2000) *E-commerce: The Land that Real Estate Forgot*, www.ey.com

Fox, S. (2000) *Virtual Tours: The Future of Real Estate* HomeGain.com. Inc

Globerman, S., Roehl, T.W. and Standifird, S. (2001) 'Globalisation and Electronic Commerce: Inferences from Retail Brokering', *Journal of International Business Studies*, 32 (4), 749–68.

Griffith, P. (2000) 'Winning in Online Marketing', *e-First: e-commerce for Business Leaders*. (Somerset: E-First Media Ltd), July, 25–27.

Gummesson, E. (1994) 'Making Relationship Marketing Operational', *International Journal of Service Industry Management*, 5 (5), 5–20.

Gummesson, E. (1999) *Total Relationship Marketing* (Oxford: Butterworth-Heinemann).

Hamill, J. (1997) 'The Internet and International Marketing', *International Marketing Review*, 14 (5), 300–23.

Ibeh, K.I.N., Brock, J. and Zhou, J. (2001) 'The Drop and Collect Survey Among Industrial Populations: Theory and Empirical Evidence', presented at the British Academy of Management Conference, Cardiff Business School, Cardiff, Wales, September 5–7.

Klump, G. (2000) *MLS® home sales start the new year on a strong note* (External Relations Department of the Canadian Real Estate Association).

Kyle, G. (2000) *The 100 Best Internet msl to Own* (New York: McGraw-Hill).

Leamer, E.E. and Storper, M. (2001) 'The Economic Geography of the Internet Age', *Journal of International Business Studies*, 32 (4), 641–65.

Lettl, C. and Schlegelmilch, B.M. (1999) 'Research on Global Marketing and Information Technology: The State-of-the-Art', in Burton, F., Yamin, M. and Bowe, M. (eds) *International Business and the Global Service Economy*, proceedings of the European International Business Academy 25th Annual Conference, Manchester.

Lyons, G.G. (1994) *Real Estate Sales Handbook*, 10th edn (Chicago: Dearborn Financial Publishing).

Lynch, P.D. and Beck, J.C. (2001) 'Profiles of Internet Buyers in 20 Countries: Evidence for Region-specific Strategies', *Journal of International Business Studies*, 32 (4), 725–48.

MacDonald, G. (2000) 'On golden pond', *The Globe & Mail*, April 1, 57–61.

Mang, P. and Stauss, B. (1999) '*Culture Shocks in Inter-cultural Service Encounters*', *Journal of Services Marketing*, 13 (4/5), 1–22.

Mikus, L. (2001) 'Internet and Business Performance', presentation at the OECD Business and Industry Policy Forum on the Internet and Business Performance, 25 September, *http://www.oecd.org/pdf/M00023000/M00023758.pdf*

Morath, P. (2000) *Success @ e-Business: Profitable Internet Business and E-commerce* (New York: McGraw-Hill).

NDP Online Research (1999) 'Property Buyers Take To The Web In Search For Homes', *www.npd.com*

OECD (2001) *OECD Science, Technology and Industry Scoreboard: Towards a Knowledge-based Economy*, (Paris: OECD), *http://www.oecd.org/pdf/M00023000/M00023758.pdf*

Oxley, J.E. and Yeung, B. (2001) 'E-commerce Readiness: Institutional Environment and International Competitiveness', *Journal of International Business Studies*, 32 (4), 705–23.

Peck, H., Payne, A., Christopher, A.M. and Clark, M. (1999) *Relationship Marketing: Strategy and Implementation* (Oxford: Butterworth-Heinemann Ltd).

Poon, S. and Jevons, C. (1997) 'Internet-enabled International Marketing: A Small Business Perspective', *Journal of Marketing Management* 13 (1–3), 29–41.

Porter, M.E. (2001) 'Strategy and the Internet', *Harvard Business Review*, 79, 63–78.

Quelch, J.A. and Klein, L.R. (1996) 'The Internet and International Marketing', *Sloan Management Review*, 37 (3), 60–75.

Segner, J. (2000) *e-Real Estate* (Indianapolis: Sams Publishing).

Sterne, J. (1996) *Customer Service on the Internet* (New York: John Wiley & Sons).

Turban, E. (2000) *Electronic Commerce: A Managerial Perspective* (New Jersey: Prentice Hall).

Ward, M. and Lee, M. (2000) 'Internet Shopping, Consumer Search and Product Branding', *Journal of Product and Brand Management*, 9 (1), 1–14.

Wilford, D. (2000) 'A Moving Story: How is the Internet Changing the UK's House-moving habits?', *e-commerce for Business Leaders* (Somerset: E-First Media Ltd), June, 6–11.

Wonnacott, L. (2000) 'Here's Why Your Brand is so Important to the Marketing Success of Your Web Site', *InfoWorld*, 21–22, 80.

Young, G., Walker, C. and Watkins, D. (2000) *Scottish Homes: Demographic Trends in Scotland*, Context Information Paper (Edinburgh: Scottish Homes).

Zineldin, M. (2000) *Beyond Relationship Marketing: Technologicalship Marketing* (MCB: University Press).

17 Political Risk and Litigation in International E-Commerce

Jedrzej George Frynas

INTRODUCTION

Is political risk of much relevance in international e-commerce? After all, political risk has traditionally been associated with foreign investment in mining or utilities. In any case, the world economy has become considerably more conducive to foreign investors than it was only 10–20 years ago. Scholars have argued that political threats to investment – especially threats of highly damaging events such as nationalization and expropriation – have markedly declined since the 1980s (Minor, 1994; Diamonte *et al.*, 1996). John Dunning (1998, p. 280) argued that the relationship between multinational corporations and host governments in developing countries has shifted from being 'predominantly adversarial and confrontational to being non-adversarial and co-operative'. With the introduction of the GATS and TRIPS agreements as part of the GATT Uruguay Round, internet firms could be expected to have little to fear from political interference. Do these developments lead to the conclusion that political risks are of little significance in international e-commerce?

Such a conclusion would be highly superficial and misleading. Political risk is still important in today's world. Major political instability in popular investment locations such as Israel or less severe but more frequent risks such as repatriation restrictions continue to present major challenges to foreign investors. Moreover, despite major advances in risk-management techniques and risk insurance, firms are frequently little protected from political risk. In a telephone survey of 122 Fortune 1000 firms by the Aon Corporation in 2001, 85 per cent of risk managers stated that their firm was well-protected from 'property, general liability and directors' and officers' risks'; yet only 21 per cent felt well-protected from political risk losses.

While Internet firms have perhaps less to fear from traditional political and legal risks such as expropriation or coup d-états, they still face other risks such as non-enforcement of intellectual property rights; uncertainty over the legal validity of electronic contracts; changes in taxation; or legal liability of Internet service providers (ISPs) for third-party content. Furthermore, as there has been increasing internationalization of e-commerce and firms increasingly derive a greater part of their income from outside the home country, internet businesses became more vulnerable to unpredictable changes in the political and legal business environments outside the home country. Meanwhile, the regulation of e-commerce has mainly developed at the national or regional level and few common global rules have been established. An Internet firm might find that the legal and political environment in foreign markets may be very different from that of the home country. Moreover, quite crucially, the confidence of online consumers depends on supportive national political-legal environments, which can ensure the integrity of e-commerce transactions (consumers need to believe that the court system can effectively deal with fraud or other illegal activities). This last point was suggested in a recent study that stated that 'the integrity of the institutional environment, particularly with respect to the "rule of law", is important for the development of e-commerce' (Oxley and Yeung, 2001, p. 706). Therefore, online firms must not ignore political and legal factors, and their cross-national differences.

Unfortunately, the rapidly expanding business and management literature on e-commerce appears to have neglected the political and legal environment. The academic writing on e-commerce in mainstream business publications concentrates on purely commercial concerns such as strategic management issues (Mellahi and Johnson, 2000; Porter, 2001), marketing issues (see Reichheld and Schefter, 2000; Rosen and Howard, 2000) or supply-chain management issues (Fraser *et al.*, 2000; Lancioni *et al.*, 2000). The legal and political environment in e-commerce has been extensively discussed in the popular media and in law journals or very narrow specialist journals on topics such as taxation. In the meantime, a small set of scholarly articles began to address the legal aspects of e-commerce in mainstream academic journals in business and management (Caudill and Murphy, 2000; Zugelder *et al.*, 2000; Kobrin, 2001; Oxley and Yeung, 2001). However, these studies are relatively small in number and, much more importantly, there is still a dearth of studies on the practical legal and political problems of international e-commerce in the mainstream business literature.

This chapter analyses several important political and legal challenges faced by internationally operating Internet firms. In order to conduct this analysis, we use a novel socio-legal approach and the chapter provides a fresh perspective on this topic by utilizing the concept of political risk. After outlining a conceptual framework and methodology the main body of the chapter consists of a discussion of three aspects of non-commercial risk in e-commerce – ISP liability for third-party content, consumption tax and intellectual property rights. These are used as exemplars of the difficulties faced by Internet firms in the international arena. Finally, some conclusions and practical recommendations are made.

THE CONCEPTUAL FRAMEWORK

Political risk denotes a bundle of expectations concerning potential future political events that have a market value and influence future earnings. This is in contrast to actual political events that are observable in the real world. In other words, political risk is a subjective perception of how events may affect the firm and it is assessed in order to predict the likelihood of different types of events (Frynas, 1998; Frynas and Mellahi, 2003).

As a consequence of the subjectivity of risk assessment, any estimate of risk depends on the standpoint of the affected individual or group. Indeed, as Shubik (1983, p. 134) argued:

> Risk is only defined in the context of a specific goal structure. It cannot be assessed independently from purpose. Probabilities or the possibility of the occurrence of an event exist independent of purpose. The risk to an individual given that something occurs depends upon that individual's goals and resources.

Following this logic and drawing on writings of other scholars (Robock, 1971; Kobrin, 1980, 1982), this chapter considers any risk to be firm-specific. Thus, potential non-recognition of electronic signatures may be a serious risk for an internet firm which relies on information exchanges involving electronic signatures, but may present no risk for a firm that does not rely on electronic signatures at all.

One of the chief conceptual difficulties is that scholars have diverse views on what precisely constitutes political risk or the sources of political risk. The utilization of the term can be so confusing and narrow that Kobrin (1979) even suggested that it might well be dropped from usage. Conventional definitions of political risk either incorporate risk related to government policy (for example Weston and Sorge, 1972, p. 60; Dunn, 1983) or a combination of government policy risk and other political risks such as war or change in government (see Shubik, 1983; Robock and Simmonds, 1989, p. 378). Unfortunately, such definitions tend to be narrow and fail to capture some of the phenomena described by the same authors. For instance, kidnapping or labour unrest have occasionally been referred to by writers on political risk even though these events failed to fit into their definition of political risk.

Building upon Miller's (1992) framework for risk management, socio-political risk is defined in the most expansive sense as 'any risk arising from national as well as international changes in the business environment encompassing political risk, government policy risk and social risk' (as defined by Miller) (Frynas and Mellahi, 2003). Following Miller's categorization, the first component of this definition is political risk, which reflects the threats and opportunities resulting from 'potential or actual changes in the political system' (Miller, 1992) including war, revolution, coup d'état, change of government or other political upheaval. The second component is policy risk, which refers to the instability in government policies that impact on the business community, including fiscal and monetary reforms, price controls, expropriation or barriers to earnings repatriation. The third component is social risk, which follows from 'the beliefs, values and attitudes of the population that are not reflected in current government policy or business practice' (Miller, 1992); these can involve changing social concerns, social unrest, demonstrations, riots or small-scale terrorist movements, which can in turn be a precursor to political or government policy uncertainty (Miller, 1992, pp. 313–15).

Dealing with the sources of all these risks would be too broad for the purpose of this chapter, so it does not deal with social risks (for example pressures by environmental or other pressure groups on website owners) or political risks (such as the potential effects of a change in government). Instead, this chapter focuses solely on policy risk (for example change in policy on intellectual property rights).

METHOD

Subjective risk perceptions are difficult to evaluate unless studied in the context of systematic questionnaire surveys of managers. However, this chapter is not aimed at analysing managerial perceptions but rather at determining the actual sources of risk in the real world. In other words, it is focused on possible events which may constitute risk for specific firms.

In order to study real situations, a socio-legal approach was used. This relies on evidence provided by litigation filed by or against internet firms on topics such as intellectual property rights and liability for website content. Rather than using court cases solely as legal material, they are also used as factual evidence of the impact of the political and legal environment on Internet firms. Since there were many lawsuits against Internet firms, court cases provide a significant number of references to particular events and disputes. Court cases were collected from publicly available legal sources in the UK and the United States (including printed law reports and court transcripts available either in print or online). Court cases were selected based on (1) their significance as legal precedents as evidenced in their discussion by legal scholars, and (2) actual availability of primary material (that is, the original court judgment and/or other court transcripts). (See the Appendix for a list of court cases cited.) These selection criteria were designed to ensure both the relevance of the reported cases and the accuracy of sources. To verify the findings of the cases use was made of information from a multitude of other sources including articles in specialised periodicals and Internet publications; this provided corroborative data from interviews and other sources. In order to increase the reliability of findings, any secondary sources were checked against a number of criteria, above all whether the source had a vested interest in a particular opinion. Thus, secondary information used in this chapter was corroborated with information from other trusted sources.

SOURCES OF POLICY RISK IN INTERNATIONAL E-COMMERCE

The three aspects of policy risk in e-commerce discussed in this chapter – ISP liability for third-party content, consumption tax and intellectual property rights – were selected because a considerable body of case law has developed in those three areas. They were not selected because of their importance to a specific type of Internet firm and it should be remembered that they affect different types of internet businesses to different degrees.

Liability for Third-Party Actions

Liability for third-party actions, which were neither authorized nor condoned by the Internet firm, is a major problem for firms using the Internet. The use of third-party content remains an important issue for different types of Internet businesses. For instance, Amazon.com offers a forum for book reviews written by members of the public; in the case *Schneider* v. *Amazon.com*, the internet bookseller faced (and won) a lawsuit in the USA arising from book reviews which defamed the author Jerome Schneider. However, ISPs face the greatest risk as they allow third parties to post material freely on their websites, chatrooms and so on. Most famously, the 1999 English case of *Godfrey* v. *Demon Internet* exemplifies the potential liability of ISPs. In that case, a university lecturer Dr Laurence Godfrey sued Demon Internet, a British ISP, for defamation. A posting to an internet newsgroup carried (in the words of the judge) 'squalid, obscene and defamatory' material about Godfrey. Godfrey contacted Demon Internet asking them to remove the posting but the firm refused. The posting remained on the server until it was automatically removed two weeks after being sent to the newsgroup. In a pretrial court ruling, the judge found that Demon Internet was liable for the defamatory content of the posting. He said that whenever ISPs transmit a posting, they 'publish' it to any customer who accesses the newsgroup. Furthermore, since the ISP was made aware of the defamatory content of the posting but chose not to remove it, the firm could not claim 'innocent dissemination'. This was despite the fact that Godfrey was not without blame as his own postings were described by the judge as 'provocative' and were 'designed to tempt people to overstep the mark and defame the plaintiff [Godfrey] so that he can sue'.

In contrast to the English case, similar cases adjudicated in the United States have not led to the prosecution of the ISP. In the case of *Cubby* v. *CompuServe*, CompuServe as a distributor was granted the protection of the First Amendment which guarantees the right to free expression. This was followed by other defamation cases in US courts which were won by the ISP. Therefore, an ISP in the UK faced considerably greater risk of liability for third-party actions than an ISP in the USA.

This discrepancy could be directly attributed to government action. In 1996, the US legislature made a conscious policy decision not to impose liability on ISPs that carry other third parties' potentially defamatory content through their servers (Akdeniz, 1999). As a consequence, in the 1997 US case *Zeran* v. *America Online*, the court stated that 'section 230 [of the Communications Decency Act (CDA) 1996] creates a federal immunity to any cause of action that would make service providers liable for information originating with a third-party user of the service'. This line of reasoning was followed in more recent US court cases including *Blumenthal* v. *Drudge*, in which AOL was sued for defamation. The case related to a gossip column providing gossip from Hollywood and Washington DC, which claimed that a confidant of President Clinton – Sidney Blumenthal – had a 'spousal abuse past'. However, AOL, which was a co-defendant in the suit, was able to claim immunity from prosecution. In some respects, the court judgment was even more unequivocal than that in *Zeran* v. *America Online*. The 'Drudge Report' was not simply an anonymous individual who posted an Internet message using AOL services, but in fact it had a written licence agreement with AOL to make the column available to AOL users in exchange for a monthly payment of US$3000, and AOL had actively promoted the Report. But, while AOL exercised the right to some editorial control over Drudge's gossip column, the court stated that ISPs had immunity from defamation claims 'even where the interactive service provider has an active, even aggressive role in making available content prepared by others'. The court added that the US Congress 'has conferred immunity from tort liability as an incentive to Internet service providers to self-police the Internet for obscenity and other offensive material, even where the self-policing is unsuccessful or not even attempted'. A US-based ISP expanding overseas would thus face greater government policy risks, as Yahoo! experienced when it was sued for hosting auctions of Nazi objects in France in line with a French law prohibiting the sale of goods which encourage racism (Kobrin, 2001).

The above cases demonstrate that ISPs are faced with different degrees of risk in different countries. The UK remains a more hostile location for network development than some other countries because of the failure of the government to protect ISPs from defamation suits. In the UK, two ISP trade associations have reportedly lobbied the UK government to change the law following the Godfrey case (Akdeniz, 1999). The uncertainty surrounding the UK government position on the issue is a major source of government policy risk for ISPs operating in the UK.

In May 2000, the policy risk for ISPs operating in the UK decreased as a result of the European Union (EU) Electronic Commerce Directive which reduced the liability of ISPs for content provided by third parties. All EU member states were required to implement the Directive's provisions by January 2002, though implementation was delayed in the UK, amongst other EU states. By the time that the e-commerce directive was due to be implemented on 17 January 2002, the directive was only adopted by three out of 15 EU states. There were also delays in implementing other directives such as the one on electronic signatures (Crossick 2002). This highlighted the EU's complex and extremely lengthy decision-making processes which proved unable to keep pace with developments in cyberspace. However, the Directive is more restrictive than the US CDA, which provides blanket immunity to US ISPs in all circumstances where third parties provide content on websites or chatrooms. In particular, under the Directive, ISPs in the EU are still liable if they have 'actual knowledge of illegal activity or information'. Following this logic, under the Directive, Godfrey would probably still have won the court case against Demon Internet because the ISP was made aware of the defamatory content and did not act to remove it. Furthermore, the European Directive does not deal with all related matters such as liability for hyper-links (Edwards, 2000, pp. 268–70). Therefore, while legislative provisions have reduced policy risk for ISPs in the EU, investment in European-based ISPs may continue to cause problems.

As mentioned at the beginning of this section, other types of businesses may also be affected by the issue of third-party content. For instance, recent UK case law suggests that information posted on the Internet by news services may be less protected from defamation charges than the print media, which again contrasts with the US position where internet-based media are not disadvantaged. In a recent case *Loutchansky* v. *The Times Newspapers*, one of Britain's leading newspapers was sued over publishing articles in which a Russian businessman was implicated, amongst others, in the smuggling of nuclear weapons. A key issue of the trial concerned the storing of articles on the newspaper's online archive. According to UK law, if a newspaper publishes an article with defamatory content, a lawsuit must be started within one year of the original publication; no libel action can start after that period. However, the court pronounced that an online article would be considered to be republished whenever it is accessed by Internet users, which contrasts with the one-year limitation period for libel enjoyed by a solely-printed newspaper. Furthermore, the court stated that a newspaper's online archive does not enjoy the so-called qualified privilege with regards to defamatory material which grants immunity from compensation for libel; this permits journalists to publish information which may be of public interest but which they may not necessarily be able to prove in court. The court suggested that *The Times* could have protected itself by attaching 'an appropriate notice [with the online version of the article] warning against treating it as the truth', which 'will normally remove any sting from the material'. However, the point here is that printed articles still enjoy protection from the qualified privilege rule and from the one-year limitation period, which puts news services with online content at a legal disadvantage.

The situation in the USA is very different where courts have extended the so-called 'single publication rule' to the internet, whereby the limitation period runs from the first publication of defamatory material in any form and it does not start again when the material is distributed in a different form such as an online version. Furthermore, unlike in the UK, online publishers enjoy the same rights to the protection of the freedom of speech as the print media. Indeed, in the case *Blumenthal* v. *Drudge* mentioned earlier, the plaintiff suggested that US online media are better protected than the print media. The plaintiff stated that the *Washington Post* (or, by implication any other print media) would have been liable to defamation charges if it had done what AOL did. There is some merit to that interpretation, which again underlines the privileged position of US Internet firms vis-à-vis their European counterparts.

If Amazon.com had been taken to court by Schneider in the UK rather than in the USA, it would probably have lost the case like Demon Internet, as it was notified of defamatory comments by the third party and failed to remove them.

Consumption Tax

Changes in future taxation of e-commerce are amongst the key policy risks facing internet firms. A KPMG survey of CFOs and tax directors of Fortune 2000 corporations found that 66 per cent of respondents would find it difficult to administer taxes properly on Internet sales. Indeed, when asked about the greatest challenges faced when entering into global e-commerce, roughly one-third of respondents felt tax and tax-related issues were a greater obstacle than cultural differences (33 per cent compared with 19 per cent). As many as 57 per cent of tax directors stated that decisions on where to locate e-business operations were affected by the jurisdiction's tax incentives (PR Newswire, 2000).

Perhaps the most contentious tax-related issue is that of consumption tax, as internet transactions differ from conventional sales. As the consumers may come from many different jurisdictions with different consumption tax regimes, the administration of tax is particularly complex in e-commerce. It is also more difficult to locate the place of consumption and the place of origin of the delivered good/service for tax purposes, particularly with regards to 'all-digital' transactions such as purchase of music files on the Internet using electronic cash (Cobb *et al.*, 2000).

Consumption tax poses significant difficulties in international e-commerce as there are major tax-related differences between the USA and other developed countries. Unlike all the other major developed countries, the United States does not have a value-added tax (VAT), though it does have retail sales taxes. However, US sales taxes are not applicable to business-to-business (B2B) transactions and the tax rates are generally much lower than, for instance, VAT rates in the EU (Cobb *et al.*, 2000). Even these relatively low rates frequently remain unpaid by US Internet buyers. In the US Supreme Court ruling *Quill Corp. v. North Dakota*, the court stated that no use tax could be imposed on out-of-state mail order or telephone sellers as long as the sellers have no physical presence in that federal state, which also applies to Internet firms as these often have no physical presence in the jurisdiction of the buyer. US consumers are obliged to self-report and remit use taxes when the seller has not charged them, but in practice they usually do not pay sales tax for Internet purchases from firms based outside their federal state. In effect, US Internet firms, therefore, have an advantage compared to brick-and-mortar businesses, as their retail prices do not include sales tax. Furthermore, the US imposed a three-year moratorium on the imposition of state and local taxes on the Internet in 1998 (Bick, 2000), which was later extended by the Bush administration for another two years, whereas other jurisdictions such as the EU strongly resisted the idea of any (even temporary) suspension of consumption taxes on Internet transactions (Loten, 2001).

Internet firms in the USA nonetheless face government policy risk with respect to future tax changes as US states (which rely heavily on revenue from sales taxes) and mainstream brick-and-mortar businesses (which fear internet competitors) continue to press the federal government to tax Internet firms. As the moratorium on Internet taxes is due to expire by 1 November 2003, Internet sellers in the USA face the policy risk of a possible higher tax burden in the future. In the meantime, there have been many court cases as a result of US states trying to extract sales taxes from Internet firms based outside its state boundaries. In a recent 2001 US case *America Online Inc.* v. *Johnson*, the controversy was whether the Tennessee state tax authorities should collect sales tax from America Online. The Tennessee court had to establish whether America Online had enough presence in the state to justify payment of sales tax. Indeed, the firm had contracts with Tennessee residents, bills were sent to Tennessee customers, America Online had a business relationship with local firms to provide access to its service for local subscribers, software was sent to thousands of Tennessee residents and the firm leased telecommunications equipment to firms in Tennessee. Nonetheless, by broadening the previous pronouncement of the Quill case, the court ruled that all these contacts did not constitute sufficient nexus to allow the state to raise sales tax from the firm, as long as the firm did not have staff, agents or premises in the state. If judged by this case, US Internet firms enjoy considerable protection from sales tax payments.

In contrast to the USA, the authorities in European countries have shown much greater willingness to tax Internet transactions. This contrast has been reflected in litigation, as exemplified by the English tribunal case *Forexia (UK) Ltd* v. *The Commissioners of Customs and Excise*. In that case, it was contested whether Forexia (UK) Ltd should pay VAT on the publication and distribution of a regular news digest related to foreign exchange and movements of currencies, which was distributed to most clients via fax, website and e-mail. Under current English law, there is no VAT payable on goods such as books, newspapers and periodicals, which would perhaps imply the principle that VAT should not be levied on the supply of information and knowledge in general. However, the tribunal ruled that the Forexia news digest constituted a 'service' rather than a 'good', so it could not benefit from the zero rate of VAT. In other words, if information were distributed by letter post, courier or by hand, it would be exempt from VAT, but electronic distribution is subject to VAT. Even though the tribunal recognized that the judgment ultimately amounted to 'distortion of competition', it was bound by the strict current legislative provisions on VAT. Therefore, it appears that UK internet firms can be disadvantaged *vis-à-vis* brick-and-mortar businesses under certain circumstances as far as consumption tax is concerned, which contrasts with the advantages of US internet firms towards brick-and-mortar businesses operating within the USA discussed earlier. Indeed, as pointed out elsewhere (Loten, 2001), online gambling in the UK has already become dominated by offshore internet firms, and other sectors may follow this trend due to the current tax disadvantages and the uncertainties related to future tax changes.

While the Forexia case only deals with one narrow specific tax issue, it illustrates the attempt by European countries to extend conventional VAT to Internet transactions. Indeed, the recent changes to indirect taxation within the EU make clear that, while the tax position of EU-based internet firms will improve vis-à-vis non-EU firms (see below), existing VAT principles are to be extended to Internet transactions (European Commission, 2002). However, policy risk arises as the detailed regulations may or may not disadvantage different types of businesses. This risk is exemplified by differences between EU and non-EU Internet firms. As it currently stands, suppliers of electronic services based in the USA do not pay VAT on services supplied to customers (B2C) within the EU. At the same time, a EU-based Internet supplier of, for instance, downloadable videos to a US consumer must charge VAT. Thus, European-domiciled Internet firms have a disadvantage compared non-EU firms.

The competitive disadvantage of EU firms will be largely eradicated as a result of the most recent EU legislative provisions. In May 2002, the European Commission (2002) officially adopted a new Directive which removes the obligation on EU suppliers to levy VAT on electronic services supplied outside the EU. At the same time, the Directive requires suppliers of digital products from outside the EU to charge VAT on sales of electronically supplied services to private consumers inside the EU. Non-EU suppliers will need to register with a VAT authority in a EU country of their choice, but to levy VAT at the rate applicable in the country where each customer is resident. Effectively, the VAT rate applicable to non-EU suppliers' B2C sales in the EU will be the same as the rate charged by local suppliers.

The Directive only applies to electronically supplied services to end-consumers including the supply of software, the supply of music, films and games, and the supply of distance teaching. As Edgar (2002) pointed out, it does not apply to the sale of goods which is relatively uncontroversial as physical goods bought over the Internet can be taxed by the customs and excise authorities when they arrive in the country of the consumer. Until the Directive is implemented in July 2003, the market distortions created by previous EU VAT provisions remain. However, while the policy risk for EU Internet firms decreased, the risk for non-EU firms increased. Previously, it was suggested that as a result of disadvantageous EU legislation Internet firms domiciled in the EU could be forced to relocate outside the EU in order to gain a level playing field vis-à-vis their competitors (Ball, 2001). Now it seems that EU firms will gain a more level playing field, while non-EU firms will face uncertainty both over the implementation of the current Directive and over the future changes to EU legislation. The Council of Finance Ministers of the EU agreed in December 2001 that the new system on VAT payments by non-EU suppliers should be initially applied for three years following implementation of the proposal and could then be extended or revised, so further policy risk for non-EU firms is already inbuilt into the proposals. This highlights the vulnerability of Internet businesses to changes in national taxation.

Intellectual Property Rights

In many instances, the application of intellectual property rights (IPR) to the Internet is not markedly different from any other area of business. When the music industry sued the music-sharing service Napster, conventional legal provisions could be applied to prosecute IPR infringements. As with any other type of business, Internet firms with a heavy reliance on protected patents or brand names face policy risks when investing abroad. For instance, Internet firms may face the same problems faced by the music industry in China due to non-enforcement of IPR. In one landmark event, members of the International Federation of the Phonographic Industry (IFPI) filed lawsuits in Chinese courts in 1999 against two Internet firms – My Webb and Tekson – that the IFPI claimed were illegally selling music files. These were the first lawsuits of that type to be brought in China (Fridman, 1999) and other Chinese cases involving Internet firms and IPR infringement have since been filed. However, the remaining uncertainty over China's policy on IPR presents a policy risk for Internet firms who might want to consider expanding in China.

Beyond these conventional problems with IPR, e-commerce may present very distinctive challenges to business. One major issue is to what extent novel business practices in e-commerce can be patented. In the highly publicized US case *Amazon.com* v. *BarnesandNoble.com*, Amazon brought a patent infringement suit against its chief rival. Amazon alleged that Barnes and Noble's 'Express Lane' feature infringed Amazon's patented '1-Click®' shopping. Both purchasing systems allow repeat customers to make a purchase of an item with a single mouse click by relying on previously entered billing and shipping information. Amazon claims that its patented purchasing system is markedly different from the previous multistep 'shopping cart' purchase system, whereby the customer would typically add items to a 'shopping cart' by clicking on each item, and would then 'check out' to complete the purchase at the end.

The Amazon case is far from being an isolated example. In another recent US case *Winston and Katz* v. *Ask Jeeves, Inc.*, two US scientists filed a patent infringement suit against the Ask Jeeves search-engine service, alleging infringement of two patents associated with methods for facilitating retrieval of computer text and database material. Other well-known firms such as Yahoo! and the Microsoft Expedia travel service have become involved in similar suits alleging infringement of a business practice patent. This recent flood of litigation was caused by a ruling in *State Street Bank & Trust Co.* v. *Signature Financial Group, Inc.* in 1998, which changed US patent law by allowing 'business methods' to be patented. While the US Patent and Trademark Office (PTO) continued issuing patents on business methods, the US Congress introduced a bill to limit the number of patents issued relating to business methods that generated government policy risk (Carlson, 2000).

In contrast to the USA, government policy risk for potential business-method patent holders has been considerably greater in other countries with a much more restrictive policy on business-method patents. In the UK, for example, the Patent Act 1977 provided for an exclusion of business-method patents (Newton, 2000). More recently, in the case of Merrill Lynch Inc's application, an English court refused to grant a patent for a trading system on the grounds that it was merely a means of performing a business method. As of March 2001, the British government categorically stated that business methods 'should remain unpatentable' (UK Patent Office, 2001). Thus, Internet firms with business method patents such as Amazon face considerable risks in the UK.

In addition to this government policy risk, the question remains which business practices in e-commerce are worthy of patent protection in the USA or elsewhere. In the lawsuit brought by Amazon, for instance, Barnes and Noble averred that CompuServe had previously offered a service called 'Trend' whereby CompuServe subscribers could obtain stock charts for a surcharge of 50 cents per chart with a single mouse click, which anticipated Amazon's 'single-action ordering technology'. Indeed, Amazon have themselves been accused of IPR infringement. Amongst others, they have been accused of devising a front page for their online toy retailing venture which was said to bear a striking similarity to the website of eToy.com (Mellahi and Johnson, 2000). Therefore, questions arise as to which e-commerce innovations are genuine and to what extent IPR in e-commerce will be interpreted and enforced differently in countries outside the United States. Such uncertainties over the future present an important source of investment risk for Internet firms, both for non-US firms and US firms expanding overseas.

Using the conceptualization of risk being firm-specific, the above cases illustrate that even if public initiatives reduce risk for some internet firms, they may increase the risk for other firms. On the one hand, legal and political change in favour of patent owners would decrease the risk for firms such as Amazon as it would deter imitation of firm resources by competitors. On the other hand, it would increase the risk for a firm which independently develops a new product and service similar to that of a competitor. In addition, if governments make patents on business practices such as '1-Click®' shopping or hyperlinks to other websites broadly enforceable internationally, internet firms will need to pay royalties to different patent owners for different purposes, which will in turn raise operational costs in e-commerce. Therefore, risk-minimizing measures by governments may not always be a win–win situation for all Internet firms. In the meantime, uncertainty over future IPR regulation remains an important policy risk in international e-commerce.

CONCLUSION

This chapter has demonstrated that Internet firms face serious political and legal uncertainties which differ considerably between different markets. The Internet is regulated very differently even in markets with similar legal systems and similar cultures such as the USA and the UK. In the age of globalization, national boundaries still matter a great deal. Indeed, e-commerce becomes more and more regulated at the national and regional-bloc level. While Internet firms face various other threats to their existence – first-mover disadvantages or high speed of innovation, regulatory differences between countries add to the purely commercial risks faced by e-businesses.

Why have Internet firms paid relatively little attention to political and legal issues so far? One reason is that, despite creating a virtual reality, managers of Internet firms live in a physical world, where they choose to establish firms in their home country/region irrespective of specific political, legal or economic risks in that location. Another reason is that, in a race to establish first-mover advantages, Internet firms may have taken risks which traditional firms would be unlikely to take. Finally, there was a lack of predictability of legal interpretations of existing regulations. When Yahoo! and Demon Internet started their businesses, it was not clear that courts would make an ISP liable for the content of individual websites designed and operated by its users. This sort of uncertainty remains in some issue-areas of e-commerce today.

Nonetheless, policy risk and its cross-country variations may have played a greater role in the expansion of e-commerce than perhaps publicly acknowledged. As Edwards (2000, p. 264) argued, one of the key reasons why the European e-commerce market developed more slowly than the US market was the 'lack of public confidence that the Internet is a safe, secure and respectable medium for commercial transactions'. This was, in turn, caused to a large extent by a less predictable regulatory framework for e-commerce provided by European countries. This would seem to be supported by a recent quantitative study that found that 'cross-country variation in e-commerce activity can in part be explained by the capacity of the institutional environment to enhance transactional integrity in online markets' (Oxley and Yeung, 2001, p. 719). With respect to risk management, the continuing differences in regulatory approaches between countries and the uncertainty over the future of regulation constitute an important source of policy risk for Internet firms.

While faced with such uncertainties, there are a number of things that Internet firms can do to minimize risk in the international political and legal environment. Managers should:

- thoroughly research and continuously monitor the legal and political developments in target markets;
- thoroughly research trademarks and patents before embracing a trademark, registering a domain name, patenting a business practice or designing a website, and continuously monitor the internet to protect the firm's intellectual property;
- design the firm's website carefully to ensure strict compliance with the law; for instance, managers should make sure that any online customer views all contract terms before submitting an order and then clicks on a button to show acceptance of the terms;

- carefully choose the jurisdiction when deciding on the home base for the internet firm, for instance a gambling website in the USA could choose a federal state with a more lenient policy on gambling;
- hire a law firm to conduct a legal audit to check if your website complies with relevant legal provisions, for example on data protection or libel;
- take out an insurance, for instance a liability insurance or an insurance covering advertising risks;
- act fast if the firm is notified of a patent-infringement, defamation charge or any other potential breach of the law;
- use legal and political weapons to fight competitors, for instance by patenting the business method in the USA and preventing competitors from using it.

In the most extreme cases, an Internet firm may be advised to refrain from establishing a physical presence in a market with high political and legal risk. For instance, some ISPs may want to avoid being based in the UK where defamation laws are particularly harsh, even compared with various other EU countries.

Nonetheless, from the perspective of society as a whole, the use of any of these risk-minimizing measures by Internet firms may in itself introduce distortions in the market. For instance, large firms may be able to afford any of these protections better than small firms; a large European-based ISP may be better equipped to install filtering methods for scanning third-party content than a smaller ISP. By implication, some smaller firms may be forced out of the market. Therefore, some types of firms may be more disadvantaged than others as a result of uncertainties in the political business environment. Some firms may even benefit from uncertainty by keeping out potential competitors, which goes back to our conceptualization of risk as being essentially firm-specific. Indeed, what constitutes a risk for one firm may be an opportunity for another firm. For instance, weak protection of ISPs may present major difficulties for some firms, but it may allow certain firms to thrive (for example peer-to-peer internet services such as Napster).

It is easy to forget that the Internet, albeit global in nature, is subject to national regulations which may vary considerably between countries. Efforts to provide a more uniform regulatory framework in international e-commerce – for example the OECD Taxation Framework Conditions agreed in Ottawa in 1998 (OECD, 2002) or the UNCITRAL Model Law on Electronic Commerce (UNCITRAL, 2002) – have had only limited success so far and lack teeth. However, there is some hope for the spread of uniform regulatory frameworks in future. Indeed, with the adoption of the new EU Directive on VAT in May 2002 mentioned earlier, the website of the European Commission (2002) prides itself that the 'EU became the first significant tax jurisdiction in the world to develop and implement a simplified framework for consumption taxes on e-commerce in accordance with the principles agreed within the framework of the OECD'. Until uniform regulatory changes are instituted on a global scale, Internet firms will face considerable policy risks in different jurisdictions. Ignoring those risks could be costly for Internet businesses.

In terms of methodology, we have portrayed how legal materials can be used to understand the impact of legal and political processes on international firms. Indeed, we suggest that future business research could make greater use of factual evidence from litigation as an alternative methodology in the study of the business environment.

Appendix: Court Cases Cited

Amazon.com v. *BarnesandNoble.com*, Case No. 00–1109, in the United States Court of Appeals for the Federal Circuit, judgment of 14 February 2001.

America Online Inc. v. *Johnson*, Docket No. 97–3786-III, Tenn. Chancery Ct., judgment of 13 March 2001.

Blumenthal v. *Drudge*, 992 F. Supp. 44 (DDC 1998).

Cubby v. *CompuServe*, 776 F. Supp. 135 (SDNY 1991).

Forexia (UK) Ltd v. *The Commissioners of Customs and Excise*, Case No. 16041, in the VAT and Duties Tribunal, London Tribunal Centre, judgment of 8 April 1999.

Godfrey v. *Demon Internet*, Case No. 1998-G-No 30, in the High Court of Justice, Queen's Bench Division, judgments of 26 March 1999 and 23 April 1999.

Loutchansky v. *The Times Newspapers* [2001] EWCA Civ 1805.

Merrill Lynch Inc's Application [1989] RPC 561.

Quill Corp. v. *North Dakota*, 504 U.S. 298 (1992).

Schneider v. *Amazon.com*, Case No. 46791–3–I, in the Washington Court of Appeals, judgment of 17 September 2001.

State Street Bank & Trust Co. v. *Signature Financial Group, Inc.*, Case No. 96–1327, in the United States Court of Appeals for the Federal Circuit, judgment of 23 July 1998.

Winston and Katz v. *Ask Jeeves, Inc.*, Case No. 99GV12584 MLW, pending in the United States District Court for the District of Massachusetts.

Zeran v. *America Online* [1997] 129 F3d 327.

REFERENCES

Akdeniz, Y. (1999) 'Case Analysis: Laurence Godfrey v. Demon Internet Limited', *Journal of Civil Liberties*, 4 (2), 260–7.

Ball, A. (2001) 'UK Vetoes EU Move to Tax E-Commerce', *The Tax Journal*, 4 June, 5–7.

Bick, J. (2000) 'The Tax Man in Cyberspace', *New Jersey Law Journal*, 161, 8.

Carlson, N.F. (2000) 'Developing Business Process Patents and Intellectual Property', *Strategic Finance*, 82 (5), 65–8.

Caudill, E.M. and Murphy, P.E. (2000) 'Consumer Online Privacy: Legal and Ethical Issues', *Journal of Public Policy & Marketing*, 19 (1), 7–19.

Cobb, P., Kobrin, S. and Wagner, E., (2000) 'Taxing E-Commerce: The Landscape of Internet Taxation', *University of Pennsylvania Journal of International Economic Law*, 21 (3), 659–78.

Crossick, E. (2002) 'EU Decision-Making and E-commerce: Time For a Change?', *E-commerce Law and Policy*, February, 4–5.

Diamonte, R.L., Liew, J.M. and Stevens, R.L. (1996) 'Political Risk in Emerging and Developed Markets', *Financial Analysts Journal*, 52 (3), 71–6.

Dunn, J. (1983) 'Country Risk: Social and Cultural Aspects', in Herring, R. (ed.) *Managing International Risk*, (Cambridge: Cambridge University Press).

Dunning, J. (1998) 'An Overview of Relations with National Governments', *New Political Economy*, 3 (2), 280–84.

Edgar, L. (2002) 'Taxing E-commerce – How Feasible are Europe's Plans', *Electronic Business Law*, 4 (2), 10–12.

Edwards, L. (2000) 'Defamation and the Internet', in Edwards, L. and Waelde, C. (eds) *Law and the Internet*, 2nd edn (Oxford: Hart).

European Commission, (2002): *http://europa.eu.int/comm/taxation_customs/taxation/ecommerce/vat_en.htm*, accessed 7 June.

Fraser, J., Fraser, N. and McDonald, F. (2000) 'The Strategic Challenge of Electronic Commerce', *Supply Chain Management*, 5 (1), 7–14.

Fridman, S. (1999) 'US Record Companies Sue Chinese Music Pirates', News Bytes News Network at *http://www.newsbytes.com*, 17 December.

Frynas, J.G. (1998) 'Political Instability and Business: Focus on Shell in Nigeria', *Third World Quarterly*, 19 (3), 457–78.

Frynas, J.G. and Mellahi, K. (2003) 'Political Risks as Firm-Specific (Dis)Advantages: Evidence on Transnational Oil Firms in Nigeria', *Thunderbird International Business Review*.

Kobrin, S. (1979) 'Political Risk: A Review and Reconsideration', *Journal of International Business Studies*, Spring/Summer, 67–80.

Kobrin, S. (1980) 'Foreign Enterprise and Forced Divestment in LDCs', *International Organization*, 34, 65–88.

Kobrin, S. (1982) *Managing Political Risk Assessment* (Berkeley: University of California Press).

Kobrin, S. (2001) 'Territoriality and the Governance of Cyberspace', *Journal of International Business Studies*, 32 (4), 687–704.

Lancioni, R.A., Smith, M.F. and Oliva, T.A., (2000) 'The Role of the Internet in Supply Chain Management', *Industrial Marketing Management*, 29, 45–56.

Loten, M. (2001) 'VAT and E-Commerce–An Opportunity Missed', *The Tax Journal*, 18 June, 5–7.

Mellahi, K. and Johnson, M. (2000) 'Does it Pay to be a First Mover in e.commerce? The Case of Amazon.com', *Management Decision*, 38 (7), 445–52.

Miller, K.D. (1992) 'A Framework for Integrated Risk Management in International Business', *Journal of International Business Studies*, 23 (2), 311–31.

Minor, M.S. (1994) 'The Demise of Expropriation as an Instrument of LDC Policy, 1980–1992', *Journal of International Business Studies*, 25 (1), 177–88.

Newton, J. (2000) 'Internet Patents: US Developments and Their Implications for Electronic Business in the UK', *Electronic Business Law*, 2 (4), 8–9.

OECD (2002): *http://www.oecd.org/*, accessed 18 June.

Oxley, J.E. and Yeung, B. (2001) 'E-commerce Readiness: Institutional Environment and International Competitiveness', *Journal of International Business Studies*, 32 (4), 705–23.

Porter, M. (2001) 'Strategy and the Internet', *Harvard Business Review*, March, 63–78.

PR Newswire (2000) 'KPMG Survey: As Global E-Commerce Expansion Continues…', 12 June.

Reichheld, F.F. and Schefter, P. (2000) 'E-Loyalty – Your Secret Weapon on the Web', *Harvard Business Review*, July–August, 105–13.

Robock, S.H. (1971) 'Political Risk: Identification and Assessment', *Columbia Journal of World Business*, July/August, 6–20.

Robock, S.H. and Simmonds, K. (1989) *International Business and Multinational Enterprises*, 4th edn, (Homewood, IL: Irwin).

Rosen, K.T. and Howard, A.L. (2000) 'E-Retail: Gold Rush or Fool's Gold?', *California Management Review*, 42 (3), 72–100.

Shubik, M. (1983) 'Political Risk: Analysis, Process, and Purpose', in Herring, R. (ed.) *Managing International Risk* (Cambridge: Cambridge University Press).

UK Patent Office, (2001): *http://www.patent.gov.uk/about/press/releases/2001/software.htm*, accessed 6 June.

UNCITRAL (2002): *http://www.uncitral.org/en-index.htm* , accessed 18 June.

Weston, V.F. and Sorge, B.W. (1972) *International Management Finance* (Homewood, IL: Irwin).

Zugelder, M.T., Flaherty, T.B. and Johnson, J.P. (2000) 'Legal Issues Associated with International Internet Marketing', *International Marketing Review*, 17, 253–71.

Name Index

Subject Index

accounting 193, 196, 199
actors 245, 246–7, 248, 250–1,
  252–3, 254–5
  internal–external 247f
Advantage West Midlands 45–6, 47,
  54, 56
advertising 10, 103, 113, 203, 254,
  264, 287
Africa 42, 42t, 44t, 44
African-Americans 25, 33
agency theory 3–4, 138–49
agents 165, 166f, 170, 171f, 171, 172,
  172f, 173f, 177, 213
agglomeration economies 26, 33, 40–1,
  50, 52, 55
AIB (Academy of International Business,
  1973–) xi, xii, 1, 6
Alcan 87, 88t
Alcoa 87, 88t
aluminium 3, 84, 95, 87–90
Alusuisse 87, 88t
Amazon.com 251, 265, 278, 281,
  284, 285
America Online Inc. 278–9, 280, 282
  AOL Time Warner 93t
American Brands 93t
Americas: net FDI in the UK (1996–2000)
  44t, 44
Amoco 94, 94t
Anaconda 93t, 94
architecture 169, 172
Asia 42, 42t, 44t, 44, 229–31t
Asia-Pacific region 45, 45t, 48t, 48, 255
Ask Jeeves, Inc. 284
asset specificity 168, 212
assets
  firm-specific 10
  fixed 196
  intangible 193
  strategic 39
'augmented product' (Kotler) 110

Australasia and Oceania 42, 42t, 44t, 44
Australia 170, 171f, 175t, 229–31t, 238
automotive sector 45, 46, 54

banks 93t, 196, 237
BarnesandNoble.com 284, 285
Bartlett test of sphericity 125, 136
behaviour (opportunistic) 144, 190,
  195, 200–1
behavioural theory 167
Belgium 154, 155t, 159, 172, 173f, 175t
Belleek (1857–) 169, 170–1, 174–81
best practice 142, 147, 266, 270
beverages/drink 14, 45, 85, 142
biotechnology 49, 120, 122, 131, 135
'bleak houses' 65, 66, 74, 75, 75t
BMW 46, 83
bonuses 145, 157
book reviews 278
'born globals' 102, 181–2
bounded rationality 200, 201
BP Amoco 84, 88t, 89, 93t, 94
brand names 15, 18, 104, 107, 108,
  111–13, 115, 116, 177, 179, 194,
  202, 265, 270, 284
  global 83, 112–13
Brazil: biotechnology companies 3,
  120–37
Brooks Brothers (USA) 153, 154
brownfield sites 74–5, 75t, 76
business services 47, 55

Canada 10, 22, 34, 89, 170, 171f, 175t
  real estate sector 5, 262–73
capabilities (role in HTSF) 187–207
capital intensity 1, 10, 15–20
Caribbean 170, 171f, 175t
cars/automobiles/vehicles 3, 24, 47, 84,
  86, 87–90, 95
  components (cars/vehicles) 84, 86,
    89, 90t